HISHAM D. AIDI

REBEL MUSIC

Hisham D. Aidi is a lecturer at the School of International and Public Affairs and the Institute of African Affairs at Columbia University. He was a Carnegie Scholar and Global Fellow at the Open Society Foundation and is coeditor, with Manning Marable, of *Black Routes to Islam*.

Also by Hisham D. Aidi

Black Routes to Islam

Redeploying the State: Corporatism, Neoliberalism, and Coalition Politics

REBEL MUSIC

Race, Empire, and the

New Muslim Youth Culture

HISHAM D. AIDI

VINTAGE BOOKS
A Division of Random House LLC
New York

Grateful acknowledgment is made to the following for permission
to reprint previously published material:

Alfred Music Co., Inc.: Excerpt from "Wake Up Everybody,"
written by John Whitehead, Gene McFadden, and Victor Carstarphen.
Copyright © 1975 (renewed) by Warner-Tamerlan Publishing Corp. All rights reserved.
Reprinted by permission of Alfred Music Co., Inc.
Tom Evans: Excerpt from "Beard Is Beautiful" by Tom Evans.
Reprinted by permission of the artist.

The Library of Congress has cataloged the Pantheon edition as follows:
Aidi, Hisham.
Rebel music : race, empire, and the new Muslim youth culture / Hisham D. Aidi.
pages cm
Includes index.
1. Muslim youth—Western countries—Social conditions. 2. Music and youth—
Western countries. 3. Protest movements—Western countries. I. Title.
BP188.18.Y68A36 2013   305.235'088297—dc23   2013028800

Vintage Trade Paperback ISBN: 978-0-307-27997-2
eBook ISBN: 978-0-307-90868-1

Book design by Iris Weinstein

www.vintagebooks.com

Printed in the United States of America
10 9 8 7 6 5 4 3 2

For Randy Weston
and
Maurice El Medioni

Contents

Prologue

One muggy afternoon in July 2003, I headed up to the South Bronx for the Crotona Park Jams, a small festival that is little-known locally, but manages to draw hip-hop fans from around the world. The annual event is organized by Tools of War, a grassroots arts organization that invites artists from across the country and Europe to perform in the Bronx, hip-hop's putative birthplace, and to meet some of the genre's pioneers, figures like Afrika Bambaataa and Kurtis Blow. I arrived at the park and asked around for Christie Z, a local promoter and activist. Christie, who has blue eyes and a ruddy complexion and wears a white head scarf, is the founder of Tools of War and a smaller group called Muslims in Hip Hop. She is married to Jorge Pabón (aka Fabel), a well-known dancer and master of ceremonies (MC), who appeared in the classic 1980s hip-hop film *Beat Street* and currently teaches "poppin'" and "lockin'" dance styles at NYU. The two—Christie Z & Fabel, as they're known—are a power couple on the East Coast's hip-hop scene, but they've become significant players internationally as well, organizing shows in Europe and bringing artists from overseas to perform in America.

Christie's story is unusual. "People always ask me," she says with a laugh, "how did a white girl from central Pennsylvania become a Muslim named Aziza who organizes turntable battles in the Bronx? I say the lyrics brought me here. I was in high school when I heard 'The Message,'" she says, referring to the 1982 breakout song by Grandmaster Flash, which vividly described life in the ghetto during the Reagan era, and was one of hip-hop's earliest mainstream hits. "I heard that track and I followed the sound to New York."

I had arrived early hoping for a pre-show interview with the French rap crew 3ème Œil (Third Eye), who had flown in from Marseille to perform that evening. The rap trio is known in France for its socially conscious lyrics. Since the invasions of Afghanistan and Iraq, the group had become even more political, rapping about what they call the West's "stranglehold" on the East. I stood around the stage waiting. A circle had formed with a group of boys clapping and dancing, as the DJ on duty that evening—another pioneer, DJ Tony Tone of the Cold Crush Brothers—spun rap and Latin soul classics. Soon Third Eye's manager, Claudine, a brown-haired woman in her early twenties, appeared and led me backstage. I explained that I was a researcher at Columbia writing about global hip-hop. Her face lit up. "We've been wanting to talk to you for a while," she said, as she walked me through a backstage tent and out into the open. Later I found out Claudine had thought I was a representative of Columbia Records, about to offer her group a contract.

The sun was setting, a blue glow had enveloped the park, and I walked up to the four young men lounging on a bench facing the spectacular Indian Lake, which sits at the park's center. Soon I was chatting with the rappers—Boss One (Mohammed) and Jo Popo (Mohammed), both born in the Comoros Islands off the coast of East Africa, but raised in Marseille—and their DJ, Rebel (Moustapha). They were dressed similarly in sagging denim Bermudas, eighties-style Nike high-tops, and baseball caps. Jo Popo gave me a copy of their new hit single, "Si Triste" (So Sad). I told him I'd already seen bootlegged copies at African music stands in Harlem. He nodded and gave me a fist bump. The song, popular among West African youth in New York, offers social commentary over a looping bass line, decrying police brutality and mass incarceration (with a special shout-out to the American death-row prisoner Mumia Abu-Jamal). I asked them how the French press responded to their lyrics, and about the anti-immigrant National Front leader Jean-Marie Le Pen's claim that hip-hop was a dangerous musical genre that originated in the casbahs of Algeria.

Boss One shook his head, "For Le Pen, everything bad—rap, crime, AIDS—comes from Algeria or Islam." This was mid-2003;

the War on Terror was in its early years. "The more Bush and Chirac attack Islam and say it's bad," said Boss One, "the more young people will think it's good, and the more the oppressed will go to Islam and radical preachers." His tone became a little defensive when talking about the *banlieues,* the poor suburbs that ring France's major cities, stating that life in France's *cités* was better than in the American ghettos. "Life is hard in France, but we have a social safety net. Here there is no such thing"—he stood up to emphasize the point—"and it will get worse with Bush, the cowboy, *le rancheur*!"

Their bluster disappeared when I asked what they thought of the Bronx. They grew wistful talking about the Mecca of hip-hop. Jo Popo smiled describing their meeting the day before with hip-hop legend Afrika Bambaataa. *"C'était incroyable!"* Bam, as he is known, is particularly loved in France, where he was instrumental in introducing hip-hop in the early 1980s. The group's music mixer, DJ Rebel, who previously hadn't said a word, suddenly spoke up. "I have dreamed of visiting the Bronx for all thirty-six years of my life. This is where hip-hop started, this music which has liberated us, which has saved us," he said with apparent seriousness. "Yesterday we met Bambaataa and Kool Herc. I thanked them personally for what they have done for us blacks and Muslims in France—they gave us a language, a culture, a community." His voice broke a little.

I was struck by the emotion and sincerity of their words, and I had a few academic questions to ask: Why was the Bronx so central to the "moral geography" of working-class kids in Marseille? Where did this romantic view of the American ghetto come from? Why were they more fascinated by Bronx and Harlem folklore than by the culture of their parents' countries of origin? Claudine suddenly reappeared and asked them to return to the tent. Grandmaster Flash, the legendary DJ and another iconic figure of global hip-hop, had arrived, and they were scheduled to meet him. "Flash invented scratching—I get paid to teach scratching in France," said DJ Rebel getting up to leave. *"A bientôt,"* and the rap trio and their thoughtful DJ walked off. Half an hour later they were on the stage, waving their arms: *"Sautez! Sautez! Sautez!"* Boss One translated: "That means, 'Jump! Jump! Jump!' "

The *Banlieues* Are Burning

European travelers visiting the Bronx is not a new phenomenon. In the early 1980s, groups of French architects and urban planners took tours of the borough's more dilapidated areas of burned-out buildings and gang warfare, trying to figure out how to avoid developing the same problems in French suburbs. In the 1990s, French and German youth would line up for the popular "From Mambo to Hip Hop" tour, which takes visitors through major sites of the Bronx's musical past. I've met young entrepreneurs who land at Kennedy Airport in the morning, rush up to the Bronx, buy two suitcases' worth of hip-hop gear (*le streetwear*), and fly back to Europe in the evening. During the 1990s and early 2000s, the French youth one encountered in Harlem and the Bronx were largely cultural tourists, and they sounded bullish: they loved the Bronx, it was hip-hop's ground zero, but French rap was more political, more cerebral; and yes, the French *banlieues* were bleak, but not as violent or segregated as America's inner cities.

The French youth one meets in Harlem today, with their Obama T-shirts, don't sound so upbeat; the riots of 2005, the right-wing surge, the head-scarf ban, the EU's financial crisis, and the election of Barack Obama have led to self-doubt and soul searching. In November 2005, riots shook France's major cities for weeks on end. Images of cars burning and youths tossing Molotov cocktails at the police were broadcast around the world, and the French understood the world could see that it was their suburbs, and not the Bronx, that were burning. The rise of Barack Obama, a leader of African and Muslim ancestry, captured the French imagination, particularly in the country's Muslim-heavy urban periphery; during the campaign it was not uncommon to see Arabic graffiti in support of candidate Obama on walls in the housing projects. Attitudes toward the U.S.—which had soured during the Bush years—quickly shifted. As the *New York Times* reported in September 2010, "anti-American sentiment, once pervasive in these [*banlieue*] neighborhoods, seems to have been all but erased since the election of Mr. Obama, who has proved to be a powerful symbol of hope here and a powerful diplomatic tool." Muslim leaders began to cite America as a model—a utopia, even—to bash Europe. If Obama's victory generated European goodwill toward the U.S., it also made painfully clear, argued activists, just how far ahead the U.S. was on matters of race: America had become the first Western nation to elect a minority as head of state, while European governments were only beginning to address issues of ethnic difference and inequality. "Obama is the incarnation of the American dream," said Patrick Lozès, who heads France's Representative Council of Black Associations. "But where is the French dream?" And across the political spectrum, pundits asked: Was America's racial past Europe's future? Did Western Europe have to go through a sixties-style phase of urban riots and burned cars to get an Obama?

At the height of the unrest, a group of young residents in Bondy, a gritty municipality in northeastern Paris, set up a blog to chronicle the events. *Bondy Blog* soon became the go-to source for understanding the republic's urban crisis. In September 2011, *Bondy Blog* reported that the outflow of French Muslims to the U.S. had increased in the last decade: "Many Arab Muslims have left France seduced by Uncle Sam's liberty of religion." The magazine's North American correspondents often do exposés on young *banlieusards* who have left France. "I'm boycotting France. The U.S. is my second country, *alhamdulillah*," said Hajer, a young French-Tunisian woman who had settled in Astoria, Queens, in 2009. "A Muslim lives better here than in France. There's freedom of expression, freedom of thought, freedom to practice one's religion. [At the mosque] we have policemen who pray with us. Women can drive wearing their niqab."

This book looks at the young European and American Muslim's search for a nonracist utopia. In the past, this quest has led the young European or American Muslim—often converts—toward Africa or the Middle East, in search of an authentic Islam; the student-traveler who heads east—traveling through space and time—in search of spiritual knowledge still exists, but today it's also common to see the young

(European) Muslim head westward across the Atlantic, to northeast Brazil or an American metropolis, in search of religious freedom or simply to immerse themselves in black history. The European Muslim transplants one meets in New York and other American cities will register their resentment of U.S. foreign policy—before lauding the civil rights movement and the American model of integration. And they are not the only ones. Today, as young French and Dutch Muslims wander through Upper Manhattan and Chicago's South Side, it's not uncommon to see European politicians, journalists, and activists in those same urban areas, visiting mosques and community centers trying to identify "best practices" they can take back home. Countless working papers and reports have been issued in the past few years in Dutch, German, and French on the "successful" assimilation of American Muslims, explaining why the U.S. has not seen the urban unrest that has recently plagued European cities. An easy consensus seems to have emerged: that America's foreign policy toward the Muslim world may be seriously flawed, but domestically it has successfully integrated its Muslim population, whereas while Europe may have a more "balanced" approach to North Africa, the Middle East, and South Asia, domestically it has failed to assimilate its immigrant populations and is faced with a young, restive Muslim underclass.

This view, of course, neglects how America's foreign entanglements have adversely affected the situation of American Muslims, and how—just as European Muslims are enthusiastically endorsing the "American model"—their American counterparts are mobilizing against the security policies and civil rights infringements of the last decade. It's debatable whether the situation of European Muslims, a largely rural and working-class migration, is even comparable to that of an affluent American Muslim migration; a more apt comparison would be Latino immigration to the U.S. But in this book, I am more concerned with the "American dream" that exists in Europe's urban periphery, how European and American Muslims view the American civil rights struggle and are drawing on black history more broadly, how American diplomacy is deploying race and diversity, rather than with whether American Muslims are better off than European Muslims, or how European governments can replicate American policies.

The European Muslim youth one encounters in American cities today—attending conventions, visiting mosques, appearing at Malcolm X's grave site a few miles north of the Bronx—are part of a larger transnational mobilization of Muslim youth in Europe and North America. This movement of Muslim youth, within and across national borders, is a reaction to War on Terror policies, and geopolitical shifts provoked by American state power, that have put enormous stress on Muslim communities in Europe and America. In *Among Empires: American Ascendancy and Its Predecessors,* the Harvard historian Charles Maier argues that empires rely not only on territorial frontiers, but also on sociopolitical frontiers, which protect stratification at home and abroad, separating "insider" from "outsider." "Empires seek to defend internal sociopolitical frontiers as well as external boundaries," he writes, warning that these frontiers invariably become contested fault lines.

In the years since 2001, Muslims have launched a range of social movements—integrationist, separatist, utopian, dystopian, secular, and Islamist—to challenge the myriad policies, narratives, and frontiers of the American imperium. They are contesting the physical borders between nation-states; the ethno-spatial boundaries between cities and their "postcolonial" peripheries; the discursive frontier between "immigrant" and "indigenous" Muslims; the institutions of racial classification that separate human populations into different racial and ethnic categories; the official geographies and mappings of the world that draw lines between Islam and the West, Africa and the Orient, the Near East and the Far East; and so on. These movements are emerging in a context of globalization, where local neighborhoods and foreign territories are increasingly linked, and states are vying to control an Islam gone global.

For European Muslims, the economic downturn, the rise of the far right, and the spread of the War on Terror have all sharpened questions of belonging. Embattled in the European countries where they were born, these young Muslims are reaching for identity and freedom beyond the borders of France, Germany, and Holland. Some join transnational movements like Hizb ut-Tahrir; others head to Pakistan or Yemen in search of "real" Islam. But there is also a movement westward, toward the Black Atlantic, and the cultures and movements of the African diaspora. An American dream exists in Europe's Muslim ghettos and it's very much a black American one. For these young Europeans, America is home to African-American Islam, the oldest Muslim presence in the West, the Islam of Malcolm X and Muhammad Ali, an Islam that played a critical role in the civil rights movement and in making America more at ease with diversity than Europe. And whether through actual migration or virtually—through the Internet and social media—Muslim youth are reaching across the Atlantic to draw on the black freedom movement and the Islam of the African-descent communities of the New World.

Asalam aleykoum—Welcome to America

The three men dressed in brown tunics, calf-length *shalwars,* and large white turbans double-wrapped around their heads cut a curious sight walking up the white steps of the Rayburn House Office Building on Independence Avenue in Washington, DC. As they made their way into its grand marble hall, a Capitol Police officer leaned over to check IDs and name tags. "And where is home for you?" she said with a smile. "Pakistan!" beamed one of the men. The three Pakistani clerics walked down Rayburn's narrow corridor, punctuated with state flags. Staffers looked on curiously as the "three Taliban"—as one onlooker called them—went down to the basement and boarded the underground train to the Capitol. Upon arrival, the guests were guided to room HC-F: a room on the basement level of the House, where Muslims in Congress hold their weekly prayer. They performed their preprayer ablution, removed their leather sandals, and sat cross-legged on the red wall-to-wall carpet, alongside staffers, interns, and lobbyists, awaiting the imam's sermon.

The three men are religious scholars from Islamabad, affiliates of the International Institute for Islamic Thought, and were invited to Washington in April 2010, part of the State Department's International Visitor Leadership Program to introduce Muslims from around the world to America. The congressional liaison for this State Department program is Jihad Saleh, legislative assistant and head of the Congressional Muslim Staffers Association, a forty-five-member group that organizes cultural events on Capitol Hill and encourages Muslims to get involved in government. A stocky, fast-talking thirty-eight-year-old with shoulder-length hair, Saleh grew up in South Central Los Angeles and embraced Islam in college. Walking around the Capitol with me, he stifles a smile when fellow staffers call, "Hey there, Jihad," or "Morning, Jay!"

"The best part of this job is when I have to give Muslim delegations a tour of Congress," he says. "We have four or five staffers meet with the group, we walk them to the Rotunda, and then we take them to our prayer hall in the Capitol Building and that's when they get the deer-in-the-headlights look. They cannot believe that every Friday afternoon a hundred Muslims come out to pray in Congress."

As the Friday service ends, interns set up tables at the back of the prayer hall, begin passing out flyers regarding an upcoming event— Muslim high-school students from Maryland will be visiting the Hill. One woman, a staffer for Senator Dick Durbin, walks to the front and makes an announcement about an upcoming hearing. The three guests seem taken aback by the gender mixing in the prayer space. "Different nations have different traditions—*likuli shu'bin qawaiduha,*" observes Ikhlaq Mansoor, one of the clerics, smiling diplomatically.

"They're wondering why there is no partition between men and women," grins Saleh.

Saleh has given walking tours to politicians from Iraq, journalists from Pakistan, female physicians from across the Middle East; but recently, the delegations he's received have been of young Muslims from France, Italy, and Holland. "I gave a tour to a group of young Muslims from Italy last year—college students of Somali, Senegalese, Tunisian background. We spoke about Muslim political engagement, and then we went to the prayer hall, and of course they asked, 'Why no partition?' The visitors always ask that. I just say, 'This isn't Saudi Arabia.' After the prayer service, a Senegalese guy stood up, choked up, almost crying, and he said that this would never happen in Europe. Muslims praying in parliament? Never."

"I know, in many ways, we're tap-dancing for the State Department," says Saleh, "that they're using us to show Muslims around the world just how affluent American Muslims are, and how tolerant America is, but I still love doing this. I bring together a group of Muslim staffers—Sunni, Shia, converts, immigrants, black, white, Asian, everyone—and we meet these delegations to show them that America is a place where the Islamic world has converged. After prayer, I take them to meet my congressman—and then they go on to visit other cities."

The French riots of 2005 were a turning point. The unrest cast doubt on Europe's self-image, and brought home the realization that Muslim youth could seriously trouble the transatlantic alliance. As France's suburban ghettos blazed, the European press warned about the "unassimilability" of certain immigrants, hand-wringing about the role of mosques in the suburbs—are they keeping youths out of trouble or radicalizing them?—and, worst of all, about how France, and perhaps Europe, was developing an American-style "race problem." In the U.S., on the other hand, the initial cable-news gloating over how the riots had discredited the French model of integration ("the final nail!") soon gave way to uneasy discussions about what might happen if the disturbances reached American shores. Pundits noted that, after all, Zacarias Moussaoui, "the Twentieth Hijacker," and Richard Reid, "the Shoe Bomber," had attended the same London mosque. American officials began warning that the alienation and segregation of European Muslims could seriously weaken European allies. The U.S.'s National Intelligence Council's report *Global Trends 2025* mentions the French riots and warns that Europe's economic downturn could lead to instability and "deepening ethnic cleavages": "Despite a sizeable stratum of integrated Muslims, a growing number—driven by a sense of alienation, grievance, and injustice—are increasingly likely to value separation in areas with Muslim-specific cultural and religious practices."

The U.S. government soon began reaching out to Muslim youth in Europe, sending prominent Muslim Americans to talk about the merits of American multiculturalism, organizing seminars on affirmative action and ethnic statistics, funding nongovernmental organizations (NGOs) in underprivileged Muslim neighborhoods across Europe. American diplomats also began inviting young European Muslims to come experience American diversity and see firsthand that American Muslims "are not oppressed," hoping these trips would soften Muslim attitudes toward the U.S. and "make terrorism's recruiters less appealing." In June 2008, the American embassy in France invited the editorial staff of *Bondy Blog* to visit the U.S. One of the three men who took up the State Department's offer was Mohammed Hamdi, a thirty-six-year-old schoolteacher from Paris. Hamdi visited a troubled neighborhood in Washington, DC, and a "Muslim clinic" in Los Angeles; he rode with police officers in Jackson, Mississippi, toured Jackson State University (a historically black institution), and met with Muslim staffers in Congress, ending his trip with a meeting with Obama himself. "I now know things are more complicated than we think," Hamdi told an American journalist. "When I have a discussion about the American situation, I can say what I saw in the neighborhoods of Los Angeles. I saw Islamic people, I saw the situation of black people and Spanish people."

The challenge for all governments with diverse populations is how to bind the communities living within their borders to the nation-state. Increased immigration has made this problem acute for Western politicians, who worry that their minorities, Muslims in particular, are more likely to identify with "embassy Islam"—that is, some state in Africa or the Middle East—or with a transnational movement like the Muslim Brotherhood, than with the country where they live. This was, after all, the thesis of Samuel Huntington's best seller *Who Are We?*, which warned that Hispanic immigration posed an unparalleled challenge because it was undermining allegiance to the American nation-state; many of the newcomers, argued the late political scientist, identified with different Latin American states and pan-Latin movements rather than with the government of their adopted homeland. Huntington's tome resonated in Europe, where leaders are deeply concerned about the allegiance of their immigrant populations. (The claim of Robert Putnam, another Harvard scholar, that diversity undermines civic life would similarly send shudders through European policy circles.) But while having European Muslim youth identify with America may be better than their identifying with transnational Islamic movements, it's still discomforting to European officials when French Muslim youth tell National Public Radio that they are "more open to help from the American embassy than anything that may come from their own government."

The American initiatives to gain the goodwill of European Muslims through financial assistance and public diplomacy signal a new era. Western states have a long history of intervening in the Muslim world to protect and empower religious minorities, but it is unprecedented for allied Western states to court each other's minorities. And yet the U.S. is spending millions of dollars to win the hearts and minds of Europe's disaffected Muslim communities, often vying with European states' own local outreach efforts (and angering local officials and right-wing parties, who see this as an infringement of their sovereignty). These public diplomacy efforts directed at Western Europe's urban periphery seem to constitute a kinder, gentler corollary to U.S. counterinsurgency initiatives in Iraq, Somalia, and Afghanistan.

The U.S. embassies, however, are not the only ones pursuing Muslim outreach strategies. Saudi Arabia, Iran, Turkey, Pakistan, and a host of other states are also monitoring their diasporas in Europe, assertively promoting their interpretations of Islam. Saudi Arabia is promoting Salafism; Iran is wooing Shia communities; Turkey is backing the Gülen movement, and so on. These state-driven soft-power initiatives demonstrate two things: For all the talk of clashing civilizations and a "de-territorialized" Islam, nation-states are still the most powerful actors shaping Islamic discourses, identities, and movements in Europe, especially since the Arab revolts of 2011. And second, the Great Game of the twenty-first century—the ideological and geopolitical tussles centered around postcolonial Africa and the Middle East—is increasingly playing out in Europe's urban periphery, and in efforts to shape Muslim youth culture.

"Islam, Not Hip-Hop"?

Globalization is in many ways Americanization—the spread of the lone superpower's ideas, trends, and products. But given the import of African-American culture in the U.S., cultural globalization is often the dissemination of African-American styles. Black art forms like spoken-word poetry and fashions like sagging jeans—which emerged in the New York prison system, when authorities banned belts after the 1971 Attica riots—have become popular with youth everywhere. The spread of American culture has also coincided with the global-ization of Islam: the increase in immigration and communication technologies means that Islam's teachings and art forms are circulat-ing worldwide, streaming into the West through media flows and minority communities. And this has created some interesting cultural fusions: Arabic country music in Alabama, punk rockers in Pakistan, and Muslim Barbie dolls. But it is the encounter between hip-hop, the lingua franca of youth, and Islam that has produced one of the most dynamic and polemical forces in youth culture today.

Islamic motifs and Arabic terms have threaded through the genre's fabric since its genesis in the early 1970s. As hip-hop went global in the mid-1990s, these allusions were transmitted around the world, and rap lyrics would disseminate the ideas of different strands of African-American Islam—Nation of Islam, Five Percenter, Sunni, etc.—to far-flung audiences. The superb documentary *Across the Bridge,* about Istanbul's musical scene, captures disparate reactions to hip-hop in one Muslim metropolis: from young Turkish artists who hang posters of Tupac in their bedroom and spray-paint silhouettes of Malcolm X on street walls, to a black-lettered slogan on the front of a building that reads "No Hîp Hop, Yes Müslüm." Religious conserva-tives and anti-globalization activists denounce the "hip-hopization" of their culture, and lament that local art forms are being marginalized, but to young Muslims, the African-American history spread by the music and other media flows represents struggle, an alternative idea of modernity and cosmopolitanism, as well as a different relationship to the West.

Yet African-American Islam is seldom included in conversations about the globalization of Islam. Scholars will talk about the transnational reach of the Muslim Brotherhood and Hizbullah, but not the Islamic and quasi-Islamic movements exported by America. Sociologist Olivier Roy, for instance, argues that "de-territorialized" Islam became an ideological alternative for Western youth after the end of the Cold War. Explaining how the accused "dirty bomber" José Padilla and the Shoe Bomber, Richard Reid, converted to Islam, Roy writes, "Twenty years ago such individuals would have joined radical leftist movements, which have now disappeared or become 'bourgeois' . . . Now only two Western movements of radical protest claim to be 'internationalist': the anti-globalization movement and radical Islamists. To convert to Islam today is a way for a European rebel to find a cause; it has little to do with theology." This portrayal of Islam as a post–Cold War outlet for the West's political malcontents ignores the powerful allure that Islamic theology and history have exerted on minorities in Europe and America since the mid-nineteenth century. It also neglects the critical elements of race and racialization. At the height of the Cold War, when communism was still in vogue, the ranks of African-American Muslim organizations were growing, drawing people who sympathized with the decolonizing "darker nations" and Third World states' attempt to create a Non-Aligned Movement.

Similarly, the scholars who rightly see political Islam as a discourse of opposition that challenges Western hegemony often underestimate the disillusionment among Muslim youth with the dominant Islamist movements. In Europe's urban periphery there is a sense of disaffection with the plight of Muslims worldwide, and a desperate need for a narrative of social justice that can make sense of local injustices and "wars abroad." The Muslim Brotherhood's integrationist approach, or the Salafist movement—with its calls for political disengagement in anticipation of divine deliverance—may offer solace to some young Muslims, but others find these movements' conservative worldviews lacking. Youth activists often ponder the dominance of the "Islamic right," asking what an "Islamic left" would look like. The young Muslims searching for an Islamic liberation theology will gravitate toward the writings of the Iranian sociologist Ali Shariati or the Egyptian philosopher Hassan Hanafi, but increasingly it is African-American Islam (as represented by Malcolm X) and the Black Atlantic more broadly that is drawing the politically restless. The young European activists who come and stand in silence in front of Malcolm X's bronze statue at the Audubon Ballroom, where he was assassinated, will state that the civil rights leader's critique of racism and state violence, his linking of race and empire, is precisely what European Muslims need today. In their eyes, African-American Islam links the local and the global, connecting the ghetto with the international state system in a way that no Islamist movement does; it also represents a melding of struggles, both anticolonial and civil rights, the era of Bandung and the 1960s, when W.E.B. Du Bois hailed Indian and Egyptian independence, and people in the Third World proclaimed solidarity with the pan-Africanism of Paul Robeson.

Muslims, in the last decade, have discovered race as a political tool, and the ghetto as a site of struggle; black internationalism increasingly provides an archive from which young Muslims in Europe and the U.S. can draw on to reinvigorate Islamic thought. Thus, what is striking about the last decade is not the emergence of Islam as a "new, post–Cold War left," but the youth's dissatisfaction with current Islamic movements and attempts to build an Islamic left by revisiting the Bandung era, mining the historic interactions between the Black Atlantic, Islam, and anticolonial struggles. African-American thinkers and leaders drew on the cultural resources of Islam and the Orient, starting in the late nineteenth century, to remake black identity, to build social movements, and to bargain with the U.S. government. The very cultural bridges that they threw to the Islamic world are today being crossed by young Muslims trying to find an entry into the West.

"Audiotopias"

The Brøndby Strand suburb in southeastern Copenhagen is strik-ing for its ordinariness. The cluster of grim high-rise buildings, the Brøndby Projects, standing in the center of this "commune," as these areas are called in Denmark, resembles the public-housing projects now widespread in European cities. The suburb is home to immigrants from Africa, Latin America, and the Middle East, and is referred to as a "ghetto" by local media and as the "Southside" by young denizens. This neighborhood has in recent years captured the attention of the pop world, giving birth to a new musical genre called "Muslim R&B" or "urban *nasheed*," producing a crop of home-grown artists like the colorful Burhan G, a R&B crooner of Turkish descent, who models himself after the American pop star Usher. Following his American inspiration, Burhan G sports a shaved head and favors tight sleeveless shirts; his most popular video shows him standing in pouring rain on a dark night, muscles glistening as he looks up at the thundering sky wondering why his woman left him. "Who is he? What is his name?" he whimpers, before shrieking, "You a straight deceivah with a cold demeanah!"

But the act that has put this Danish suburb on the world-music map is the trio Outlandish. The group is made up of a Moroccan, a Pakistani, and a Honduran, all the Danish-born progeny of immi-grants who settled in Brøndby Strand, and their music reflects the neighborhood's demographic composition with lyrics sung in Danish, English, Spanish, and Urdu, and tracks mixing R&B with "Islamic" and Latin rhythms. Part of Outlandish's international appeal is the artists' cosmopolitanism, their easy mixing of the local and the global. The three singers make clear that they are patriotic Danes—and have done albums in Danish only—but they carefully balance their citi-zenship and allegiance to Denmark with solidarity with the *ummah,* the worldwide Islamic community. They perform at rallies for Dar-fur and Palestine, write songs about HIV among Muslim youth, and collaborate with lesser-known Muslim artists around the world. Their message is a curious sort of Islamic universalism, or, more precisely, Andalusian humanism. Only two members of the group are Muslim—the third, Lenny Martinez, is a Catholic—but the three describe themselves as "Moros" (Moors), and have embraced (and popularized) a neo-Moorish identity that puts a hip-hop spin on the *convivencia* of Moorish Spain, when Muslims, Jews, Christians, and other groups coexisted in relative peace.

Talk of 1492—the year Islamic Spain fell to the Reconquista, and Columbus set sail to the New World—and a common Andalusian past, and the appearance of neo-Moorish cultural trends are part of a larger tendency that can emerge when Muslim and Hispanic immigrants or Muslims and Jews encounter one another in Europe and America; but few expected such a discourse to emerge from a housing project near Copenhagen. The precedent of Muslim Iberia—like the history of the black freedom movement in the New World—is a fount that young Muslims are drawing on. Groups like the Murabitun, based in Chiapas, Mexico, or the Alianza Islámica, active in the Bronx and East Harlem during the 1990s, see continuities between Islamic Spain and the New World, and their narrative connects Andalusia with the Black Atlantic. The banner hanging at the Alianza's center in the South Bronx celebrates the African and Islamic roots of Latin America: against a red, white, and blue backdrop stands a sword-wielding Moor, flanked by a Taíno Indian and a black African. The Spanish conquistador is conspicuously absent.

In Europe today, Muslim youth are weaving Islamic, Afrocentric, Asian, and Latin American elements to produce new identities and movements in an example of what Yale anthropologist Arjun Appadurai has described as "culturalism": "the mobilizing of cultural material and cultural differences in the service of a larger national or transnational politics." This culturalism is both fascinating and unsettling for Europeans. The American ghetto has long been recognized for its cultural pluralism. (In 1929, sociologist Harry Zorbaugh described the Near North Side slum in Chicago as one of "the most cosmopolitan areas in a distinctively cosmopolitan city.") But the cultural diversity of the European Muslim "ghetto"—in fact the very notion of a "Muslim ghetto," a contested idea—is relatively new. European commentators are taken aback when artists and youth leaders in these urban spaces put together narratives that embrace different causes (Darfur, Kashmir, Mumia Abu-Jamal) and connect local places—specific neighborhoods and housing projects—with past eras (Timbuktu, Islamic Spain, the Harlem Renaissance) and far-flung geographic regions (Africa, the Orient, the South Atlantic) to show that this minority community can transcend its local isolation and be part of a global majority.

Music is a powerful lens through which to view the identities and movements emerging in Muslim communities. Music has long been used by youth to protest, proclaim identity, build community, and interpret the world. But the dominant Salafi movement—with its opposition to music—has meant that debates about music, its permissibility and purpose, are paramount in contemporary Muslim youth culture. In *What the Music Said,* Mark Anthony Neal observes that in the 1970s, the dance floor became the place where the African-American diaspora reintegrated itself. I would argue that today music is the realm where Muslim diaspora consciousness and identity politics are most poignantly being debated and expressed. Music can offer a snapshot of local movements and trends as well as the larger cultural politics of America's encounter with Muslim youth and Europe's relationship to its postcolonial citizens. Moreover, while music may not, as Jacques Attali claims, presage larger social political change, it is a mechanism of social control, increasingly deployed by states to "moderate" Muslim youth. As the Canadian-based neuroscientist Steven Brown argues in *Music and Manipulation,* through its "affective" power and ability to communicate ideas, music can shape identity, ideology, and group solidarity; and states aim to control music flows as a way to homogenize mass behavior. In Europe, as Islam-inflected cultural forms reach the mainstream, state officials, diplomats, and counterterrorism officials are carefully watching, wondering if these music flows are undermining national cohesion and how they can be incorporated into a politics of counterextremism.

After I met the French rap trio Third Eye in the Bronx in July 2003, I wrote that Islam was increasingly providing an anti-imperial idiom and an imagined community of belonging for marginalized groups in the West. I also noted that French officials were worried about the spread of hip-hop—and black culture, more broadly—among French Muslim youth. French and American observers have blamed hip-hop for bringing social ills associated with the American ghetto to France, including "belligerent Afro-American lifestyles," and the "African-Americanization" of the speech patterns of French youth. In 1994, the French government had passed a law limiting the amount of American hip-hop that could be played on French radio stations.

Anxiety over the combined influence of Islam and hip-hop only grew louder after the 2005 unrest. Before the riots were over, two hundred members of parliament submitted a petition to the French Ministry of Justice calling for the prosecution of seven hip-hop groups whose lyrics allegedly provoked the unrest. Nicolas Sarkozy, then minister of the interior, would bring a lawsuit against the French-Algerian artist Hamé of La Rumeur for the group's anti-police lyrics. After his first court appearance, the rapper left Paris for New York, enrolling in a master's program at NYU film school. More recently, the German and Dutch governments have been cracking down on rap artists with Islamist inclinations, but other European governments have been using music to promote a "moderate" Muslim identity. State officials have come to believe that acceptance or rejection of music is a quick way to separate "moderates" from "extremists," and music has become central to policies aimed at promoting Sufism, to countering Salafi and Islamist discourses, and to deradicalizing "at-risk" youth. The U.S. is deploying music overseas for public diplomacy, for counterterrorism, and for democracy-promotion. American officials are keenly aware of the hunger for African-American history among Europe's minorities, and the emotional pull of black music; various soft-power projects have been launched that tap this awe for the black freedom movement.

· · ·

In his *Discourse on Colonialism*, first published in 1950, the late French-Caribbean poet Aimé Césaire wrote that after World War II, Europe was politically ruined and culturally bereft, unable to deal with the two main problems it was facing: the challenge of late colonialism (European empires were crumbling, despite attempts to cling to territories in Africa and Asia) and the question of the proletariat and mass inequality. As the Truman administration launched the Marshall Plan to rebuild a war-ravaged continent, Europeans, Césaire observed, sought to culturally renew themselves by absorbing African-American cultures—the jazz, literature, and art—that had emerged in America's ghettos, accompanying and chronicling the Great Migration, the Harlem Renaissance, and the incipient civil rights movement.

Today, it is Europe's minorities, its Muslim underclass—the progeny of immigrants from former colonies—who are looking toward the African-American experience for regeneration. African-American artists and their art were always embraced in Europe with an element of moral smugness: race, after all, was an "American dilemma." Now, as the continent's disaffected Muslims deploy those same admired African-American art forms to critique Europe and mobilize politically, it's injecting dissonance into the transatlantic alliance. Forty years ago black artists and radicals found refuge in Paris's intellectual circles. In 1978, France refused to extradite four Black Panthers who were wanted in the U.S. for a hijacking. The militants became a cause célèbre among French intellectuals, who mounted a legal case to fight their extradition, putting together a book in their defense titled *Nous, Noirs américains évadés du ghetto* (We, Black Americans, Refugees from the Ghetto).

Now it's young French Muslims who are fleeing to the U.S. and writing missives denouncing France as a country where minorities are "drug dealers, imams, soccer players, budding writers turning out stories about the ghetto, or buffoons on cable TV." Today's Black Panthers are local Muslim youth in Antwerp, Athens, and Stockholm who are organizing in self-defense against far-right groups, reviving the discourses of black radicalism to critique their governments. And, as in the postwar era, the U.S. earlier in this decade launched a new enterprise—what French journalists call "a Marshall Plan for the *banlieues*"—to shore up European banks, counter the far-right "nativist surge," and help integrate its Muslims.

The cultural and political ferment in Europe's urban periphery at the moment is reminiscent of the period almost exactly a century ago, in the 1910s, when Islamic and proto-Islamic movements began emerging in American cities. The Great Migration sent hundreds of thousands of African-Americans to northern cities. The abysmal conditions of the "new" American ghetto and the dispiriting situation of blacks worldwide (by 1920, almost all of Africa and the Caribbean had been conquered and colonized) produced a deep sense of malaise and a search for deliverance in the African-American community. The ideological ferment of these densely populated northern ghettos gave rise to assorted groups and movements—Marcus Garvey's UNIA (Universal Negro Improvement Association), the Moorish Science Temple, and the Nation of Islam—which emerged between the 1910s and 1930s, providing services and security, organizing communities, and putting forth narratives to make sense of a global situation where people of African descent everywhere seemed besieged.

A century later, Muslims in Europe and the Americas are undergoing a similar process of moving into the peripheries of major Western cities with an emerging racial consciousness. If it was the confluence of local and global processes—the rise of the African-American ghetto, and the transnational flows of ideas and people—that fueled the rise of Islam in America's northern metropolises, similar processes are producing Europe's Muslim ghetto. There is a sense of besiegement: Muslim communities in the West, rebuffed by economic crises, find themselves wedged between surveillance states and rising xenophobic movements. The international situation for the last decade has been equally dispiriting: wars in Iraq and Afghanistan; drone strikes in Somalia, Pakistan, and Yemen; ongoing conflict in Sudan and Syria; and the wave of revolts that swept North Africa and the Middle East in 2011 that has been suppressed by a massive counterrevolution launched by Saudi Arabia and her allies. Movements are emerging to make sense of the "global Muslim predicament"; and as these youths agitate, they are drawing on cultures and traditions from around the world, but especially the cultural-historical archives of Harlem and the Bronx. Today it is more common to hear of Malcolm X and the Black Panthers in Europe than in America.

The connectedness of these histories is not surprising. The story of American Islam is one of race, empire, and urbanism; it's the tale of the descendants of African slaves running aground in northern cities and encountering immigrants from different corners of the colonial world. The European Muslim experience echoes this history: it's a story of newly arrived migrant communities from former colonies settling in decrepit urban areas, and never fully belonging in the nation-states where they reside. As the European-born generation comes of age, their search for freedom and a modern Muslim identity is leading them to reach out across continents and oceans. Muslim youth on both sides of the Atlantic are, along with their non-Muslim counterparts, building movements and narratives that casually traverse history and geography to imagine a utopian future for themselves.

Rebel Music

1

The Enchanted Mooress

Thousands of little ramshackle brick houses with flat metal roofs cling to the hillsides of northeast Rio de Janeiro, in an area known as Complexo do Alemão, one of the largest favelas in Brazil. Just a twenty-minute cab ride from the beaches of Copacabana and Ipanema, this cluster of shantytowns of four hundred thousand people faces south toward the massive statue of Christ the Redeemer watching over Rio. Residents joke darkly that God has turned his back on the northern outskirts, his outstretched arms embracing only the city's affluent "South Zone." The Alemão favela was until 2010 ruled by rival gangs, the Red Command and Friends of Friends. These criminal organizations engage in drug trafficking, but also provide protection, adjudicate conflicts, and fund neighborhood associations. The gangs openly challenge the authority of the state. And every so often the Brazilian military will launch a "pacification" operation, sending hundreds of troops in armored vehicles to drive out the traffickers and regain control of the area. Yet on this balmy Friday afternoon in late October 2012, it wasn't armored vehicles that were making their way into the hills of Alemão, but refrigerator trucks. Residents and shoppers looked on curiously as the trucks came to a halt, and volunteers sporting T-shirts that read "Brasil-Turquia" began unloading boxes and handing out plastic bags to passersby. The occasion was Eid al-Adha, the Muslim festival of sacrifice, when a sheep or goat is slaughtered, and volunteers from the Brazilian-Turkish Cultural Center were distributing halal meat to residents of Alemão.

"It's not much. The meat may last a few meals, but it's the gesture of solidarity that's important," says Mustafa Goktepe as he helps hand out the bags. Mustafa directs the Brazilian-Turkish Cultural Center in Rio, set up by Gülen, a Sufi movement that runs schools and charities around the world. "We're not preaching, we're not doing propaganda. We're just serving. Our center provides classes, scholarships, and aid to the needy." Mustafa's center distributed twenty thousand kilos of halal meat to ten thousand people in Alemão, while volunteers fed another forty thousand in other favelas in Rio and São Paulo.

One reason Alemão residents were awed by the sight of people in T-shirts with Turkish flags passing out food was because it seemed as though life were imitating art, that characters from a telenovela had walked off screen and into their neighborhood. Just days earlier, TV Globo, Brazil's main television channel, had begun broadcasting, to much fanfare, *Salve Jorge* (Save George), a soap opera set in Brazil and Turkey. The plot of *Salve Jorge* revolves around a love story between Théo, a captain in the Brazilian military sent to pacify a favela, and Morena, an eighteen-year-old favela-dweller and single mother, who ends up migrating to Europe and then Turkey in search of work. Théo heads to Turkey to find Morena, and their tale overlaps with another love story, that of Bianca, who visits Turkey as a tourist, and falls in love with her tour guide. *Salve Jorge* is by no means the first soap to be set in the "Orient," but it is the first to be filmed in a favela, in Alemão. The opening episode shows Théo, the army captain, riding in on horseback, removing the drug gangs' flags, and planting the Brazilian national flag, just as the military actually did after its operation in November 2010.

The story line moves from Brazil's urban periphery to the Middle East and back. The noise and confinement of daily favela life are contrasted with the vastness and quiet of the Anatolian mountains; shots of Rio's breathtaking coastline are intercut with the warrens and alleyways of the Grand Bazaar of Istanbul; the throb of favela funk gives way to images of whirling dervishes and Anatolian dance. The Orient is presented in sensuous detail, from the courtship dances to the women kneading bread to the smoke-filled hookah lounges; and the favela is depicted as communal, culturally lush, and ascendant. The aim seems to convey that Brazil and Turkey are two rising nations that have much in common. St. George, after whom the soap is named—and who is Théo's patron saint—was after all born in Cappadocia, in eastern Turkey.

The ongoing telenovela—a story of love, betrayal, and organized crime—set off a mania for Turkish music, fashion, even "Ottoman" plates and cutlery; viewers have begun incorporating expressions used by actors into their speech—"*merhaba*" and "*mashallah, mashallah*"; travel agencies are offering special package tours of Turkey. Soap operas in Brazil, as in other developing states, do more than entertain: they hold up a mirror to society and try to alter public attitudes. *Salve Jorge* touches on the improving conditions in a "pacified" favela; the problem of sex trafficking; tensions between Brazilian evangelicals and devotees of Afro-Brazilian religion; the country's deepening ties with Turkey and the Middle East; and of course Muslims, and how they are part of the Brazilian nation. In the Brazilian telenovelas that deal with Islam, there is a complete absence of the issue of terrorism, or Muslims as a threat, unlike popular American television series like *Homeland, 24,* and *Sleeper Cell.* They seem mainly intended to educate the public about Brazil's growing Muslim population, and to highlight the cultural elements in the world of Islam that can be borrowed and made Brazilian.

This cultural representation is not accidental. Brazil has long sought to show that it's different from Europe and America in its relationship to the developing world. President Luiz Inácio Lula da Silva made it clear that Brazil in the twenty-first century would be pursuing an "independent foreign policy," and emphasized his country's historic ties to Africa and Islam, through the transatlantic slave trade and the legacy of Muslim Iberia. This type of pan-Islamic rhetoric from Latin American leaders and nationalists is not new. At various political moments in Latin American history, when South American states have chafed under Spanish or American domination, leaders have declared solidarity with the Arab world and Africa. The argument that Brazil is culturally indebted to Africa and Islam was first made in the 1930s by Gilberto Freyre, a leading Brazilian thinker, and adopted as official policy by the populist regime of Getúlio Vargas (1930–1945). Today this discourse has been revived, as the Brazilian government, under Lula and Dilma Rousseff, has sought closer relations with Africa and the Middle East. This diplomatic maneuvering has made cultural ripples at home. Rio's Carnival, a metaphor for the nation, is increasingly strewn with Oriental and Islamic elements—from Middle Eastern–themed floats to veiled, burkaed, and fake-bearded street dancers. Samba queens, long symbols of national identity, adorn their bodies with Middle Eastern ornaments, as if to signal Brazil's growing immersion in the Muslim world and ability to seduce anyone. And "the enchanted Mooress" (*a moura encantada*), a centuries-old trope in Portuguese and Spanish folklore, is making new appearances in Brazilian public life.

The experience of Brazil's Muslims shows the degree to which the fate of Muslim communities in the West is determined by policy and geopolitics; and Brazilian policy—foreign and domestic—has created a situation where the country's Muslims face little hostility and no state repression. Yet ironically, for all its efforts to distance itself from the War on Terror and build alliances to counter U.S. power, the growth of Islam in Brazil today—through migration and conversion—mirrors the rise of Islam in the United States in the early twentieth century, and is in fact deeply influenced by American cultural politics. As Brazil's democracy enters its third decade, newly empowered Afro-Brazilian movements are reclaiming the Islam brought by African slaves in the 1500s, just as African-Americans did a century ago. Carnival in Bahia, in northeast Brazil, is exhibiting a Black Muslim consciousness reminiscent of North America. The Brazilian state, like the American government, is discovering that its early Muslim history is a useful diplomatic asset. And Muslim youth in Europe and elsewhere are increasingly charmed by this cheerful nation.

Sensual Mysticism

In October 2009, President Lula launched the campaign to bring the Olympics to Rio. In a televised speech, the head of state addressed the

Olympic committee and millions of viewers and counted off Brazil's advantages. "We are a people in love with sports, in love with life. Our men and women come from every continent—we're all proud of our origins," he said. "We are not only a mixed people, but a people who likes very much to be mixed. That is our identity." In underlining Brazil's mixedness, Lula was invoking an idea essential to Brazilian national identity: that Brazil can absorb any culture and "indigenize" it, that Brazil is a country where immigrants are always welcome, seen as saviors who, in the words of one 1940s state official, would make the nation "bigger, stronger, and more respected."

But this wasn't always the case. In the late nineteenth century, Brazilian elites saw the racial mixing between Native American, European, and African that had produced Brazil as a drawback, the cause of myriad afflictions, from corruption to poverty to national disunity. Prominent intellectuals like the historian Cezar Magalhaens would argue that Brazil's "backwardness" was rooted in a "Muslim passivity" inherited from the Portuguese. And Brazilian immigration policy would reflect these views. The government, from the 1880s through the 1920s, encouraged mass immigration from Europe, hoping that would help "whiten" the country.

But in 1933, Gilberto Freyre, a young Brazilian scholar who had studied at Columbia University with the anthropologist Franz Boas, published his book *Casa-grande e senzala* (later translated as *The Masters and the Slaves*). Freyre turned the conventional wisdom on its head. He argued that Brazil was a rich mix of Amerindian, African, and Portuguese; that the country was saturated with African culture, and that every Brazilian had within his "soul" the mark of the African and the native. Freyre coined the term "Luso-tropicalism," arguing that the Portuguese, unlike other Europeans, had an affinity for dark-skinned peoples and an ability to adapt to the tropics. But to fully understand the Portuguese talent for mixture, Freyre argued, one must look to the influence of the Moors in Iberia, because it was the overflowing Muslim presence that saved the Iberian peninsula from "Nordic obliteration," and brought about a "Portugal influenced by Africa, conditioned by the African climate, and undermined by the sensual mysticism of Islam." It was the "interpenetration" between

Iberians and Moors that made the Portuguese a syncretic people, who are fatalistic but energetic, modern yet Oriental in their voluptuousness and sense of longing.

The sexual dynamics of Muslim Iberia, according to Freyre, continued in the New World. It was Portuguese men's love for the "Moorish brown girl," and the fantasy of the "enchanted Mooress," that propelled them across the Atlantic. "Long contact with the Saracens had left with the Portuguese the idealized figure of the 'enchanted Moorish woman,' a charming type, brown-skinned, black-eyed, enveloped in sexual mysticism, roseate in hue, and always engaged in combing out her hair or bathing in rivers or in the waters of haunted fountains," writes Freyre in the opening pages of *The Masters and the Slaves,* "and the Brazilian colonizers were to encounter practically a counterpart of this type in the naked Indian women with their loose-flowing hair . . . Only, they were a little less coy and for some trinket or other or a bit of broken mirror would give themselves, with legs spread far apart, to the '*caraibas,*' who were so gluttonous for a woman." The Moorish era was critical to understanding Brazil: Islam had softened Portuguese slavery, giving life on the sugar plantation its sensual character; slaveholder identified with the enslaved, since both had "Negro" and "Moorish" blood.

This idealized, eroticized view of the colonial encounter is not unusual. Across Latin America there are such "foundational fictions," which locate the birth of the nation in a romantic union between European man and Native American woman. Yet Freyre's account was distinctive, for the encounter that produces Brazil begins, not in the Americas, but in the Moorish empire; and the Moorish past is not only the "seed" for Luso-Brazilian civilization but an antecedent for Brazilian national unity and *convivencia.* Freyre's book caused alarm at first, but the author was also seen as daring and revolutionary; the young scholar had used cutting-edge social theory (distinguishing between race and culture) to counter the discourse of eugenics and give Brazilian national esteem a much-needed boost. Brazil's history was now a story of cultural affinities and sugar production; her hybrid character, a national virtue and a comparative advantage linking the country to Africa and the Orient. Soon Getúlio Vargas, the strongman who ruled Brazil for fifteen years beginning in 1930, would pick up Freyre's ideas and make them central to the New State that he was building. The concepts of "racial democracy" and "Luso-tropicalism" became state ideology, disseminated in the media, in classrooms, and in official proclamations.

Freyre's book drew attention in the U.S. as well, from activists who thought Brazil's mixing was "more humane" than Jim Crow segregation and from scholars who were doing fieldwork in Bahia in the 1930s and saw Freyre's ideas as an antidote to Nazi ideology. American diplomats, in turn, viewed the South American nation as an ally that could contain German influence in Latin America. In 1942, the House of Representatives discussed the importance of the Brazilian example and "Brazil's fascinating three-way blending." Speakers praised Freyre's "monumental works," saying that English translations were urgently needed to demonstrate the importance of the "Negro to the life, culture, and defense" of both Brazil and the United States; and in 1946, an English version of *Casa-grande e senzala,* retitled *The Masters and the Slaves,* finally was published in the States. American lawmakers were intrigued by the "Brazilian solution," in part because Vargas, who was implementing Freyre's ideas, was a staunch anticommunist.

The Vargas regime fully embraced Freyre's nationalist vision of Brazil as mixed, exotic, and better than the Great Powers. From the mid-1930s onward, Afro-Brazilian cultural forms—samba, carnival, capoeira—became national culture. The *mulata,* the embodiment of miscegenation, would become a national icon. The *mulata,* it's worth noting, was at the heart of Freyre's analysis of Brazil; she was the reincarnation of the "Moorish brown girl," a culture-bearer and, like rum or molasses, the precious product of the sugar economy. It was because of her that all Brazilians had a mark of Africa. "Practically all of us bear the mark of black influence," writes Freyre, "from the slave or the nanny who raised us. Who nursed us. Who fed us . . . the mulata . . . who initiated us into physical love and gave us, on a coarse cot, the first sensation of being a man." The Vargas dictatorship would make the *mulata* a symbol of Brazil's hybridity and virility. The regime would also mobilize samba, a music born in the shantytowns of Rio, broadcasting songs laced with patriotic lyrics across the country. Carnival, with its drummers and samba dancers—usually *mulatas*—flitting atop floats, would come to signify Brazilian conviviality. In 1935, the Vargas regime opened up cultural centers in New York and European capitals to improve the country's standing; and slowly—starting with the samba singer Carmen Miranda and her tutti-frutti hat—Brazil would come to be seen as a tropical paradise.

The images of Brazilian "racial democracy" in films like *Black Orpheus* and the soft sounds of bossa nova that circulated globally in the 1950s cut a sharp contrast with the pictures of degradation emanating from the American South. Brazilian diplomats and intellectuals began to envision their country as the first racially mixed Great Power, one that could compete with the U.S. Brazil was, after all, on the right side of the "racial curtain," opposed to European colonialism and American racial segregation. In the early 1960s Brazilian leaders attempted an "independent foreign policy," making diplomatic forays into Africa; but the country, relatively weak and dependent, could not resist pressure from its former colonial master, and ended up siding with Portuguese colonialism in Africa, alienating dozens of newly independent African states. António Salazar, the Portuguese dictator, would actually adopt Freyre's theory of Luso-tropicalism, using the scholar's ideas to justify colonial rule over Angola and Mozambique.

By the mid-1970s, Freyre was a cause célèbre in the Portuguese-speaking world, serving as an advisor to Brazilian and Portuguese leaders. *Casa-grande e senzala* would appear in nine languages and forty editions, inspiring a comic book, a television series; even floats at Carnival celebrated the book's message. But the scholar's defense of Portuguese colonialism brought heavy criticism. And in the 1930s, Freyre's ideas were used to counter white supremacists; by the 1970s, the ruling junta would invoke his name to silence Afro-Brazilian activists, depicting them as militants who opposed mixing. Meanwhile, Brazilian scholars had begun producing research showing that racial inequality was entrenched in Brazil, and feminists were contesting his idealized, eroticized picture of colonial violence, so that by the mid-1970s, few Western policymakers were talking about the "Brazilian solution."

And yet Freyre keeps returning, oscillating, as one scholar put it, between canonization and excommunication. Still recognized as the "inventor of Brazil," and one of the greatest Latin American intellectuals of the previous century, in the last decade or so, he has been enjoying a revival. In 2000, President Fernando Henrique Cardoso, who as a young sociologist had slammed the idea of "racial democracy," declared the year, the centenary of Freyre's birth, the "National Year of Gilberto Freyre," stating that with the transition to democracy, Brazil was coming closer to the ideal. The rise of genomics and genealogy testing has also brought renewed interest to Freyre's ideas, as Brazilians who identify as white discover that they have African blood. But most important, many Brazilians (and non-Brazilians) think Freyre's ideas of mixing and Moorish antecedents can counter the clash-of-civilizations talk, and that in the post-9/11 world Brazil can offer a solution.

The Story That Broke All the Rules

There are roughly one million Muslims in Brazil, scattered in the cities of São Paulo, Rio, Curitiba (in the southern state of Paraná), and Foz do Iguaçu, a city in the tri-border area near Paraguay and Argentina in the east. Most Brazilian Muslims are the descendants of immigrants from the Middle East, though that's changing due to conversion and recent migration from Africa and South Asia. "There was no anti-Muslim backlash here after 9/11," says Rasheed Abou-Alsamh, a Brasília-based correspondent for the newspaper *O Globo.* "Muslims in Brazil are generally viewed positively. I think that's partly because they're lumped with the Syrian-Lebanese community. The Lebanese have been here for over a century, they're integrated, they're represented in the arts, in politics. They paved the way for the Muslims."

Brazil's Syrian-Lebanese community, estimated to be seven million strong, is affluent, influential, and largely Christian. Arab Brazilians own multimillion-dollar businesses such as the luxury-goods conglomerate Grupo Monalisa and SBT, Brazil's second-largest television network, and make up an estimated 10 percent of the city council in

São Paulo and the federal congress in Brasília. In public perceptions, Arabs and Muslims in Brazil have historically been more associated with business savvy and affluence than with political violence. Yet in the weeks after 9/11, Brazil's Muslims felt vulnerable. The Arab Brazilian Chamber of Commerce received a bomb threat; a cultural event in the city of Guarulhos, just outside São Paulo, was postponed. Brazilian Muslims were interviewed on the evening news. In October 2001, CNN and the *New York Times* began reporting that the Muslim community in Foz do Iguaçu was being monitored for terrorist activity, a claim repeated by Brazilian media outlets. At the root of these allegations was a photograph: American troops in Afghanistan had found a photo of the Iguazu waterfalls—a major tourist attraction in eastern Brazil—at an Al Qaeda training camp. Muslim Brazilians nervously wondered how the spectacle unfolding on their television screens would affect them. "I was anxious day and night," says Leila Chamaa, a Lebanese-Brazilian community leader in São Paulo. "I got caller ID, I kept my daughter home from school for two days, worried she would be harassed." She recalls the post-9/11 weeks vividly. "I was really worried—but then the soap opera started," she smiles.

Leila is referring to *O Clone* (The Clone), a popular telenovela that began airing on October 2, 2001. The soap told the story of Jade, a young Brazilian Muslim who returns to her mother's homeland of Morocco after her mother's death in Brazil, and tries to adapt to life in an extended-family setting in the old city of Fez. There she falls in love with Lucas, a Christian Brazilian who is born after his brother (Diogo) dies. Diogo's heartbroken godfather clones the dead boy's tissue cells and plants them in an unsuspecting Moroccan woman, who then gives birth to Lucas, who looks just like the deceased brother. Filmed in Rio, Fez, and Miami, the telenovela offered a profusion of Orientalist imagery—from veiled belly dancers swaying behind ornate latticework to dazzling shots of Marrakesh and Fez spliced with footage of scantily clad women on Rio's beaches—and of course, incessant supplications of *"Ay, por favor, Allah!"* from Jade's neighbors in the medina.

O Clone was scheduled to air on Brazil's TV Globo in September 2001. The first episode was postponed after 9/11, as producers debated how to portray the Muslim characters. They decided the series, originally intended to address the issue of cloning and genetic engineering (a topic of interest in Brazil), would be recast to educate the public about Muslims in Brazil and Islam in general. "We need to say no to prejudice, to stop feeding this ignorance," explained the screenwriter, Glória Perez, at the premiere. "We're showing common people that there is terrorism in all countries and between all peoples, and the Muslims are people like us."

O Clone captivated viewers. It ran for two years (250 episodes), leading up to and through the invasion of Iraq. Eighty-five million Brazilians, and tens of millions across Latin America, tuned in weekly to watch this Moroccan-Brazilian love story that played out alongside the War on Terror spectacle, which sometimes would seep into the story line. The earliest episodes aired just as American media outlets were raising alarms about the Muslim community in Foz do Iguaçu. In October 2002, an article appeared in *The New Yorker* by Jeffrey Goldberg, a prominent American journalist, claiming that "Middle Eastern terrorist groups" had bases in the eastern Brazilian city. The allegations snowballed, and soon the *Washington Post* was claiming that Osama bin Laden had spent time in Brazil in the mid-1990s. The telenovela would change the subject to a Brazilian concern: intermarriage. In the first season, Jade has an affair with Lucas, a Christian Brazilian, but her uncle has promised her in marriage to a young Muslim named Said. She is forcibly married to the latter, but there's no love there. On the night of their wedding, Said, decked in a white djellaba, removes Jade's silver slippers, bathes her feet, dries them with rose petals and a woven cloth; but he cannot win her heart. Year after year she tries to escape from him. Only after twenty years—and in a finale reminiscent of García Márquez's *Love in the Time of Cholera*—is Jade reunited with Lucas in Brazil. For four seasons, the producers seemed most interested in probing Muslim family life and showing that Muslim immigrants to Brazil were intermarrying just like earlier Christian immigrants from the Middle East.

In a show of Brazil's cultural reach, *O Clone* was translated and broadcast in fifty-three countries. In Portugal, the soap was screened by social workers in workshops on immigration and intermarriage;

in Kyrgyzstan, where Islam was suppressed for seventy years of Soviet rule, viewers saw *O Clone* as an introductory course on Islam. In Turkey and the Arab world, women loved Jade, the protagonist. On blogs and in chat rooms, fans groaned at the cliché story of a captive Muslim girl trying to escape to be with a Christian prince, but they enjoyed watching bejeweled Brazilian actors in face veils and belly-dancing outfits appeal to Allah, and traditional family gatherings turn into dance-offs. In Brazil, the producers defended the story lines as humanizing, a challenge to the idea of Muslim women as passive. Glória Perez said her soap aimed to show that "Muslim women love, too. Muslims do not have anything against sexuality . . . If you take the women of Islam, they transgress rules the entire time." The series was responding to American discourses about Islam, showing that Brazilian Muslims were part of Brazil and more secure than their American counterparts (one episode specifically addressed reprisals against Muslims in the U.S.). The Brazilian Muslim community by and large welcomed the soap; at least it didn't link Muslims to terrorism.

O Clone's cultural impact was astonishing, triggering what *Latin Trade* magazine called "Mideast fever." In Brazil, belly dancing and Middle Eastern–style jewelry became "the rage in Rio and São Paulo"; Brazilians began throwing "A Thousand and One Nights" parties; "Talk to a Sheikh" chat rooms cropped up online; and tourism to Morocco increased by 300 percent. A journalist visiting Quito, Ecuador, found viewers of the series "wide-eyed and drop-jawed for all things Arab." In the States, *O Clone* (dubbed into Spanish and titled *El Clon*) was picked up by Telemundo, an American Spanish-language channel, but almost canceled due to potential controversy. When it was finally broadcast, "the story that broke all the rules"— as Telemundo billed the series—would reach an estimated 2.8 million Hispanic households in the U.S. and exert a palpable influence on Latino youth culture. In one memorable episode, Jade does an elaborate dance for Lucas: she tiptoes from behind a smoking candelabra, draped in veils, twisting, writhing, a silver sword balanced on her head; she balances the sword on her right hip, on her bustier, and then shimmies toward him; she lies down, gazing up at her Christian lover, the blade bobbing dangerously on her bare stomach—*"Por que, habibi?"* That dance would rivet viewers. "Made in Brazil but with airs of a Morisco past," crowed the Miami-based *Nuevo Herald.* In New York, the Spanish daily *El Diario–La Prensa* would report an *El Clon*–triggered fashion for Arab jewelry and hip scarves, overflowing belly-dancing classes teaching the dance of "Jade y Lucas," and a recently opened beauty parlor in Queens called El Clon.

The soap, a celebration of the Orient's appeal for Brazil, was part of a larger pushback against Western representations of Islam—but also of Brazil. In the 1980s and 1990s, Brazil's image had suffered. With the rise of favela violence and films like *City of God,* media stories were depicting Brazil as an urban dystopia, a cautionary tale to other countries. With 9/11, international media fueled the idea of a lawless Brazil, speaking of terrorism on the country's borders. Brazilian activist groups began to counter the American and European media flows. When CNN aired a report in November 2001 alleging terrorist activity in the tri-border area, Foz do Iguaçu's public prosecutor sued the Atlanta-based network for defamation. Groups like Peace Without Borders and MV Brasil mobilized to protect Muslim Brazilians from "cultural aggression." An advertising agency in Foz decided to respond with parody to reports that bin Laden had visited a local mosque. It printed posters with bin Laden's face on them: "When he's not blowing up the world, he spends some pleasant time in Foz. You come too." Across Brazil, the Al Qaeda leader's face began appearing in unexpected places. A tavern opened up in Niterói called Bin Laden's Cavern ("Where the Taliban Gather!") with a promotional poster of a grinning Osama floating on a pool mattress in swim trunks. In February 2002, in Rio's Carnival, a troupe of street dancers called Bin Laden's Harem would dance around, then raise their burkas to show off their thongs. Irony, Orientalist kitsch, and cultural fusion became a way to disrupt War on Terror talk.

The Brazilian state promoted the idea of solidarity with Muslims. Upon assuming office in January 2003, President Lula would distance the country from the United States' War on Terror policies. Brazil did not pass the antiterrorism bill that the U.S. requested. According to American diplomats, the Brazilians feared the bill would be used to target Arab Brazilians and "members of what they [Brazilian officials] consider to be legitimate social movements fighting for a more just society." Brazil would also refuse "multiple requests" to take in a group of released Guantanamo prisoners—Uighur Muslims—that the U.S. did not want sent back to China. Brazilian officials also "vigorously" rejected American claims of terrorist activity in their country. A 2009 dispatch from the American embassy in Brasília states, "The USG [United States Government] is regularly accused of making unsupported assertions that malign TBA [Tri-Border Area] residents and have a negative impact on tourism in the [tri-border] region." Lula also reached out to Arab and Muslim Brazilians, appearing at events, assuring them that they were the pride of Brazil's "racial democracy." At Arab community functions, the head of state would don traditional headdress and perform a Lebanese *dabka* dance, twirling a cane over his head.

Lula also launched a number of South-South initiatives to, as *Foreign Affairs* put it, "rebalance the global order in favor of the developing world." He began building ties with African and Asian states to lobby for a reform of World Bank and IMF rules. In December 2003, he took a nine-day tour of the Middle East, the first time a Brazilian head of state had traveled to the Arab world since Dom Pedro II, the emperor, visited in 1876. Lula visited Syria, Lebanon, the UAE, Egypt, and Libya, with an entourage of Lebanese-Brazilian businessmen. "If, alone, none of us can compete with the rich countries, together we will have a lot of strength," he told his hosts. His foreign minister, Celso Amorim, was more explicit, saying the objective of the trip was to create "a new world economic geography," so that "to go from Brazil to Cairo, you won't need to pass through Washington and Paris." In 2005, Lula hosted the first South American–Arab nations summit in Brasília. Brazil also became a sponsor of the "Alliance of Civilizations"—a United Nations initiative launched by Spain and Turkey, two states that see themselves as a bridge between Islam and the West. In May 2010, Brazil and Turkey brokered an agreement with Iran to delay UN sanctions.

Yet Turkey was wary of Brazilian soft-power initiatives in its backyard and began to push back. In the early 2000s, Brazilian and Mexican soaps were watched across North Africa and the Middle East.

By 2008, the Turkish soap *Gümüş* (known outside Turkey as *Noor*) had edged out the Latin America telenovela. Risqué and glamorous, the soap focused on the relationship between Noor and her doting husband, Mohannad, who challenged every stereotype of the "traditional" Muslim husband; Noor's independence and rags-to-riches tale signified Turkish society's growing affluence and changing gender roles. A subsequent series, *Magnificent Century,* focusing on sexual and political intrigue in the harem of Suleiman the Magnificent, would bring the glory of the Ottoman Empire to viewers from West Africa to Pakistan, eclipsing all U.S., Latin American, and Arab competition. "U.S. cultural imperialism is finished. Years ago we took reruns of *Dallas* and *The Young and the Restless.* Now Turkish screenwriters have learned to adapt these shows to local themes with Muslim story lines," says Sina Kološlu, a Turkish television critic. "Asians and Eastern Europeans are buying Turkish series, not American or Brazilian or Mexican ones. They get the same cheating and the children out of wedlock and the incestuous affairs but with a Turkish sauce on top."

Samba Citizenship

It's February 2011, and Ana Paula Minerato is standing in front of a gaggle of journalists and cameras at the edge of the Sambadrome parade ground in São Paulo. She's wearing a pearl-studded crown, stiletto-heeled gladiator boots, braided gold chains around her neck, and nothing else. "I represent the Arab wedding tradition," she says, and smiles, as a body artist dabs touches of black paint on her stomach. "*O casamiento do Dubai.*" Her breasts are painted black and red, speckled with pearls and sapphires; a band of black paint loops diagonally around her thighs and buttocks. Arabesque calligraphy adorns her stomach and forearms. "I'll now show you the Dubai samba, *samba do Dubai,*" she says, hopping off and doing a quick foot-step. She disappears into the throngs of dancers and drummers.

The nineteen-year-old Ana Paula is a member of the Gaviões da Fiel (Hawks of Faith), a top-level samba school, and an aspiring samba queen. (Her title now is *musa* (muse), hence the massive feathered wings attached to her shoulders.) In Carnival, samba schools perform different themes or plots (*enredos*), telling stories about Brazil. In 2011, the Hawks made their theme a celebration of Dubai, "the El Dorado of the Orient," and staged a raucous, visually stunning show mixing tropicalism and Orientalism. The extravaganza featured four thousand drummers and dancers, twenty-six dance companies, and five floats that paraded down the Sambadrome, hailing "the City of the Future" and "the Dream of King Maktoum." Samba singers—in satin robes, Arabian headdresses, and dark glasses—strummed their mandolins, chanting "*Riqueza, beleza, e cultura árabe*—riches, beauty, and Arab culture!" Dancing nomads on stuffed camels, harem boys in embroidered vests, and drag queens with palm trees sticking out of their turbans pranced in between floats.

The floats, depicting Dubai's ascent from ancient kingdom to economic power, are deliberately satirical and outrageous: a newborn baby blinking at the world, a massive golden hawk with headphones, a sphinx glaring down at a spinning Ferris wheel, a cluster of gleaming skyscrapers representing Dubai's financial power. The last float is an Oriental palace with golden minarets and arches. Looming above the towers is the turbaned effigy of Sheikh Mohammed bin Rashid al-Maktoum, the current ruler of Dubai. The sight of near-naked samba queens—in thongs, plumage, and loose head scarves—frolicking beneath Sheikh Maktoum's bearded visage, as his robotic arms wave to people, is striking. But no one else seems surprised. The thirty thousand spectators—many dressed as sheikhs or veiled women themselves—are dancing, banging tambourines, and cheering the "Arab Spring" float, as it was dubbed. Thousands of miles away, Mubarak of Egypt and Ben Ali of Tunisia had just been toppled. The Orient, like Brazil, was rising; or so it seemed.

Since the 1930s, Carnival has been a metaphor for Brazil. The floats and samba schools are supposed to narrate where the country is at the moment. "The naked, seductive women mark the transformation of public space into one big house," writes a Brazilian scholar. For the four nights before Lent, the pageantry of the Catholic Church, the drumming and dancing of Afro-Brazilians, and the elaborate Native American costumes blend into one symbolic family. Brazilian officials—and cultural elites—see samba as the sound of the nation, soaking up new cultures and maintaining social peace. It's not surprising that the post-9/11 craze for things Middle Eastern would find its way into Carnival. Now one sees more Orientalist *enredos,* more references to things Arab and Islamic, whether it's head scarves and turbans or dancers called *habibas,* who mix samba and belly dancing. Also, part of the local response to War on Terror discourse has been to highlight Arab and Muslim contributions to Carnival. In June 2010, a group of Rio-based dance activists published a study on "Arab-Muslim" influences in the city's "corporal culture," noting the Moorish origin of various musical instruments used in samba, and parsing the *marchinhas* sung at Carnival that refer to the East (such as the Lebanese singer Antônio Gabriel Nássara's 1941 jingle "Allah-lá-ô / We crossed the desert / We had to pray / My good Allah"), all to show that Muslims were present at the birth of samba in Rio's favelas.

This pop Islamophilia was spurred by Brazil's new diplomacy. In his first foreign-policy speech in 2003, President Lula declared, "The rich heritage of the Arab-Islamic civilization was present at Brazil's birth, given its powerful influence on the Iberian Peninsula, where the Portuguese heralded." Freyre became part of the national dialogue again. Celebrations of Freyre and his works were held at Brazilian embassies in Africa and the Middle East. At the launch for the Arabic translation of Freyre's *New World in the Tropics,* the Brazilian ambassador to Morocco praised the intellectual who had "fashioned the Brazilian way of being." At home, Brazilians began—as seems to happen every few decades—searching for traces of "Moorish presence" in their Lusified selves. Freyre was now vindicated as a visionary. "Freyre saw the Oriental pattern in Brazil, he foresaw the resurgence of Islam in the world," declared scholar Antônio Campos at the opening of a literary festival in November 2011 in honor of the late anthropologist. "He foresaw a new, rising Brazil, a mestizo Brazil, with greater tolerance, racial and cultural convivencia." And the enchanted Mooress, a figure of Portuguese folklore that has, over the centuries, drifted in and out of the Brazilian imagination, has in the last decade been making more appearances: in the guise of the iconic *mulata* (now dabbed with Arabic tattoos); as the veiled temptress in a telenovela; as the flash-mob *habibas* doing the *dança mourisca* in São Paulo's city square; as a spirit summoned at poetry readings.

The legend of *a moura encantada* appears in Portuguese and Spanish folklore from the 1500s through the early twentieth century. It's not clear how or when the enchantress emerged: some historians say she appeared in southern Iberia during the Moorish era; others claim she was born during the Reconquista, after a Moorish princess fell impossibly in love with a Christian knight. The Mooress was seen frequently in Portugal's and Spain's southern- and westernmost regions, usually on the eve of the feast of San Juan (St. John the Baptist). The dark-haired damsel would be spotted, near a river or a cave, grooming her hair with a golden comb. She would appeal for help, speaking Portuguese (or Spanish) with a Morisco accent. The *moura* would be carried by Spanish and Portuguese colonists to the Americas and soon be sighted across the New World, making her way into Cuban poetry and Brazilian fiction.

But the enchanted Mooress was not simply a figment of the Portuguese male imagination. The Inquisition, as recent scholarship has shown, reached the New World and targeted the Moor and Mooress. In 1501, less than a decade after Columbus landed on the island of Hispaniola, Queen Isabella of Spain issued a decree instructing the governor of Hispaniola to ban Jews, Moors, "New Christians," and heretics from entering the Americas. The queen had just quelled the Morisco rebellion of Alpujarras (1499–1501), and as Muslims and Jews fled eastward toward the Ottoman Empire, the Spanish monarchs feared that these religious outcasts would board ships in Seville and escape to the Americas. The last thing Ferdinand and Isabella wanted was for their centuries-old battle with Islam to continue in the New World. And they took great measures to ban the importation of Muslims. Several church decrees, *cedulas,* were passed (in 1501, 1532, 1543, 1550, and 1577) to stop the flow of "white slaves" (*esclavos blancos*), as Moors were called, and to deport those who had trickled into the New World. The Spanish and Portuguese conquistadors saw the Moors as "agents of Islam," "intractable and rebellious," and feared their radicalizing influence over West African slaves.

But Moorish women did not face the same persecution. In 1512, King Ferdinand issued an order to send *moriscas* to the Americas in order to avoid "carnal relations between the colonists and native women." Spanish and Portuguese officials issued licenses to have these *mujeres publicas* ("fallen women") transported from Iberia to the Americas to serve in brothels. No sooner had they arrived than the colonists established these *casas publicas* throughout the Americas. In 1526, Charles I authorized the establishment of a brothel of *moriscas* (*"casa de prostitutas blancas"*) in San Juan, Puerto Rico, again to avoid mixing between Spaniards and indigenous women. The demand for Moorish women actually made the Church decrees difficult to implement. In 1543, when an order calling for the deportation of enslaved Moors was issued, settlers in Hispaniola requested its annulment, "because slaves and free persons from this background were few and very useful in a variety of occupations." The order was rescinded in 1550.

This Orientalist fantasy would come to play a critical role in forging a Brazilian national identity. It's certainly possible, as Freyre claims, that the indigenous woman reminded the Portuguese colonists of the *moura,* the Moorish girl. The conquistadors, after all, believed that they were near the "Orient," and often interpreted what they saw in the New World in terms of the Muslim enemy. Native American women were often mistaken for *moriscas.* In New Mexico, the Spanish conquistador Hernando de Alvarado would describe the Zuni Indians' huts (*kivas*) as "mosques" and their wives as "Moorish women." But the conquistadors encountered the indigenous woman at a time when *moriscas* were around and playing a specific social role. The *moriscas* brought to the New World would gradually—through marriage—be absorbed into the Spanish and Portuguese category, and not endure the violence that African women suffered; by the seventeenth century, the term *morisca* would simply mean the daughter of a *mulata* and a Spanish man. Yet the Moorish seductress would remain part of Catholic lore—and national mythology—in Latin America.

· · ·

Brazilian Muslims have long loved Freyre and his notion of Moorish continuities across the Atlantic. Muslim migrants were, in fact, making such arguments before he began writing. In 1929, when the Muslim Beneficent Society was raising funds to build a mosque in Rio, community leaders described Brazil as "our second Andalusia." During the Vargas years, when the government first latched onto Freyre's ideas, Arab Brazilians would tout the official line, that they're familiar yet exotic, because "ancient Arab culture infiltrated itself in Brazil through the Portuguese and Spanish." Today there are Arab and Muslim community leaders who see Carnival as vital for greater recognition, and speak giddily of their community's presence in the samba tradition.

"You can hear Moorish influence in Carnival," says Oswaldo Truzzi, a sociologist at the University of São Carlos. "The Brazilian mandolin (*bandolim*) used in samba is a descendant of the *oud*, the lute—we call it *alaúde* in Portuguese. That instrument has children across the Americas—the Cuban *tres*, the Andean *charanga*." Truzzi speaks proudly of the Arab elements that Carnival has ingested. "The *adufe* as well: the square tambourine used in samba comes from the Arabic *daff*. The instrument traveled from North Africa to Iberia, then across the Atlantic and mixed with everything else."

But this discourse of miscegenation and samba cordiality is troubling to others. And it's not so much the public erotica that's causing contention. Brazil's main Muslim organizations are conservative— either Salafi- or Tablighi-oriented—yet there has been no Muslim protest around depictions of Islam in Carnival, even after the Brazilian government, in 2010, overturned a law banning religious symbols from being displayed on floats, prompting more religious references. Conservative Brazilian Muslims—like their evangelical and Orthodox Jewish compatriots—cringe at the idea of Brazil being an "erotic democracy," and will leave town during Carnival week, taking their children to "halal retreats" and "Islamic camping."

"It's really curious. The very things that will cause Muslims to protest in Europe—public sexuality, cartoons, etc.—cause no outrage in Brazil," says Samy Adghirni, a correspondent for *Folha de S. Paulo*, who relocated from France to Brazil in the mid-2000s. "And that's because Muslims are very comfortable here. I really think Brazil is the best place to be Muslim in the West. The Muslim population has grown, and there is very little hostility. The problem is that this narrative of celebration, of a rising Brazil and a rising Orient, ignores the rise of Islam among low-income communities here."

And this is what's unsettling to younger Muslims. Brazilian officials and cultural elites will deploy samba, Carnival, and Afro-Brazilian culture to create a spirit of tropical cordiality, but in so doing they are glossing over a great deal of history. The trope of the Moorish brown girl—whom Freyre made a linchpin of Brazilian national mythology, capturing the nation's Iberian, Oriental, African, and Native American components—is, after all, rooted in the *morisca,* a figure of sexual indulgence, who transmutes into another erotic character, the *mulata,* who would be similarly exploited by the colonists. Why exactly, feminist critics are asking, did Brazil's intellectual founding father transform the "enchanted Mooress," usually seen sitting by a river with her legs crossed in a sign of Islamic modesty, into a woman "with legs spread far apart"?

In his fiction, Alberto Mussa, a Lebanese-Brazilian scholar, and one of the country's leading novelists, probes the ironies of Brazil's national mythology, examining the violence, the brothels and "erotic crimes," that made the nation. A respected historian of Carnival, Mussa has long argued that the samba plot (*enredo*) is the only true epic form created in Brazil, and was crucial in diffusing Afro-Brazilian history. But today he is openly critical of the "functional samba" of Rio and São Paulo's mega-Carnivals, lamenting the "lost poetry" of Carnival that helped uplift marginalized communities.

And this seems to be the growing view among Brazil's Muslims: Carnivalesque depictions of Muslims are important for cultural inclusion, but portrayals focusing on Syrian-Lebanese affluence, Muslim intermarriage, the rise of Turkey or Dubai, tend to sweeten the past.

2

Sugar's Secrets

In the autumn of 1865, two steamships sailed into the harbor of Rio de Janeiro. The vessels had set off from Constantinople in September, and were heading to Basra, in modern-day Iraq, but powerful winds pushed them away from the African coast and toward South America. The Brazilian emperor, Dom Pedro II, long fascinated by the Orient, a student of Arabic and Sanskrit, welcomed the Ottoman navy ships with elaborate protocol, including military parades and firing cannons on the streets of Rio. When the navy officers went ashore to sightsee the next day, they were accompanied by a religious scholar, Abdulrahman al-Baghdadi, a man born in Baghdad and appointed by the Ottoman sultan to lead prayers for the sailors.

As al-Baghdadi strolled through Rio, marveling at the city's beautiful "gardens and promenades," he was approached by a black Brazilian, who said, "'As-salamu 'alaykum.' He specifically addressed this greeting to me because I was wearing official attire with a turban, showing my status as a scholar," al-Baghdadi would observe. "I did not answer his greeting thinking that he had learned it just to mock."

The Brazilian persisted, but the language barrier prevented any further communication. Later that day, various Brazilians came aboard the ship to welcome the Ottoman visitors, including some "Sudani" people, and they too gave the Muslim greeting. When afternoon prayer time came around, writes al-Baghdadi, "We stood to pray and all of them stood with us . . . We became convinced that they were Muslims and that they believed in the unity of God. We were greatly enchanted but also astonished. We welcomed them and showered them with our best attentions."

Through his translator—a Moroccan Jew who had settled in Rio—al-Baghdadi would learn about the situation of "Blacks in America." He learns that more than fifty million Africans were brought from West Africa in "Frankish ships" to North and South America; that slavery had caused a war between the northern and southern United States that had liberated America's slaves; that most of the slaves in Brazil were free, but others remained in bondage. He is also told that the Muslims in Rio—an estimated five thousand—are forgetting their traditions, and desperately want to learn from him. Al-Baghdadi visits their homes, and is dismayed to see that, indeed, these Muslims who came to Brazil when they were very young are not praying correctly and are drinking wine regularly.

Al-Baghdadi decides that it's his duty to reacquaint the Brazilians with the basics of their faith. The commander of his ship, fearing a diplomatic crisis between the Ottoman and Brazilian Empires, disagrees. "You must know that the protocol between states makes it clear that each country controls the religion in its land, between its regions and valleys," says the commander, telling al-Baghdadi that the Muslims of Brazil "unwillingly hide their Islamic beliefs, and fear the Frankish communities very much because the latter know them publicly as Christians." He cautions the scholar, "If I tell you to go to these people and the leaders of this Christian group catch you, I will not escape from the blame of the Ottoman authorities."

Al-Baghdadi decides to stay anyway. He learns some Portuguese and for the next six months the imam travels across Brazil, visiting different Muslim communities, and jotting down his observations. The manuscript that al-Baghdadi wrote in 1871, following his sojourn, titled *The Amusement of the Foreigner*—recently discovered at the Berlin State Library and translated—is a gem of a document, offering a rare view of Latin America through the eyes of a nineteenth century Arab traveler, who is enthralled by Brazil's architecture, the steam train, the landscape, the "fifty species of fruits, which do not exist in the Orient," the cuisine (the *farinha* that Brazilians eat reminds him of the *asida* porridge he grew up with), and the ways of the Native Americans. The text also offers a rich vignette of Muslim life in Brazil following the slave revolt of 1835 and in the wake of the American Civil War, as Pedro II ponders abolition.

A significant number of the slaves—7 to 8 percent by some estimates—brought to the New World were Muslim. In the last two decades, historians have uncovered texts written by Muslim slaves in Arabic, English, and Portuguese, shedding light on a far-flung population of Muslim Africans enslaved across the Americas. Many of these individuals were literate in Arabic and struggled to maintain their faith, fasting Ramadan, writing out the Quran from memory, sometimes even launching jihads against their overlords. Since the late 1980s, most of the scholarly writing on Muslim slaves has centered on North America; but in the last decade, scholars of Latin America—partly inspired by American academic debates—are revisiting their region's early colonial period. Historians point out that in North America and the English-speaking Caribbean, Muslim slaves were often given relatively privileged positions on the plantation, whereas in Latin America, the lives of Muslim slaves were characterized by "severe political repression." The Iberian colonists, as mentioned, saw Moorish slaves as particularly intractable and would shift to importing West African slaves. Yet even the latter were persecuted when suspected of being Muslim. The French and English settlers, on the other hand, viewed African Muslims positively; their encounter with Islam in the Americas was new, and not a continuation of the Reconquista.

The fascination with the African Muslims in the antebellum American South was due to the latter's literacy in Arabic. Bilali Muhammad, a slave on Sapelo Island, off the coast of Georgia, made a lasting mark on the American cultural imagination. Due to his literacy and leadership qualities, he would be appointed the manager of his master's plantation, overseeing approximately five hundred slaves; he gained notoriety after the War of 1812, during which he and eighty slaves successfully fought and prevented the British from invading Sapelo. He is also remembered for an Arabic text that he wrote about Islamic law, which he had placed in his coffin along with his Quran and his prayer rug. Bilali's literacy was always a source of fascination; he would become the subject of children's books, praised in contemporaries' memoirs, but his learnedness also posed a challenge to the ideology underpinning the system of bondage that saw Africans as incapable of reason.

Antebellum writers and plantation owners would expend a great deal of energy in coming up with a nonthreatening—"Oriental"— genealogy for Muslim slaves. Bilali of Sapelo Island would be described as "an Arab—man of the desert—slave hunter." Omar ibn Said—a Muslim slave in North Carolina, who wrote a fascinating autobiographical essay in 1831—would be similarly "Orientalized": "He is an Arab by birth of royal blood," who had been enslaved by Africans, "whom he had always hated," explained the *Providence Journal* in 1846. Muslim slaves—most of whom were of Wolof or Fula ancestry—were thus separated from other Africans, not only physically, in the work and positions that they were given, but also ideologically and epistemologically. In North America, writes Sylviane Diouf in her now classic *Servants of Allah,* "African Muslims were seen as owing their perceived superiority not to their own 'genes,' not even to their culture or proximity to the Arab world, but to foreign 'blood.'"

The experience of Muslim slaves in Latin America was radically different. There was no popular fascination with the writings of Muslim slaves; they were not co-opted upward. "The Spaniard was accustomed to the threatening presence of Islam," writes the Colombian historian Jaime Borja, describing the persecution of African Muslims in the country's northern coast. "But Islam and blackness were truly a dangerous combination." Repression, in the name of Catholic purity, however, only fueled defiance.

In the wee hours of January 25, 1835, the last day of Ramadan, Muslim slaves wearing *abadas* (gowns), skullcaps, and silver rings gathered in the basement of a two-story house in Salvador in northeast Brazil. They were making last-minute preparations for an uprising set to start in a few hours. Discontent had simmered among Bahia's Muslims for years, and events had brought matters to a boil: the Brazilian police had two months earlier disrupted a Muslim gathering to celebrate Lailat al-Miraj, the night when the Prophet ascended to heaven; then they publicly destroyed the community's makeshift Vitória mosque, and arrested two respected community leaders. A revolt was planned for the day after the "Night of Power" at the end of Ramadan, when the Quran was revealed. The Brazilian authorities, however, were alerted to the conspiracy ahead of time, and they broke into the lodge, attacking the insurgents. Violence erupted all over the city of Salvador, leaving seventy people dead, among them fifty slaves, and scores wounded.

Bahia in northeast Brazil, like the American South, was the primary destination for slaves transported from Africa. During the 1800s, thousands of Muslims, mostly Hausas, captives of the wars then raging in northern Nigeria, were imported from the Bight of Benin to Bahia. As their numbers increased, the Muslims (*imales,* as they were called), imbued with a religious fervor from the wars in Hausaland, grew restive. Insurrections erupted frequently, culminating in the rebellion of 1835. The Malê Revolt, as it came to be known, failed, but its Muslim character captured the attention of American and European publications, like the *Times* of London. The court trials and hearings that took place in Salvador afterward would reveal the complexity of Muslim communal life in nineteenth-century Bahia. Objects confiscated—amulets, documents, dozens of wooden writing boards—showed that the Muslims had mosques and schools, where students studied under community elders called *alufás.* Bahian Muslims celebrated the end of Ramadan by sacrificing sheep and, like their counterparts in North America, exchanging rice cakes, called *saka.* As historian Michael Gomez has observed, the material collected after the Malê rebellion revealed the similarities in cultural practice between Muslims in Brazil and their co-religionists elsewhere in the New World, showing that "Muslim dress and diet in Bahia were also distinctive, as they were in coastal Georgia and South Carolina."

The decades following the Malê Revolt were difficult. Many Muslims fled Salvador for Rio; others were exiled to Lagos, Nigeria. It was during this period that al-Baghdadi arrived in Brazil. The Ottoman scholar saw that Muslims were baptizing their children while secretly practicing their faith. The Muslim men pleaded with the Ottoman "priest" not to dress in Oriental attire when with them, so as not to attract attention. Al-Baghdadi, in turn, was struck by the way their wives dressed. "They do whatever they want just like Christian women who spend their time sleeping," he wrote. "They go to the markets without covering themselves; they drink what is forbidden." The Brazilian women would reject the changes in inheritance practice that al-Baghdadi wanted to introduce.

When al-Baghdadi travels north to Bahia, he remarks that there are more Muslims, that the men "shave their mustaches and leave their beards," and each Muslim "faction" has an imam with the title *alfa*. He is again taken aback by the sexual permissiveness, regretting that Muslim women in Salvador give alms to church and "do not veil themselves." He is particularly aghast at a custom whereby men can "try out" prospective wives by living with them before marriage, and states that he successfully put an end to that practice. From Salvador, the Ottoman scholar heads to Pernambuco, where he finds more Muslims, who, he notes, pray correctly and fast Ramadan. The Muslims of Brazil, who had hosted and benefited from his learning during his six-month stay, paid for his trip back to Constantinople.

Today, as the Orient beckons again, as Muslims from Africa and the Middle East migrate to Brazil, and as Afro-Brazilians mobilize politically, al-Baghdadi's manuscript and description of Muslim life is often cited. Islam would endure among Afro-Brazilians until the 1920s, and disappear just as Islamic and quasi-Islamic movements began emerging among African-Americans in the U.S. Today Islam is appearing again among Brazil's Afro-Brazilians, in movements that are building on the Malê's history of literacy.

Prophets of the City

"Allah says in the Quran that for every people there is a prophet who speaks their language. So who knows? A young black kid full of swagger and rhymes could appear in the favelas?" says Valter Gomes, a sixty-two-year-old community elder in São Bernardo do Campo on the outskirts of São Paulo.

This *município* is home to almost two million people, of whom many are laborers in the Ford and Volkswagen plants nearby and live in thousands of redbrick houses that line the hills. Gomes, who works at a halal slaughterhouse, is understandably upbeat. A veteran activist in São Paulo's Afro-Brazilian politics, throughout the 1990s he urged bickering factions to come together into one Islamic movement, and now they have. Today he's part of a community of Afro-Brazilian Muslims that has drawn a lot of media attention. "Islam has fallen into the mouth of the *periferia*," he says, referring to the urban periphery, "and we don't know what will follow."

The São Bernardo community is centered around the Abu Bakr Assidik Islamic Center, founded by Ahmad Ali Saifi, a Lebanese-Brazilian philanthropist and close friend of President Lula, who built his fortune exporting Brazilian halal beef to the Middle East. Attached to the Islamic center is Posse Hausa, an arts collective founded in the mid-1990s, just as São Paulo was becoming the capital of Brazilian hip-hop. Members note casually that it was through American hip-hop—particularly the Afrocentrist rap of the early 1990s—that they discovered Islam and Brazil's Muslim past.

"I got my political education through rap," says Honorê Al Amin Oaqd, the founder of the organization. "Through the music I discovered Malcolm X, and then the history of the Malês. I saw that Muslim slaves were at another level. They were learned, didn't drink, didn't smoke, knew how to write. I became Muslim and made hajj when I was twenty-one. I do believe had the Malês taken over Bahia on that 25th of January in 1835, they'd have had this country in their hands—and Brazil would be an Islamic state."

Posse Hausa's center is decorated with paintings of nineteenth-century Bahia—women in white head wraps, a man wearing a fez kneeling in prayer—and murals celebrating the uprising. The organization provides social services, but it's also trying to create a new identity for black Brazilians. Honorê thinks Islam can create solidarity, "The Hausas who led the revolt were on different sides of the wars in Nigeria—but they came together in Bahia." Activists at the center learn Arabic and hold workshops on the history of Bahia, teaching neighborhood youth how in 1807, a group of Malês tried to commandeer a fleet of ships and sail back to West Africa; how the 1835 revolt was inspired by the Haitian revolution of 1799–1804; and how history can dignify and empower. They're aware of how their narrative challenges the discourse of "racial democracy." "We're not promoting a racist discourse," explains Ali Jamal Shabazz, a recording artist who moved from eastern Brazil to join the group in São Paulo. "But we have countless Trayvon Martins killed every day in this country, black youth killed by police violence, by gang violence—and no one talks about it. We have problems that go all the way back to the plantation. And honestly those who die young in Brazil are those who never knew their history."

Sugar has a bittersweet meaning in this community. In the Freyrian narrative, sugar epitomizes the Oriental sensuality of the Brazilian plantation. For these young converts, sugar is linked to the Orient, but in a different way: *açúcar* was the essence of plantation slavery, but it's also what connects them to history and the wider world. They speak excitedly about how sugar was the handmaiden of Islam; that it was Muslim conquerors in Persia who brought the crop to the western Mediterranean and Iberia. (In his classic *Sweetness and Power,* historian Sidney Mintz writes, "And wherever they went, the Arabs brought with them sugar, the product and the technology of its production; sugar, we are told, followed the Koran.") Talking to these young men, I recalled the words of Orestes Fonseca, the imam of Havana, who tells his congregation, "Every time we hear Cubans proudly say 'I'm as Cuban as the sugar cane, *tan Cubano como la caña,*' we Muslims should smile, because sugar cane is not Cuban, it's Arab, it came from the Middle East to Andalusia to the Caribbean." Posse Hausa members echo this thinking: *sukar* is a Moorish legacy, brought by the conquistadors to the Americas, where it was cultivated by machete-wielding African Muslims. Sugar in the narrative of Afro-Brazilian Muslims—and Afro-Latino "reverts" in general—is thus not a byword for interracial intimacy, but a reminder of a history of oppression and a lost Muslim identity, where a retrieval of the latter can redress the effects of the former.

"Since I became Muslim, I don't drink, or smoke, my children have a father and mother, education, and a regulated life [*vida regrada*]," says Abdullah Malik Shabazz, who heads the Center for the Development of Brazilian Islam (NDIB), also in São Bernardo. "Islam gives us the instruments to combat social problems that afflict those of us who are the majority, but have less than everyone else."

The growth of Islam in Brazil has been noticeable. "In 2000, there were 32 mosques in Brazil; now there are 150 mosques in the country," says Paulo Pinto, an anthropologist at the Fluminense Federal University in Rio. "The War on Terror, the war in Iraq, the soap operas, with positive Muslim characters—all sparked an interest in Islam. It came to be seen as a form of resistance to globalization, to empire. And many people decided to convert—especially people who historically vote left—Trotskyites, socialists—they saw Islam as a new Third Worldism. Today, in Rio, for example, the majority of Muslims are converts."

But this view of Islam as a "new left" was rare in the nation's favelas, where for the last thirty years it has been evangelical movements that have made inroads. Yet in January 2009, *Época* magazine ran a cover story with the headline "Islam Is Growing in the Periphery of Brazil's Cities," and asking, "Young blacks are becoming Muslim activists in response to racial inequality. What do they think and what do they want—the Muslims of the ghetto?" The American embassy in Brasília would similarly report that "conversions to Islam are rising among non-Arab citizens." The irony here is that it is partly American cultural flows—hip-hop and Spike Lee's film on Malcolm X—that sparked an interest in Islam among favela youth.

"It's not surprising that you're seeing Islam in São Paulo's favelas," says Honorê, smiling. "This is the birthplace of Brazilian hip-hop—and in this country, hip-hop has a moral advantage over funk."

With Brazil's transition to democracy in the late 1980s, hip-hop and funk emerged as the sound of the favelas, challenging the hegemony of samba. Rap took root in São Paulo, while "funk carioca" developed in Rio; both genres would mock the performance of democracy represented by Carnival. Funk musicians, in particular, laced their lyrics with references to poverty, gang violence, and vigilantism. Brazilian funk grew out of two American musical genres: a type of rap called Miami bass (also known as "booty bass" for its sexually explicit lyrics) and an electronic dance pop known as Latin freestyle, also born in south Florida. In the mid-1990s, Rio-based DJs would fly up to Miami to pick up the latest rap mixtapes, and they created a musical crossbreed different from the original George Clinton–style funk of the 1970s. The *funkeiros* began throwing open-air parties in Rio's favelas, drawing youth from far away and inspiring clever new dances. In 2001, the "train dance" (*trenzinho*) became popular: young men and women would line up, crouching, and bounce forward, cheering, barking, thrusting their pelvises to the beat. In 2008, *creu* became the craze: an MC would rhyme while one or two female dancers in tiny shorts would show how rapidly they could thrust, *"Creu, creu, creu!"*

These dance steps—often accompanied by barking and spanking—are a far cry from samba's more subdued eroticism. As middle-class youth began doing the train dance, and songs like "My Little Mare" and "A Little Slap Doesn't Hurt" got more radio play, a backlash started. Funk would be blamed for civil unrest and social breakdown. "I Got Pregnant in the Train Dance," read a headline in the conservative magazine *Veja*. "Funk with a Police Record," read another. It didn't help that drug gangs were sponsoring weekly funk parties and mixtapes to attract young recruits; and DJs gave shout-outs to gangs like the Red Command. The police began raiding favela parties. And in 2007, a law—later repealed—was passed that made it all but impossible to hold open-air funk parties in the favelas.

Hip-hop and funk exposed rifts in Brazilian society and brought a note of discord into the national harmony that samba was supposed to broadcast. Hip-hop artists were more political, though, building organizations and working with party officials. The Posse Hausa activists genuinely believe that through an Islam-inflected hip-hop—and with support from the Workers' Party, which has supported rap organizations—they can draw attention to racial inequality, "convert the *funkeiro* tribe," and even challenge the evangelicals in the favelas and prisons. Honorê and his posse hold workshops on Malê history in prisons nationwide; they send books, gowns, and skull caps to inmates who have converted; they set up prayer rooms (*musallas*) in various favelas; they are currently lobbying local government to recognize "Black August" as a month to celebrate Afro-Brazilian history.

Brazil watchers will observe that middle-class Brazilian converts encounter Islam through Sufi organizations, whereas in the favelas it's African-American youth culture that sparks interest. American culture—religious and profane—plays an undeniable role in Brazilian religious life. The Pentecostal movement—which grew out of a storefront church in Los Angeles a century ago—has millions of followers in Brazil, and one of its star evangelists is the Grammy-winning gospel artist Aline Barros. It is rather ironic that American diplomats are worried about the rise of Islam among African-descended communities in Brazil and the Caribbean when it's American cultural exports that are triggering that interest. But such America-centered accounts of favela Islam ignore a critical domestic factor: President Lula's educational reforms and the political ferment in Bahia today.

Pelourinho, as Salvador's historic center is called, is dazzling in the summer twilight. A cluster of low colonial buildings overlooks the clear blue water of the Bay of Bahia. The cobblestone lanes are lit by hanging streetlamps; the pastel-colored stucco town houses and baroque church façades beam with history. As banners of African masks flutter in the wind, the sound of trombones and trumpets grows louder. Carnival in Salvador's old city is a quiet affair compared to Rio's or São Paulo's. The procession tries to replicate an earlier era: brass bands stroll through the alleyways; teenagers pound drums tied around their waists; young girls with white bandanas carry effigies of different *orishas*—African gods—"disguised" as Catholic saints. No floats or trucks are allowed into the historic area. Also absent is the near-naked samba queen. The female protagonist in this Carnival is the Bahian woman, with her distinctive head wrap and white hoopskirt. Whether walking with the procession; selling water, food, *baiana* dolls; or teaching tourists how to wrap their *rodilha* around their heads, the *baiana* with the embroidered dress covering up her body is a ubiquitous presence in northeast Brazil.

Gilberto Freyre, not surprisingly, saw the *baiana* as an important symbol. The anthropologist, born soon after abolition in Pernambuco, just north of Bahia, was captivated by the Malês and their institutions. In the "dark of the slave huts," he wrote, they ran schools and cooperatives to purchase each other's freedom. The revolt of 1835 would shape his view of Brazilian identity. If antebellum North Americans gave African Muslim slaves an "Oriental" origin, Freyre thought, the Muslim presence in Bahia afforded the entire Brazilian nation an Oriental pedigree. The Malês, with their "Mohammedan fire," brought another injection of Moorish civilization into Brazil. And the African Muslim woman of Bahia would—like the "Moorish brown girl"—enchant the Portuguese man, and come to stand as a reminder of Islamic influence. Freyre extolled the *baianas*—"tall, heraldic-appearing, aristocratic in bearing"—with their long white shawls and "Mussulman turban on their heads." That turban—the *rodilha*—is making a cultural comeback in northeast Brazil.

The musical group Ilê Aiyê came together in Salvador in 1974. Their aim was to "re-Africanize" the city's Carnival, which had become tourist-and-samba-dominated, and so they set up floats celebrating different African countries and carried signs that read "Black Power." "We wanted to call our group Black Power," says Antônio Carlos Vovô, the school's seventy-year-old founder, "but the federal police and the military said no, they saw us as too radical, too American." Through their activism, Ilê Aiyê and other Afro-Brazilian *blocos* were able to revitalize Pelourinho—long neglected by the government— and prompt UNESCO to declare Salvador's center a World Heritage Site in 1985. Yet as pioneering and brazen as they are, it was only in 2002 that Ilê Aiyê decided to celebrate the Malê Revolt in Carnival. In February of that year, squadrons of school members, women in beige turbans and long print skirts flanked by young men in white robes, marched behind a float with red-white Moorish arches, chanting, "Night of glory perhaps . . . in the name of Allah." The song, composed for the occasion, imagined how the world would have "turned" had the revolt of 1835 not been betrayed. Ilê Aiyê set a precedent. Their *enredo* received high marks from the festival's judges, and soon other *blocos afros,* like Olodum and Malê Debalê, began recounting the Muslim revolt. Brazil's post-9/11 interest in Islam thus manifests itself differently in Bahia than in the Carnivals of Rio and São Paulo. In 2012, leaders of Malê Debalê stood atop a float truck, leading thousands in chant, "We're Black, Muslims/Warriors and revolutionaries—*Somos negros, Muçulmanos/Guerreiros e revolucionários.*" It's hard to imagine a similar war cry sounding at Rio's Carnival.

The growing references to Bahia's Islamic past are also due to Lula's reforms. In 2003, the Brazilian congress passed Law 10/639, requiring public and private schools to teach "the black struggle in Brazil, black Brazilian culture and the role of blacks in social, economic and political aspects of the history of Brazil." The law mandated that schools celebrate a "National Day of Black Consciousness." This initiative sparked a wave of research and advocacy to bring Afro-Brazilian figures into history textbooks. Activists are now trying to find out more about the lives of individuals like Luísa Mahin, a Muslim *baiana* who fought in the revolt of 1835. The memory of this "Queen of Brazil" has been preserved in song and chants: she was, according to local lore, a vendor by day, an Arabic scribe by night, who participated in the rebellion but then disappeared, possibly deported to Angola. The political ferment in Bahia has spread to other cities as well. Today in Brazil, as in the U.S., there is a keen interest in the Islam of the plantation: Afro-Brazilians and the children of Muslim immigrants are studying the writings of slaves and the rituals of Afro-Brazilian religion, looking for "Muslim retentions." Is the white cloth that is laid down in the middle of the room during a Candomblé ceremony a Muslim legacy? Does the chant "*É barika é barika*" derive from the Arabic *baraka,* meaning "grace"? Is the holding of Umbanda ceremonies on Friday a Muslim remnant? Is the Afro-Brazilian distrust of Catholicism—and attraction to Protestantism—a Muslim holdover, as Freyre suggested?

The Brazilian government has made Bahia's past central to its cultural diplomacy. When addressing Muslim audiences, Lula celebrates the history of the northeast: "Muslims who came to Brazil as slaves laid the foundation of the country." In November 2009, he received the Palestinian leader Mahmoud Abbas in Bahia, the latter praising Brazil as an example of *convivencia* that the world could learn from. Bahia is also pivotal to Brazil's new Africa policy. Lula—and his successor, Dilma Rousseff—opened more embassies in Africa, expanded trade ties, and built a symbolic fiber-optic cable running from Bahia to West Africa. Lula's and Rousseff's overtures to Africa and the Middle East are intended to show how far Brazil has come toward achieving "racial democracy," but also to integrate the Islam of upwardly mobile migration—represented in Rio and São Paulo's Carnivals—with the protest Islam seen in Salvador's street processions.

As in the U.S., where there are now tours of Georgia's Sea Islands, for people who want to meet the descendants of Bilali Muhammad and witness Muslim traces in local Baptist traditions, Bahia is drawing a curious kind of "Muslim roots" tourism. It's not unusual these days to see Dutch or French Muslims inside the Church of Our Lady of the Conception of Lapinha, in downtown Salvador, looking up in awe at the church's mosquelike interior: the bright-colored Moorish tilework and floral patterns; figures of a crucified Christ and statuettes of Mary placed inside engraved arches; hues of blue, orange, and beige. Just above one corner arch, a black-and-white Arabic inscription unfolds counterclockwise around the edge of the ceiling: "Behold, This is the Miracle of God and This is the Door of Heaven." The church brochure says this house of worship was founded in 1771; the church's tour guide tells visitors the edifice served as a shelter for fleeing Muslim slaves after 1835; other sources say the church was designed and built in the 1860s by a Muslim (*inmale*) named Manoel Friandes. And that is all we know: Is the Arabic inscription a Muslim adage that Friandes buried in the Morisco patterns, or a biblical verse translated into the language of the Quran? And is the church facing east toward Mecca, the direction of Muslim prayer, or toward West Africa?

The Moorish Atlantic

The cultural memory of Islamic Spain—and the question of Moorish influence in the Spanish- and Portuguese-speaking worlds—has long divided Latin American intellectuals and leaders. The Mexican novelist Carlos Fuentes rejoiced in the cultural mélange that Spain poured into Latin America, and the "river of voices" heard in the *cante jondo* song, which absorbed centuries of influence, "from the Arab call to prayer to the latest tropical rumba." But his compatriot the Nobel laureate Octavio Paz saw Moorish influence—specifically the "Hispano-Arab idea" of caudillo—as the root of the militarism that plagued Latin America during the 1970s. In Brazil, the conservative economist and diplomat Roberto Campos never bought Freyre's theories, and lamented the vestiges of Arab despotism on Brazilian society. Throughout the past century, particularly during the Cold War, Latin American leaders from Cuba's Fidel Castro to Argentina's Juan Perón would call for Muslim-Latin solidarity in the face of imperial domination, highlighting historic ties to the Orient, while their political opponents would call for a distancing from Africa and the Middle East. When the nationalist left is ascendant in Latin America, as it was after the Cuban Revolution, there is talk of solidarity with the Orient, and the Moor (or Mooress) invariably makes an appearance.

The *mulata* has been central to Cuban nationalism since the colonial era. As in Brazil, there was an association between sugar, sensuality, and darker skin. To woo foreign customers, exporters in the nineteenth century would place pictures of *mulatas* on cigar and sugar packages, referring to light *mulatas* as "first-rate" sugar or "second-rate white." As Cuban nationalists began agitating against Spanish rule, the *mulata* became a symbol of colonial exploitation, but also a source of pride; she represented the miscegenation that distinguished the island from its Spanish oppressor. The Cuban nationalists expressed solidarity with the Muslims then also struggling against colonial rule. In 1893, as the Berbers of northern Morocco rose up in revolt against

Spanish rule, the poet José Martí would declare, "*Seamos moros!* Let us be Moors . . . we [Cubans] who will probably die by the hand of Spain." The Spanish overlords withdrew in 1898, but the U.S. gained control of the island's sugar economy. Havana became a tourism destination, playground for American artists and mobsters. In 1926, the novelist Waldo Frank would wax poetic about the *mulata:* "The hips and the high heels are jazz; the arms and breasts swath her in Andalusian softness; under the blare of her rouge Africa mumbles." The miscegenated woman would again become a reminder of the island's sexual and economic exploitation.

When Castro came to power in 1959, he shut down Havana's glitzy, mob-operated casinos and promised to provide sex workers with legal jobs. But the music of 1950s Havana—*danzóns* like Eliseo Grenet's "La Mora," which spoke of Moorish beauties and enchanting eyes—had already spread around the world. In Cairo, the Sudanese crooner Sayed Khalifa shook his maracas and band members in bow ties banged on congas as he sang "Al Mambo Sudani"; this chirpy Latin tune became a hit as Castro and Che Guevara's revolutionary fervor reached the Arab world. Castro made a philo-Muslim pan-Africanism central to his regime's ideology and policy initiatives. In his famous 1959 speech on race, the *jefe maximo,* echoing Freyre, underlined Cuba's Moorish origins: "We all have lighter or darker skin. Lighter skin implies descent from Spaniards who themselves were colonized by the Moors who came from Africa. Those who are more or less dark-skinned came directly from Africa. Moreover, nobody can consider himself as being of pure, much less superior, race."

Almost a half century after the Cuban Revolution, a new mix of tropicalism and Orientalism would surface. In 2002, a group called Hanine y Son Cubano appeared on the international music scene. Their debut album, a collection of classic Arab compositions set to the rhythms of *guajira* and *son montuno*—evoking belle époque Cuba and pre–civil war Beirut—climbed the Arab pop charts. Produced by the eccentric Lebanese politico and club promoter, Michel Elefteriades, who was exiled in Havana during the late 1990s—and friendly with Che Guevara's daughter, Aleida—the group appeared just as the Cuban regime began restoring pre-revolution casinos to draw tourists, and a new discourse of Arab-Latin solidarity was emerging. Hanine y Son Cubano's performances made creative use of Cuban lore: The vocalist, Hanine Abou Chakra, plays the role of an Arabic-speaking *morisca,* in one video ambling languidly through a colonial-style mansion, singing of exile and homeland. Afro-Cubans dressed in white call on Shango, the god of thunder, and convert into trumpeters in white suits and fedoras. As they kick and twirl around her, the *morisca* raises her arms above her head, swaying her torso.

When he returned to Lebanon, Elefteriades, known for his anarchist views—he likes to be called "the Emperor of Nowheristan"—opened a Cuban casino in Beirut called Amor y Libertad, whose theme is revolution: the walls are decorated with quotes from Castro and Che; cigars and flyers on the injustice of the embargo against Cuba are passed out to clients. The post-9/11 tropicalism-Orientalism wave would take different manifestations, but it was the cultural effect of Latin America's response to the War on Terror.

September 11—like 1492—has a two-edged meaning in Latin America. It was on September 11, 1973, that a CIA-backed coup by General Augusto Pinochet led to the death of Chile's Marxist president Salvador Allende. Pinochet would put in place Operation Condor, a joint effort that authorized the intelligence services of Argentina, Brazil, Uruguay, Paraguay, and Chile to hunt down leftists across Latin America; for the next decade, the campaign would lead to the torture or disappearance of tens of thousands. When the Cold War ended, Latin American democracies began the arduous task of dismantling the secret prisons and setting up truth commissions. Thus, when Donald Rumsfeld flew to Santiago, Chile, in November 2002, to persuade Latin American defense ministers of the merits of a coordinated security policy—to integrate "various specialized capabilities into larger capabilities"—he received a cool response. A handful of military officials liked the idea of fusing the War on Drugs with the War on Terror, but left-leaning leaders—many of them former political prisoners—were wary of a continent-wide war on "narco-terrorism." In early 2003, Lula took office in Brazil, and Néstor Kirchner was voted president of Argentina; and over the next few years Ecuador, Bolivia, Paraguay, and Uruguay elected leftist leaders who decided to pass on Rumsfeld's offer.

The majority of South American states voted against the invasion of Iraq. Brazil led the opposition to American efforts to create a region-wide version of the Patriot Act and to the rendition system. In February 2013, the *Washington Post* published an astonishing map highlighting (in red) the fifty-four countries in the world that contributed to the U.S. program of "extraordinary rendition," either by hosting CIA prisons or by allowing their airspace to be used for secret flights, and showed that the only region in the world that did not participate was Latin America. Even Colombia, the sole South American nation to vote for the Iraq War, and a staunch U.S. ally in the War on Terror, was untainted; the only speck of red in the region appeared on Cuba's eastern coast, at the Guantanamo Bay naval base, claimed "in perpetuity" by Teddy Roosevelt in 1903. Latin America's left turn revived the South-South discourse of the 1960s. In Bolivia, Evo Morales would set up a "Ministry of Decolonization." Latin American leaders would reach out to Asia, Africa, and the Middle East, especially as it emerged that in Iraq, the U.S. was using methods of counterinsurgency developed in Central America ("the Salvador Option"), deploying paramilitary squads trained by Reagan-era veterans of the Central American "dirty wars." In December 2010, Brasília would lead a number of Latin American states in recognizing Palestinian statehood at the UN. And speaking at the Security Council in September 2012, Dilma Rousseff lambasted Western states for their "Islamophobic prejudice."

In truth, it was Venezuela's Hugo Chávez, elected in 1998, who was the first of this crop of leaders to adopt a discourse of Arab-Latin solidarity, urging his compatriots to "return to their Arab roots." But his support for the repressive regimes of Iran, Libya, and Syria alienated many. Brazil had the soft power to charm and the hard power to rearrange regional alliances. Brazil's rise would pull a number of South American states out of the U.S.'s orbit, foiling Washington's security strategy; the second Bush administration in turn would pull back, solidifying its "security corridor" further north, running from Colom-

bia through Central America to Mexico. Colombia would emerge as
the anchor of Washington's security policy in Latin America. It was
also Colombia that would produce Shakira, the global cultural icon of
the 9/11 decade, and the "enchanted Mooress" par excellence.

The Lebanese-Colombian singer brought Middle Eastern
culture—albeit with a Latin rock pulse—to millions. Advised after
9/11 to drop the belly dancing and the Arabic riffs from her music
because it could hurt sales, she refused, expressing horror at the
hate of "everything that's Arab, or seems Arab." In dozens of venues
around the world—concerts, sporting events, MTV—she shimmied
blindfolded, crawled around inside a cage growling like a she-wolf,
explained her "oral fixation" to fans, and famously humped a speaker
onstage in front of three billion viewers at the 2010 World Cup final.
In Europe, the United States, South America, and the Middle East,
the chanteuse fostered a fashion for hip scarves with coins and tassels. In a random check of Cairo nightclubs in 2003, Egyptian government officials confiscated twenty-six Shakira outfits, weighing no
more than 150 grams (five ounces), and deemed "scandalous."

In some ways, Shakira was catapulted by the post-9/11 interest
in the Orient, and her performances often took an explicitly political
tone; but she managed to transcend the political rows that touched
other global divas. During the run-up to the Iraq War, her onstage
dancers would wear masks of Tony Blair and George W. Bush. Backdrop screens would flash images of Bush and Saddam Hussein as two
puppets playing a sinister game of chess, with the Grim Reaper as the
puppeteer. Yet while Beyoncé and Mariah Carey were apologizing for
performing private shows for Muammar Gaddafi (the former forced
to cancel a tour in Malaysia due to protests), Shakira was strolling
through the Pyramids crooning in Arabic. She took a highly publi-
cized tour of the Middle East, visiting her father's ancestral village in
the Bekaa Valley in eastern Lebanon. She was appointed a UN goodwill ambassador and invited to share the stage with Presidents Santos
and Obama at the Summit of the Americas in 2012.

Public diplomacy notwithstanding, Shakira's greatest impact—
like Jade's in the Brazilian telenovela—has been to popularize an aesthetic of Mideast-inflected miscegenation (*mestizaje*), personified by

the tanned, limber girl with a hip scarf and an upper-arm cuff; and to bring a pop tropicalist-Orientalist syncretism—long present in the gay underground—into the mainstream. After 2002, Arab-Latin fiestas and "1001 Valentino Nights" began popping up from Los Angeles to Beirut, a curious sideshow to the War on Terror.

Whether it's the "Brazilian example," the politics of solidarity, or the Muslim slave manuscripts that continue to appear in places like Panama, Trinidad, and Bahia, Latin America is viewed warmly by Muslims these days, as a progressive region, a place where Islam endured quietly after being suffocated in Iberia in 1492. Young Muslims looking for a place to be openly Muslim are idealizing Brazil, as that rare Western state that has no issue with Islam. Racial and ethnic tensions do abound in Brazil, but what the South American giant does illustrate, richly, is the extent to which Western states understand Islam through their own identity. In France, Islam is perceived as a threat to secularism; in Holland, it's a menace to multiculturalism; in Austria, people speak of the "gates of Vienna" and Ottoman reconquest. But in Brazil, a nation that views itself as hybrid and anti-imperial, the standard wisdom is that "mixing" with Islam will only make the country more mixed and voluptuous and anti-imperial. Visiting Brazil during the 9/11 decade, one is struck by the absence of organized hostility to Muslims and the absence of conflict around Islam and music as it has raged in Europe and the U.S. This state of affairs is contingent, the product of a political moment, and could shift with a change of government or an act of violence; then Brazil will turn her back on the East, and the Mooress will vanish again.

3

Ghettos in the Sky

One chilly Sunday in January 2011, hundreds of youths—Moroccans, Tunisians, Turks, Congolese—lined up outside the Elckerlyc theater in downtown Antwerp. Young men in jeans and skullcaps, ankle-length tunics and Timberland boots, some in military fatigues and kaffiyehs wrapped around their heads, and young women, mostly in hijab, a few in face veils, filed into the auditorium through separate doors. The event was titled "De Terugweg" (The Way Back), a discussion about hip-hop and Islam set up by a local organization called Al Ihsaan. The listed performers were popular Dutch rapper Salah Eddin, British reggae artist Muslim Belal, and Napoleon, once a member of Tupac Shakur's crew the Outlawz.

The emcee for the event was a Dutch Muslim activist known as Al Khataab. Wearing a white robe and a scraggly beard, he came onstage, welcomed everyone, and apologized that the rapper Salah Eddin had not been able to make it. He introduced the first act: a Jamaican youth from South London who had embraced Islam as a teenager and changed his name from Ashley Chin to Muslim Belal walked onstage, dressed in a black *shalwar kameez,* a red turban, and leather sandals. Pacing back and forth, he described his difficult upbringing in Brixton, how he quit rap for the Quran, and how he now does a cappella rap as *da'wa;* and then, in a lilting, melodic voice, he sang what can be described as a roots-reggae *nasheed,* describing his spiritual journey. "I'm a man on a mission / Who made the transition," he intoned.

Al Khataab then came back onstage and, speaking in rapid-fire Dutch, explained why he had also quit the hip-hop lifestyle. He spoke breathlessly for twenty minutes, sprinkling his sermon with American hip-hop phrases ("gotcha!," "there's gonna be a paaaaartay!," and "uh-uh-uh!"), pausing only to recite, in beautifully melodious style, verses from the Quran to underline his point.

And finally, Napoleon, the headliner, came on.

Wearing a brown robe, white skullcap, and combat boots, Napoleon recited a prayer in impeccable Arabic and, feet crossed, sat down to speak. He talked about personal responsibility and the urgent need to return to Islam. "Whatever evil happens to Muslims in Belgium or Holland is because of *our* deeds, because of what *we* are doing. Don't blame anyone else—don't blame the Jews in Palestine." He then explained how he had left the music business. "Tupac was a good friend of mine, but he died upon misguidance." The audience clapped at the mention of Tupac. "Why do you clap for Tupac, but not for the *sahaba*?" Napoleon interjected, referring to the prophet Muhammad's companions. He began quizzing the audience members about their favorite rappers. "How many people here like Nas?" Loud cheering. "Did you know that Nas said, 'I'm God's son—you are my children.' Did you know Nas said, 'There's heaven for atheists.'" He went on: "How many people here like Biggie Smalls?" Applause. "I don't want you to think I'm picking on Biggie because he was my enemy," he said. "But did you know Biggie said, 'When I die, I wanna go to hell!'? And Jay-Z? You know Jay-Z says, 'I am God with the flow. Jehovah is his name'?"

Napoleon shook his head. "Muslims be repeatin' these lyrics—and the angels are recording."

In his preacherly tone, he continued. "Every year thousands of people from around the world make *hijra* to Vegas—to wait for Tupac to reappear." He shook his head. "The *sahaba* should be our role models, not these rappers!" he said, his voice growing agitated. "God praised the *sahaba* in the Quran—he did not praise Nas or Jay-Z!" The former rapper asked his audience, "What are we doing, remixing Islam? Arab tribes used to be into music. But the Prophet did not say, 'Yo, Abu Bakr, go get drums! Now you and Abu Waqas go and sing the Quran to that tribe!' He didn't!"

His tone softened. "I had millions of dollars when I was in the music industry, and *walahi*, man, I went to sleep depressed every night." He described his religious awakening and his move to Saudi Arabia. "The first time I made hajj, I loved the *deen*, the *shahada*. Man"—he smiled—"I thought I was high off the *zamzam*, but then I realized it was the *iman*." Napoleon ended with words of advice for the youth. "The *shabab* here is cool. But in this city you have Muslims breaking into stores," referring to recent unrest in Antwerp and Brussels. "You don't want people to say, 'Why do these Muslims come to this country?' You need to have shyness for Allah and his religion."

The event ended, and the audience exited quietly. The young men and women, gathering in the theater vestibule, seemed stunned. "He's on our side, but I don't know," one youth said, and shrugged. Napoleon's pep talk was passionate, witty—and with its mix of classical Arabic and urban slang, tailor-made for the audience. But the kids had not expected the "show" to be a diatribe against their favorite hip-hop artists—and against music itself.

The speakers' calls for a return to the pure Islam of the *sahaba*, their frowning upon music and disdain for politics, and particularly Napoleon's belief that young Muslims had placed hip-hop icons on a par with the Prophet's companions, conveyed their Salafi beliefs. The ex-rapper was touring Europe and giving a lecture titled "Is There a Ghetto in Heaven?" He had stopped in Antwerp, where there were intense ideological battles between Sufis, Islamists, and Shiites, and in effect used his hip-hop credentials to dis the music and promote Salafism. His tour wrapped up in early 2011 just as the protests were spreading from Tunisia to Egypt, and he would soon return to his base in Riyadh and begin speaking—and tweeting—against the uprisings and in support of the Saudi regime.

American converts to Salafism have appeared on Arabic-language Saudi religious channels since the early 1990s. But the rise of the hip-hopper-turned-Salafi-evangelist—like Napoleon of Tupac's Outlawz, Loon of Bad Boy Records, and Sean Cross of Ruff Ryders Entertainment—who tours Europe and Muslim-majority states speaking out against music and hip-hop culture is recent, and shows how different regimes are trying to direct Muslim youth culture. After

9/11, both the Bush and the Blair government would begin to promote Sufism as a counter to Islamist influence among British Muslim youth, setting up Sufi institutions, bringing American Sufi scholars and musicians to speak in England. This was part of a broader War on Terror strategy that extended from West Africa to South Asia, where the Bush administration and its allies sought to mobilize local Sufi brotherhoods and institutions as a way to check the transnational Salafi movement. Music was at the heart of this "Sufi solution," with various regimes—the U.S., Britain, Pakistan—deploying Sufi-inflected musical practices from *qawali* to "Muslim hip-hop" to alter perceptions, calm passions, challenge Islamist narratives, and draw youth away from extremism. The emergence of the rapper-turned-Salafi-ambassador in the late 2000s, and Salafism's steadfast opposition to hip-hop, thus tells a larger story about the relationship between Islam and urban disillusionment, political identity and music, and the resilience of Islamist movements in the face of "state-sponsored Sufism."

Thobe-Wearin', *Miswak*-Chewin'

The roots of Salafi thought lie in the Wahabi movement, which appeared in eighteenth-century Saudi Arabia; the Salafi movement today is trying to return to the "pure" Islam of the Prophet's companions and the first three generations of Muslims who experienced the rise of Islam. Salafis see themselves as defending the timeless Islam of the "pious forefathers" (*as-salaf as-salih*) from change and innovation, and as such contest the authority of all four schools of Sunni law, which together constitutes centuries of jurisprudence. The Saudi state began to spread Salafi ideology internationally in the early 1960s with the establishment of the Muslim World League. These efforts were stepped up following the Iranian Revolution. The Saudi regime would answer Khomeini's revolutionary Shiism by exporting an ultra-conservative Sunni Islam, through media, the funding of mosques and schools, and student scholarships.

The 1990s were a critical decade in the shaping of Muslim youth movements in the West; it was in this decade that second-generation Muslims—the children of migrants—came of age, began building organizations, pushing for rights, and triggering very public debates (especially in France and Britain) about integration and Islam. It was also in the 1990s that the Saudi regime, after the Gulf War, seriously escalated efforts to spread Salafism. King Fahd's decision to host the U.S. military in 1990 gave rise to an antigovernment movement within the kingdom that split the country's religious establishment, pitting those for and those against the decision to allow American troops on holy land in a conflict that reverberated among Muslims around the world. This rift would eventually give rise to Al Qaeda (which grew out of Salafism's jihadi fringe). Salafi ideology would continue to make inroads in Europe and America, as the Saudi regime exported dissident clerics, and students who had received scholarships to study at the University of Medina returned home, setting up mosques and centers to spread their message of doctrinal purity. By the late 1990s, the bearded man wearing an Arabian robe (*thobe*) that ends mid-calf and the woman in a niqab had become familiar figures on the American and European urban periphery.

In *Global Salafism,* Dutch scholar Roel Meijer observes that Salafism is not explicitly revolutionary; it does not aim to overthrow a political order, but rather it is "iconoclastic in the name of conservatism," aiming to build a superior moral order by resocializing the individual, the family, and community institutions. Salafism usually appears in areas where social relations have broken down. In parts of the developing world, where nationalist causes are strong, the Muslim Brotherhood, with its attempts to control the nation-state, tends to dominate; but in areas where states have failed or social breakdown exists, as in post–civil war Algeria or Somalia, Salafi groups will emerge and try to bring political order to these conditions of *fitna* (anarchy). For similar reasons, Salafism has an appeal in the ghettos of Europe and America. In areas of high unemployment and urban violence, where state institutions are absent and families are fraying, Salafism tends to take hold. With their strict social code and ability to enforce Islamic norms, Salafis are seen as a force for order and moral rectitude.

While there is a jihadi-Salafi fringe, made up of de facto revolutionary anarchists who believe in using violence to overthrow a social or political order (Al Qaeda is the best-known jihadi-Salafi organization), Salafism is "activist while being (mostly) quietist." Most Salafis in Europe and America avoid politics and political participation, saying it leads to *fitna*, factionalism, and loss of identity. But many are active in *da'wa* (outreach) and in trying to bring Islamic norms to the spaces they inhabit. And it is this focus on society rather than the state, and on resocializing youth, that has given the Salafis an advantage over other groups like the Jamaat-i-Islami and the Muslim Brotherhood (who are more focused on gaining state power). In the early 1990s, for example, Salafi activists in Britain began competing for young hearts and minds with other organizations, the Jamaati Islami's Young Muslim Organization (YMO), the Muslim Brotherhood–inspired Muslim Association of Britain, and the pan-Islamist Hizb ut-Tahrir (HT). The Salafis—with their command of Arabic and religious scripture, and the support they had from top Saudi scholars—easily edged out the "clean-shaved kids" from Hizb ut-Tahrir and the Young Muslims.

Rather than lobbying the state, British Salafi groups focused on "purification and education," building institutions and Islamicizing their communities. In Birmingham and Luton, for instance, they delivered services, provided security, confronted drug dealers and far-right groups like the English Defence League. (Some of the Salafi leaders had fought in Afghanistan after the Soviet withdrawal and built reputations as defenders of the *ummah*.) They also advocated a return to a "pure" Islam: urging young men and women to fast, pray, and dress Islamically; speaking out against gender mixing, consumption of alcohol, and socializing with non-Muslims; and denouncing the practices of "folk Islam," from the veneration of saints to using music for worship. And this approach succeeded. The youth who gravitated to Salafism during their late teens and early twenties were more interested in building new identities and community than in capturing or overthrowing the state. The fixed, "authentic" Islam that the Salafi activists taught resonated with the children of immigrants who were culturally disconnected from the Sufi Islam of their parents. From the start, young Salafi converts in Britain and elsewhere were clashing with their parents, who were often steeped in the old country's Sufi traditions. The youngsters saw their Islam as authentic and free of any "folkloric" innovation, and were openly contemptuous of Sufism's ritual practices, referring to Sufi Muslims—often their own parents and community elders—who visit grave sites or saints' tombs as heretics and "grave worshippers."

Across Europe, Salafis with their opposition to political participation have clashed with other Muslim organizations. In France, while the Muslim Brotherhood–leaning French Council of the Muslim Faith calls on French Muslims to vote and integrate, the Salafis advocate separatism and a boycott of elections, and no engagement with the French republic. As in Britain or Holland, the French Salafi will claim to be Muslim first, and adopt a borderless, transnational outlook that bypasses the nation-state, identifying a local neighborhood (*quartier*) with the global *ummah*. Salafism's aversion to political participation and the nation-state is reminiscent of another urban (quasi-Muslim) movement, the Nation of Islam (NOI). And in the U.S.—as in Britain—the rise of Salafism was linked to the declining fortune of the NOI.

For the Love of Philly

Every Ramadan, in what is now a yearly tradition, Aman Ali, an Indian-American comedian and Reuters journalist, drives across the U.S., visiting far-flung Muslim communities from Alaska to Florida, writing about different mosques and their varied ways of celebrating Ramadan. (His blog, called *30 Mosques in 30 Days,* is keenly followed by youth in the U.S. and Britain.) On August 15, 2010, as he drove into South Philadelphia, the comedian-turned-ethnographer observed, "Apparently it's not an uncommon sight in Philadelphia to see female parking meter attendants that cover up their faces in full niqab. It's that kind of 'I'm Muslim, so you're just going to have to deal with it' attitude that's so refreshing to me."

Visitors are often struck by Philadelphia's Muslim-influenced youth culture: from the Quranic references that local popular artists like the R&B diva Jill Scott invoke in their songs to what *Philadelphia* magazine dubbed "Muslim-inspired menswear." It's not uncommon, in the City of Brotherly Love, to see young men wearing scraggly, mustache-less beards—called a "Sunni" in Philadelphia, or a "Philly beard" outside the city—combined with calf-length trousers and long shirts. Conservative Muslims mock these stylish youngsters as "wannabes" and "assalama-faykers," but these youths see Islam as cool, "street," and politically conscious. "I'm not Muslim," says one young man, smiling and stroking his beard, "but I'm righteous." The untrimmed Sunni—popularized in hip-hop culture by local rapper Freeway—even became a political issue in early 2006, when a local police officer was fired for refusing to clip his facial hair down to the required quarter-inch. When the officer appealed, Philadelphia's police commissioner, Sylvester Johnson—the only Muslim police chief in the country—declared, "You don't wear religion on your face, you wear it on your heart and mind." Philadelphia's oft-commented-on Muslim styles—the rolled-up pant legs, beard, etc.—are Salafi influences on street culture (though the rolled-up pant *legs* are to be distinguished from the *single* rolled-up pant *leg,* which is more a style associated with the Bloods and Crips gangs and popularized by rapper LL Cool J).

One garment that strikes Aman is the kiltlike *izaar,* which he dubs "the Muslim Man Skirt." He notices young men wearing it in the downtown area. At the United Muslim Mosque, the comedian quips, "I woulda worn one too tonight, but I didn't get a chance to shave my legs." Aman asks mosque attendees—a question that often arises—why an Islamic aesthetic is more visible in Philadelphia's streets than in other cities. A community elder explains that Islam's appeal is tied to the Nation of Islam's decades-long presence in the city. "In the 1960s," Aman writes, "the Nation of Islam in Philadelphia got respect from just about everyone on the block because they cleaned up the violence and drugs in the neighborhoods. So when the Nation of Islam transitioned into mainstream [Islam] here in Philly, they held onto those views of demanding respect and having no tolerance [for] things like drugs and violence." Aman wraps up his trip, saying, "I was sitting among some certified Muslim badasses. Maybe if I ever get to their level of toughness, I could pull off wearing a man skirt too."

Philadelphia is not the only place where Salafism is clashing and mixing with hip-hop in unexpected ways, but the city is a microcosm of a larger debate about Islam, music, and urban blight.

> Wake up all the builders,
> Time to build a new land
> I know we can do it
> If we all lend a hand . . .
> —*Written by Luqman Abdul Haqq*
> (aka Kenny Gamble)

Philadelphia draws curious young Muslims as well as urban planners from Europe, not only because the city is home to the country's largest Salafi community, but also because it boasts a unique urban development model that uses music and religious capital. At the center of the initiative is Luqman Abdul Haqq, a real-estate developer who has harnessed the energies of diverse Muslim groups to revitalize the city's southeast area. When Luqman walks down Fifteenth Street, wearing his traditional black robe, with his ample white beard and his skullcap, returning people's salaams, it's hard to believe that this sheikh is one of the fathers of disco music and R&B—more specifically, a subgenre called the Philadelphia sound. Luqman's given name is Kenny Gamble. He is the founder of Philadelphia International Records (PIR), and in the 1970s he and his partner, Leon Huff, recorded dozens of R&B and disco hits for artists like the O'Jays, the Delfonics, Teddy Pendergrass, and Patti Labelle, winning Grammys and producing almost two hundred gold and platinum records.

Even before he became Luqman Abdul Haqq, Gamble's music had a social message. In 1977, he wrote "Let's Clean Up the Ghetto," recorded by the Philadelphia International All Stars, calling on communities to "do for self" and not "depend on the man downtown." So it was perhaps no surprise when, in the early 1990s, this music mogul moved back to South Philadelphia, where he grew up, and plunged into community organizing. He established Universal Companies, a nonprofit that includes a housing-development initiative, a charter school, and a social services agency. Working with the Philadelphia Chamber of Commerce, he began buying up plots of land and vacancies in the city's south-central area, building houses, schools, clinics, and senior homes. Since its founding, Universal has refurbished over a thousand homes and created areas where Muslims own businesses and live near mosques.

Luqman's Islam and urban renewal project bears the influence of various movements. The land ownership and do-for-self aspects obviously echo Nation of Islam practice. "We are continuing the cultural revolution that began among African-Americans in the 1960s, a cultural revolution based on Islam," says Luqman. "The Nation of Islam was a vehicle that came to the need of African-Americans, teaching do-for-self." His economic conservatism (he addressed the Republican National Convention in 2000) appeals to Republican-voting Muslims as well as Salafis, who don't want to rely on the state, though Luqman does partner with city government and urges his community to vote.

Luqman's belief that Islam can elevate the ghetto has won him admirers around the world, and resonates with conservatives who think religion can "clean up" the streets. But his music initiatives have ruffled Muslim feathers. As part of his urban revival project, Luqman aims to make South Philadelphia, a heavily Muslim area, the epicenter of R&B—similar to what Memphis is for the blues. Luqman convinced the Rhythm & Blues Foundation to move from New York to his hometown. He purchased a plot of land where he plans to build a $50 million National Center for Rhythm & Blues, along with a complex that will house a concert hall, a music academy, and a Hall of Fame. For this Muslim leader, faith, music, and economic uplift go together. He sees no contradiction. "It's because of my music sensibility that I am sensitive to human affairs," says Luqman. And the universal appeal of his music helps counter the critics who think he is a separatist, building a Muslim enclave. But his social project, and efforts to replicate it in other American cities, have raised thorny theological questions.

The Message Is in the Music

One humid Friday afternoon in June 2010, dozens of artists—break dancers from Paris, graffiti artists from London and Montreal, *qawali* vocalists from Pakistan, drummers from Algeria—left their rehearsals and filed into a non-air-conditioned gymnasium at Marquette Park in Chicago. The French dancers—members of the renowned Pockemon Crew—had performed ablution and thrown white robes over their B-boy outfits. They were now sitting on the floor on prayer rugs and flattened cardboard boxes, next to the "red turbans," members of a local African-American Sufi order, known for their head wear and the Arabic "Allah" tattoo on the right side of their necks. Soon they were all listening raptly to Imam Talib of the Mosque of Islamic Brotherhood in Harlem talk about the responsibilities of Muslim artists.

"This is blessed work, prophetic work that you are doing, indispensable to the future of Islam," said the imam. "Islam can have a cleansing role in the global hip-hop nation." Talib—known lovingly as "the hip-hop imam"—had flown in from New York to deliver the Friday sermon on the eve of Takin' It to the Streets, an urban arts festival that brings artists from across the Islamic world to Chicago's South Side. The festival—a three-day event, with over a hundred performers scattered across five stages—is organized by the Inner-City Muslim Action Network (IMAN), a social services organization that tries to use Islam and music for community building and urban development. The group sponsors turntable battles between rival gangs, will bring in a DJ and have a performance and a barbecue on a street corner plagued by drug dealers to show how positive music and Islam—an "urban Muslim aesthetic"—can reverse urban blight.

Muslim activists doing this kind of work have to contend with the centuries-old debate of whether music is permissible in Islam. At the root of the polemic is the question of Quranic recitation—whether melodious recitation of the Quran is acceptable—which developed into a debate about musical audition (*sama'*) more generally. A large body of commentary emerged over the centuries on listening and whether music is antithetical to the ideals of Islam, with opinions and guidelines from legalists, literalists, and Sufi scholars on how to regulate the power of music. To simplify this complex debate, there are two positions on music and Islam, with a range of opinions on each side. The first position flatly rejects music on puritanical grounds, saying that the pursuit of pleasure does not contribute to salvation and distracts from the focus on God. This side will make an exception for devotional incantations, but warns against "vain" singing. Today the Salafis are the most well-known proponents of this view; and from Mali to Afghanistan, Salafi groups have been known to disrupt weddings, set fire to music shops, destroy CDs and MP3 players, and even ban music altogether (as happened in northern Mali in 2012).

The second position recognizes the pleasure of listening to music, but cautions that it must be handled "carefully and sparingly," as it can lead to behavior unacceptable in Islam. The most authoritative exponent of this view was the eleventh-century jurist Imam Al-Ghazali who argued that it is the social context that determines the lawfulness of *sama'*. He and subsequent commentators would caution against the use of stringed instruments, the *daff* drum, and the *mizmar* (a reed wind instrument) because they can lead to the drinking of wine. Thus, today it is common to attend Muslim weddings with strictly a cappella entertainment; or voice and drums, but no stringed instruments; or, alternatively, wind instruments but no drums, which, conservatives caution, can stir the body to dance. These debates continue to this day: when the British teen heartthrob and *nasheed* singer Sami Yusuf launched his hit album *My Ummah* (2005), he released two versions—one with percussion and one with "voice only" for his more conservative fans.

Sufi thinkers, who see music and even dance as a way to worship and achieve union with the divine, have been the most accepting of music, though they too outline a set of rules—a musical *adab*—and argue that it is the social situation and state of mind that determine when music is permitted. As the ninth-century Baghdad mystic al-Darani put it, "Music does not provoke in the heart that which is not there." The most liberal commentators, again often Sufi, accent the link between music and poetry, noting that the prophet Muhammad enjoyed poetry, even if he didn't practice music, and opine that a song is judged as licit or *haram* (illicit) depending on the meaning of the text, not necessarily the instruments. Sufism's use of music to achieve spiritual transcendence has for decades, if not centuries, angered Muslim conservatives. But today, it is hip-hop more than any other genre that has preoccupied Salafis and other Muslim conservatives. This is not only because of the dominance and globalization of the genre, but because of Islam's central role in the evolution of hip-hop.

African-American music's coupling with Islam goes back at least to the 1910s and the emergence of (quasi-) Islamic movements in American cities. In the 1920s, anthems written for Marcus Garvey's Universal Negro Improvement Association used symbols of Islam; one musical composition was titled "Allah-Hu-Akbar," and stated, "May He our rights proclaim / In that most sacred Name / Allah—one God, one Aim, one Destiny." Islamic motifs and notions of pan-African solidarity have been heard in jazz and soul music since the 1940s, a reflection of Ahmadi and Nation of Islam influence. In the 1960s, as members of soul and R&B groups like the Delfonics, the Five Stairsteps, the Moments, Earth, Wind & Fire, and Kool & the Gang embraced Islam, the ideas and tensions between Sunni Islam and the Nation of Islam would find expression in their music. Kenny Gamble was at the forefront of this trend. As critic Nelson George writes in *The Death of Rhythm and Blues,* "By the mid-seventies, Gamble no longer saw [Philadelphia International Records] as merely a musical enterprise but also a platform from which to proselytize, espousing a world view that obliquely revealed his private belief in the tenets of Islam." Philadelphia International's slogan became "The message is in the music," soon the title of a song by the O'Jays; in songs and liner notes, Gamble would express his views on everything from family structure to abortion, alluding to his belief in "the Brotherhood of Man and the fatherhood of Almighty God."

With Elijah Muhammad's death in 1975, the transition from the Nation of Islam to Sunni Islam would also be reflected in the music of groups like Kool & the Gang. The two brothers who started the band, bassist Robert "Kool" Bell and saxophonist Ronald Bell, grew up in New Jersey, attending the Nation of Islam's "Muslim bazaars" in Jersey City; and they soon incorporated NOI ideas about the Orient and African spirituality into their recordings, with songs like "Open Sesame" and "Ancestral Ceremony." After the Bell brothers embraced Sunni Islam, the references changed. One morning, after reading a *sura* in the Quran that celebrated life and the creation of man, Ronald Bell (aka Khalis Bayyan) wrote the track "Celebration." "The initial idea came from the Quran," says Ronald Bell, the Gang's musical director. "I was reading the passage, where God was creating Adam, and the angels were celebrating and singing praises. That inspired me to write the basic chords, the line, *Everyone around the world, come on, celebration.*" This song inspired by Islam would become an international hit heard regularly at ball games and political rallies in the U.S., and ironically was played by the Reagan administration on February 7, 1981, to welcome home the hostages held by the Islamic Republic of Iran.

Islamic motifs and Arabic terms have threaded the fabric of hip-hop since its genesis in 1973, when Afrika Bambaataa founded the Zulu Nation, reflecting the range of Islamic and quasi-Islamic ideologies and cultures that have coexisted for decades in America's urban centers. As hip-hop sidelined disco and R&B, the Islamic references would be channeled into rap songs and videos. The 1987 video of Eric B and Rakim's hit "Paid in Full" featured images of Khomeini and Muslim congregational prayer. In a later track, Rakim would flow: "In control of many, like Ayatollah Khomeini . . . I'm at war a lot, like Anwar Sadat." In March 1991, the hip-hop magazine *The Source* devoted an entire issue, titled "Islamic Summit," to the relationship between Islam and hip-hop. In that golden age of "politically conscious hip-hop," Rakim and Public Enemy peppered their rhymes with Arabic phrases invoking Islam—"*alhamdulillah,*" "*as-salamu 'alaykum*"—and excerpted the speeches of Malcolm X and Elijah Muhammad. As the Five Percent Nation, an offshoot of the Nation of Islam, gained ascendancy in the 1990s, mostly among youth in the Northeast, the movement's wordplay found its way into the lyrics of Gang Starr, Poor Righteous Teachers, and Brand Nubian. As hip-hop went mainstream at about the same time, these allusions were broadcast around the world, transforming cultures and identities. Through hip-hop, Muslim youth were exposed to black history, and non-Muslims were introduced to Islam. Such is the prevalence of Islam in rap that for many white hip-hoppers in the U.S. and Europe, acceptance in the hip-hop community (the "ghetto pass") comes only with conversion to Islam, which is seen as a rejection of being white. The white rapper Everlast, formerly Erik Schrody of House of Pain, claims that conversion to Islam allows him to visit ghetto neighborhoods he could never enter as a non-Muslim white. (Curiously, his espousal of Islam caused static with another white rapper, Eminem, who accused him of becoming Muslim to deny that he is a confused "homosexual white rappin' Irish.")

How do Muslim leaders feel about what the media today calls "Muslim hip-hop"? Opinions hark back to the classical debate about Islam and spiritual listening. In general, Muslim clerics criticize hip-hop for reasons not unlike those mentioned by non-Muslim conservatives: that the genre promotes values of materialism, arrogance, violence; that the videos of "clothed yet naked women" are derogatory. The Salafis are particularly opposed to hip-hop, seeing the culture with its raw lyrics, imagery, and graffiti as a cultural pollutant that sullies the Muslim's already dilapidated neighborhood. This view grows out of their belief in doctrinal purity. Opposed to cultural innovation, Salafi imams condemn the heterodox Five Percent and Nation of Islam references carried in rap lyrics, saying they teach *kufr* (unbelief), even Satanism. "It's basically *jahaleeya* poetry translated into ebonics," says one critic, comparing today's hip-hop culture to the "Days of Ignorance" before the arrival of Islam.

Salafi converts, who spend years studying overseas learning to speak the elevated classical Arabic that the Prophet's companions purportedly spoke, cringe at the youth argot that mixes Arabic and Islamic references with urban slang. "The poets mentioned in the Quran spoke perfect Arabic," fumes Umar Quinn, a Richmond-based imam. "These folks change their language every day." Quinn, whose sermons circulate widely online, implores Muslims not to support the hip-hop-industry "monster" that has encroached on every aspect of a Muslim's life. He recalls being at a prayer service at the Masjid Al-Nabawi, the seventh-century mosque in Medina, when he heard Jay-Z on somebody's ringtone. "And I was sitting near the door of the masjid, and could hear youth beatboxing outside!" says Quinn, aghast. Salafis see hip-hop's dominance as a sign that Muslims have gone seriously astray. "What is going on, when real gangstas are leaving hip-hop for Islam, while Muslims are leaving their religion for gangsta culture?" asks Napoleon. Conservative clerics have even developed programs to help the young "person who's [*sic*] heart is infested with the termites of hip hop" get off the music and back "on the *haqq* [truth]," by making prayer a priority, avoiding commercial radio, going on "regular music fasts," and slowly "transitioning" to "instrumental" hip-hop.

But there are more nuanced opinions. The imams and activists (like those at Posse Hausa in São Paulo) who believe that the lawfulness of music depends on the intent (*niya*) of the artist and the culture that the music promotes do not dismiss rap so quickly. Imam Talib, in his Chicago *khutba* (sermon), invoked a *hadith* in which the Prophet did not object to the performance of music, and argued that Muslims can practice hip-hop depending on its musical form and content. Responding directly to the Salafis who emulate the Prophet's companions, Talib gave the example of one of them, the poet Hassan ibn Thabit, known for his rhetorical eloquence. "Ibn Thabit was the Bambaataa of the Salaf!" says Talib, referring to the Bronx-based hip-hop pioneer. "Poetry was a source of comfort for the Prophet, he made *dua* for ibn Thabit, even had a little *minbar* built for him at the mosque." Ibn Thabit's verbal skills were so superior that the Prophet summoned him "in the midst of a propaganda war against Muslims, and asked him to respond." Imam Talib thus defends "Islamic hip-hop" as the cultural expression of an "authentically American" Muslim identity, arguing that Muslim MCs in America can play a role similar to the poets of seventh-century Arabia, responding to the rhetorical attacks on Muslims. "As Muslim artists, you are the guardians of the hip-hop nation, and you have a job to do—to introduce *tazkiya* (purity) into the hip-hop matrix," he told the young artists gathered in front of him. Music can bring uplift and enlightenment, if imbued with Islamic values.

Bringing Allah to Urban Renewal

The paradox is not only that many of the Salafi evangelists who are today *deenin* and *tableeghin* against hip-hop came to Islam through rap, but that, as activist Umar Lee has argued, rap music paved the way for the rise of Salafism in the United States. It was the Malcolm X fad of the early 1990s—sparked by Afrocentrist hip-hop and Spike Lee's biopic—that led many young Americans to read the civil rights leader's autobiography and become interested in African and Islamic history. "There was a strong yearning to be part of something positive," observes Umar Lee, an activist who embraced Islam during the early 1990s. But the political excitement triggered by Afrocentrist rap and the Malcolm X fad, he says, ended "in disappointment" following the Million Man March of 1995. With the decline of the Nation of Islam, these young converts gravitated toward Salafism, which in the early 1990s was being taught by Saudi-trained, American-born converts, who spoke American English and understood the issues of social breakdown and urban exclusion that drew inner-city converts to Islam. They were able to present Salafism as the most authentic Islam, and not an "Arab Gulf thing."

The Nation of Islam's receding influence in favor of Sunni Islam was the result of post-1965 immigration from Muslim-majority states as well as the geopolitics of the Middle East. During the early 1960s, a period of ideological competition between the socialist pan-Arab alliance led by Egypt and the conservative Islamist monarchies led by Saudi Arabia, the Nation of Islam was solidly allied with Egypt, receiving political and economic support from Nasser. After the 1967 War, Elijah Muhammad would find himself bereft of Nasser's backing and under growing criticism from Sunni Muslims for his heterodoxy, while emissaries of the Saudi-sponsored Muslim World League began to spread Salafi Islam in America. After his death in 1975, his son Warith Muhammad would dismantle the Nation of Islam and embrace Sunni orthodoxy. Sunni organizations in the U.S. gained even greater influence after the Camp David Accords in 1978 and with the rise of the "Egyptian-Saudi axis."

Louis Farrakhan, long suspicious of whether immigrant Muslims really understood or cared about the plight of African-Americans, revived the Nation of Islam in 1981, just as Reagan's policies were beginning to wreak havoc on America's already struggling inner cities. Farrakhan brought back Elijah Muhammad's message of black economic empowerment (appealing to many poorer blacks) and began rebuilding the NOI's business empire. Throughout the 1980s and into the mid-1990s, an intense competition ensued in American cities—particularly on the East Coast—between Nation of Islam and Sunni Muslim activists for the "hearts and souls" of the youth. Although the Nation of Islam delivered services and economic benefits, soon after the Million Man March the organization began to decline, partly because of infighting, mismanagement, and Farrakhan's intolerant rhetoric. The African-American and Latino youth who were drawn to the Nation of Islam's message of solidarity and self-reliance—one amplified by the hip-hop of the late 1980s and early 1990s—would increasingly be drawn to Salafism.

A very small minority—an estimated 8 percent—of American Muslims favor Salafism over other schools of Islamic thought, and the majority of these are African-American, who appreciate their goal of bringing order to battered urban areas and their emphasis on economic self-reliance. Salafi activists, by most accounts, do show more interest in mentoring young converts, teaching "self-rectification," explaining the practices of "authentic" Islam, down to the details about how to dress like the *sahaba,* how to grow a beard with a low mustache, and how to make sure prayer lines are straight. The Salafis, who were also pioneers in using social media (e-mail Listservs, taped lectures, CDs, etc.), had a better rapport with young converts than the larger Muslim organizations like the Islamic Society of North America, founded by Muslim Brothers (Ikhwan) who had migrated to the U.S. The Ikhwani mosques, writes Lee, "just weren't interested in converts except where they could help speak out on issues such as Palestine."

By the late 1990s, Salafi organizations, benefiting from steady intellectual and financial support from Saudi Arabia, were leading the most influential Islamic movement in North America, with followers across the U.S. The largest communities, boasting mosques, community centers, and bookstores, were concentrated on the East Coast—in East Orange, New Jersey; Philadelphia; Washington, DC; and New York. The East Orange community, home to the Islamic Center of America, was often described as the center of Salafi life in the U.S., with the communities of Philadelphia and New York as extensions. But the political rift in Saudi Arabia—between pro- and anti-regime clerics—soon reached the shores of New Jersey. The imams who were more loyal to the Saudi throne (and who would open their lectures by stressing the "importance of obeying the rulers") attacked those who were more critical of Al Saud. One community member recalls, "I was not, and am not, anti-Saudi per se, but I grew tired of brothers trying to force the Saudi throne down my throat."

The infighting and the rhetoric began to take their toll. By 2000, even before 9/11, the East Orange community began to splinter, and Salafism's influence across the U.S. began to wane. After September 2001, government prosecution would end Salafism's hegemony. Law enforcement shut down a number of Salafi organizations in northern Virginia. Citing "intolerant rhetoric," the State Department would also revoke the diplomatic visas of more than twenty individuals at the Saudi embassy working in religious outreach. In response to American pressure, officials in Riyadh declared that the Saudi government planned "to shut down the Islamic affairs section in every embassy." With the crackdown on centers in Washington, DC, and Virginia and the disintegration of the East Orange community, members migrated to Philadelphia, which today boasts the largest Salafi community in the U.S. In Philadelphia, as in other cities, Salafism filled a political void left by the decline of the Nation of Islam.

. . .

The interaction and parallels between the Nation of Islam and Salafism paint a larger picture of religious movements, welfare cuts, and declining state services in America. Commentators often describe Salafis as "the Protestant reformers of Islam" because of their economic asceticism and attempts to "purify" society; but a more apt comparison would be with the Nation of Islam. The Salafi message of social conservatism and self-rectification, political withdrawal and geographic separatism is similar to the Nation of Islam's narrative of self-help, racial separatism, and divinely ordained salvation. Under Elijah Muhammad, the Nation of Islam essentially functioned as a development organization emphasizing thrift and economic independence among poor African-Americans, and with such success that it turned many followers into affluent entrepreneurs. The Salafi movement has a similar message of economic thrift and salvation: the concept of *hijra* refers not only to migration (to Arabia), but also to economic ascendance. But the most striking parallel between the two movements is their disdain for political participation and the nation-state, and their embrace of a transnational community that transcends the state and identifies with the East. In the NOI, followers identified with a mythical place where Asia and Africa met; the Salafis claim to belong to a "counter-community" that bypasses the nation-state, and owes allegiance to a global *ummah* anchored in Saudi Arabia, the "land of the two Holy Sanctuaries."

The public debates about Salafism in Europe and America today are also reminiscent of the last century's conversation about the Nation of Islam. Before 9/11, Salafism was not seen as a threat. The movement was, in fact, deployed by Western states during the Cold War as a response to leftist and Shia groups. In the U.S., Salafi and the Muslim Brotherhood–affiliated groups were seen as a force to moderate black nationalist groups like the Nation of Islam. Moreover, from the late 1970s until 2001, policymakers in the U.S., Britain, and elsewhere in Europe viewed the Salafis' "traditional values" as an asset to rebuild communities and clean up the streets; their economic conservatism was a resource, a way to revive run-down urban areas. In suburban Detroit, for instance, during the 1990s, conservative Yemeni mosques were so successful at turning around neighborhoods— patrolling the streets during the crack cocaine epidemic and revitalizing a dormant housing market—that public school officials in neighboring towns began competing to attract Muslim students, in the belief that their conservative social mores and intact families could contribute to upward mobility, owner-occupied houses, and "strong ethnic co-residence."

The Salafis' libertarian political attitude—not asking the state for anything—fit well with the Reaganite and Thatcherite free-market thinking of the 1980s and 1990s: as the state stopped providing services and amenities, religious groups, including Islamists, stepped in to fill the vacuum. The Salafis' ultraconservatism and intolerant rhetoric, though recognized as a potential problem, was, proponents argued, mitigated by their political quietism. Similar arguments were made in the 1960s in defense of the Nation of Islam's economic and social conservatism. In their pioneering study *Beyond the Melting Pot,* Nathan Glazer and Daniel Patrick Moynihan lamented the NOI's "nationalist and racist" tendencies while lauding the movement's "traditional values" and "Horatio Alger" entrepreneurial spirit, stating that "no investment of public and private agencies on delinquency and crime prevention programs will equal the return from an investment by Negro-led and Negro-financed agencies." In the 1990s, the Salafi groups' ability to patrol the streets, rehabilitate young men, restrain anti-state sentiment, and mobilize capital through their economic networks was seen as an asset to cash-strapped city governments. After 9/11, however, as it became evident that the quietest Salafis could not control the violent anarchists in their midst, the Bush and Blair governments cracked down on Salafi organizations and began to look for an alternative Islam to back.

Big Up, *Mashallah*

No Muslim movement in Europe grates on liberal sensibilities the way the Salafi movement does. Despite their small numbers, Salafi attempts to Islamicize public spaces in European cities—by banning music and dancing, alcohol consumption, and gender mixing—draw intense media and public attention. "The Salafis are culturally disruptive," says Michael Privot, a young historian, and director of the Brussels-based European Network Against Racism. "For the fragile youth, Salafism offers an easy alternative, a rupture with the past. Yesterday they were listening to rap and dealing drugs, today they're against music, calling people infidels, passing out leaflets telling Muslims not to wish Merry Christmas to the *kuffar,* telling their mothers to not shake hands with non-Muslims, to not cook for Christians."

In France, authorities estimate that there are only five thousand individuals who follow the Salafi movement (less than 0.1 percent of the Muslim population), but the presence of women wearing face veils triggered a groundswell of panic and led to the 2011 law banning the burka in France. The Salafi mandate not to mix with non-Muslims (often called *kuffar,* or infidels), and not to venture out of their enclaves to other parts of the city for fear of being morally contaminated, have drawn strong criticism from other Muslims, who think such separatism sets back the integration of all Muslims. "[Salafism's] aim is to plant a wedge between young Muslims and larger British society," says Sheikh Musa Admani, the imam of London Metropolitan University and a strong critic of this movement.

The Salafis tap into a deep ambivalence about the nation-state that exists among Muslim youth. This doubt is due not only to American and European foreign policy toward "Muslim lands," but is also a reaction to domestic policies involving policing, welfare, employment, and housing. Sociologists continue to debate whether the Muslim neighborhoods in European cities constitute enclaves—spaces that immigrants move into voluntarily for a sense of community and identity, and will eventually "graduate" from after achieving a level of economic success—or ghettos, the more stigmatized zones where ethnic or racial concentration is not voluntary, but the result of external constraints and discriminatory urban policy, and where social mobility is stunted. For Muslim youth, however, the debate was resolved after 9/11: the desolate zones they inhabit, the grim housing projects ("estates" in England, "HLM" in France) they grew up in, are—like the heavy police presence, the anti-burka and anti-mosque laws, and the drone strikes in Somalia—the result of hostile state policy. And the term "ghetto" is embraced by French and Dutch Muslims and used often—sharply, proudly, playfully, tenderly—to refer to the European Muslim's geographic segregation; to embarrass politicians (who hate the term); to claim kinship transnationally with similarly situated people in Brazil's favelas or America's inner cities, with whom they share a distrust of state power and a common ghetto-centric hip-hop aesthetic. French rapper Kery James speaks proudly of a *patrimoine du ghetto,* a culture and consciousness extending from the Caribbean to Europe.

Muslim integrationists find such talk of ghettos and borderless identity juvenile: it's through political engagement that damaging policies can be reversed. The Salafi movement took the debate over Muslim integration in a new direction, in effect, giving anti-state sentiment a theological boost. Salafi activists, of course, scoff at all talk of ghetto nationalism. But they are not advocating integration, just a different kind of separatism, an anti-statism based not on a hip-hop-inflected class or racial solidarity but on a conservative Islamic internationalism. Related to this, Islamists reject the term "diaspora," another contested and much-used word in Muslim communities. As with "ghetto," young Muslims speak of the "Muslim diaspora" to express a particular sensibility of exclusion and to claim solidarity with other marginalized communities. European- and American-based Muslim theologians will accept that ethnic and nationalist diaspora communities exist, but note that the term "diaspora," which grows out of the Jewish experience, is anathema to Islam. "There is no theology of the land in Islam," explains Professor Mahmoud Ayub, a theologian at Hartford Seminary. "The Islamic view is that the whole earth belongs to God, and all of God's broad earth is a *masjid,* a mosque—so there is no diaspora in Islam." For Salafis, the concept of diaspora, especially when people speak of ethnic or national diasporas, fractures the Muslim community. They prefer the word *ummah* and try to direct all allegiances and anti-state sentiment toward this global community of belonging, which transcends any territory.

Unlike in America, where it was state authorities who began

expressing concern over Salafi extremism, in Britain and Holland, where Salafis have a much larger following, a coalition began to form in the early 2000s against the influence of Salafism that included feminists, secularists, critics of multiculturalism, and liberal Muslims, who argued that the Salafis' "theology of separatism" inflames xenophobia.

The British and American Salafi movements shaped each other (as would the reactions to these movements). The ideological struggles taking place on the East Coast of the U.S. were also playing out sharply in Great Britain, and alliances formed across the Atlantic. In Birmingham, the pro-Saudi-regime camp led by "purist" Abu Khadeejah battled Abu Muntasir, who was sympathetic to the *sahwa* movement that opposed the Saudi monarchy. Abu Khadeejah, who established the Salafi Institute and Salafi Publications in Birmingham, aligned his side with the Islamic Society of North America in East Orange. Abu Khadeejah publicly attacked other Muslims, calling them deviant, singling out Shia Muslims and Sufis for censure. The conflict between the two camps in Britain grew ugly and redounded back to the U.S. As British Salafi groups like Al Muhajiroun grew more assertive, an offshoot appeared in Queens, New York. The group, called Islamic Thinkers, would gather on the streets of Jackson Heights, Queens, every weekend burning American and Israeli flags and, through a megaphone, calling on Muslims to boycott elections.

After the invasion of Iraq, a Salafi-jihadist camp appeared in England that openly incited British Muslims to violence. This group was centered around the Jamaican convert Abdullah al-Faisal (né Trevor William Forrest), the one-armed Abu Hamza al-Masri (whom the British press dubbed "Captain Hook"), and Omar Bakri Muhammad, the former leader of Hizb ut-Tahrir. In a Friday sermon in 2004, Bakri vowed that if Western states did not change their foreign policies, Muslims would give them "a 9/11, day after day after day." This rhetoric—and the London bombings in July 2005—prompted a government crackdown that was supported by a broad coalition of Tory and Labour politicians as well as secular and liberal Muslims, dismayed by Salafism's growing influence among Muslim youth. The Blair government imprisoned or expelled the clerics who called for violence, including Trevor William Forrest, who was deported to his birth land of Jamaica. Forrest's trajectory (he had embraced Islam as a teenager in Jamaica and studied in Trinidad on a Saudi scholarship before moving to Medina, then settling in England in the early 1980s) illustrates the transatlantic aspect of the Salafi movement, and the role played not just by American Islam but by Caribbean migration in the evolution of British Islam.

In the late 1980s, as Sunni organizations in America were competing for influence with the Nation of Islam, a similar contest was playing out in British cities. British Sunni organizations—particularly Hizb ut-Tahrir and Salafi mosques—were engaged in a turf war with the Nation of Islam and to a lesser extent the Rastafari movement, which had emerged in Jamaica in the 1930s and was brought to the United Kingdom by West Indian migrants in the 1950s. The Nation of Islam had developed a small following in Britain in the early 1960s, but was soon overwhelmed by the Rastafari movement. "Before the emergence of Rastafari, it was the Black Muslims who set a platform for post-war religio-political movement amongst the Caribbean diaspora in Britain," observes the English theologian Robert Beckford. But in the 1970s and 1980s, Rastafari and reggae became the dominant counterculture among black and Asian youth in England, shaping and interacting with the punk movement, which emerged in the mid-1970s. When Bob Marley died in 1981, the Rastafari movement began to decline as did the conscious roots-reggae of the 1970s. With the advent of hip-hop, Islam would again emerge as an identity option.

If reggae music disseminated Rasta culture, hip-hop exposed young Britons to the teachings of the Nation of Islam, the Five Percenters, and Sunni Islam. "I was a Rastafarian for a while," says Yasmin Mohammed, a British-born woman from Enfield who joined the Nation of Islam in the early 1990s. "Being a Rastafarian was a religion for me but when I realized that it was simply a fashion statement to others I became disillusioned." Soon dozens of Rastas would cut their locks, embrace Islam, and, for reasons explained below, become vehement critics of Rastafarian theology. Thus, while in the U.S. the hip-hopper-turned-Salafi is an increasingly common figure, British Salafi evangelists are more likely to have been Rastafarians in their youth—figures like Abu Hakeem Bilal Davis of Birmingham, who now tours the Caribbean speaking to audiences about the dangers of reggae, gang violence, and Rastafarian distortions of the story of Judas. By the early 2000s, Salafism had emerged as the adversary of reggae, hip-hop, jungle, punk rock—that is, most musical subcultures in Britain, a fact not lost on state officials who were contemplating how to roll back Islamist influence.

4

9,000 Miles . . . of Sufi Rock

In March 2004, the Nixon Center, a Washington-based policy think tank, organized a conference on Sufism's "potential role" in American foreign policy, chaired by Princeton historian Bernard Lewis, who had become an advisor to the Bush administration. The participants—academics, policy wonks, and representatives of various government agencies—praised Sufism's tolerance, talked about Salafi hostility to Sufism, and pondered how the U.S. could ally with Sufi brotherhoods. Panelists noted how unlike the Salafis and Wahabis, who have a global *ummah*-centered outlook, Sufis value local and national loyalties. One participant cautioned that "due to the secular nature of the American political system, it is difficult to imagine U.S. policymakers openly endorsing the value of Sufism"; yet various policy recommendations on how the U.S. could take a "proactive stance" in supporting the revival of Sufism were put forth, from funding the preservation of Sufi shrines to supporting Sufi centers of learning that can help "retrain" youth influenced by Salafism. In the keynote, Lewis praised Sufism's openness to other religions, and argued that while Sufi brotherhoods may have spearheaded anticolonial struggles in Africa and Asia—and even today Sufis in Chechnya are fighting Russia—it is "highly unlikely" that Sufis would use violence against Westerners today.

The idea of Sufism as an ally of the West has a long history in European colonial thought. Late Victorian intellectuals, like Sir William

Jones, the eighteenth-century scholar of India, saw Sufis as "cosmo-politan pantheists," who, unlike other Muslims, practiced a mystical, universal Islam. Colonial treatises written in the nineteenth and early twentieth centuries would describe Sufism as the antithesis of Islamic orthodoxy, and rooted in local (non-Arabian) culture. This view of Sufism as an ally was partly encouraged by the fact that although it was Sufi brotherhoods who resisted early colonial expansion—Abd al-Qadir fought back French incursions in Algeria, Muhammad al-Sanusi confronted the Italians in Libya, Usman dan Fodio battled British troops in Nigeria, and so on—once these Sufi movements were defeated, French and British colonialists ruled through the Sufi brotherhoods, who in turn helped the Western powers establish an "official Islam." In 1900, the French ethnologist Edmond Doutté described France's Islam policy in West Africa: "In purely administra-tive matters the *marabous* [holy men] have been of service to us: we have seen them order their followers, in the name of God and at the behest of an administrator of a *commune mixte,* to follow an admin-istrative ruling."

Bernard Lewis had long argued that the U.S. should see Sufi brotherhoods as comrades-in-arms. More than fifty years earlier, in September 1953, Lewis, then still at the University of London, was invited by the State Department to a conference at Princeton, where he presented a paper—now at the National Security Council archives at the Eisenhower Presidential Library—arguing that the Naqshbandi Sufis living in the Caucasus region could be used as a fifth column inside the Soviet empire. After 9/11, Washington was more open to Lewis's ideas on Sufism. With the crackdown on Salafism at home, American officials came to view Gülen, the Turkish-based Sufi move-ment, with favor. The movement, which has several million adepts and runs schools, hospitals, and cultural centers in 140 countries, had emerged as a formidable player on the transnational Muslim scene. Its leader, Fethullah Gülen, who had been living in voluntary exile in the United States since 1998, was granted permanent residency, and the movement, after 2001, expanded its institutional presence across the country, continuing the urban development that the Salafis had been doing, except on a broader scale and without the religious proselytism. As one senior American official told the *New Republic,* "It was 2003, two years after 9/11; we were just in the beginning of the Iraq War, and here's this ecumenical Muslim movement that seems to be open to modernity and science and is focused on education. It seemed almost too good to be true."

Government agencies and leading think tanks began producing papers and policy memos on how to mobilize Sufism against Salafism, in Asia, Africa, and even Europe. In 2004, the RAND Corporation issued a report titled "Five Pillars of Democracy: How the West Can Promote an Islamic Reformation," arguing that the West should support those who practice a "folk Islam" against the "fundamentalists" by encouraging Sufism, "a traditionalist form of Islamic mysticism that represents an open, intellectual interpretation of Islam" and by inciting "disagreements between traditionalists and fundamentalists." A monograph published by the U.S. Defense Intelligence Agency would similarly speak of Sufism as "an exploitable fissure in the bulwark of Islam."

A year earlier, in 2003, the National Security Council had established a program called Muslim World Outreach, with a budget of $1.3 billion aimed at "transforming Islam from within" by supporting organizations in Muslim countries that are "moderate" and compatible with democracy. Much of this money was distributed through USAID and spent on programs to train new Muslim clerics, reform school curricula, set up schools to counter what the madrassas taught, and to shape public discourse through radio and satellite TV channels. This ideological project resembled—and was in some ways modeled on—the State Department's Cold War strategy of supporting opposition currents in the former Soviet Union, except that the post-9/11 campaign had an "overt theological agenda." USAID's programs explicitly sought to reform Islamic religious thought and practice. As the promotion of Sufism became a centerpiece of this theological campaign, the U.S. began supporting Sufi leaders and institutions in far-flung countries, from Ethiopia to Indonesia; but it was in Pakistan and Britain that the "Sufi strategy" would be most deeply implemented, and draw the most opposition.

Mystical Power

By fall 2005, some months after the London bombings, the Blair government was scrambling for a new Islam policy. Arguing that Britain was losing the "battle of ideas" with Al Qaeda and that British Muslims were drifting toward "voluntary apartheid," state authorities began looking for new interlocutors in the British Muslim community. Salafi activists, riled by the Iraq War, were no longer seen as a quietist, restraining force; fringe groups like Muslims Against Crusades and Islam4UK had appeared, protesting military parades and burning poppies on Remembrance Day. The long-established Muslim Council of Britain (MCB) was viewed as politically recalcitrant and not doing enough to combat extremism. In August 2006, shortly after the Lebanon-Israel war, the MCB submitted an open letter to Tony Blair stating that his foreign policy in Iraq and support for Israel offered "ammunition to extremists." The letter was rebuffed and relations with the Muslim Council of Britain were downgraded. Blair declared that it was the duty of moderate Muslims to stand up to those with a "false sense of grievance" against the West. Downing Street then began to empower Sufi leaders to counter Islamist influence, funding various organizations, including the Muslim Sufi Council, Radical Middle Way, and the Quilliam Foundation, a "counter-terrorism think tank" led by two former members of Hizb ut-Tahrir.

These new organizations offered a counter-narrative that rejected key Salafi ideas. In his best-selling memoir, *The Islamist,* Ed Husain—one of Quilliam's founders—recounts how as a youth, he left the Sufi Islam of his parents and joined the militant Hizb ut-Tahrir, only to return to Sufism; the author repudiates the idea of an *ummah* as a "big lie," stating that for British Muslims to identify with the *ummah,* or Saudi Arabia or Pakistan, instead of the British nation-state, is folly. Prominent British converts to Sufism began appearing on television vigorously and publicly criticizing the Salafi movement in Britain. "I regard what the Saudis are doing in the ghettos of British Islam as potentially lethal for the future of the community," declared Abdal-Hakim Murad (né Timothy Winter), a professor of Islamic studies at Cambridge. He decried Salafi attacks on Sufi practice, "Just as the Protestants wanted to get rid of the saints and shrines, the Aristotle and Aquinas of medieval theology, so the Salafis declare as 'unbelief' most of the practices which are normative to Islam in the Indian sub-continent." The government's Preventing Violent Extremism pro-gram organized a "road show" of British and American Sufi scholars who traveled around Britain speaking to young Muslims.

The newly founded Sufi organizations like Quilliam and the Mus-lim Sufi Council were close to Washington, and openly backed by the State Department. The Sufi Council's spiritual head was Sheikh Hisham Kabbani of the Naqshbandi-Haqqani order, who consulted with President Bush after 9/11 and addressed think tanks in Washing-ton on the political potential of Sufism. Soon American clerics with Sufi leanings, like Hamza Yusuf and Nuh Keller, would fly to London and begin working with Radical Middle Way to present an alternative Islam. Yusuf, a prominent American imam and an advisor to President Bush, traveled to Britain in October 2001 and addressed the House of Lords. He echoed Margaret Thatcher's criticism that British Muslims had not denounced extremists loudly enough; to the young Muslims who criticized the West, Yusuf said, "I would say to them that if they are going to rant and rave about the West, they should emigrate to a Muslim country. The goodwill of these countries to immigrants must be recognized by Muslims."

The Sufi offensive spearheaded by American clerics—along with government prosecution—persuaded some hard-line British Salafis to nuance their understanding of Islam; but more important, it encour-aged other Sufi groups to speak up. Hamza Yusuf in particular pre-sented what one sociologist calls "an intellectual, activist form of classical Sufism" that appealed to a large number of Muslim youth: one result of this Sufi "counter-response" was that it emboldened the traditional South Asian Sufi groups, who had until then been cowed by the Islamists. By the mid-2000s, a number of British Salafi leaders had abandoned their incendiary rhetoric, stopped attacking Sufi prac-tices such as *mawlid,* and dropped the title "Abu" preferred by Salafis and adopted the honorific "Sidi" instead. After the London bombings, Abu Muntasir—the "Super Salafi," as he was then known—publicly and tearfully apologized for his rhetoric; he and other prominent Salafis began sharing the stage with Yusuf, trying to reverse the political polarization of the 1990s.

Music—and music's role in the public sphere—was from the start a key component of the Sufi counteroffensive. In the 1990s, Hamza Yusuf had been harshly critical of popular music, referring to popular culture as the "culture of zombies," excoriating its *kufr* and lambasting hip-hop. In the 2000s, he relaxed his opposition to popular culture and music, perhaps in a realization of how important hip-hop was in reaching youth. The Prevent program, in addition to sponsoring its tour of Sufi imams, would also begin funding music events and programs, from "Muslim hip-hop" at Radical Middle Way to the all-woman Ulfah Collective in Birmingham. For Sufi activists, music was a way to proclaim their difference from Salafis, win over public opinion, and touch "at-risk" youth. Music featured prominently at the Sufi Council's public events as well, with performances by the Naqshbandi Ensemble, who often traveled with Sheikh Kabbani. At the Tariqa Conference and the United Colours of Sufis convention in London in 2009, where the Sufi Council sought to build a coalition with other *tariqas,* there were performances by male and female performers, including Chico Slimani, a pop artist and former stripper (who had been discovered on the British talent show *The X Factor*), a male group called Aashiq Al-Rasul, and a female duo named Pearls of Islam, who sang accompanied by drums and guitars.

It's not clear how British policymakers or Sufi activists thought music could counter militancy or reach at-risk youth; religious gatherings starring female performers playing stringed instruments were a surefire way to alienate conservative Muslims, always wary of music at religious events and of being forcibly exposed to music. (In July 2010, hundreds of parents in London withdrew their children from music class in primary schools so as not to have them playing musical instruments during Ramadan.) The disaffected youth targeted by the Sufi Council were seldom impressed by the organization or the speeches of American converts. For urban Muslim youth, in Britain and the

U.S., Sufism is just "too white"; it's the Islam that white converts have been drawn to since the nineteenth century. Many young Muslims especially resented Hamza Yusuf telling them to leave Britain. The magazine *IslamOnline* dubbed the American cleric the "Great White Sheikh"—defender of the "pick-up driving, flag-waving, good ole boys yelling, 'America: love it or leave it.'" (In fairness, Hamza Yusuf soon broke ranks with the Bush administration and began publicly expressing discomfort with the Sufi-Salafi juxtaposition.)

Slowly opposition began to build against the Blair government's Sufi policy and the new Sufi organizations. Critics charged that the government preferred to talk to marginal Sufi institutions that had little grassroots support, rather than to more established organizations like the Muslim Council of Britain, which denounced extremism while criticizing British foreign policy. Local activists, like Salma Yaqoob, a city councilor from Birmingham, publicly stated that Prevent money only went to those who didn't say that British foreign policy foments domestic extremism. Others worried that mobilizing Sufis as the "good Muslims" was sowing discord and could provoke a "civil war" within the British Muslim community.

Britain's policy of promoting Sufism extended to South Asia, where it was argued that British Muslims were being radicalized in Pakistan's and Afghanistan's madrassas. As the Pervez Musharraf government and USAID began supporting Sufi institutions in Pakistan, opposition mounted against "state-sponsored Sufism." In October 2006, Musharraf established the National Sufi Council to bring an "enlightened moderation" to Pakistani politics and to improve the country's image overseas. His successor, Prime Minister Yousaf Gillani, established a seven-member Sufi Advisory Council in June 2009 to counter the Taliban's resurgence by spreading Sufi thought through conferences and festivals. Promotion of Sufi music and institutes like SayArts that produce *qawali* was at the heart of these initiatives, locally and internationally. (In July 2010, a couple of months after a Pakistani national tried to explode a bomb in Times Square, the Pakistani Mission at the UN organized a *qawali* festival in New York's Union Square to show the world the Pakistan of "love, peace, and tolerance.") Pakistani officials argued that one way of responding to the

Taliban and Wahabi zealots who were attacking shrines and denouncing music (in 1998, the Taliban had confiscated and publicly burned musical instruments) was by mobilizing the poetry of the great Sufi masters; poetry and music could disseminate the discourse of Sufi Islam. Tensions between Sufis, Islamists, and the Pakistani regime had been playing out in Pakistan's youth culture since the mid-1990s, but when Musharraf decided to deploy Sufi music for deradicalization, this interaction took an unexpected turn.

The Taliban and the Guitar

Pakistan's leading rock band is Junoon ("Obsession" in Urdu), a group founded by Salman Ahmad, who spent his teens in New York listening to Led Zeppelin and Van Halen before returning to Lahore in 1981. As a youngster, he experimented musically, fusing the poetry of Sufi mystics like al-Rumi and Bulleh Shah with the rock he had heard in America, mixing fluid guitar solos with *qawali*, the devotional singing accompanied by tabla drumming and hand clapping. Salman, who grew up during the Soviet-Afghan war and watched the rise of Wahabism in Pakistan, dreamed of launching a "cultural jihad" to "take us back to our Sufi roots of coexistence, acceptance, and musical ecstasy." When Junoon's album *Azadi* (Freedom) became a best seller in 1997, the group was catapulted into the international spotlight; Salman saw his influence grow and his "Sufi rock" drew the anger of government officials.

Pakistan has a long tradition of protest through poetry, and Junoon saw themselves in that tradition, as musical guerrillas, using verse to challenge the government of Nawaz Sharif. But when they released tracks about corruption and accountability, singing verses from one of Pakistan's greatest poets, Muhammad Iqbal—with electric guitar riffs blaring over a Peavey 5150 amplifier—they outraged the government *and* the mullahs. The use of Sufi poetry seemed to cause more anger than the lyrics about accountability. "We were promoting Pakistan's authentic Sufi heritage—the antithesis of the Wahhabism that had been grafted onto the country by Sharif's mentor, General Zia," writes Salman Ahmad in his *Rock & Roll Jihad*. The band was celebrating a heterodox Sufi Islam that clashed with the more narrow interpretation of the faith that state officials were using to consolidate the Pakistani nation-state and to appease myriad Islamist groups that had emerged during the Cold War. Junoon were subsequently banned from television and radio stations, charged by the government of "belittling the concept of the ideology of Pakistan." In a concession to the country's religious conservatives, Nawaz Sharif went on to ban all pop music from the airwaves later in 1997.

The ban on Junoon was lifted in October 1999, when General Musharraf overthrew Sharif and began a process of political reform. Junoon suddenly found themselves on several domestic channels, paraded as proof of the new regime's openness. Musharraf called on Junoon to perform at the mausoleum of Muhammad Ali Jinnah, Pakistan's founder, on the latter's birthday. The United Nations appointed Salman a goodwill ambassador and invited the group to play at "peace concerts" around the world. After 9/11, Sufi-inflected cultural diplomacy came to be seen as an answer to the "clash of civilizations." The "Alliance of Civilizations" launched by Turkey, Spain, and Brazil would claim inspiration from thirteenth-century Sufi poet Jalal al-Din Rumi. In honor of Rumi's eight hundredth birthday, the UN would declare 2007 the Year of Mevlana [Our Master] and Tolerance. In this climate, Junoon assumed an even bigger diplomatic role, releasing a song in English condemning political violence, and performing at the United Nations General Assembly with an Indian band.

But as the Musharraf years wore on, Pakistani and British Asian youth began to turn against Junoon: these pioneering rockers who were inspiring and oppositional in the 1990s were now part of Bush and Blair's "Sufi strategy." When the Home Office and the Quilliam Foundation invited Salman Ahmad to perform at British universities and told the press, "You counter radicalization through telling the truth, and if that comes from the power of a guitar, then do that," it proved to be the last straw for many. "The latest folly to come out of the Prevent Programme," wrote London Muslim, a popular blogger, ". . . is to use an aging Muslim Pakistani rockstar to sing a few songs which apparently should do the trick . . . What a bunch of idiots the establishment are and it's no surprise that the comedians over at Quilliam had a hand in this. Rather than honestly explaining about the hatred generated by this country's foreign-policy adventures in Muslim lands, the advice the men in suits get from . . . Quilliam is to play us a few songs." Even British kids who had no problem with music or Sufism were suspicious of government deployment of Sufi music, seeing it as a diversionary tactic. Blair's "false grievances" remark still stung.

In response to this Sufi policy, a fascinating counterculture emerged in the transnational Muslim youth scene. Stretching from North America to Britain and Pakistan, a movement called Taqwacore (combining *taqwa* (piety) and "hardcore"), emerged of Muslim punk rockers—about a dozen or so bands—who were sickened by both the Islamists' hostility to music and government use of music, whether for diplomacy or for torture. Despite their use of the Islamic term *taqwa,* these punk rockers have an agnostic, anarchist, anti-establishment attitude reminiscent of 1970s punk groups in England. "In Islam, *taqwa* means 'fear of God,' but to us it stands for 'Terrorists Are Quite Well-Adjusted!' " says Basim Usmani, the lead guitarist and vocalist for the Kominas ("scoundrels" in Punjabi), the most well-known band of this Taqwacore subculture.

The Kominas are made up of three Pakistani-American kids raised between Boston and Lahore in the 1990s, who came together—like other "Punkistanis"—to contest attitudes to music in the American Muslim community. In 2007, they were thrown out of the Islamic Society of North America's annual convention for playing their guitars and singing a song about the Prophet's wife Aisha at the conference. But this politically engaged trio soon turned their attention to the American and Pakistani governments' deployments of Sufi poetry; they honed in on Junoon. For these working-class boys from Boston, Junoon's jet-setting lifestyle, hobnobbing with heads of state and sampling the country's precious Sufi heritage for diplomatic purposes, was too much to bear. Things came to a head when the conservative Colorado-based author Asma Gull Hasan, who is the cousin of Junoon's Salman Ahmad and a Republican donor, launched "Muslims for Bush" to support the former president's reelection campaign in 2004, and she used Junoon's "Sufi rock" as a sound track. The Kominas were appalled: Pakistan's treasured Sufi verse was being used to drum up support for President Bush. Basim Usmani, who writes a column for the *Guardian* in London, published an article denouncing the "exploitation" of Sufism. Musically, the group released two crass "dis songs" against Junoon and Asma Hasan; the first ("I Want a Blowjob") rebuked Junoon, and the second ("I Want a Handjob") accused Hasan of giving "very sloppy" manual sex. (Hasan filed a lawsuit against the group which is still pending.) The Kominas would also travel to Britain, appearing on BBC Asia radio, where they would try to respond to the Salafi opposition to music—telling youth about how punk and reggae emerged together, giving voice to Britain's impoverished urban youth. In Pakistan, they would write songs against the landed elite and the patriarchal system. Basim would pen an angry column on how Sufis in Pakistan had "paid dearly" for Musharraf's embrace.

Beyond musical protest, political commentators in Pakistan were baffled by an American strategy that targeted Islamist militants from the skies while trying to establish a tolerant Sufi Islam on the ground, promoting festivals and building a Sufi university. Historians generally agreed that Sufism could help counter Salafism; the hundreds of shrines and *pir*s (saints) across Pakistan were venerated by Sunnis and Shias, and their "trans-communal nature" could bridge the Sunni-Shia divide and dampen sectarian extremism, but not when linked to American policies; that association simply exposed Sufis to violent reprisals. When two young men blew themselves up at a shrine in Punjab province in April 2011, the *Times of India* observed that Pakistani Sufis had become victims of the "West's great expectations."

The larger American attempt to shape Islamic belief and practice across Africa and Asia also came under criticism. After 9/11, the State Department spoke openly of galvanizing "indigenous moderates" and counterterrorism czar John Brennan cultivated warm relations with Imam Feisal Abdul Rauf, leader of the American Sufi Muslim Association, sending him on diplomatic missions around the world; but domestically, despite overtures to Gülen, the U.S. did not openly endorse Sufi Islam over other branches of Islam, because of the First Amendment and the Establishment Clause, which declared the state's neutrality in the face of all religions. But overseas, American embassies and development agencies covertly (and not-so-covertly) supported interpretations of Islam deemed favorable to American interests against those that weren't. As one American official explained, "If you found out that Mullah Omar is on one street corner doing this, you set up Mullah Bradley on the other street corner to counter it." When American Sufi clerics, like Hamza Yusuf and Feisal Abdul Rauf, were sent abroad, they were chosen according to "theological criteria." Likewise, when American officials in Iraq, working under General Douglas Stone, compiled and distributed "the world's most moderate Hadith" to mosques in Baghdad, they were laying down a scriptural interpretation compatible with American strategic objectives. If these theological interventions were prohibited in the U.S., critics asked, why was the U.S. government "establishing" religion in Europe and Asia? Commenting on how USAID was financing various Islamic organizations in Indonesia, legal scholar Jesse Merriam argued that if the United States had underwritten these kinds of organizations at home, the funding would have been considered unconstitutional.

Even in Britain, which does not have the same Establishment Clause as the U.S., the Blair government came under fire for trying to force theological change. In June 2009, when Hazel Blears, a member of Blair's cabinet, broke off ties with the Muslim Council of Britain because of comments made by its deputy secretary about the Gaza War, and tried to force the official's resignation, critics charged that the government was attempting to establish an "official Islam," and that theology should not be part of counterterrorism policy. British security officials would also critique the "Sufi policy," albeit from a different angle, arguing that Salafis have a street credibility and capacity for social control that the government-funded Sufi organizations lack. Robert Lambert, then head of the Met's Muslim Contact Unit in South London, who worked closely with the Ibn Taymiyyah mosque in Brixton, denounced the general vilification of Salafi Muslims in public discourse, and the Labour policy of encouraging Sufis to take on "counter-radicalization" work against Salafis and Islamists, saying it doesn't work and simply gives ammunition to those who argue that the UK and the West use "neo-colonial tactics of divide and rule when engaging with Muslim communities." The Sufi organizations' ties to neoconservative circles in the U.S. did not help either. Rumors still circulate among British Muslims that the Muslim Sufi Council is a CIA front.

With David Cameron's rise to power, the government would reestablish ties with the British Muslim Council and cut funding to Quilliam, whose leaders then moved to Washington. Likewise, in the U.S., by the time Obama came to power, the "Sufi strategy" was being shelved; Sufi clerics and musicians would continue to be deployed as goodwill ambassadors, but the U.S. government was no longer mobilizing Sufis against Salafis.

Beard Is Beautiful

> As a boy, my beard was coy
> Now it's in your face, shouting Oyyyy!!
> You're annoyed
> You can't avoid—
> Bristles!
> It's official,
> They're everywhere
> From Bradford to Bristol!

—*Tommy Evans*
(aka Abu Safa), ex-hip-hopper

The aesthetic styles on the streets of Birmingham, England—young men in white tunics and Run-DMC Adidas sneakers, women in colorful robes and face veils—are reminiscent of Philadelphia. What is different about the Salafi enclave in central Birmingham is its astonishing diversity; it's home to adherents from around the world—West Indians, Americans, Berbers, Somalis, Swedes, Bengalis, and others—who have gravitated to this city in the West Midlands, which has emerged as Europe's center for Salafi thought and life.

"How do we create an urban Islamic spiritualism?" says Mohammed Ali who heads the Hubb, a Birmingham art gallery, as he walks down Coventry Road, a street lined with Islamic-style boutiques and stores, including the world-famous Salafi Books. Even in Birmingham, young activists are contemplating how to deal with the excesses of hip-hop culture, Islamist strictures against music, and government efforts to use Sufi art. "I'm no longer proud of my earlier artwork," says Ali, a world-renowned artist whose colorful murals—verses from the Quran on compassion and resilience, spray-painted in an ornate Arabic calligraphy—dot the Birmingham cityscape. He stops at a wall with the word "Knowledge" hovering over an intensely hued skyscraper scene, painted in yellow, orange, and black. "I used to do hip-hop-style graffiti," he says. "One day I was spraying a wall with bubble letters and all, and an American brother came up to me and said, 'Why are you turning our neighborhood into the Bronx?' And he was right. My earlier work was too flashy, didn't respect the environment. Besides, hip-hop graffiti is the voice of the American ghetto, and this is not the American ghetto." Ali's murals today exhibit softer colors and subtle Mauresque designs—no more clashing tones and bubble letters—reflecting, perhaps, a widespread exhaustion after two decades of strife.

Salafism may not have rolled back or cleaned up hip-hop, but it has forced some young Muslims to think about the genre's excesses. And hip-hop culture, already a bricolage, seems to have simply absorbed Salafi influence. In European cities, what journalist Richard Reddie calls "the righteous look"—the untrimmed beard, the skullcap, the long-sleeved shirt with Arabic writing—is common, and often combined with some jewelry and activities that would not be endorsed by Muslims. Thus, contrary to Olivier Roy's claim that Salafis reject all "cultural variations," even the Salafi evangelists who are implacably opposed to hip-hop betray the culture's influences in language, dress, and entrepreneurial drive. Indeed, the "getting paid" ethic is one trait that, ironically, Salafis share with mainstream hip-hop culture. For all his critiques of the materialism ailing pop culture, after finishing his European tour Napoleon returned to Saudi Arabia to promote his streetwear business, Trendz. It is this innovative, entrepreneurial drive—halal pizza, halal McDonald's, halal beer, Mecca-Cola, "Islamic streetwear"—and the Salafis' links to transnational economic networks that make them attractive to state officials, who see these groups as crucial to reviving blighted neighborhoods and to containing Muslim youth.

By the late 2000s, the incendiary rhetoric inciting violence or excommunicating other Muslims was rarely heard in mosques in Europe or America, and jihadist networks were largely dismantled; but Salafism is still influential in Europe's Muslim ghettos, particularly in Britain. The disaffected youth of Birmingham and Bradford were never taken by Britain's Sufi Muslim Council or by the speeches of American converts. The political mood today is not unlike that of the early twentieth century, when Islamic reformers argued that imperial domination and the subdivision of the *ummah* into different nation-states was a punishment for straying from the true path. Colonialism led to an aversion to Sufi leaders, many of whom cooperated with imperial rulers. With the rise of anticolonial movements, reformist thinkers like al-Afghani and Rashid Rida began calling for a return to the scriptural and prophetic foundations of Islam—the Quran and *hadith*—shedding all the cultural rituals and "innovations" that had accrued since the seventh century. Salafis today have an identical reading of history: Muslims around the world are living under oppressive states and Western hegemony because they have strayed from the straight path and allowed cultural practices—from *mawlid* celebrations to hip-hop—to pollute their Islam.

But it's this hostility to Sufism—along with the animus toward Shiism, liberalism, socialism, and feminism—that also alienates many young Muslims from the Salafi movement. The truth is, for all its ideological dominance, Salafism still does not fulfill the young Muslim's desire for a narrative of social justice that addresses inequality, racism, and imperialism. Left-leaning Muslims argue that Salafi movements, in their separatism and political disengagement, are essentially a mechanism of social control that allows governments to contain

Muslim youth; and the claim that Salafism transcends the nation-state or a particular culture is belied by their attachment to Saudi Arabia and embrace of a Gulf Arab identity. The American and British effort to mobilize Sufism against Salafism led to much soul searching among Muslim youth. Western governments will mobilize Islamism overseas—as is occurring in Libya and Syria—and yet will crack down when these conservative currents reach European or American cities, while granting a space in society to ultraconservative Christian or Jewish groups with similarly conservative, separatist tendencies.

And how did Sufism come to be "the client faith of the American Empire"?, asked the *Samosa,* a local London magazine. How did Salafism, an ultraconservative Islam that opposes politics, hates stringed instruments, and is funded by the most reactionary regime in the Middle East, emerge as *the* counterculture for Muslim youth? The absurdity of this situation is sent up brilliantly by the dark jihadi film comedy *Four Lions* (2010), which follows four wannabe suicide bombers from Sheffield, England, to Pakistan and back to England, where they accidentally self-detonate. The film mocks the Salafis' sense of moral superiority, the jihadi's love-hate relationship to hip-hop, and British Sufi organizations. One of the boys, a raging, rapping white convert, at one point shouts, "Islam is cracking up! Women are talking back, people are playing stringed instruments!" When he gets his nose bloodied, his mates chuckle: "You have the Sufi Council running down your nose!"

5

The Jazz Caliphate

The only jazz critic to note the complex links between jazz, Islam, and American expansionism is the late English historian Eric Hobsbawm. A lifelong jazz aficionado, Hobsbawm was from the 1930s an incomparable chronicler of Great Power politics, and the cultural trends and struggles triggered by the rise of America. In his autobiography, *Interesting Times,* he muses on what jazz meant to him—as an uprooted, isolated youth in London who had fled Weimar Germany—and to other Europeans who were watching the skies darken across the Continent. "After the excitements of Berlin, England was inevitably a come-down," he writes; London in the early 1930s lacked any "emotional charge." But there was one passion he discovered in the English capital: "hot jazz." The music was an affecting reminder of the Berlin life he had left, where his mother and aunts had shimmied and fox-trotted to the gramophone sounds of Gershwin, as well as a powerful portent of America and its possibilities. To Europeans of his generation, jazz symbolized America: the music was in films, it had a democratic appeal, it was modern and cosmopolitan—perhaps even more so in Europe than in the States, where the music was still linked to the South. For a young member of the Communist Party (Hobsbawm had joined its youth organization in Berlin at age fourteen), to be a jazz fan was to be progressive, "to be against racism and for the negroes" and a supporter of Roosevelt's brand of liberalism, specifically the New Deal. Roosevelt and jazz made it possible for a teenage Communist "to approve of both the USA and the USSR."

Hobsbawm would go on to become jazz critic for the *New Statesman* for a decade in the 1950s, covering the explosion of jazz in postwar Europe. He wrote under the pseudonym Francis Newton, and in 1959 he published *The Jazz Scene,* a landmark study of the origins and rise of the genre, tracing the postwar jazz revival that he had witnessed. In it, Hobsbawm would famously compare jazz's conquest of Europe to the spread of Islam: "Jazz was born. But the unique thing about it is not its existence—there have been plenty of specialized musical idioms—but its extraordinary expansion, which has practically no cultural parallel for speed and scope except the early expansion of Mohammedanism." Jazz, he argued, had spread around the world through Hollywood's films, and through government sponsorship as American officials realized the power of jazz as "an agent of propaganda for the American way of life" during the Cold War.

Less well-known are Hobsbawm's thoughts on the role of Islam within the world of jazz. What the jazz musicians he studied "shared with other Northern big-city negroes was mass conversion to Mohammedanism." He watched jazz musicians embrace Islam, read the Quran, and attempt to speak Arabic, and saw this as a "revolt against inferiority," part of a "new intellectualism" that tried to remake traditional forms of jazz identified with the South ("Uncle Tom music"). The English historian tries to be respectful of the conversion ("It would be easy, but wrong, to make fun of such gestures of revolt"), but ultimately he saw the embrace of Islam as a misguided form of rebellion, luring these artists away from their southern roots, where jazz's origins and "cultural situation" lay; he predicted that just as Zionist Jews rejected Yiddish culture because of its link to *shtetl* oppression only to rediscover it later, and early feminists rejected "feminine fripperies" only to make their peace with pretty dresses, with time and distance from the South, the jazzmen who had rejected their southern origins by opting for "Mohammedanism" would re-embrace the South, and eventually there would be a New Orleans revival.

It didn't quite turn out that way. The spread of Islam in the American jazz community from the 1940s through 1960s was, as

Hobsbawm observed, indeed rapid and indeed an attempt to break with a southern past; but it turned out to be no brief uprising but a critical part of the movement for black emancipation. Recalling his youth in his memoir, Hobsbawm wrote, "Jazz turned out to be the key that opened the door to most of what I know about the realities of the USA, and to a lesser extent of what was once Czechoslovakia, Italy, Japan, postwar Austria and, not least, hitherto unknown parts of Britain." Islam played a similar role for African-American jazzmen from the 1940s onward, providing a psychological and cultural escape from the severity of the northern ghetto, the "key" that opened up the cultural and political worlds of Africa, Asia, and the rest of the colonized world then also struggling for self-determination. But the story of Islam and jazz begins in the 1910s with the Great Migration.

The Sun Never Sets

On September 20, 2008, the twentieth day of Ramadan on the Islamic calendar, the midwestern branches of the American Ahmadiyya community gathered in Milwaukee to celebrate a hundred years of the *Khalifat*. The Ahmadiyya is a heterodox Islamic movement that emerged in the late nineteenth century in Punjab, in the western part of British India. Its founder, Mirza Ghulam Ahmad, saw himself as a *mujaddid*—a renewer, sent by God in order to reinvigorate the faith and to promote the unity of all religions through Islam. Ghulam Ahmad would proclaim himself the Mahdi of Islam, the promised Messiah of Christianity and Islam, and an avatar of Krishna for the Hindus, and put forth an inclusive, ecumenical message that emerged in response to the religious sectarianism of India. Through missionary outreach, he gained more and more followers, so that by the 1920s, Ahmadi leaders were setting up missions in various parts of Africa, Australia, China, and the United States.

For decades the Ahmadiyya community's headquarters were in Pakistan—first in the Punjabi city of Qadian and then in Rabwah, but the group has long been the target of persecution. The founder's claim that he was the Mahdi—a figure who would appear at the end of times—and his belief in "continuous prophecy," that the prophet Muhammad was not the last and seal of the prophets, made his group heretical in the eyes of mainstream Muslims. When the Pakistani government amended its constitution in 1974 to define a Muslim as "a person who believes in the finality of the prophet Muhammad," it in effect declared the Ahmadis non-Muslim. The community suffered increased repression. In 1984, General Muhammad Zia-ul-Haq passed an edict making it possible to imprison Ahmadis for "posing" as Muslim; the community's headquarters were moved to England.

On this warm Saturday afternoon, hundreds of Ahmadi Muslims from mosques across the Midwest gathered at the University of Wisconsin campus in Milwaukee, to break fast together and to celebrate the caliphate's centennial. The atmosphere was joyous: boys in colorful skullcaps running down the stairs of the student hall; teenagers carrying platters of saffron rice and tandoori chicken, jugs of milk, boxes of dates, and bright-colored desserts. The range of head covering was striking, each a proclamation of identity, an indicator of age, social status, national background, level of piety and presumably wisdom: boys in gold-embroidered muslin caps with the front cut out to reveal their bangs; young women sporting (depending on age) dark or pastel head scarves wrapped in a variety of ways; fathers in pakol-style hats made of Afghan wool, and grandfathers in white turbans, some loosely folded, others tautly bound with a raised end.

The attendees, mostly Pakistani and African-American, filed into the main hall to hear Mirza Masroor Ahmad, the fifth khalifa (elected in 2003), deliver a televised message from London; the Ahmadiyya community's spiritual leader gave a message of support to the *jamaat* (congregation) of America, congratulating them on their work and wishing them a blessed Ramadan. Hassan Hakeem, a prison chaplain who heads the community's Illinois chapter, then began to speak, congratulating the midwestern mosques on their various initiatives and outreach efforts in their neighborhoods, from food pantries to health counseling; and he handed out academic awards to high-school students sitting in the front row. An air of melancholy settled over the hall as Hakeem informed the audience that a week earlier, two members of their community—Pakistani-American doctors who had returned to their land of birth to serve the poor—had been murdered. The killings came on the heels of a speech given by a Pakistani religious scholar, the host of a popular television program, who declared on the air that it was a Muslim's duty to kill Ahmadis. Hakeem underlined the Pakistani government's failure to protect the Ahmadiyya community. "Never has our community produced a single terrorist in the world," he said. "And yet we are persecuted and tortured simply because of our beliefs." He offered words of consolation, asking the attendees to support the families of the slain doctors. "We converted to Islam because the khalifa reached out to us," he said in an uplifting tone, holding up a copy of the community's century-old publication, *Muslim Sunrise.* "You'll notice it says, 'The sun never sets on the Ahmadiyya movement.' We will continue our work. We have Muslim missionaries around the world—missionary is not just a Christian concept."

Various speakers took to the podium, including a representative of the local NAACP chapter, an editor of the *Milwaukee Community Journal,* and the leader of the Ahmadi branch in St. Louis. The speeches invariably focused on the violence in Pakistan and the problems afflicting Milwaukee's inner city. One speaker mentioned the high school dropout rate, the joblessness, and the family breakdown in inner-city Milwaukee. "Our mission is to uphold the downtrodden African-American Muslim. We missionize to all Americans, but especially to African-Americans who are not privileged." A letter was passed around for signing, to be sent to Dish Network, which carried the channel where on September 7 the host had called for the killing of Ahmadis. Hakeem then led a prayer for Pakistan; an explosion earlier that day had left forty dead: "Let us pray for a country in turmoil." The attendees bowed their heads.

The curious relationship between black America and Pakistan goes back to the early twentieth century, decades before Pakistan was created, and has its origins in the Muslim communities that emerged in the Midwest—Detroit, Chicago, Milwaukee—in the 1910s, and the interaction between African-Americans recently arrived from the South and Ahmadiyya immigrants from India. This encounter between two marginalized communities—African-Americans and a small, persecuted sect of Islam—on the margins of American cities, would produce a cultural and political intermingling whose effects are felt to this day.

The Ahmadis were the first to send Muslim missionaries to the United States. In February 1920, Mufti Muhammad Sadiq arrived in New York, hoping to establish an ecumenical Ahmadiyya mission in America. But his encounters with law enforcement, segregation, and the Asian Exclusion Act would make him more race-conscious. He began advancing a worldview that joined Indian nationalism with global Islam and pan-Africanism, setting up a mission in Harlem in 1920 and linking Muslims in the U.S. to other excluded minorities and to oppressed peoples of color overseas. Sadiq began speaking against racial discrimination and the immigration laws—once quipping that if Jesus appeared at Ellis Island, he would be turned away because "he comes from a land which is out of the permitted zone."

Sadiq established mosques in New York and Detroit, building small communities of converts in these cities, before setting up his headquarters on Wabash Avenue on Chicago's South Side. In 1921, he launched the *Moslem Sunrise,* a publication to counter the way mainstream American newspapers depicted Islam. The *Sunrise* portrayed Islam as a color-blind faith and multiracial community of believers that stood in contrast to the segregated society in which he now lived. One of his columns presaged Malcolm X's racial epiphany some forty years later, contrasting America's segregated religious life with the Orient's multiracial centers of worship: "What sad news we came across . . . about the conflict between Blacks and Whites in this country . . . There are people fairer than North Europeans living friendly and amiably with those of the darkest skin in India, Arabia and other Asiatic and African countries . . ."

Unlike their orthodox Sunni counterparts, Ahmadiyya missionaries were not incensed by the quasi-Islamic black groups they encountered, possibly because of their own minority status within Islam. The Ahmadiyya's global outlook and ecumenical message (which emerged in response to religious sectarianism in India) were not unlike that of movements—Noble Drew Ali's Moorish Science Temple and Marcus Garvey's Universal Negro Improvement Association—that had appeared in northern cities, drawing parallels between the emerging ghetto and the colonized world, and defining the identity of these new black urban communities in terms of self-determination and internationalism. Noble Drew Ali's claim to prophethood was not dissimilar from that of Ghulam Ahmad. The message of Garvey's UNIA movement seemed particularly compatible with the Ahmadi vision. As early as 1914, Garvey had been calling on "all people of Negro or African parentage" to join the movement "to reclaim the fallen of the race; to administer to and assist the needy . . ." In addition to the welfare organization that he founded, Garvey also called for the creation of a transnational black republic in Liberia to unite Africans and join them with "the darker races of the world."

The Ahmadis also noticed that Garvey's journal, *Negro World,* had a clear affinity for the Muslim world. Garvey had been exposed to Islam when he moved to London in 1912 from his native Jamaica, hoping to study at Birkbeck College. In the English capital, he met and began working with the Egyptian-Sudanese journalist Dusé Mohamed Ali, who published the influential *Africa Times and Orient Review* (1912–1920). This monthly anticolonial publication "devoted to the interests of the coloured races of the world," joined pan-African and pan-Islamic discourses, and circulated from India to Egypt to the West Indies.

Garvey worked for the *Africa Times* briefly (as a messenger), before heading to New York where in 1918 he founded the *Negro World.* In 1921, Dusé came to the United States, joined the UNIA as head of its African affairs department, and wrote regularly for the *Negro World* before he moved to Detroit, where he founded the Universal Islamic Society and America-Asia Society.

Garvey never officially embraced Islam, but the UNIA's rhetoric was suffused with Islamic themes and motifs. The *Negro World* would refer to Garvey as a "child of Allah" and compare him to the prophet Muhammad with "his inexhaustible incandescent energy." And throughout the 1920s the publication hailed the anticolonial agitation in India, Egypt, and Morocco, seeing the uprisings as a portent of the coming triumph of Islam. Not surprisingly Sadiq began to focus his proselytizing efforts on African-Americans: speaking at UNIA gatherings, teaching that Arabic was their original language, presenting Islam as the solution to America's race problem. "The spread of El Islam cannot help but benefit the UNIA," declared the *Moslem Sunrise* in April 1923. "With millions of Moslems in India, China, Arabia, Persia, Afghanistan, Turkey, Negroes would find valuable allies." African-Americans, in turn, were increasingly drawn to Sadiq's message of Islamic tolerance. Between 1921 and 1925 most of the 1,025 converts to the movement were African-Americans in Chicago, Detroit, St. Louis, and New York. Garvey's followers, in particular, found Sadiq's anti-imperial pan-Africanist rhetoric attractive. The Indian-inspired Ahmadiyya movement's membership became increasingly African-American, with many rising to occupy high-ranking positions in the organization. Not surprisingly, the movement was irreparably damaged by Garvey's downfall. Sadiq suspended publication of the *Moslem Sunrise* between 1924 and 1930, the period when Garvey was imprisoned and deported. The missionary himself returned to India in September 1923, but the Ahmadiyya community continued its outreach to African-Americans.

Sadiq's most enduring influence would be seen in a movement that appeared shortly after his departure—the Nation of Islam. Fard Muhammad, who helped found the Nation of Islam, was by most accounts an Ahmadi, born to a Pakistani father and an English mother. When he arrived in Chicago, Fard attended an Ahmadi mosque on the city's South Side before joining the Moorish Science Temple. When he relocated to Detroit, Noble Drew Ali had recently died, and on July 4, 1930, Fard Muhammad founded the Lost Found Nation of Islam, as the movement was first called, with a message intended for the late Moorish Science Temple leader's thirty thousand followers. In August 1931, Elijah Poole, a migrant from Georgia and a corporal in the UNIA's Chicago chapter, heard Fard speak, and shortly thereafter joined the Nation of Islam. Poole dropped his "slave name" and became Elijah Muhammad (he briefly went by the name Ghulam Bogans in honor of the Ahmadiyya founder) and eventually became Fard's Supreme Minister. The Ahmadiyya movement and the Nation of Islam would henceforth have close ties, though the two groups competed for followers. Elijah Muhammad taught that blacks, before their subjugation by the white race, were the original people of the earth, descendants of the Tribe of Shabazz who inhabited the Holy City of Mecca; and that W. D. Fard was the *Mahdi*, "God-in-person," who appeared in 1930 to "mentally resurrect" the black man and bring him back to Islam. It's not uncommon still to meet people who embraced Islam in the 1940s and 1950s and were initially members of the NOI before moving toward the Ahmadiyya community.

Today the American Ahmadi community remembers "Dr. Sadiq" with great reverence, as the first Ahmadi missionary, the man who lit the flame of Islam in America. One reason I came to attend the convention in Milwaukee was to interview community elders, particularly the eighty-six-year-old Rashid Ahmad, the patriarch of the Ahmadi community, who received the Mufti Muhammad Sadiq Lifetime Commitment Award in 2007 and who knew Sadiq personally.

Freedom Dreams

As the speeches were winding down, I was told that Rashid Ahmad—"Brother Rashid," as he's called—was waiting to see me. I walked down the hall to a large seminar room in the student center and was introduced to a slight, older gentleman seated at the end of a long table. He was wearing a collarless beige shirt topped by a dark brown Nehru vest and a beige "Jinnah cap," a fur hat named after the founder of Pakistan, Muhammad Ali Jinnah. His attire bespoke the influence of the ideologies of Afro-Asian solidarity and the era of decolonization and Bandung, which molded his generation. Born in East St. Louis, Illinois, Ahmad joined the Ahmadiyya community in Chicago in 1945; it was then under the leadership of Sufi Rahman Bengalee, Sadiq's successor.

"I was a young man in 1940s Chicago," Rashid reminisced. "I was street smart, I wore the finest clothes, hung out at the taverns. I thought I knew everything. I was a showman—you know we African people are showmen, it's in us to perform. I heard Garveyites teaching on the street, I saw Elijah Muhammad's followers—they taught black superiority, gave us philosophies that said blacks had superior qualities, but they gave us little otherwise. The Garvey movement had nothing in it. The man took equipment to go build Liberia but couldn't do it. One day I was walking and I heard a street preacher say, 'Jesus did not die on the cross!' I stopped and went to talk to him; he told me to go to the *Moslim Sunrise* on 220 South State Street"—the headquarters of the publication—"or to the mosque on 4448 South Wabash." Rashid shrugged. "I went. I didn't know what I was doing; I was looking to make some money. At the mosque, a man in a white cotton shirt opens the door and tells me to come back later. I could smell curry cooking. I had never smelled that—I thought they were smoking opium in the back," he chuckled. "But then I went back again and again. I went there regularly for three years—and just read."

Brother Rashid quickly gained a reputation for his honesty and talent at *tabligh* (outreach). In 1949, when the Khalifa Bashiruddin Ahmad, then based in Punjab, invited American converts to come to Rabwah to study Islam, the twenty-six-year-old Rashid was one of those selected to go. "I headed for Pakistan. We changed flights in Iraq," he recalled, "and I got arrested in Baghdad. I had no visa for Iraq, and the security officials saw in my suitcase that I had a radio, two overcoats, pen sets—all gifts I was carrying for people in Pakistan. So they thought I was a spy with a wireless radio—spying for America! I finally got to Karachi, days later. No one was there to meet me, so I went to the Karachi *jamaat*. I stayed in Pakistan for five years. The country had just gained its independence; the Ahmadi missionaries had lost their allowance—the government had cut their money. I stayed to help. I learned Urdu, I married there, I learned all the greetings and rituals—I made them treat me well."

I asked about Sadiq. "Dr. Sadiq was in the United States between 1920 and 1923. Marcus Garvey, Noble Drew Ali, and Elijah Muhammad all met him—and borrowed points from him. When I was in Rabwah, in 1950, I used to go for long walks with him. Sadiq was an old man when I met him." Rashid smiled mischievously. "When

I first met him in Pakistan and I saw his newborn son, they looked the same—both bald and with only one tooth! Sadiq was a very determined man. He always wore white robes and colorful turbans. He—the Ahmadis in general—felt very comfortable with African-Americans, and we thought they had something that could pull us up. The Arabs in Chicago back then were very low-key, interested in making money—didn't teach anyone, unless to make money. The Arabs would change their names too—Rahman became Raymond, Dakhil to Daykil, Daoud to David. In 1947, it was the Pakistanis who were teaching us the *alif ba ta,*" Rashid said, reciting the Arabic alphabet. "We took classes for fifty cents an hour, so we could learn Arabic."

His memories of Chicago sixty years ago were vivid. "Back in the forties and fifties, Pakistanis would often be mistaken for African-Americans because of their complexion—their complexion is no brighter than ours. But they wanted to be accepted as white. They stopped covering their hair, and wore no hat—even if it's *sunnah*—just to show that their hair was different, and not be taken for a local black." He shook his head. "And back then we were straightening our hair, putting grease and so on—trying to look like foreigners."

By now the sun had set, prayers were over, and people were entering the room with plates of food and sitting down around the seminar table. I asked Brother Rashid if he wanted to break his fast. "Don't worry," he grinned. "I have a cookie. But you can go get some food." He pulled out a small paper bag with chocolate chip cookies and began nibbling on one. His grandson came up to chat.

The conversation soon turned to jazz, and Rashid's days in the Chicago jazz scene. "Jazz musicians were attracted to the Ahmadis, because they taught a life of equality. Jazz musicians were also independent-minded. Pakistan had just gained independence, and that was inspiring for the artists. Before I began working in retail and wholesale, selling jewelry, I was a front man for Ahmad Jamal," he said, referring to the acclaimed jazz pianist from Pittsburgh. "I'd handle his publicity, PR, I'd book shows, hotel reservations." Rashid began naming the jazz musicians he knew who had converted to Ahmadi Islam. "I taught Yusef Lateef the primer, the Arabic alphabet, and the *suras,*" he said. "I knew Miles Davis. He wasn't Muslim, though. We went to the same high school in East St. Louis—he was younger than me. I used to roll with the big boys, and he began to adopt my style. I was cooler than him." He grins again.

Some older gentlemen and teenage boys had entered the room and were listening to Brother Rashid talk about their community's history. Most of the older men had also migrated from the South, leaving Georgia, Mississippi, and Tennessee in their teens, embracing Islam in Chicago, Detroit, or Milwaukee. They began to recall their childhood in the South, how they left, and their arrival in northern cities half a century ago.

"Life in the South is something else, hard but slow, mixed but separate," said Abdul Kareem, a sixty-seven-year-old furniture maker, also in a collarless shirt and Nehru jacket. "I picked cotton until I was sixteen, and then I came to Chicago. I quickly started getting into trouble. I stopped going to church. It was all too hypocritical." He shook his head. "Sultan, my barber, was a Muslim, and he used to hang out with jazz musicians. So I started hanging out with them too—Art Blakey, Mustafa Dalil, Sulieman Saud, and Amin Lakan, who was an excommunicated Ahmadi. Jazz makes people think— that's why jazz artists liked Islam, they were thinking of ways out. Islam for them, for me, was just more honest. But many of the immigrants didn't like jazz—I remember one Pakistani missionary said jazz was the worst art form," he says, laughing.

The seminar room had filled with boys: the girls and women were in a room across the hall. Toddlers were rolling on prayer rugs on the floor, young boys hiding under the table; but mostly it was teenagers, listening intently to their fathers and grandfathers talking about their childhood in the South and why they turned to Islam.

Abdul Kareem went on. "I got drafted into the military in 1963. Before we set sail from Port Authority to Germany, I picked up a copy of Pickthall's translation of the Quran. I was stationed in France. There I had time to read, and I wrote a letter to Elijah Muhammad. He asked me to come see him after I got out."

A middle-aged gentleman sitting around the table, a native of Cuba known in Milwaukee as Imam Nasrallah, recalled moving to Wisconsin at the age of fourteen from the Caribbean. "Those were revolutionary times," he smiled, stroking his large salt-and-pepper beard. He was wearing a gray Afghan hat and a *shalwar kameez.* "The civil rights struggle was in full force, the Black Panthers were just down the street—I joined with them for a few months. We read Lenin, Marx, Mao, Nietzsche, Plato to see what they had to offer. I was drafted to fight in Vietnam. I read Ghulam Ahmad's *The Teachings of Islam* and I liked the ideas. I saw the Ahmadi community going into the ghetto, which other Muslims weren't doing. I recently gave a *khutba* about the significance of Sadiq, of leaders like him who can attract all people. He spoke to the disenfranchised in the ghetto, but also at universities—he could speak in the ghetto and then Times Square."

"Islam in the 1920s filled a vacuum," observed Abdul Kareem. "The NAACP was dormant back then. Garvey and Elijah brought awareness of justice, but they were not teaching brotherhood for all men, and Islam did that. Dr. Sadiq advised Marcus Garvey. Dr. Sadiq bought the building on 4448 South Wabash, the first property purchased in America by the Ahmadiyya movement. The building was torn down and a mosque built in its place in 1993—the mosque still stands on those grounds."

Listening to these "pioneers," as they're known in the American Muslim community, I was reminded of Ralph Ellison, who in 1948 wrote that African-Americans had been "swept from slavery to the condition of industrial man in a space of time so telescoped (a bare eighty-five years) that it is possible literally for them to step from feudalism into the vortex of industrialism simply by moving across the Mason-Dixon line." These southern-born, Urdu-speaking septua- and octogenarians arrived in the northern ghetto as uprooted young men, fleeing the South with its religious traditions and institutions; they landed in an urban miasma where they were exposed to a variety of ideas and cultures—mostly radical, Third-Worldist ideologies which stressed Afro-Asian solidarity and decolonization. Jazz, to paraphrase Abdul Kareem, imagined a space that Islam would come to fill: Muslim prayer and dietary rules provided structure in a world suffused by drugs and alcohol; languages like Arabic and Urdu opened up the texts and cultures of other civilizations and provided a connection to a rising postcolonial world. By identifying with the Islamic world, the African-American converts could go from being a downtrodden minority to being part of a global "colored majority."

The experience of these pioneers also shows just how closely the history of Islam in the West is entwined with empire and racial exclusion: it was European colonial powers that first brought African Muslims to the New World. It was the Fugitive Slave Law of 1850, granting federal agencies "unlimited powers" to apprehend runaway slaves—and often freed slaves as well—that pushed many African-American leaders toward the "back to Africa" movement and eventually Islam. The Immigration Act of 1917 restricted immigration to the United States, prompting northern industrialists to turn to southern blacks as a source of cheap labor. African-Americans in turn migrated northward, seeking work and fleeing Jim Crow laws. As millions of African-Americans flooded northern cities, they encountered migrants from various parts of the colonized world—from Asia, the Middle East, Africa—who were fleeing conflict and colonial rule. This "Asiatic Barred Zone Act" as it also was known, would push thousands of undocumented Muslim migrants—like Dr. Sadiq— from South Asia and elsewhere to seek refuge in these "new" African-American communities across the U.S. (in an eerie foreshadowing of what would happen after 9/11).

They Turn East

The cultural ferment produced by the Great Migration and the Harlem Renaissance would propel the rise of Islam and jazz, two forces that spread rapidly and concurrently in pre- and postwar urban America. And in a trend that still intrigues historians and music critics, after World War II scores of jazz musicians embraced Ahmadi Islam. In 1947, the drummer and bandleader Art Blakey, who had spent time in West Africa studying Islam, formed a group called the Messengers, a name with a clear religious connotation. This seventeen-member, all-Muslim band was centered around the Ahmadiyya center in Harlem. Later, as the band's personnel changed, its name became the Jazz Messengers, but at the start, it was led by Blakey (Abdullah Ibn Buhaina) and included trumpeter Idrees Sulieman (Leonard Graham) and saxophonist Yusef Lateef (Bill Evans). Other artists who embraced Islam were pianist Fritz Jones (Ahmad Jamal), drummer Kenny Clarke (Liaqat Ali Salaam), pianist McCoy Tyner (Sulieman Saud), trumpeter Oliver Mesheux (Mustafa Dalil), bassist George Joyner (Jamil Nasser), trumpeter Kenny Dorham (Abdul Hamid), alto saxophonist Edmond Gregory (Sahib Shihab), pianist Walter Bishop (Ibrahim ibn Ismail), trombonist Howard Bowe (Haleen Rasheed), vocalist Dakota Staton (Aliyah Rabia) who was married to trumpeter Alfonso Nelson Rainey (Talib Dawud), and tenor saxophonists Orlando Wright (Musa Kaleem) and Lynn Hope (El Hajj Abdullah Rasheed Ahmad)—the latter would perform in a turban and talk about his travels to Mecca.

The mass conversion of jazz musicians to Islam prompted *Ebony* magazine in 1953 to publish an article on these two hundred or so "Moslem musicians" with the headline "Ancient Religion Attracts Moderns," which not inaccurately described the conversion as a response to segregation. This was a common view among journalists in the 1950s, that Muslim identity helped blacks in America sidestep (legal) racial barriers, especially down South.

Dizzy Gillespie never embraced Islam, but he understood the cultural and political work that it did. He noticed that the converts who changed their names and donned turbans were perceived as African or Middle Eastern and treated better. In his memoir *To Be or Not to Bop,* the trumpeter recalls Ahmadi converts in the 1940s telling him, " 'Man, if you join the Muslim faith, you ain't colored no more, you'll be white . . . You get a new name and you don't have to be a nigger no more.' So everybody started joining because they considered it a big advantage not to be black during the time of segregation . . . ," he writes. "When these cats found out that Idrees Sulieman, who joined the Muslim faith about that time, could go into these white restaurants and bring out sandwiches to the other guys because he wasn't colored—and he looked like the inside of the chimney—they started enrolling in droves." Most poignantly, Gillespie recounts how his friends who converted had their Muslim names and, under "race," *W* for white printed on their police cards: "[Drummer] Kenny Clarke had one and he showed it to me. He said, 'See, nigger, I ain't no spook; I'm white, "W." ' "

Though ambivalent about this identity shifting, Gillespie winced when journalists dismissed his Muslim cohorts as "weird" and "exotic." Hobsbawm recounts an interesting exchange between the trumpeter and his arranger Gil Fuller, who is puzzled when a band of "Moslem boppers" break rehearsal to bow toward Mecca:

> Dizzy's eyes filled with tears.
> "They been hurt," he explained, "and they're tryin' to get away from it."
> "It's the last resort of guys who don't know which way to turn," said Fuller impatiently.
> "East," said Dizzy. "They turn east."

Gillespie understood how turning east could shield one from daily indignities. And he was impressed by the Muslims' discipline. He admired their refusal to accept discriminatory pay standards and their pride in African history. He saw how Ahmadi jazz converts propagated Islam within the jazz world in different cities (despite the resistance of some of the Indian and Pakistani Ahmadis who frowned upon music), raised money to bring teachers from Pakistan, and even developed their own jargon—a blend of bebop and Arabic. He saw how their internationalist outlook helped expand and regenerate their art, and how their interest in Africa and the Orient opened up new musical worlds, as church-raised musicians began incorporating Eastern rhythms into the syncopated structure of the blues and church-based gospel numbers.

Yet both Gillespie and the *Ebony* article were remarking on a pattern—of Muslim blacks being treated better than their non-Muslim counterparts—that went back to the plantation. Not only did Muslim identity and literacy in Arabic bring better treatment, but in the 1820s, as the United States established Liberia and began venturing into Muslim areas of West Africa, Muslim slaves would gain a political significance. The State Department thought they could help negotiate the release of Americans held captive on the Barbary Coast, and the American Colonization Society, which advocated the repatriation of blacks to Liberia, saw them as a valuable tool for opening up West Africa to American interests. The Muslim slaves were seen as natural intermediaries with the Muslims and pagans of the West African coast, and a number of African Muslim slaves literate in Arabic—individuals like Ayyub bin Suleiman, Ibrahima Abdul Rahman, and Lamine Kaba—earned their liberty by feigning conversion to Christianity and offering their services to American and British colonial projects in West Africa. The preferential treatment—and in some cases manumission—afforded Muslim slaves encouraged other blacks to claim Muslim or Oriental ancestry in the hope of gaining passage to Africa.

The association of Islam with preferential treatment and "passing" would irk a number of prominent black leaders, especially those opposed to the "back to Africa" movement. Booker T. Washington, in his autobiography, *Up from Slavery,* scoffs at how a "dark-skinned man . . . a citizen of Morocco" is allowed into a hotel from which he, "an American Negro," is banned. But Islam would be used not only to "exit" or separate from America but also as a way to integrate politically. In 1913, Noble Drew Ali founded the Moorish Science Temple in Newark; he relocated to Chicago in 1923, saying the Midwest "was closer to Islam." The MST would use a heterodox Islam and an Oriental genealogy to navigate the racial hierarchy (the same strategy adopted by Muslim slaves to gain manumission) and to reconstruct black identity. His aim, however, was to build a movement that would integrate African-Americans into America. He thus taught his followers their true genealogy (Asiatic), nationality (Moorish), and faith (Islam), all of which had been stripped from them by slavery. Like Garvey's UNIA, Noble Drew Ali's movement had a strong social services mission, feeding the needy and rehabilitating people with drug and alcohol addictions. But unlike Garvey, he did not believe in returning to Africa—or Morocco, specifically—and was not anti-nation-state.

A firm believer in civic and political engagement, he exhorted his followers to vote, to participate in the American political system and to respect the law of the land, while awaiting God's deliverance. Noble Drew Ali did not reject America the way Garvey did. The Moorish Science movement was culturally separatist, but only to the extent that such a stance could help its members integrate.

Noble Drew Ali saw how rapidly immigrants from Europe were assimilating into American society, and figured that if he could convince the American government and the white majority that he and his followers were Moroccan nationals, they could escape discrimination. The ethno-national label "Moorish" was as such more empowering and functional than the racial designation "Negro." As he put it, "If you have a nation you must have a national name in order to be recognized by the [American] nation as an American citizen." He tapped into the "national origins" discourse of the day, teaching his devotees that they were Moorish Americans, "descendants of Moroccans and born in America." Across the country, Noble Drew Ali's followers were given the Arabic or Turkish honorifics *El* or *Bey* to accompany their names, and wore silk robes, turbans, and red fezzes, a style of dress meant to imitate the attire of Muslim slaves of the previous century. Members also carried identity cards ("passports") that underlined their association with Morocco, but stated, "I am a citizen of the United States." All the talk of Morocco and Moorish nationalism proved vexing to some. "What a terrible gang. Thieves and cutthroats!" said one Detroit police office. "Wouldn't answer anything . . . Pretending that they don't understand you, that they were Moors from Morocco. They never saw Morocco! Those Moors never saw anything before they came to Detroit except Florida and Alabama!"

But the language of national origins was strategic. Decades before 1960s-style identity politics and before groups started claiming minority status, Noble Drew Ali calculated that if the idiom of nationalism and difference was helping anticolonial movements challenge their colonial masters, imbuing his movement with passports, Moroccan-style flags, and a proto-Islamic ideology could help him bargain with the U.S. government for inclusion in America.

The Moorish Science Temple is critical to understanding the evolution of Islam in America and subsequent cultural trends. Noble Drew Ali was the "bridge over which the Muslim legacies of the eighteenth and nineteenth centuries crossed over into the Muslim communities of the twentieth and twenty-first." His movement was the first organization to appear in the American ghetto teaching that Islam was the "black man's religion" and introducing an association between Islam, urban marginality, and race consciousness that persists to this day in Europe and the Americas.

The Muslim jazz artists who wore turbans and adopted Muslim names and Oriental genealogies must be understood with this history in mind. The Brooklyn-born bassist Ahmed Abdul-Malik (né Jonathan Tim), who became a distinguished oud player, was long believed to be the son of a Sudanese migrant; but in fact both his parents were born in St. Vincent in the Caribbean. Likewise, the Juilliard-educated Sheikh Daoud Faisal (né David Donald), a leading Sunni figure in postwar New York, who would claim Moroccan ancestry and be appointed representative of Morocco at the UN, was a Trinidadian national. Dizzy Gillespie never claimed Oriental ancestry, but he enjoyed toying with Oriental identities and people's preconceptions. On tour in Europe, he'd wear a turban and pretend not to speak English. "People would see me on the streets and think of me as an Arab or a Hindu. They didn't know what to think, really," writes the prankish trumpeter. "Sometimes Americans would think I was some kind of 'Mohammedan' nobleman. You wouldn't believe some of the things they'd say in ignorance." Gillespie would end up embracing Bahá'ism, a religious movement that emerged in nineteenth-century Iran; he would go on to set up the United Nation Orchestra, inspired by the Bahá'i belief in the unity of mankind. The irony is that Gillespie, a Muslim-sympathizing former member of the Communist Party, was tapped to become America's first jazz ambassador to the Soviet bloc.

Jazz to the Rescue

After World War II, as French and British colonies gained their independence, they found themselves courted by two superpowers eager to expand their spheres of influence. Forty states had become sovereign by 1960. Washington's efforts to attract them into its orbit were complicated by Soviet propaganda, which focused on racial discrimination and strife in the American South. Images of the killing of Emmett Till in 1955 and the violent backlash to *Brown v. Board of Education* a year earlier were broadcast around the world, and President Dwight Eisenhower, who had been rather complacent about civil rights, began to see that internationally, race was America's Achilles' heel. The State Department began organizing high-profile jazz tours to alter impressions. The tours were the brainchild of the Democratic congressman from Harlem Adam Clayton Powell, who conceived of jazz as a Cold War weapon after attending the Afro-Asian Conference of Non-Aligned Nations in 1955 in Bandung, Indonesia. Powell was repelled by the Third-Worldist rhetoric he heard and the claims that the Soviet Union was more progressive on race than the U.S. Upon returning, he proposed to the State Department that bands led by Dizzy Gillespie, Count Basie, and Louis Armstrong be sent abroad to improve America's image. As Powell would tell Eisenhower, "One dark face from the U.S. is of as much value as millions of dollars in economic aid."

Top diplomats welcomed the idea. The main goals of the tours were to bolster alliances and persuade nonaligned states that the U.S. was different from European colonial powers and the Soviet Union. "Before long, jazz will become an arm of this country's foreign policy in such places as the Far East, Middle East and Africa," observed the *New York Times* in November 1955. "Bands will go into countries where communism has a foothold." In March 1956, Gillespie and his arranger, a young trumpeter named Quincy Jones, embarked on the first tour; their first performance took place in Iran, where three years earlier a CIA-backed coup had reinstalled the shah to power. With the Soviet Union expanding into the Middle East and an insolvent Britain unable to keep troops in Greece, the U.S. assumed the role of containing communism and protecting oil resources in this region. Gillespie's eighteen-piece band performed in Iran before moving on to Syria, Lebanon, and Pakistan and ending in Turkey, Greece, and Yugoslavia. The jazz tours targeted areas where communism was gaining a foothold and zones rich in oil and uranium; as Penny Von Eschen writes in her seminal study *Satchmo Blows Up the World*, the tours often moved "in tandem with covert CIA operations." The "jambassadors" were often dispatched as first responders to trouble spots. In 1958, John Foster Dulles extended a tour that sent Dave Brubeck's band into Iraq, the only Arab state in the anticommunist Baghdad Pact, hoping that while the jazz ambassadors performed, U.S. officials could help quell the discord within the Iraqi army's ranks.

"They sent us to every post where there were problems and [we] got nothing but raves: we were the black kamikaze band," writes Quincy Jones in his memoir. "The American embassy in Athens was getting its ass kicked, being stoned by the Cypriot students, so they rushed us over there from Ankara, Turkey, and the Greek people loved it." The "jambassadors" had their mix of fun and adventure, posing in Arab headdress near the Pyramids, partying in Lebanon and Turkey while dodging local police. In July 1958, Paul Desmond, Dave Brubeck's saxophonist, skipped the concert in Iraq and went to Beirut to unwind. One morning he woke up to see fourteen thousand Marines wading ashore amid the sunbathers: Eisenhower had sent troops to bolster Lebanese president Camille Chamoun against his leftist opponents. In Damascus, trombonist Melba Liston—one of the few women to participate in the tours—would learn the Syrian national anthem from a group of schoolchildren, then perform her own version to the delight of local audiences; during his performance at a fair in Damascus, Duke Ellington was hailed with shouts of *"ash al-Duke, ash al-Duke"* (Long Live Duke). A running joke among the male ambassadors revolved around the perils of flirting with local girls. Recalls Quincy Jones, "We'd meet so many fine women that all you wanted to do was dream about giving them one lick on the back of the neck because sometimes in the Middle East, that's as close as you could ever get."

Integrated bands led by Gillespie, Armstrong, Ellington, and Benny Goodman visited the Soviet Union and parts of Africa, Asia, and the Middle East, their performances aimed at generating goodwill and getting citizenries to identify with "the American way of life." The bands were intended to be symbols of the triumph of democracy, with jazz serving as an embodiment of America's liberal ideals, in its improvisational pluralism and its universal, race-transcending quality. The irony, of course, is that these black musicians were deployed to improve the country's image and legitimize policies at a time when the U.S. was still a Jim Crow nation. And vast swaths of the American public opposed the tours, in fact, leading the State Department to disguise their full extent. Yet the tours, which ended in the 1970s, are widely considered a success. Harvard scholar Ingrid Minson speaks of the "extraordinary success of the jazz tours." Pianist Brubeck thought the jazz ambassadors helped end the Cold War.

The jazz tours are deemed to have been so successful that the State Department has recently tried to revive the program, sending American jazz artists to play the music of Ahmadi jazz musicians for Muslim audiences. Saxophonist Chris Byars, one of the new jazz ambassadors, described the response he gets when he plays the pieces by Basheer Qusim (né Gigi Gryce), a New York–based altoist who became Muslim in the early 1950s. "When I announce that I'm going to play compositions by the American jazz musician Basheer Qusim, that gets their attention," he said, referring to a performance in Saudi Arabia in February 2008. "Afterward several people came up, very appreciative, saying very intensely, 'Thank you for coming to our country.'"

"Searching for Noble Drew Ali"

One chilly night in November 2005, the Kominas, the punk rockers from Boston, stood outside the Burr Oak Cemetery in southwest Chicago, the city's first African-American cemetery, wherein lay the remains of blues singer Dinah Washington and of Emmett Till, the youth whose murder helped galvanize the civil rights movement. This trio of musicians had hitched their way to Chicago, bumming rides and sleeping in parking lots. They were accompanied by the author Michael Muhammad Knight (whose novel *The Taqwacores* had inspired the rock movement so named); by Muhammad, a member of the Moorish Science Temple in Chicago; and by another fellow, a member of the Five Percent Nation. Since the main gate was locked, the group entered through an opening in the fence and began combing the graveyard. ("We were using our cell phones as lights," recalls band member Shahjehan Khan.) These young men were trying to locate the grave of Noble Drew Ali. The group formed a prayer line in the cemetery and recited verses from the Quran in remembrance of this early twentieth-century leader. Knight had visited the cemetery a year earlier and now had brought his fellow rockers to visit Noble Drew Ali's grave. "We stood at a flat plaque with Noble Drew Ali's face on it, with a 7 and 2 shaking hands," he would write. "I sang a Fatiha over his bones and sang it for everyone else in that yard too."

What sets the Kominas apart from other rock groups on the Muslim youth scene is their keen interest in the heterodox movements of early American Islam, an interest usually associated with hip-hop, not rock. The Muslim youth today borrowing from Noble Drew Ali are living in a context obviously dissimilar from that of a hundred years ago, but the challenges of exclusion, empire, and religious nationalism that produced the Moorish Science Temple are still facing Muslim communities from Lahore to Boston, albeit in a different guise. After Noble Drew Ali's death in 1929, the Moorish Science movement split, and Fard Muhammad founded the Nation of Islam, absorbing many of Noble Drew Ali's teachings.

The NOI would also advance a "moral geography" centered around the Orient, placing emphasis on personal decorum and a healthy diet, setting up temples across the country to teach discipline and bring a message of uplift to followers. But unlike the MST, the NOI was staunchly separatist under Elijah Muhammad and Farrakhan, and opposed to integration and electoral participation. (Farrakhan came close to breaking with this practice in 2008, when he exhorted his followers to support then candidate Obama, describing the senator's meteoric rise as a divine sign and likening him to Fard, the Nation of Islam founder, a "black man with a white mother [who] became a saviour to us.") The MST still exists, with temples across the country and a presence in the prison system. Members still don robes and fezzes and brandish the Moroccan flag; but the movement lacks the influence it had in the 1920s, when it had tens of thousands of members. But young American Muslims—the children of immigrants—are intrigued by Noble Drew Ali's syncretism and views on nationalism and integration, and are using his ideas and the practices of early Black Muslim groups to expand the boundaries of contemporary Muslim identity.

After immersing themselves in Five Percenter and Moorish Science teachings and visiting temples around the country, in 2007 Basim Usmani and Shahjehan Khan returned to Lahore. They set up a new band—this time a punk-ska group called Noble Drew. They sang only in Punjabi, so that their political lyrics could reach the lay listener. "I chose the name Noble Drew for many reasons," explains Basim, "but in particular, I loved that the man had created his own Islamic culture. Noble Drew changed my view of Islam. And it felt great to raise the flag of American Muslims in Lahore. My Marxist friends loved Noble Drew because he was resisting hegemony. The big word among Pakistani students is *hegemony,* and they could see that Noble Drew was anti-hegemonic. He was a Muslim resister, who reached back to rescue the Islam beaten out of the African slaves."

As a journalist, Basim tried to use the ideas of Noble Drew Ali to critique Pakistani society. But the Islam that the American religious leader preached was rather unorthodox. The Moorish Science Temple's holy book was the Circle Seven Koran, which Noble Drew Ali compiled in 1927. The 139-page book is divided into forty-seven chapters and borrows from the Bible, the Quran, Marcus Garvey's teachings, medieval German Christian mystic thought, and in particular a volume called *The Aquarian Gospel of Jesus the Christ,* written by onetime Civil War chaplain Levi H. Dowling. The Circle Seven Koran didn't contain a single verse from the Quran that Muslims around the world revere; aside from the aversion to pork, there was actually very little that was Islamic about the Moorish Science Temple's teachings. But this is what excited the Kominas. Basim wrote an article for the respected *Friday Times* comparing the impact of Noble Drew Ali's Circle Seven Koran and the poetry of the eighteenth-century Punjabi poet Bulleh Shah.

"The great Sufi poets like Bulleh Shah bad-mouth the clergy all the time, they say things like the 'Love of God is the enemy of sharia.' They say there's a divine in all of us—*ana al haq,* 'I am the truth.' In the article I tried to show how to this day in Bulleh Shah's village [Sheikhpura, thirty minutes north of Lahore] people will cite passages from Shah's commentary, thinking that it's the Quran; people confuse his elaborations with the Quran. Because his commentary was in Punjabi and resonated with people, people think it's the Quran itself. And I was arguing that Noble Drew's Circle Seven Koran, considered so blasphemous by Muslims, did the same: Drew spoke his people's language, he understood their culture and adapted Islam to his community in Chicago." The *Friday Times* editor wouldn't run the story, citing a fatwa issued against Noble Drew Ali in 1930. "They found the fatwa on the Internet, and said the article would be deemed blasphemous. Blasphemy laws in Pakistan are very unpredictable."

That the offspring of Muslim immigrants to America, who were outraged by the Moorish Science Temple's heterodoxy, are today unearthing Noble Drew Ali's teachings is ironic enough; but it's astounding that newspaper editors in Pakistan in 2008 would invoke a fatwa from eighty years earlier to censor their young compatriots. Noble Drew Ali's movement emerged at a time when immigrant Muslim communities in the Northeast and Midwest were growing. By and large, the immigrant Muslims and the Moorish Americans kept out of each other's way; but the interaction between Noble Drew Ali and Satti Majid, a Sudanese imam in New York, captured the communities' clashing interpretations of Islam, and in many ways foreshadowed encounters to come between Sunni Muslim immigrants and African-American Muslims.

Satti Majid was born in Sudan and trained as a scholar of religion at the prestigious Al-Azhar University in Cairo. He traveled to London before moving to New York in 1904, at the age of twenty-one, to spread the message of Islam. He founded a slew of pioneering Muslim organizations in New York, Detroit, Pittsburgh, and Buffalo. Visiting the Midwest, he came across Ahmadi centers, and was displeased by their heterodoxy; but he was particularly incensed by the Moorish Science Temple, with its sacrilegious Circle Seven Koran and Noble Drew Ali's claims to be a prophet. Satti wrote to Noble Drew Ali asking him either to recant his beliefs or to perform a miracle (*mu'jiza*) that, according to Islamic belief, only prophets could perform. The Sudanese imam then tried to sue Noble Drew Ali in an American court for "bringing the Islamic faith into disrepute." Unsuccessful, he returned to Cairo, and in January 1929 he requested a fatwa from Al-Azhar University to censure the Chicago-based leader.

Satti Majid would never return to the United States, but he succeeded in getting three fatwas issued against Noble Drew Ali: the first promulgated at Al-Azhar in 1929, the second in Omdurman, Sudan, in 1930, and the third in Khartoum, Sudan, the same year. The fatwas denounced him as "a liar and a charlatan and unbeliever (*kafir*) [who] deserves eternal and everlasting punishment in Hell." There's no evidence that any of these fatwas reached the U.S. In any case, Noble Drew Ali died in July 1929, but this was the legal precedent that the Lahore-based editor invoked—through Google Books—to block the publication of Basim's article, noting that mullahs could use the fatwa to bring charges of blasphemy against the newspaper.

Hostility to the band grew. The musicians' praise of Fard Muhammad, founder of the Nation of Islam and widely believed to be an Ahmadi, and their use of the pentagram, the five-point star—an emblem of the Moorish Science Temple and the Nation of Islam, but also a symbol favored by neo-pagan and Satanic groups—raised hackles. In December 2008, the band Noble Drew was invited to the World Performing Arts Festival in Lahore's famous Alhamra Arts Centre. Basim was onstage when, midway through his second number, two blasts went off right outside the stadium, followed by another two explosions. Media reports said gas cylinders had been placed outside the complex. "I don't know if they were targeting us, or sending us a message. The bombs went off just when we were onstage. After that we didn't know who to trust." The group began considering leaving Pakistan. Soon after, the musicians—this time as the Kominas—were invited to perform at South by Southwest, one of the largest arts festivals in the U.S., which takes place every year in Austin. In early 2009 Shaj and Basim returned to America.

Allah Supreme

It's not unusual to see young American Muslims huddled around their iPod docks and speakers, trying to make out the exact words that John Coltrane utters during "Acknowledgement," the first part of his thirty-two-minute-long masterwork organized around a simple four-note bass routine and, seemingly, the words of the album's title, *A Love Supreme*. The believers swear that you can hear Coltrane chanting "Allah Supreme" in a breathy voice reminiscent of Sufi *dhikr*, "*Allah* Supreme, *Allah* Supreme"—the literal English translation of the Arabic expression "Allahu Akbar."

The skeptics demur: you can clearly hear the man utter the consonant *v* toward the middle of the song when he starts singing "A love supreme." The believers then describe how Coltrane was influenced by the Ahmadi Muslim jazzmen with whom he performed. They cite his biography, which describes how "Islam was a positive force in [1950s] Philadelphia," the musician's adopted city; how Coltrane had long discussions about Islam with his friend Hasan, the piano player; how Islam helped him shake off his heroin addiction; how Yusef Lateef, his saxophonist, encouraged him to pursue Islam; and how his wife, Naima, known in the community as Sister Coltrane, was Muslim. The skeptics roll their eyes: Coltrane was drawn to Sufism as well as to other Eastern philosophies—so what? To seal their case, the Coltrane-said-"Allahu Akbar" camp point to the record's liner notes, which mention the saxophonist's "spiritual awakening" in 1957 and point to a few lines that should excite any Muslim. "NO MATTER WHAT . . . IT IS WITH GOD. HE IS GRACIOUS AND MERCIFUL. HIS WAY IS IN LOVE, THROUGH WHICH WE ALL ARE. IT IS TRULY—A LOVE SUPREME. Al-Rahman, al-raheem.

The Gracious, the Merciful," writes Coltrane, and he ends with "ALL PRAISE TO GOD," a translation of another Muslim expression.

Both State Department officials and Muslim youth are scrutinizing the connections between Islam and jazz, but for different reasons. American Muslim youth are studying the compositions of Lateef, Gillespie, and Coltrane, trying to understand, for example, how Malcolm X's speaking style was influenced by the big-band sounds of the 1940s, and how, in turn, this fiery Muslim leader's rhetorical cadences would influence jazz artists like Coltrane, whom Amiri Baraka dubbed "Malcolm in the New Super Bop Fire" and who, coming a generation after bebop, rejected political moderation, identifying, rather, with Malcolm X's militancy. Coltrane's relationship to jazz has long intrigued jazz aficionados and elders in the Muslim community. Rashied Ali, who was Coltrane's drummer, says rather cryptically that the saxophonist was "a real country boy" and that "he was into being a Muslim and everything like that, but boy Trane liked his collard greens with his fat back in it." For today's kids, whether Coltrane is saying "Allah" or "A love" is of critical importance. If the former, that would mean one of the greatest jazz compositions of the twentieth century—the manuscript for the album is one of the National Museum of American History's "treasures"—is a tribute to or was inspired by Islam.

The last living member of the Jazz Messengers, the group founded in 1948, is the saxophonist Yusef Lateef, currently the spokesperson for the worldwide Ahmadi community. Between 1963 and 1966, he was signed to Coltrane's label, Impulse, when Coltrane was experimenting with Eastern sounds in his free-jazz recordings. Every youth I spoke to in Milwaukee suggested I talk to "Brother Lateef Saheb," as they call him, and ask about *A Love Supreme*. In Ramadan 2009, almost a year to the day after my trip to Wisconsin, I got to meet Lateef. I arrived at Roulette in Tribeca in Manhattan just after sunset. The concert space was packed; the musicians were in place, the audience was waiting quietly while Lateef, dressed in a gray robe and a skullcap, was to the right side of the stage in full view, saying his evening prayers.

He broke his fast with a drink of water and came onstage. As always, he played various instruments—saxophone and some Eastern instruments, such as an *arghul* (bamboo flute). He softly sang spirituals, accompanied by a Gnawa *sintir,* a three-stringed instrument made of camel skin.

When I spoke to Lateef, I was struck by how similar his biography was to those of the other "pioneers" I had spoken to in Milwaukee. He was born in Chattanooga, Tennessee, in 1920, his family migrated north, settling in Paradise Valley, Detroit's historic black neighborhood, where Arab peddlers came selling their wares. He was exposed to Islam while playing with the Wally Hayes Band in Chicago, where he met trumpeter Talib Dawud. He began attending the now historic Ahmadi mosque on 4448 South Wabash. In 1955, while he was working at a Chrysler factory, a fellow laborer—a man from the Middle East—gave him a stringed instrument called a *rabat,* saying that King David played it during his prayers more than five thousand years ago. On another occasion, while strolling through the city's Syrian spice market, he discovered instruments like the *arghul,* which along with the *rabat* he incorporated into his music. Lateef went on to tour with Gillespie's band and played with Coltrane and Charles Mingus. He would go on to record *Nile Valley Blues* and *Prayer for the East,* capturing the cultural and ideological winds of the postwar era. Today, Lateef is recognized as an American Jazz Master by the National Endowment for the Arts, and credited with creating the subgenre of "world music jazz," blending music from Africa and Asia with bebop and hard bop.

As he autographed records for a line of fans, I asked about the Gnawa instrument—the *sintir*—that accompanied his singing. "It's a spiritual instrument," he whispered. "It produces auto-physio-psychic music—music from one's physical, mental, and spiritual self—which is what I call jazz."

When I mentioned *A Love Supreme,* Lateef gave me the same self-effacing response he offers in his memoir, *The Gentle Giant:* that the inspiration for the composition came from Coltrane's late Muslim wife, Naima. Coltrane heard her recite the *fatiha* five times a day. "I can only say that John and I, we were dear friends, we were trying to advance our music together. I don't know if I encouraged him to read the Holy Quran. My guess is his wife, Naima, encouraged him to read the Holy Quran, Khalil Gibran, and Krishnamurti. The prayer that John wrote in *A Love Supreme* repeats the phrase 'All praise belongs to God no matter what' several times. This phrase has the semantics of the second sentence of the *fatiha*. The Arabic transliteration is 'Al Humdulilah,' and that means 'All praise is due to God.'"

6

The Blue Spirit Chose Me

Some day a wonderful new music is destined to come out of North Africa.

CLAUDE MCKAY, 1931

Six men file quietly into a modest villa in Saint-Denis, a *banlieue* in northern Paris. It is a chilly spring evening; the sun had just set. Once behind walls, they don their gowns—red, yellow, green, black, dark and light blue—with shells and beads hanging from the sleeves. The body of a recently slaughtered goat hangs in the corner of the courtyard; a pool of blood has formed on the floor. They dab their hands in the blood and whisper a prayer. One of the young men begins to pound his snare drum to announce their arrival. He is hushed by another, the group's apparent leader, "Not so loud." Hearing the drums, four young women in caftans appear, holding candles of different colors, and accompany the men into the house. As the procession enters the living-room area, the snare drums grow louder. Thirty or so women are seated on the floor. The men form a circle and begin a swirling dance to bless the space of ritual. Individual dancers break from the circle, kicking, squatting, dropping to their knees, and giving reverence.

The men are Gnawa practitioners who have arrived to perform a healing ceremony. The Gnawa are a Sufi order in Morocco that identifies with the descendants of formerly enslaved West Africans. They venerate Bilal al-Habashi, the freed Ethiopian slave who became one of the earliest converts to Islam, a companion of the Prophet and— blessed with a songful voice—the first muezzin, caller to prayer. To this day, adepts speak of Sidna Bilal's ability to heal through music, and relate how once when Fatima, the Prophet's daughter, and her husband, Ali, were arguing, Sidna Bilal appeared, dressed like a Gnawi, playing the *qraqeb*, twirling the long tassels on his cap—and made them smile.

Gnawa music is believed to heal people afflicted with spirit possession. In Islam, the jinn (spirits) are said to be made of vapor or flame. The jinn are not necessarily evil; like human beings, spirits have different personalities and temperaments—they can be kind or cruel. But what they all have in common is an ability to trail humans and afflict their subjects with madness, infertility, and lifelong misfortune. In popular Islam, spirits inhabit people; sometimes they can be exorcised, at other times the possessed must simply surrender to them. The Gnawa are called upon to appease the spirits, which they do through animal sacrifice, incense, and colors but especially through music and chants in praise of God, the Prophet, and the saints in their pantheon. The intoxicating rhythms of the Gnawa—produced by the repeated bass line of the *sintir,* and the heavy clacking of large metal castanets (*qraqeb*)—have the ability to reconcile the possessed with their spirit; once the possessed submits to the jinn, that spirit is mollified and the inhabited person can avail herself of the spirit's powers.

A Gnawa healing ceremony—a *lila,* as it's called—is an intense, all-night affair, often starting shortly after *'isha,* the night prayer, and lasting until sunrise. Traditionally the musicians are men, led by a *ma'alem,* a master of the stringed instrument, an older man who has memorized the Quran and is a custodian of the Gnawa tradition; an older woman called a *mqadema* (often translated as "priestess") supervises the ceremony; and the possessed are generally women. But at this *lila* in northern Paris, as the *ma'alem* sits down, one sees that the master is not an older man, but a boyish thirty-two-year-old with a goatee and a ponytail. His name is Jawad. He plays with a local group, and if he's nervous, he's not showing it. A brazier, a piece of cloth, and ceramic bowls filled with different kinds of incense—sandalwood, myrrh, frankincense, benzoin—are placed in front of him. Drops of blood from the sacrificed animal are sprinkled on the cloth. Jawad whispers a blessing and picks up the *sintir*. He has prepared the instrument for the ceremony: its camel-skin front was rubbed with a teaspoon of milk, decorated with henna, and held over a brazier of burning sandalwood. As Jawad begins to strum the strings, a powerful thwacking bass line vibrates through the room. The musicians praise the Prophet, calling different saints and invoking the spirits of Bambara, Hausa, and Fulani, an allusion to ancestors from West Africa. One of the musicians gets up and does a dance imitating a hunter or warrior, another reference to the Gnawa's West African origins. He collects money from the women seated. Jawad throws incense into a hot coal brazier. Each jinn demands a particular incense; a fragrant smoke fills the room, setting the stage for the spirits, who upon hearing the musical notes will descend through the *sintir*'s long neck and into the instrument's belly.

Seven spirits are usually invoked by the Gnawa—not all of them will manifest in a *lila,* but one can tell which spirit has arrived by the emotions and movements of the possessed. Among the main jinn are Sidi Musa of the sea, whose color is blue—and when he manifests, the possessed begin to dance as if they are swimming or drowning—and Sidi Hamou, the spirit of the slaughterhouse, whose color is red. Lala Mira, whose color is yellow, is known for her joy and vanity—when she appears, the possessed begin chuckling and laughing; Sidi Mimun, whose color is black, guards the forests. The last spirit to manifest is Aisha Kandisha, the most tyrannical and terrifying of them all. Voracious and voluptuous, this she-demon dwells near rivers and pools of water and captivates men with her beauty, especially at night, when, struck by her looks, they fail to see her camel hooves; by the time they do, it's too late—she has possessed their bodies. Her colors are red and black.

Jawad is playing and chanting, "*Sali 'ala nabi ya rasul allah!* Pray for the Prophet, O Messenger of God!" This *lila* is celebrating the prophet Muhammad's day of birth (*mawlid*), a propitious time for believers to renew their ties with saints. The priestess, an unsmiling middle-aged woman in a beige caftan and gold bangles on both wrists, orders a younger woman in need of healing to get up to dance; the woman—in her early forties—kneels over, slowly tossing her hair left to right. Every rhythm has a color, and every color represents a spirit. The color now is green in honor of Moulay Brahim, the saint of Marrakesh. The priestess throws a white-and-green cloth over the possessed woman's head. The rhythm gains pace; the woman begins trancing. Castanets clacking, *sintir* pulsating, the woman's head thrashes from side to side, her feet stomping rhythmically on the carpet. As the music reaches a crescendo, the castanets stop and all one hears is the powerful, repetitive thwacking of the *sintir's* bass line, pulsating through clouds of incense. The woman is handed a bundle of lit candles, and she begins to run the flames across her arms and neck. The chants grow louder, the women sitting down ululate, and the possessed woman collapses to the ground. She is pulled away by two women and placed on a mattress; they wipe her face with orange-blossom water and whisper prayers until she comes to. The priestess gestures to Jawad to change rhythm and incense.

The Gnawa solicit money again, give blessings, and begin to summon the yellow spirit. More incense is offered—this time musk, to attract Lala Mira. The priestess orders two more women to get up to dance and throws them yellow scarves. They toss their hair, stomp their feet, and soon start to giggle—the women sitting around them begin to smile: Lala Mira, the coquettish spirit, has arrived. She is known for her frivolity, her love of perfume, henna, and pretty clothes; a mirthful ambience fills the room, the women are dancing and laughing. The mood begins to shift as the Gnawa start to invoke Sidi Hamou, the red spirit. Angry and bloodthirsty, Sidi Hamou is the guardian of the slaughterhouse, and he demands blood; the two women know this and pull out their red scarves and their daggers. They throw their hair and dance. As the rhythm builds, one woman begins to strike her calves with the dagger, and blood trickles down the side of the blade; entranced, she collapses and is carried into an outer room. The priestess signals to Jawad again. The final spirit summoned is Aisha Kandisha, the raging and domineering she-demon, a central figure in Morocco's pantheon of spirits. She manifests in a *lila* just before sunrise, when everyone is exhausted. The priestess turns the lights off as the ceremony reaches its peak; bass line throbbing, the Gnawa are chanting, "*Haya jat, haya jat!* She's arrived, she's arrived!" More women get up to trance. Those who are feeling Aisha dance aggressively throwing their limbs out, swinging their heads side to side. Three women collapse and begin to writhe almost in agony, calling God's name and sobbing for mercy, "*Allah ya Allah!* God O God." Through the smoke, one can see bodies spasming on the floor, convulsing in the dark. The *mqadema* embraces one girl who seems to have passed out, and is holding a small brazier of incense directly under the girl's nose. Closing prayers are said, ending the *lila;* milk and dates are served; meat from the sacrificed animal is divided up and given to the guests before the Gnawa depart. The sun has risen; the French capital is beginning to stir.

These types of trance-healing ceremonies are not unique to the Gnawa. Other Sufi brotherhoods—the Issawa, the Darqawa, the Hamadsha, and other North African orders—have similar rituals, used to heal conditions that Western psychiatrists call bipolar disorder, schizophrenia, and epilepsy. North African state officials have long looked down upon these devotional practices, not only because they depart from official interpretations of Islam, but also because during the colonial era, French administrators supported these Sufi orders against the nationalist movements which embraced a more puritan version of Islam. French rule encouraged Sufi rites and festivals to control populations, but also to promote tourism: Europeans were intrigued by Sufi hysteria. Sufi trance ceremonies were staged at the 1867 Universal Exposition in Paris. Eugène Delacroix's famous painting *The Fanatics of Tangier* painted after his visit to Morocco in 1838, shows trancers, as he put it, "spreading through the streets" in "a state of ecstasy which allowed them to walk on red-hot coals, eat scorpions, lick red-hot irons and walk on sword blades." The growing nationalist movement in Morocco resented the colonial use of Sufism and denounced the "imperial imposters who exploit [the masses'] ignorance and poverty." The Sultan Mohammed V—though largely a figurehead—would support the nationalist position, and in 1946 he passed a decree banning the processions of brotherhoods like the Issawa, and prohibiting the establishment of new Sufi lodges (*zawaya*) without his authorization.

Upon independence, the Algerian and Tunisian governments outlawed a host of Sufi brotherhoods, including West African–derived orders like the Stamboli in Tunisia. But in Morocco, partly because of their close ties to the palace—many Gnawa were descendants of the king's slave guard—the government never banned the Gnawa. The Gnawi was seen as a healer, not an agitator, and adepts continued performing *lilas*. Gnawa music would become particularly popular among Moroccan youth in the 1970s, when groups like Nass El Ghiwane mixed traditional Gnawa rhythms with Middle Eastern genres to create a powerful protest sound.

For Westerners, though, it is still the trance aspect that fascinates. In April 2005, the Cinémas d'Afrique festival was held in Angers, France, a charming northeastern town of cobbled streets and twelfth-century chateaux. For the festival's parade, a Gnawa troupe was invited to perform, and quickly caused a stir when a Senegalese lady in the crowd went into trance as she heard their rhythms. "This lady was older, and at that age you don't go into trance in public just for fun," recalls Seydou Guèye, a Senegalese-born restaurateur from Paris and the artistic director for the World Festival of Black Arts, who witnessed the crowd's reaction. "The rhythms reminded me of a *ndeb* [*ndeup*] ritual we have in Senegal." Attendees were mystified: Why was a Senegalese woman going into trance upon hearing Moroccan rhythms? If this was sacred, religious music, why was it being played at an outdoor festival?

Gnawa music—whether in "traditional" form or in various blends of Gnawa jazz, Gnawa reggae, and Gnawa rock—has captivated listeners. Gnawa chants about suffering and oppression are now sampled by scores of producers and DJs. Healing ceremonies are staged at prestigious venues across Europe and North America—at the Institut du Monde Arabe in Paris, New York's Symphony Space, and festivals promoting religious tolerance in Sarajevo, Turin, and Jerusalem. Every year since 1997, the Cabaret Sauvage of Paris, a massive tentlike nightclub in Parc de la Villette, hosts its annual "Folles Nuits Berbères" (Crazy Berber Nights), a cultural extravaganza with belly dancers, acrobats, fire eaters on stilts, and jugglers, promising "an Oriental voyage that will enrapture the young and old!" The show prominently features "Gnawa jams" with "*lila* dancers" feigning trance for the hundreds of revelers. Because of the success of the Cabaret Sauvage, fashion shows in Paris now invite "*lila* dancers" to trance on the catwalk as models strut alongside.

Devoted practitioners of *tagnawit* are horrified to see not only their music played outside its ritual context, but also how their religious practices are being commodified and marketed as "trance dub" and "*jedba* beat." Believers are particularly stunned by the recklessness of the Western artists and entertainers who toy with powerful spirits, chanting their names at dance parties. In 2008, the American actor David Carradine starred in a French-made film called *Kandisha,* a "supernatural thriller" about Aisha Kandisha, the "fourteenth-century evil spirit." (The plot revolves around a lawyer who must defend a woman accused of killing her husband, when in reality the man was decapitated by Aisha Kandisha.) This film would be Carradine's last: a few days after the film won an award at the Mexico International Film Festival, the seventy-two-year-old actor was found dead in a Bangkok hotel with a rope tied to his neck, wrists, and genitals. As fans and film critics speculated on this mysterious death, believers had no doubt: the deed was vintage Aisha Kandisha—the film had mocked and provoked the spirit and she had exacted her revenge grotesquely.

After independence, the cultural and political elite of Morocco rarely celebrated Gnawa music, seeing it as lowbrow, a little embarrassing—nowhere near as urbane as the country's stately Andalusian repertoire (*'ala*), held up by the intelligentsia and government as testament to Islamic Spain's refinement. Likewise, prominent feminists like Fatima Mernissi argued that the folk belief in Aisha Kandisha, a "repugnant female demon" with "pendulous breasts" who inhabits men, was symptomatic of a wider misogynist fear of female sexuality. Yet in the last fifteen years or so, as Gnawa music has become one of the most popular "world music" genres in Europe, it has boomeranged back to the Gnawa's land of origin, giving the genre a higher status. Upper-class Moroccans will have Gnawa music at their social gatherings and weddings; the government sponsors an annual Gnawa festival, one of the largest music festivals in the world; and formerly impoverished Gnawa masters are invited on television shows after returning from world tours. The popularity of Gnawa music at home and abroad has raised all kinds of questions in North Africa: Why have Moroccans and Algerians allowed the Western fetish for Sufi trance to alter national tastes and cultural hierarchy? Why are governments now sponsoring Sufi ceremonies?

The rise of Gnawa music provides a particularly clear lens through which to view the complex—often mimetic—relations between America and the Islamic world. Anthropologists and scholars of religion debate how globalization is affecting Gnawa culture, what is traditional and what is authentic *tagnawit* nowadays; but more interesting is to trace the rise of Gnawa music and how it's currently being contested and pulled in different directions: by Moroccan officials trying to counter Islamism, by European city officials interested in integration, and by European Muslim youth intent on building a transnational community. Why did this music go global in the first place? Of the numerous Sufi orders that use faith healing, and of the countless North African music genres with polyrhythmic syncopation, why has this music captivated Western listeners? As will become evident, it was jazz that elevated Gnawa to its global status. Jazz met Islam in several places: in American cities, in European capitals, and in Europe's colonies in Africa and Asia. It's noteworthy that one of the first Americans to be struck by Gnawa music, was the Jazz Age poet Claude McKay, who witnessed a Gnawa healing ceremony in Casablanca in the 1930s and would write movingly about how the rituals of these "Guinea sorcerers" reminded him of a similar ceremony practiced by peasants in his native Jamaica.

With America's postwar expansion, jazz—carried by artists, servicemen, and diplomats—traveled across the Atlantic, to Africa and

Asia, absorbing the discourses of Bandung and Afro-Asian solidarity and taking in the rhythms of various parts of the Islamic world. In the 1960s, American jazz musicians would be captivated by the *sintir*'s low-range sound, seeing it as a relative or ancestor of the bass, and would incorporate it into their repertoire. Today European Muslim youth are using the music to forge a new pan-African culture, building on the legacy of African-American artists who decades ago took their music to Europe, then to Africa. The story of Gnawa culture is thus a consummately postcolonial one, born out of the encounter between the Black Atlantic and French colonialism in North Africa. It begins during the Jazz Age, when both France and Islam began to appeal to African-Americans.

Harlem to the Kasbah

It's been said that 1920s Paris was the literary capital of America, drawing writers like Ernest Hemingway, Gertrude Stein, and F. Scott Fitzgerald. The advent of the radio transmitted American music across Europe, and American travelers and expats brought the latest rhythms and dance steps to France. After World War I, an African-American community emerged in Paris, bringing the Harlem Renaissance to France. The Great War had not generated substantial political gains for African-Americans, but it did produce the "New Negro" movement, as seen in the writing and activism of Marcus Garvey, W.E.B. Du Bois, Zora Neale Hurston, and Claude McKay, all of whom helped ignite the Harlem Renaissance. This cultural explosion spread to France, sparking a period of cultural efflorescence that the French still call *les anneés folles*—the French equivalent of the Roaring Twenties. Jazz replaced ragtime as the dominant music in Harlem, just as it did in Paris. In New York, the affluent from Greenwich Village ended their nights at Harlem's clubs and speakeasies; in Paris the residents of Montparnasse, or even the Sixteenth Arrondissement on the southern side of the Seine, would head north to Montmartre, a working-class neighborhood on the Right Bank, and home to legendary nightclubs like Zelli's and Bricktop's, which became Harlem's reflection in Paris.

France's appeal to African-Americans goes back to the eighteenth century. In 1787, Sally Hemings accompanied Thomas Jefferson to Paris, and seeing that she was legally free on French soil, refused to return to America, spending twenty-six months in the City of Light, until her master promised to emancipate all her children once they came of age. The African-American interest in France, like the French fascination with black American culture, is thus not just artistic, and must be viewed in light of what the late Michel Fabre called "the myth of a colorblind France." The notion of France as a color-blind society gained popularity in the latter half of the nineteenth century— interestingly, around the same time that the perception of a color-blind Islam began to gain influence among African-Americans. Black travelers like Frederick Douglass, who visited in 1859, were struck by the treatment they received, and praised France as the embodiment of "*liberté, égalité, fraternité.*" Partly because of this perception, an African-American presence emerged in France after World War I. Almost half of the four hundred thousand African-Americans who served in the American armed forces during World War I fought in France. In their segregated units, these black GIs fought with distinction; but while the army tried to restrict their interactions with the French, fearing that such mixing would anger southern interests back home, the French, on the other hand, were grateful and welcoming to these soldiers who had defended their soil. The French government even bestowed the Croix de Guerre on the legendary 369th Infantry Regiment in October 1918, a black regiment from New York, which included a forty-four-piece jazz band, led by James Reese Europe, one of Harlem's finest bandmasters and the man who introduced jazz to France.

After the Armistice, some black soldiers stayed on in France. Others returned to the States, where unemployment ran high. American cities were rocked by race riots in 1919, as working-class whites feared the returning soldiers would take their jobs. Such mistreatment only reinforced the myth of French color-blindness, and led many African-American soldiers to return to France to settle. As Tyler

Stovall observes in *Paris Noir,* a seminal history of African-Americans in France, "the idea of France as a refuge from American racism had far more to do with conditions in the United States than conditions in Paris." The spread of jazz in France also had much to do with conditions in the States. In the 1920s, the genre was still shunned by the black church and white concert halls; but in Paris, with *les années folles* in full swing and French surrealists having developed a strong "neo-primitivist" interest in African art, African-American jazz musicians found a hospitable place to work and flourish. Thus, despite France's brutal colonial policies—including the importation of more than half a million immigrant workers from its possessions in North Africa and Indochina, who were treated abominably—the idea of French color-blindness would persist on both sides of the Atlantic. French leaders and intellectuals would, over the course of the twentieth century, insist that their nation was immune to the racial practices that existed in America, pointing to the growing African-American presence in France as evidence. (The French government, for instance, publicly banned the white-supremacist film *The Birth of a Nation,* which triggered riots in the U.S. and was screened at the White House for President Woodrow Wilson.) It's thus ironic that it was the Paris-based African-American expats who visited France's colonies and began to challenge their adopted homeland's self-image.

France's Jazz Age soon reached Africa's shores. In 1933, the Hot Club of France, a society of jazz musicians and aficionados, established branches in Morocco, Algeria, Egypt, and Senegal. Publications like the *Gazette du Jazz* and the *Bulletin du Hot Club de France* circulated throughout French-speaking Africa. The Paris-based African-American expatriates, fascinated by the Orient, often visited North Africa. In 1908, the Pittsburgh-born romantic-realist painter Henry Ossawa Tanner spent several months in northern Morocco painting street scenes and landscapes, including *Palais de Justice* (1908), where the biblical flight to Egypt takes place against the background of a Moorish palace in Tangier. He then traveled across North Africa to Egypt, where he painted a portrait of Prince Muhammad Ali on horseback and was honored at a reception by the ruler. Jessie Fauset, novelist, editor of *The Crisis* (the magazine of the NAACP), Sorbonne alumna, and one of the few female luminaries of the Harlem Renaissance, also visited North Africa. She sailed from France to Gibraltar aboard an Italian liner and, arriving in Tangier, "the doorsill of the East," was impressed by how "un-European" the town was compared to Algiers, "where one is constantly reminded of France." Like other Western travelers, Fauset also saw Morocco as a land where spirits ran wild. Fauset and her shipmates spot a storyteller in the medina fervently recounting a tale to an engrossed crowd: "Our little group drew as close as it might, its members hoping and fearing that they might be assisting at some ritual, some exorcism of evil spirits, some quaint and different manifestation of Oriental belief and practice." But the storyteller's eyes open suddenly and he tells Fauset's party not to photograph him. Later that evening, she ran into friends she knew from Greenwich Village who had settled in Tangier. Another American writer drawn to Tangier was Gertrude Stein. She and her partner, Alice B. Toklas, hosted a popular literary salon at 27 Rue de Fleurus in Montparnasse and regularly summered in northern Morocco in the 1920s. It was at Stein's suggestion that the aspiring novelist Paul Bowles visited the northern Moroccan seaport and ended up building a literary community and living there for almost seventy years. But it was the Jamaican-born poet and novelist Claude McKay, who had published a well-regarded volume of poetry, *Harlem Shadows* (1922), a defiant proclamation of black pride, who would take on the notion of France as a color-blind society and become one of the earliest chroniclers of Gnawa music.

McKay never bought into the myth of a color-blind France. Rather sympathetic to the Bolshevik revolution, he had spent time in the Soviet Union and didn't find the racial attitudes of the French so different. He lived in the port city of Marseille among people from all corners of the French empire—what he called a "gang of black and brown humanity"—and saw how the French drew distinctions between African-Americans, on the one hand, and West Africans and Arabs from the colonies, on the other. It was in Marseille that he was inspired to write his novel *Banjo,* a classic of New Negro literature, which envisioned a pan-African world community that included the Senegalese dockers and Algerian longshoremen he had encountered. In 1928, he traveled from France to Spain and spent months in Morocco. From 1930 to 1934, McKay lived in Tangier, following the Harlem Renaissance in local European-language newspapers. He kept his distance from the expat community, which he called "European society," and though intrigued by the protégés Gertrude Stein kept sending down to Tangier, he preferred to venture outside the international zone and mingle with the local population. Paul Bowles describes McKay in the early 1930s as "plump and jolly, with a red fez on his head," and living "exactly like a Moroccan."

It was in 1928, at the home of a Martinican friend in Casablanca, that McKay first witnessed a Gnawa ceremony. "The Gueanoua were exorcising a sick woman and they danced and whirled like devils," he writes in his memoir *A Long Way from Home*. "I watched them dance a kind of primitive rumba, beat their heads against posts, and throw off their clothing in excitement. But I did not see the end, when the devils would be driven forth, because a dancing woman frightened me by throwing herself in a frenzy upon me. They said I was a strange spirit and a hindrance to the magic working. So I had to get out." As a Trotskyite, McKay did not care for religion, and maybe the Gnawa had sensed his lack of faith, but he was clearly moved by this music and impressed by the prominent role women played in this Sufi order. In 1934, prompted by his friend, the novelist James Weldon Johnson ("We, the Negro writers, need you here"), McKay returned to Harlem and did not travel overseas again, but his work would have a far-reaching impact internationally. *Banjo,* completed in Tangier in 1934, would before long inspire the Négritude movement, the French-speaking world's equivalent of the "New Negro" movement, led by poets Aimé Cesaire and Léopold Senghor. And the connections that this self-described "internationalist" drew, in the 1930s, between the Caribbean and North Africa, and his rejection of the "fine distinctions" European colonials drew between North Africa and sub-Saharan Africa, foreshadowed a larger black internationalist movement toward Islam and the Orient.

Tangier to Tahiti

Randy Weston is almost seven feet tall; standing on the stoop of his Brooklyn brownstone in June 2009, he looks like a twelve-foot-tall giant as he welcomes his Moroccan guests. *"Labas alikom."* He leans over to kiss Malika Zarra, a petite French-Moroccan sporting a short red caftan and long, spiraling silver earrings, who, even counting her six-inch Afro, stands at about five foot three. "Please, come on in," Weston says. "I've lived in this house since my father bought it in 1946." He introduces his wife, Fatou, from Senegal, *"Bonjour, comment ça va?"* He taps the lid of a black grand piano in the living room: "It's a Bösendorfer," he says, and smiles. "Let's go down to the office." Weston walks down the staircase to the basement, where he keeps his archives and music collection. Weston is a renowned jazz pianist and, along with Quincy Jones, the last surviving musician to have participated in the State Department's Cold War jazz tours.

Weston is also the first Western musician to take an interest in Gnawa culture, and to introduce Gnawa music to the world of jazz and beyond. His Brooklyn home has become a stop on the international Gnawa circuit with musicians from around the world stopping by to pay tribute to this celebrated ambassador of North African music. Zarra is one such visitor. A jazz vocalist who sings in French, Arabic, and Tamzight (Berber), she's a rising star in the world of European jazz and one of the few women in the Gnawa jazz scene. She was born in a village deep in southeast Morocco, not far from the M'hamed oasis on the edge of the Sahara; her family immigrated to France when she was three, and she grew up in the gritty neighborhood of Mantes-la-Jolie. As a teenager she started writing Arabic lyrics to jazz classics. "When I started to sing in Arabic, writing new lyrics for jazz standards, I found that people reacted really strongly," she says. Zarra began performing at local jazz bars in Paris and soon found herself invited to sing at the Montreux and London jazz festivals. After a performance at Carnegie Hall, she relocated to the United States. (CNN filmed a half-hour special on her, titled *Morocco's Jazz Jewel*.) Today she has traveled from New Jersey to give Weston her new recording.

Born in 1926, Weston has lived the sweep of the twentieth century's black freedom struggles, domestically and internationally. Portraits hang on the wall of various friends and other figures. He points at a black-and-white portrait of a stylishly dressed couple. "My parents," he says. "My father came from the Caribbean, from Panama—he was a Garveyite—and my mother from Virginia, from a black church tradition. Every Sunday!" He picks up a framed photo. "This is Langston Hughes. He was a good friend—we went to Nigeria together in 1961. When he died, it was in his will that I get a trio and play at his funeral. And so I played an hour of blues." He points to a portrait across the room. "That's James Reese [Europe]—the man who introduced jazz to Europe." Weston sits down, fitting his imposing frame into a leather office chair. A map of Africa and a knitted Gnawa skullcap with beads hang on the wall behind him.

Weston began playing the piano in his Brooklyn high school, often accompanying his classmate the drummer Max Roach. He loved Duke Ellington and his evocations of Africa, as well as the "attacking" piano style of his friend Thelonious Monk. The struggles against apartheid and colonialism in Africa would leave their stamp on the music of this era's jazz artists. Max Roach recorded *We Insist!*, subtitled "Freedom Now Suite," about South Africa. In 1960 Weston recorded *Uhuru Afrika* (Free Africa), which celebrated Africa's independence, with lyrics and liner notes by Langston Hughes and Max Roach on percussion. The album would be banned by the South African regime. Whether it was his rising profile, his expansive personality, or his pan-African consciousness, Weston was soon tapped by the State Department to participate in its jazz tours.

"When I was chosen to do the State Department tour," Weston says, "I was reluctant. I had written music about Africa, which didn't mean anything until I played the music for Africans. But this was early '67, and at home we had the civil rights struggle. I didn't know what to do, I spoke to Mom and Pop. I decided I would do it, but only if I could teach the history of jazz music." In early 1967, Weston, along with his trio and his fifteen-year-old son, Niles, embarked on a three-month tour that took them to thirteen African states and Lebanon. "On tour we taught history. I took along a traditional African drummer. In the beginning of every show I'd say, jazz's history begins in Africa, not in New Orleans. We begin with the drum, then move on to the bass—from Africa, to the Caribbean, to New Orleans, then the 1930s through the 1960s, and then close with my composition 'African Cookbook.' We start in Africa and end there, to show, as my father used to say, 'Africa is past, present, and future.'"

As Weston talks, a small boom box is playing a scratchy recording of a live Gnawa performance. Like those of the other jazz ambassadors, Weston's tour landed him in the roiling politics of Africa and the Middle East. An appearance in Nigeria was canceled because of the bloody Biafra war. He performed in Cairo shortly before the 1967 War broke out. He performed in Beirut, and was struck by the beauty of what was then called "the Geneva of the Middle East." "The sea, the people, the weather, the diversity. And there I heard incredible Arab music." In Beirut, Weston met Fairuz, one of the greatest singers of the Middle East, and the Rahbani Brothers—Assi, her husband, and Mansour, two eminent composers who launched her career. "Fairuz, and the Rahbani brothers took me to a benefit concert, and there I met Sabah," he says, referring to another Lebanese diva, who at eighty-five is still performing. "She was wearing a magnificent caftan. I had dinner at Fairuz's house, then we had a jam session." He laughs. "They had a quarter-tone piano in their home which a Lebanese guy named Chamoun had invented. I tried to play it." He sighs, "I almost settled in Beirut."

Weston ended up settling in a port city, but at the other end of the Mediterranean. The State Department tour ended in the Moroccan capital, Rabat, but he soon took both his children and relocated to the northern town of Tangier, a cosmopolitan hub, which had been an international zone until 1960, and had the same balmy weather as Beirut. By the time Weston arrived in 1967, there was a budding jazz scene and several European-owned clubs, the genre having seeped down from France to its colonies in the 1930s. There was jazz programming on a local affiliate of Radio Luxembourg and other radio stations. American soldiers who fought on the North African front had brought the music with them. During the war, Tangier was an ideological battleground and active center for espionage between the Allied and Axis powers, and as in Vichy France, jazz in Morocco and Algeria emerged as the musical idiom of the *résistance*.

When the Nazis occupied Paris in June 1940, cultural life came to a halt. The Nazis saw the black presence in France as symbolizing everything that was depraved about the country; jazz was quickly declared a decadent music and outlawed. Black artists were prohibited from performing in Parisian nightclubs. Jazz was driven underground and became the music of the Resistance, as it became across much of occupied Europe. Many of the African-American musicians who lived in France returned home or relocated to North Africa. (The singer and actress Josephine Baker, who had played the role of a Tunisian girl in the 1935 film *Princesse Tam Tam*, moved to Algiers in January 1941 and became a lieutenant in the Resistance army.) When Paris was liberated in August 1944, jazz resurfaced, the musicians returned, and a new community of African-Americans, mostly writers, settled into the city's cafés and nightclubs, though this time on the Left Bank, around the Latin Quarter and Saint-Germain-des-Prés. Authors like Richard Wright, William Gardner Smith, and James Baldwin would live in Paris just as Algerians began agitating for independence. The celebratory mood that swept France with liberation soon gave way to gloom and self-doubt, as intellectuals pondered the military defeat, the Occupation, and the extent of collaboration with the Germans. France also soon found itself embroiled in two unwinnable colonial wars—first in Indochina and then in Algeria—facing the reality that not only was the French empire crumbling, but France was now reliant on American economic largesse and protection, and experiencing Americanization on a rapid scale.

In postwar France, America was a source of fascination—the land of optimism and possibility that had liberated Europe, but also the cause of much cultural angst. As American culture and consumer products poured into Europe, French youth embraced all things American, wearing blue jeans and frequenting jazz clubs, while left-leaning intellectuals deplored American consumerism and worried about the "Coca-Colonization" of France (members of the Communist Party even urged the government to ban sales of the soft drink). Jean-Paul Sartre and other intellectuals thinking back to the bombings of Hiroshima and Nagasaki, argued that the U.S. was the greatest danger to world peace. The growing acrimony between the French left and the U.S. gave the civil rights struggle and African-American culture a particular appeal: French hipsters embraced jazz in a gesture of solidarity with African-Americans, seen as the victims of American state power, but whose cultural expression represented the very best of the country. Yet the French public's relationship to jazz was full of contradictions. Critics loved the genre but bemoaned the State Department tours as propaganda. (They couldn't criticize the tours too much, since they helped promote jazz in France and brought recognition to local artists.) French critics argued that because jazz was "black," it did not threaten French national identity, and in fact they saw it as a way to revive a moribund continent. (In 1947 Sartre, who had helped establish the magazine *Présence Africaine,* argued that black culture could circulate "a little bit of fresh blood in this old body [of Europe].") Ironically, jazz soon became a tool with which French intellectuals could attack America.

The American musicians who visited or lived in France often took their music to her colonies (like clarinetist Sidney Bechet, who toured Algeria in 1952). By the 1950s, French-style *caves*—basement clubs where live jazz was played—were appearing in Algiers, Casablanca, Tangier, and Tunis. When the Soviet authorities banned the broadcast of jazz, Tangier became central to American jazz diplomacy. The U.S. government set up two powerful Voice of America stations to accompany the State Department tours: one in Munich, to broadcast behind the Iron Curtain, and the other in Tangier—a city that was under international rule, but became part of Morocco proper in 1960—to broadcast across the Mediterranean and the Middle East.

Willis Conover, whose show *Jazz Hour* on Voice of America radio went on the air in 1955, was said to reach 100 million listeners from North Africa to Polynesia.

Blue Note *Ma'alem*

After he had lived in Tangier for a few months, people noticed Randy Weston's interest in traditional Moroccan music, and introduced him to Abdellah El Gourd, a twenty-eight-year-old English-speaking engineer who worked at the Voice of America's jazz programming section—and who happened to be a Gnawa *ma'alem*. Weston heard the music and, like many a jazz artist who would come after him, was struck by the bass register of the *sintir*. "I saw Abdellah play the *sintir*, a different style of playing the bass. I suddenly understood the bass differently—I saw a horizontal bass, one played without a bow. The Gnawa only have five notes, but they take one note and they play it again and again."

Since the mid-1950s, a community of American writers had made Tangier their home—Paul Bowles, William S. Burroughs, Gore Vidal, Allen Ginsberg, Ira Cohen—and a few had taken an interest in this music. Cohen, a Lower East Side poet, even launched a literary magazine called *Gnaoua*, printed in Brussels, which published Beat authors, local storytellers, and translations of Gnawa songs. But it was the partnership to come between Weston and El Gourd that brought Gnawa to the international scene and created the genre today known as Gnawa jazz. El Gourd and Weston began having jam sessions at the latter's apartment. "What the Sufis taught me," Weston says, "is that Allah is the real musician—I'm just an instrument. I had settled in Morocco, not speaking a word of French or Arabic or Spanish or Berber, just for the music and the love. And then I met Abdellah and realized why the Creator had chosen me, to meet the black people of North Africa, people who had made the same trip as my ancestors, and who had preserved their traditions in this incredible music.

"I met the veteran Gnawa masters in their eighties. They told me about Sidna Bilal. I was in Tangier for two years before they let me attend a *lila*. Then in 1969 they were preparing for the start of Ramadan, and I went up to this old guy, Fatah—his color was red—and asked him if I could attend." Remembering the ceremony, Weston smiles. "Ooooh, man! We began at six in the evening. People were dressed in different colors. I was sitting there in my djellaba, which got smaller and smaller as the ceremony went on." He laughs. "The ceremony lasted from 6 p.m. to 6 a.m.—until the sun came out. I couldn't go back the next night. I was in trance for two weeks." He shakes his head. "I had heard our ancestors, I had heard the universe. And I realized that my color was blue, the color of Sidi Musa, the spirit of the ocean. The color blue caught me—in it I heard jazz, the blues, the black church all at the same time." To Weston, Sidi Musa's rhythm and sovereignty over the oceans evoked not only the history—and music—of Afro-Atlantic crossings, but also the biblical trope of Exodus, which has long resonated among African-Americans, wherein the prophet Moses ("Musa" in Arabic) leads the Israelites across the Red Sea into the land of Canaan. He would compose a piece called "Blue Moses," but Fatah, the eldest master, forbade him from playing it in public.

In 1969, Weston opened a jazz club in Tangier called the African Rhythms Club, where he would play piano, his son Niles the drums, and a local Gnawi the *sintir,* a stand-in for the bass, since they lacked the funds to hire a bassist. Niles learned how to play Gnawa melodies on percussion, the first musician to ever do so; deeply impressed, the Gnawa community had a ceremony and named him Azzedine, adopting the Brooklyn teenager as one of their own. Weston's clientele included Moroccan middle-class professionals as well as Paul Bowles, Tennessee Williams, and the English novelist Evelyn Waugh ("a regular at the club"). Weston's friends—renowned jazz artists like Max Roach and Poncho Sanchez of the Latin Jazz Band—would visit and perform in the city. Charmed by the musical culture and the white-domed Sufi shrines dotting the landscape of northern Morocco, various Ahmadi jazz musicians—among them Ahmad Jamal, Idrees Sulieman, and Jamil Nasser—would spend time in Tangier.

In 1972, Weston and his local business partner decided to organize a large African music festival. The festival was a success, show-casing acts from Africa and the U.S., but having received no support from the American embassy or the Moroccan government—"I think pan-Africanism was just too radical a concept for them"—Weston found himself in deep debt. Weston sold his club and the "blue-note *ma'alem*," as the local press had dubbed him, returned to New York. That same year Weston released *Blue Moses*—a tribute to Sidi Musa. The album chronicles many of Weston's experiences in Tangier, and the title track, "Ganawa (Blue Moses)," is based on the chord sequence used in a *lila* to invoke the blue spirit. "I left Morocco in debt, but I did *Blue Moses* and had a hit record. And because of the royalties of that record, I was able to pay off all my debts in Morocco. Allah works in mysterious ways."

In 1974, Weston was invited to perform at the Montreux Jazz Festival in Switzerland. "All jazz musicians back then were moving to Europe. I played Africa before I played Europe, and my time in Africa made my life in Europe richer." He ended up settling in a small village in northeastern France, close to the Swiss border. "I lived in France from 1974 to 1985—about forty-three kilometers from Geneva, and that's when I started bringing the Gnawa to perform in Swiss villages," he says, chuckling. He began by inviting his friend Abdellah El Gourd, who had now set up a cultural center for the Gnawa in Tangier, to perform with him regularly at festivals all over Europe, at local clubs in France and Switzerland, and at little cultural gatherings. "We took the music to the *banlieues,* to schools, park festivals. The students whose parents had emigrated from Africa loved it. We were bringing them their culture. And when I moved back to New York, we continued playing the music. When Melba [Liston] was sick, I brought the Gnawa to play for her at Harlem Hospital. When my sister was in the hospital in Brooklyn, I brought the Gnawa—they spent four days with her." Weston still tours regularly with the Gnawa ensemble from Tangier. Days before the September 11 attacks, he and El Gourd's troupe performed at the National Cowboys of Color Museum in Texas, where the Moroccan *ma'alem* used a chart with different colors to explain the *lila* ceremony to a group of students.

Increased immigration from North Africa, combined with Weston and El Gourd's grueling tour schedule—performances at highbrow jazz festivals and in immigrant neighborhoods in Europe—slowly raised the profile of Gnawa music. Other jazz musicians—Archie Shepp, Pharoah Sanders, Don Cherry—headed to France or Morocco to find Gnawa collaborators; rock musicians like Robert Plant and Peter Gabriel soon followed. The international interest in the genre rebounded back to Morocco. As hordes of tourists, anthropologists, disc jockeys, and other hipsters came searching for the "traditional" Gnawa and "authentic" *lila,* the Moroccan government began to invest in the music, promoting local artists and producers to cater to the new demand. Today Randy Weston is widely acknowledged as the man who, along with his partner, El Gourd, put the Gnawa on the world-music map. In May 2000, the pan-African festival that the pianist had organized in 1972 was revived as the annual Tanjazz Festival, drawing musicians from around the world to Tangier; every year in early fall, murals of Ella Fitzgerald and Billie Holiday begin to appear on the sides of apartment buildings.

Malika Zarra, who has been silent all this time, decides to speak up. "So what do you think of the new Gnawa generation?" Weston draws a deep sigh. "I'm not happy with the new generation." He shakes his head. "People now tell me about French Gnawa and German Gnawa and Chinese Gnawa—I know it cannot be the same. You can't improve the traditions passed down by the ancestors. The West always comes in and tries to make it better."

Zarra smiles, a little nervously, and pulls out her CD, an album of jazz vocals set to Gnawa back rhythms. "I hope you like it." "I'm sure I will." He laughs. "I'm just not sure about the term 'fusion,' all this talk of fusion. It never made sense to me—what I was doing was a conversation, a dialogue between different parts of African music." By now, others have arrived to see this jazz legend. He promises to come see Zarra's performance at Le Poisson Rouge in Greenwich Village in a couple of weeks.

He calls a few days later to say her album is "very interesting."

7

In Trance We Trust

Les 4 Frères is probably the most popular *couscousserie* in Paris. Situated between a computer parts store and El Mehdaoui Musique, a small CD shop on the Boulevard de la Vilette, the restaurant looks sleepy and struggling, but in the evening it comes to life with a young clientele eager to sample the seasoned semolina cooked with squash, turnips, carrots, and lamb. This restaurant, which serves no alcohol and only halal meat, had French (Muslim) tongues wagging a few summers ago because of its "Layali Ramadan" (Ramadan Nights) series, which brings North African pop groups to entertain a hip young crowd that breaks fast at sundown and then revels deep into the night. At issue was the Orchestre National de Barbès (ONB), the group that in the mid-1990s brought "Gnawa fusion" to France and onto the world stage. The ONB hails from the working-class neighborhood of Barbès in the city's eighteenth arrondissement, home to a large Muslim community and the largest souk in the capital, a place—not far from Les 4 Frères—where shoppers can find everything from red and green henna to Senegalese peanut fish stew. The group prides itself on representing the mix of cultures that exists in Barbès, which they call the capital of the Parisian nation.

When the ONB performed at the restaurant on the third Friday of Ramadan 2009, they did not disappoint: backed by drums and guitars, the vocalists shifted from Gnawa chants to *chansons d'amour* accompanied by an accordion and back again to Gnawa chants. "*Ba'ouna wa shrawana*—they bought us and sold us!" The dance floor was crowded with young men and ululating women. Larbi Dida, the group's vocalist, shouted instructions to the dancers, "*Les épaules, surtout les épaules!*—shoulders, shake the shoulders!" Snare drums, *darbuka*s, *sintir* mixed with electric guitars, trumpets, and saxophones made for a heady blend. In between dance instructions, Dida praised the Prophet: "*Ya Rasul Allah.*" As usual, the ONB were mixing North African and West African music with rock and sentimental love songs. The entire evening was broadcast live on Beur FM, a Paris-based radio station that caters to the Maghrebian community, and the next day listeners called in to have their say. Defenders of the ONB argued that it was this kind of fusion, this mingling of genres ("*le couscous musicale*") and a nonreligious approach, that had allowed the band to bring Maghrebian rhythms to the musical mainstream. But it was also this mélange that made other listeners cringe. To the *tagnawit* practitioner and believer, playing the *sintir* outside its ritual context, calling God's name on the dance floor, mixing chants about slavery with syrupy cabaret songs, summoning spirits on a Ramadan night in a nightclub setting with men and women shimmying together, makes light of a venerable tradition—and is sacrilegious.

It's not clear where the myth of Aisha Kandisha comes from. Some folklorists believe the she-demon came from the Sudan and "married" the eighteenth-century saint Ali Ben Hamdouch, whose shrine lies in central Morocco; others say she is a figure of Iberian provenance, known as Aisha la Condesa—a character similar to the "enchanted Mooress," who fled Portugal with the Moors after 1492 and fought alongside Muslims when the Portuguese invaded Morocco in the early 1500s. Whatever her origin, Kandisha's changing significance is at the heart of debates about Gnawa. The youth don't particularly fear the she-demon. In 2011, a group of Moroccan feminists launched a magazine named *Qandisha,* casting her as a strong female heroine. ("The fact is, any time a woman claims her rights in Morocco, she is called Qandisha," says the editor.) In the United States, at North African nightclubs—Tagine in Manhattan and Gazuza in Washington, DC—one can see young women dancing opposite each other, holding hands and thrashing their hair left to right as if possessed by Kandisha until they drop to their knees.

Yet in those same cities, *lilas* are held to appease Lala Aisha. The truth is that when people migrate, so do their saints and spirits, and in recent years Kandisha, with her bewitching beauty, has been spotted in Brussels, Madrid, and even San Francisco; in Paris, there is a place where the seductress has been sighted so often that it's now called Aisha's Place, and North African migrants will stop by with food, candles, and other offerings. In September 2005, Hassania El Badissi, a thirty-three-year-old Moroccan woman living in San Francisco, began to feel the need for a *lila*. Raised in a Gnawa household in Rabat, she and her family had a ceremony every year before Ramadan. "I felt Ramadan coming, and I needed a *lila* for Bouderbala—I felt it in my bones," she told friends, referring to her patron saint. Hassania approached various mosques in the Bay Area, but none of the imams knew how to lead a possession ceremony. So she contacted Tim Abdellah Fuson, an ethnomusicologist at Berkeley, a Japanese-American convert to Islam, and one of the leading scholars and practitioners of Gnawa music in North America.

"Growing up, she always had a *lila* in Shaban [the month before Ramadan] to renew her ties to the *mluk* [the spirits]," explains Fuson, a former bass player. "I've attended many *lilas,* so I offered to put together an event for her. I said, we'll go with *niya* [good intention] and *inshallah* it'll go well." Fuson organized a ceremony for Hassania in an apartment in the East Bay. "No animals were slaughtered, I promise!" He laughs. "I had two *qraqeb* players, both Americans, one of whom knew the response vocals for a handful of songs. But for the most part of the night, I had to play the role of *ma'alem,* overseer, and choral responder at the same time—directing helpers to burn the proper variety of incense and giving trancers the proper color of cloth." Fuson sounds a little uncomfortable being cast in multiple roles. "It turned out all right for what we tried to do. She tranced. Lala Mira went well, with a crescendo. But it wasn't ideal, that's for sure. I assumed the role of the *ma'alem* for the event, and the role of overseer, but they're not roles I'm qualified to inhabit or titles that I would claim."

In Europe, where Sufism is generally seen as more compatible with liberalism and even good for what British officials call "social cohesion," Sufi practice has been encouraged. In 1999, the mayor of Brussels authorized the building of a Gnawa *zawiya* in the neighborhood of Molenbeek, which adepts describe as the first such lodge in Europe. Located on the first floor of an apartment building, the center holds *lila* ceremonies only twice a year, but works regularly with neighborhood associations, and offers its space to other Sufi groups in the city. In August 2004, a tragedy brought unwanted attention to all of Brussels's Sufi orders. Unable to have children, a twenty-three-year-old Muslim girl, Latifa Hachmi, was taken by her husband to see a sheikh, who decided to perform an exorcism. In between prayers and incense burning, the imam literally tried to beat the jinn of infertility out of his patient with a baseball bat. Latifa died in the process. "She was drowned and beaten to death by the exorcists," declared the judge, Jean-Paul Tieleman, at the trial in May 2012, after handing down a thirty-year sentence that found all six accused "exorcists" guilty of torture. "The main message here is that whatever the religious pretext, we do not violate the integrity of another human being." Although it wasn't clear if Latifa's exorcism was carried out by a Sufi *ma'alem* or by a Salafi sheikh (the latter have also begun to engage in exorcism to demonstrate that it is Quranic verses and piety—and not heathen drumming and saint veneration—that drives away the jinn) or by one of the "jinnealogists" who now advertise online, Muslim ceremonies that involve animal sacrifice and self-mortification, where people burn their skin and cut their flesh, would come under greater government scrutiny.

In France in particular, the ritual slaughter of sheep by Muslims during the annual feast of Eid al-Adha, or on other occasions, has become a flashpoint. Animal-rights groups have called for the state to regulate the practice, while anti-immigrant groups have long denounced the ritual as barbaric. The actress Brigitte Bardot was tried and fined five times since 1997 for "inciting racial hatred" with her comments about sheep-slaughtering Muslims. In his presidential campaigns, former prime minister Nicolas Sarkozy spoke of cleaning up the *banlieues,* referring directly to immigrants slaughtering sheep in their bathtubs. All this hasn't lessened the appeal of Gnawa. As law enforcement patrols Muslim neighborhoods on religious holidays looking for the odd sheep or goat, European city officials have found creative ways to use Gnawa music to celebrate "multiculturalism." State officials like the presence of women in the "brotherhood" and see Gnawa as pacifiers of spirits—and humans. In their eyes, Gnawa culture is malleable and useful—it's African, Arab, Muslim, Berber, Mediterranean—and Gnawa musicians are invited regularly to perform at "festivals of diversity." In June 2010, the socialist politician Philippe Moureaux recruited Brussels's Gnawa troupe for his reelection campaign.

But there is a new subgenre—Gnawa reggae—that has emerged in France and Belgium and is brazenly political, advocating a cross-ethnic, transnational politics that is more radical and is challenging the liberal multiculturalism that the Gnawa-loving city officials call for.

Gnawittude

The spirit of the decades-long interaction between France, North Africa, and black America is today most evident in Gnawa reggae, a genre that circulates through various channels between France's urban periphery and North African cities. At the helm of this wave are a crop of left-wing artists hailing from Morocco, Algeria, Senegal, and the diaspora communities in Europe, and who are in effect the ideological children of McKay, Weston, and Nass El Ghiwane, the 1970s Moroccan group. *Le Monde*'s music critic Véronique Mortaigne has accurately described the "Gnawa youth" she sees in Europe and North Africa: "They are the mixed-race children of a Maghreb—that is, black, Berber, and Arabophone—of a rebellious Jamaica and of working-class neighborhoods in the West." These youths draw on

Islamic and Rastafarian cosmogonies, evoking Muslim saints and Caribbean cultural icons, and use the language of Third-Worldism and Ethiopianism to explain their liminal position on the edges of Islam and Europe.

The most well-known Gnawa reggae artist is Amazigh Kateb of the group Gnawa Diffusion, known as much for his sharp tongue as for his musical arrangements. Amazigh, as he is called, is the son of the Algerian novelist Kateb Yacine (1929–89), an early voice of the Algerian anticolonial struggle. (Yacine's most famous novel is *Nedjma,* published in 1956, an allegorical story about a mysterious woman whose mother is raped, so that upon birth, Nedjma is claimed by four fathers, her disputed identity symbolizing the hybridity and violent instability of Algeria.) Early in his career, Yacine was criticized for writing in French. He always responded that to him the French language was the spoils of the Algerian war (*butin de guerre*); by the end of his life, he was being denounced for his advocacy of the Berber language, his opposition to the head scarf, and his outspoken atheism. Yacine purposely named his son Amazigh, which means "Free Man" in the Tamzight language of North Africa.

"My father gave me the name Amazigh so I would never forget who I was," explains the forty-one-year-old son. "My name is an electroshock to the Arab nationalists." The same can be said of his music. Amazigh came to France as a sixteen-year-old to dodge military service in Algeria. In 1992, as a protracted civil war tore his homeland apart, he set up his band, Gnawa Diffusion, and from Grenoble, at the foot of the French Alps, began writing songs about oppression, anarchism and—putting his father's words to the *sintir*—launching musical attacks on Islamism, Arab nationalism, and the policies of different North African states, infuriating the Algerian authorities. Amazigh has his father's anticolonial politics, though with a contemporary twist: if the father was a Communist Party member sympathetic to the Bandung movement—he wrote an essay called "Our Brothers, the Indians"—the son is explicitly against globalization (read: Americanization) and imperialism. While sharing his father's opposition to Arabization, the son has a more pan-African vision that links the French *banlieues* with Africa and the Caribbean.

Amazigh's worldview is typical of the new Gnawa generation. "We Algerians, we're African," he says, "but we have forgotten it, we are wedged between two models of superiority—the West and the Orient. If we keep looking east or west, we lose our balance. Algeria needs to look south and within—only the Gnawa, this country's African tradition, can offer a solid base of identity." Like his father, Amazigh's nationalism celebrates North Africa's native cultures, resenting both Western and Eastern hegemony. (He has a song about how his Algerian ancestors used to ambush Ottoman tax collectors.) His political awakening came when as a teenager, he visited Timimoun, in southern Algeria. Amazigh recalls standing on the edge of the desert: "I was living a poem. I saw an Algeria unmasked." At that moment, he remembered Bob Marley's universalist appeals for African unity, and the Sahara and the African diaspora met in his mind. "I then realized that those who best understood freedom were the slaves and their descendants." Like other musicians in the Gnawa reggae movement, Amazigh maps the Caribbean onto the southern Mediterranean, melding Rastafarianism with North African culture (as seen in his album *Bab El Oued Kingston*).

Onstage Amazigh is chatty and informal, but like many politicized Gnawa of his generation, there is a palpable indignation. A self-described "Truther," after 9/11 he turned his lyrical fire onto the Bush administration. On tour around Europe, Amazigh would sing long Arabic *mawals*—extended, almost whimpering songs about Algeria's agony—and then begin to strum and whack his *sintir*, and as the drums and guitars build, growl, "Dance is the beginning of an insurrection." From there he leads his mostly under-thirty crowd on a jumping dance-and-chant of "Fuck, fuck, fuck American power!"

Gnawa music initially flowed from North Africa to Europe's jazz clubs and immigrant neighborhoods; today it's running in the opposite direction, carried by new media and so-called returnees (the children of immigrants), so that the music produced in Marseille and London is altering the genre in North Africa. The gnawa-reggae fusion popular in France's *banlieues* is now widely heard in Maghrebian urban centers. In the early 1990s, the gnawa reggae artists ruffled political feathers with their critiques of Arabization policies, but today they fit well into the larger Sufi revival.

Le Top Gnawi

Loud "rub-a-dub" beats blare from a bootleg-CD shop at the entrance of the medina. Vendors hawk fez hats, Rasta caps, and T-shirts with silhouettes of Bob Marley's face shrouded in a cloud of smoke—"The King," the shirts read. A portly bald man in a Hawaiian shirt introduces himself as the "main distributor" of Gnawa music in Poland.

Some yards away, a circle has formed around a guy waving small bottles of something. "They're standing up now, but they'll go down," says Khalil, pointing to the hairy Coolio-style tentacles sticking out of his head. "This is the first stage." The thirty-four-year-old in a red, green, and yellow tank top is a self-described *m'rasta,* which is what Moroccan Rastas call themselves. He's peddling an elixir, the contents of which he won't reveal, but assuring the group gathered around him that it could quickly turn their hair into dreadlocks. With the current Gnawa reggae trend, it's not uncommon for Maghrebian youth to grow their hair into dreadlocks. These Gnawa-heads will visit local barbers, ask for the mysterious *produit,* and begin "locking" months ahead of the annual Gnawa festival in Essaouira.

Every year in late June, tens of thousands of local and foreign visitors will descend on the city of Essaouira for a music festival that's been dubbed "the Moroccan Woodstock." This windswept, coastal town has long been popular among tourists interested in exploring the twisting alleyways of the old medina, where Orson Welles filmed *Othello* in the early 1950s. As the city has become a stop on the international gnawa and reggae circuit, it's drawing a new kind of visitor. Today one can see small clusters of youths, hair done in dreads or cornrows, strolling through the medina, *sintirs* slung over their shoulders; some will hold impromptu jam sessions on the ramparts of the sixteenth-century Portuguese fortress at the medina's edge. Off the coast, windsurfers are bobbing up and down on the waves. Essaouira's choppy Atlantic shore has become a favorite for French, German, and Dutch windsurfers. (Local tour guides brag that this is the only place in the world where you find Rastas who surf.)

"I'm *not* a Rastafarian," insists Khalil, the *produit* vendor, "I'm a *rasta,* which means one thing—freedom, *freedom!*" he says, rolling the *r.* "I believe in Allah and his prophet Muhammad, praise be upon him." A youth representing a Gnawa posse from Agadir, a city farther south, spoke up. "We are not Rastafarians, we're Muslim—we don't believe in Haile Selassie. We're like Jimmy Cliff—he's a Muslim Rasta," he says, referring to the 1970s Jamaican reggae star, who for some reason is very popular in North Africa. I asked what his father thought of his long hair. "He can't tell me anything. The prophet Muhammad had long hair." For all their insistence that they are *m'rastas* but not Rastafarian, these Gnawa youths have absorbed quite a bit from the culture that emerged in the impoverished shantytowns of Jamaica in the 1930s: hairstyle, mode of dress, a language combining Rastafarian concepts with Jamaican patois ("Babylon," "downpressor man," "Exodus," and "bad bwai"), and, most significantly, a pan-African worldview.

Up on the ramparts, away from the crowds, I find Jamal, who runs the Mama Africa Café in Marrakesh. Dressed in a suit jacket with a top hat tilted on his head—like his icon the late reggae vocalist Gregory Isaacs—he explains the contents of the dreadlock-making elixir. "It's a mix of soap, banana, coconut pulp, and a hair product called Dax Wave and Groom, which we get from Gibraltar."

The Rastafarian movement was born in November 1930 when Ras Tafari Makonnen was crowned Emperor Haile Selassie of Ethiopia. A number of Christians and Garveyites thought Selassie was the liberator whose coming was prophesied in the Book of Revelation, the redeemer who would restore the black race to Mount Zion in Africa. The Rastafarian belief system fuses the teachings of Marcus Garvey and the Old Testament, rejecting the power of the oppressive, secular establishment called Babylon, which is believed to have corrupted the Bible's teachings and rebelled against God ("Jah"). Inspired by passages in Leviticus, the Rastafarians grew dreadlocks, representing the Lion of Judah's mane; adopted the colors of red, green, and gold; began to eat chemical-free foods and smoke cannabis ("ganja") for their rituals. Smoking, justified by a reference to "herb" in Revelation 5:5, often accompanied their Bible study and was considered necessary for healing and to transcend the oppressive circumstances of Babylon.

The Muslim youth in Europe and North Africa who insist that they are Rastas or *m'rastas*, but not Rastafarian, are obviously aware of the theological debates raging online over whether one can be a Rasta and a Muslim: those who say yes argue that Rastafarianism is an off-shoot of Christianity, and its followers should be respected as "People of the Book," since Islam teaches tolerance toward Jews and Christians; the naysayers argue that Rastafarians see Haile Selassie as God personified, which fundamentally contravenes Islam. The Muslim Rastas then respond that Christianity also sees Jesus as God incarnate, and that the Rastafarian description of Western society as Babylon, a corrupt, godless political order, is close to the Islamists' representation of the West and of secular Arab regimes. "The Prophet's first *hijra* was to Abyssinia," notes Mouaz Mustafa, a Palestinian-American political organizer, who attends a largely Ethiopian mosque, the First Hijra, in Washington, DC. "If King Najashi had not granted refuge to the prophet Muhammad and the first Muslims in 614 A.D., there would be no Islam today. I've spent time with Bobo Rastas up in the Blue Mountains in Jamaica. They don't drink, don't eat pork, they say God's name with every breath. If the Prophet found refuge in Abyssinia, why can't we find a home in Ethiopian culture?" The debate continues over whether Islam is compatible with Rastafarianism, but Gnawa reggae culture is one area where Bible-inspired Ethiopianism has blended with Sufism.

Different types of music have been associated with the Rastafarian movement, but it was reggae, a mix of Jamaican folk music, American soul, and R&B born in Trenchtown, a poor slum in Kingston, that brought the movement global exposure and hundreds of thousands of adherents. In the 1970s, Bob Marley and other Rastafarian singers (Peter Tosh, Burning Spear, Black Uhuru, Third World) toured constantly, bringing reggae to different parts of the world. Marley visited Essaouira in the early 1970s and, according to local lore, appreciated the native herb and jammed with Gnawa musicians. Whether he performed with local artists or not, Bob Marley today is a cult hero in Essaouira, described by youngsters as "*le top Gnawi.*" In *lilas* and in the *qa'das*—informal jam sessions that young Gnawa aficionados organize—Marley has in effect been inducted into the pantheon of spirits, with his name chanted out along with those of various other spirits and saints. "Bob Marley translated the discourse of Aimé Césaire and Frantz Fanon to make it accessible to the youth," says Amazigh, referring to the French Caribbean poet and his most famous student. "His discourse of Négritude was addressed to the world." The Rastafarian practice of absorbing music and cannabis together meshes well with the local culture, where young Gnawa will puff on cannabis joints or nibble on *majoun* (a delectable paste of almonds, walnuts, honey, and finely crumbled hashish) while playing their *qraqeb*.

The Essaouira festival showcases mainly two genres: Gnawa jazz and Gnawa reggae. Twice a day, massive stages are set up in the large public squares, drawing thousands to see the country's most acclaimed Gnawa masters: Mahmoud Guinea, Hamid el Kasri, Mustapha Baqbou, and others perform with *les grands jazzmen*—Archie Shepp, Ornette Coleman, Pharoah Sanders—and star musicians from across the African continent and diaspora. At night, at pricey, no-cameras-allowed sessions, ceremonies are staged, and one can see the occasional Australian or German tourist, after hours of *sintir* and incense, go into trance, shaking and shouting. And every year—it's almost a custom—either the Wailers or one of Bob Marley's sons will perform. In June 2008, fifteen thousand filled the public square to see Ky-Mani Marley perform numbers from his recent album; but the loudest roar rose when he began to sing his father's "No Woman No Cry": women from nearby villages, wearing djellabas and face-covering lithams, only their eyes visible, toddlers in their arms, dancing alongside European tourists and hundreds of teenagers in red, green, and yellow shirts, all celebrating the legacy of *le top Gnawi.*

The Ghost Doctor

After being scorned for decades, Gnawa music today is arguably the most popular music among Moroccan youth and is part of simmering debates over the country's identity and political future. The government's embrace of Gnawa music reflects a stunning about-face and represents a new phase in the country's postcolonial evolution. As various cultural historians have shown, French colonial administrators in Morocco promoted Amazigh language and culture, and Sufi brotherhoods, with their processions and rituals, against the Salafi and Arab nationalist groups that advanced a more puritanical Islam and claimed solidarity with the wider Arab-Muslim world. French cultural policy also suppressed Morocco's Andalusian heritage, seeing it as unhelpful evidence of the land's civilizational pedigree, preferring to promote and catalogue the traditions of local Amazigh communities and local Sufi orders—and as a way to distance the country from the Middle East.

Upon gaining independence, Morocco's nationalist leaders, mostly from northern Arabic-speaking cities, set out to overturn this colonial classification of Moroccan cultures and established a ministry of cultural affairs to promote the very Arab-Andalusian culture that the French had relegated. Deeply suspicious of the Berber and Sufi groups, which had figured into France's *divide et impera* policies, and still had an ability to mobilize people, Moroccan state-builders moved to marginalize these institutions—including their music. Their vision of a "new Morocco" was based on a particular Arab nationalist interpretation of Islamic Spain. As the Italian ethnomusicologist Alessandra Ciucci has observed, "The [Andalusian] culture which had in fact suffered the most under colonization exactly because it did not reflect the image of Moroccan backwardness—began to be promoted as national culture." If colonial policy had preferred to mobilize Berber and Sufi culture, seen as an "indigenous" counterweight to "alien" Arab influence, postcolonial leaders relegated these traditions, which with their heterodox mix of Arab and non-Arab elements just did not fit into the new official historiography and narrative of a Morocco that shared a past and a future with a larger Arab nation. And political Islam would be mobilized against local Marxist-Leninist groups.

But starting in the early 1970s, various processes began to bring Berber and Sufi music—particularly Gnawa music—out of the shadows. The global popularity of music associated with black freedom struggles in the U.S. and the Caribbean, from reggae to jazz, would spark an interest in pan-Africanism and Morocco's links to the African world, just as jazz musicians like Randy Weston were disseminating Sufi music in Europe and America. And increased urbanization in Morocco gave rise to groups like Nass El Ghiwane, who would use Gnawa music to challenge the state-imposed cultural hierarchy; finally, increased emigration from rural parts of Morocco and Algeria to Europe meant that the very rhythms that were frowned upon in the *bled* (old country) were suddenly being played in parks and housing projects in Western Europe.

Nass El Ghiwane is the most popular group to emerge in post-independence Morocco. Founded in 1971, the group drew on various types of Moroccan and Middle Eastern music as well as Bob Marley, Led Zeppelin, and the Rolling Stones to create a "folk music" that provided commentary on issues from repression in Morocco to Palestinian suffering. Their songs resonated strongly with youth in working-class areas, the children of families who had migrated from rural parts after independence and felt no particular attachment to the Andalusian music that the government media were broadcasting. From the start, Nass El Ghiwane used Gnawa rhythms and the *sintir* in addition to drums and the banjo; but it was after 1974, when Abderrahman Paco, a musician from Essaouira, joined the group, that the Gnawa influence became more pronounced. Paco, already known as a gifted *ma'alem,* was nicknamed the "Ghost Doctor" (*tabib al ash'hab*) by none other than Jimi Hendrix, who visited Essaouira in July 1969 and watched Paco use his astonishing skills as a *sintir* player to calm a man who was contorting violently at a ceremony. (According to local lore, Hendrix's "Castles Made of Sand"—like Frank Zappa's album *Trance-Fusion*—was inspired by hashish-filled nights in the city.)

Nass El Ghiwane drew on a variety of local sources, including songs from the seventeenth and eighteenth centuries, but it was their use of the repertoires of disfavored religious brotherhoods like the Gnawa and the Issawa that resounded with the lower classes. In their lyrics and string arrangements, the group evoked the Gnawa themes of sacrifice and transformation and brought them to bear poignantly on the concerns of their generation. This also drew the interest of law enforcement. Nass El Ghiwane were, after all, developing a following at a time of extreme repression, when Sufi and Amazigh cultures were tightly monitored. In the mid-1970s, the police were patrolling the streets of Essaouira looking for youth with Afros or dreadlocks—*la coiffe rasta,* as it was known. (Paco famously refused to cut his hair.) Most troubling to the state authorities was that Nass El Ghiwane were very publicly disturbing the official classifications of high and low culture: the group performed the elite urban Andalusian music with its traditional ensembles to the accompaniment of the Gnawa *sintir* and Issawa drums, and they sang Gnawa songs in a unison group style associated with the Andalusian ensemble—except that instead of embroidered white djellabas and fezzes, they wore bell bottoms, Hendrix-style floral open-necked shirts, and unruly hair. Nass El Ghiwane were, in effect, taking music from the bottom of the country's cultural pyramid—associated with the Gnawa and their heterodox practices—and apposing it to the Arab-Andalusian heritage with all its greatness, subtly highlighting the inequality and not-so-subtle exclusion that characterized post-independence Morocco. Nass inspired other Gnawa-inflected groups, like Jil Jilala and Lemchaheb; and soon it became common to see Gnawa performers at street celebrations in low-income neighborhoods, pounding their drums, twirling the black tassels on their caps, and chanting praises not just to saints and spirits, but to Bob Marley, Jackie Chan, and their favorite football players.

Politics of Trance-Fusion

When in the late 1990s the Moroccan government began opening up politically and organizing Sufi and Berber festivals in different parts of the country, these popular and underground types of music came forward. The objectives of the new policy were varied: to encourage cultural tourism and economic growth in different corners of the kingdom and to promote the country's self-image as a crossroads of civilizations, but also to activate various genres of Sufi music and Berber culture against the growing Islamist movement and the increased influence of Saudi Salafism and Iranian Shiism. The government first held the Gnawa Festival in Essaouira in 1998. Now an estimated seventy festivals take place annually in Morocco, often staged as modernized versions of ancient Sufi *mawasim,* to which families can make an annual pilgrimage. The sounds of fusion, it is hoped, will drown out the purist call of Salafism.

The Gnawa Festival has turned out to be the most popular. And the more aficionados flock to Morocco, the more fashionable the music becomes overseas; and then—to the dismay of many—the more Moroccan youth, activists, and marginalized groups like the Ismkhan in the country's southeast region begin to identify themselves as Gnawa in the hopes of drawing Western attention. "Tourists like Gnawa music because it's all they can relate to. They're culturally illiterate; they don't understand other genres," states Mohamed Ouriaghli, a young poet and director of an arts association in northern Morocco. "But does that mean *we* have to make Gnawa central to our identity?"

It is true that the American listener is drawn to Gnawa music because it resonates with American history and with an American musical palate. It's seen as a genre parallel to the African-American blues: polyrhythmic, West African–derived and "diasporic." In her book *Performing Africa,* anthropologist Paulla A. Ebron notes how Western aficionados have a fixed notion of African music as percussive and having the ability to heal the "numbness" of the Western body and mind, so that they will dance to the beat of African drums even if it is string or wind instruments that are being played: the percussion is in their heads. Likewise, with Gnawa music, Western consumers tend to carry preconceptions—the blues, the "one-drop rule," and the transatlantic history—in their minds, all of which leads to much confusion: any percussive local sound is consequently seen as Gnawa, an "African retention," and therefore of particular moral significance. North Africa in this context is seen not as part of Africa, but as an extension of the African diaspora; if light-skinned Berbers perform Gnawa music, then they are "appropriating" black music just as whites did in the U.S. And more broadly, the Sahara is seen as a divide akin to the Atlantic Ocean, separating Africa from her diasporas. By the mid-1990s, the idea of Gnawa as the sound of a borderless Africa, put forth by Randy Weston in the sixties and Nass El Ghiwane in the seventies had given way to the notion, widespread in "world music" circles, of Gnawa as displaced Africans and the Maghreb as an "outpost of the African diaspora."

The cultural liberalization of the late 1990s brought to the fore politicized Amazigh and Gnawa reggae groups—Hoba Hoba Spirit, Darga, Barry, Amarg Fusion, Ganga Vibes—that explicitly challenged this understanding of Gnawa as the music of the African diaspora in North Africa. Like their counterparts in France, the North African–based Gnawa reggae artists wrote lyrics about love, poverty, American foreign policy, but mostly they sang about history and geography, denouncing all political actors and ideologies—politicians, Islamists, Arab nationalists—who deny North Africa's ethnic diversity and its historic links to sub-Saharan Africa. These groups acknowledge their debt to Nass El Ghiwane, who were the first to begin celebrating local musical forms and challenging the dominance of Middle Eastern music. The Gnawa reggae bands likewise celebrate Morocco's ethnic and linguistic pluralism, and insist on singing in local vernacular, accenting Morocco's linguistic distance from the wider Arab world, all of which has riled Islamists and Arabs.

But today's neo-Gnawis are more strident in their Maghrebian nationalism, barely acknowledging music from the Middle East. "In most Middle East countries, the Maghrebian is seen as an Arabic-speaking African," Amazigh Kateb told an interviewer. "He is a lesser Arab. I know because part of my family is in Syria and Lebanon." The Gnawa reggae artists regularly target the official historiography of postcolonial North Africa. In their track "The Story of Africa" ("Qissat Ifriqya"), the group Darga—a Jamaican-style sound system from Casablanca—call on the youth to reach across the Sahara and to rise above the colonial separations that still haunt Morocco and split the African continent ("We're all standing on African soil, drenched with the blood of our ancestors"). Racism within the Arabic-speaking world is also a recurring issue. The Mediterranean figures prominently in their musical imagination. For those in Europe, the Mediterranean is the blue expanse that separates them from their land of origin; for the African-based, it's the perilous body of water they must brave to flee tyranny. Songs make reference to the steady flow of boat people (*haraga*) from North Africa and the human flotsam that washes up on Spanish shores; but unlike Randy Weston, rather than summon Sidi Musa, the spirit of the oceans, they will use the Rastafarian concepts of "Exodus" and "Babylon" to explain these tragic incidents.

Islamists regularly denounce the Gnawa reggae culture: the dread-locks, the cannabis, and the references to Zion that pepper reggae songs (though in Rastafarian cosmology, "Zion," another Bible-inspired idea, represents the utopian world the Rastafarians would establish upon returning to Ethiopia—not historic Palestine). In June 2006, when Ahmed Raissouni, a prominent member of the Islamist Party of Justice and Development (PJD)—an offshoot of the Muslim Brotherhood—declared the annual Gnawa Festival a moral outrage and an "intellectual perversion," the response came not from another politician or state official but from Reda Allali, guitarist of Hoba Hoba Spirit, the most popular Gnawa reggae group of this decade. "Who would resent festivals that have revived Gnawa culture and brought Amazigh culture back to the center of Moroccan cultural life?" he asked. "What the Islamists and Arab nationalists are resenting is that today there is no more media monopoly on music. [For a long time,] there was one and the same voice reminding us ad nauseam that we are Arabs, that our [local] popular music is unworthy" and encouraging imitation of the Middle East. "Diversity has emerged after a long silence"; it's time to admit "that we are Arabs, but also Amazigh, Africans . . . fans of Umm Kulthum [the legendary Egyptian singer] but also Bob Marley." The Gnawa reggae groups' insistence on using local vernacular as opposed to modern standard Arabic—the lingua franca of the Arab world—is also a political dig at the government's policies of Arabization. "This whole 'we are Arabs' discourse is rather heavy on the heart," says Allali. "Onstage we try to show how our national music is founded on African rhythms, and we deliberately sing in *darija* [Moroccan dialect] because we want to reach the millions of people here in Morocco who don't master Arabic—before making ourselves understood in the Arab world."

Yet for all their agitating the neo-Gnawa groups in Morocco and Algeria fit squarely into the governments' policy of using local music and Sufi festivals to counter Islamism and media flows from the Middle East. In Morocco, the fusion of genres performed is presented as evidence of the country's cultural openness and malleability. To a lesser extent, even Algeria would begin celebrating local "African" music as part of a broader Sufi policy. After the civil war of the 1990s, Algerian Sufi orders that had been outlawed for decades were praised as otherworldly "sanctuaries of peace" and received permits to open educational institutes, just as the Sufi hierarchy was mobilized as a counterforce to the "imported" political Islam of the Islamic Salvation Front. The Algerian government also launched Sufi television and radio stations, and in July 2009 organized a massive pan-African music festival—to commemorate the first pan-African festival of 1969—prominently featuring Algerian Gnawa artists.

In 1933, as Claude McKay traveled around Morocco absorbing Gnawa rhythms, Sultan Mohammed V passed a (largely symbolic) decree banning Sufi brotherhoods so as to "rehabilitate the international reputation of Moroccans." Nationalists opposed French Sufi policy because it reinforced a centuries-old image of Morocco as a land of sorcery in the eyes of the "Arab East." Almost eight decades later, when protests erupted in February 2011, the exact same arguments would be made by Islamists who declared Sufism an "opiate," denounced the festivals as un-Islamic, promoting an image of Moroccans as fire-eating performers and the country as a decadent tourist playground. These arguments would also be made by leftist activists in the February 20 opposition movement, who saw the festivals as wasteful and a diversionary tactic to keep youth away from protests. ("Shame, shame! Mariah [Carey] gets a billion while we drown in the seas!" chanted demonstrators.) The festivals went ahead anyhow, in 2011 and 2012—with "fusion" on display on dozens of stages across the kingdom as debates raged across North Africa around music, national identity, and cultural hierarchies.

In June 2011, at the height of the Libyan uprising, a radio station appeared in Jado, in the country's western Nafusa Mountains, broadcasting in Tamzight, a language that Gaddafi had banned for decades. Across the Maghreb, Amazigh communities began demanding rights; as Saudi Arabia and the Gulf monarchies pushed back against the uprisings, tensions between Sufis, Islamist, and Berber activists boiled over. Sufi shrines were attacked from Egypt to Mali. Salafis took particular exception to expressions of pre-Islamic identity. In Morocco, zealots would damage an eight-thousand-year-old Amazigh carving in the High Atlas called the Plaque of the Sun. Pro-regime Sufi orders—like the powerful Boutchichiya in Morocco, who had marched in support of government reforms in June 2011—were denounced by anti-regime brotherhoods. Tensions broke out between pro- and anti-regime musicians (mostly hip-hop artists) as well.

At the regional level, Saudi Arabia would counter the protest music and expressions of Berber and Kurdish nationalism unleashed by the revolts with a host of pan-Arab talent shows; in December 2011, the Saudi-owned MBC1 channel launched *Arab Idol;* a year later, *The Voice* arrived; and then Rotana, a music-video channel owned by Saudi prince Waleed Ibn Talal, began broadcasting *The X Factor.* At the same time, Saudi-owned religious channels like Iqraa TV stepped up their religious programming. (The running joke became that the young Muslim women who don head scarves with low-riding jeans—a look popularized by actress Jennifer Lopez—were simply wearing their favorite TV channels: Iqraa above the waist and Rotana below.) The Saudi government's "Anti-Witchcraft Unit," charged with apprehending sorcerers and jinn worshippers, also went into overdrive in 2011, setting up nine offices across the kingdom, and arresting hundreds of largely foreign workers from Africa and Indonesia, accused of practicing black magic and "recourse to jinn." In all this turmoil and whirlwind of media flows, the Gnawa again emerged unscathed, spared the wrath of Islamists and leftist protest, perhaps because Gnawa today is more of a youth culture than a brotherhood, and lacks the infrastructure and membership of other Sufi orders. The Gnawa reggae artists have also been carefully navigating the culture wars, presenting themselves as political healers. "What we are doing is highlighting the Africanness of Arab-Andalusian music," explained Abdou, the guitarist for Djmawi Africa, a wildly popular Algerian Gnawa band, in an interview with Tunisian television in June 2011. "We want to focus on the Africanness of all the musical scales crossing Algeria." As ethnic and racial tensions run high—with horrific attacks against sub-Saharan Africans in Libya—the Gnawa reggae artists have adopted a conciliatory approach, of not wanting to upend the national music hierarchy but simply pointing out its African character. The Gnawi, in their view, is a redemptive figure of Maghrebian nationalism, of North African *mestizaje,* who can reconcile different communities and subtly trouble three dominant narratives: the Arab nationalist discourse that suppresses African identities in North Africa; the American and European discourse that sees the Sahara as separating two civilizations; and the liberal multiculturalism and "fusion" talk of European and North African diplomats.

State elites are also seeing the Gnawi as a figure of inclusion, and have their own idea of fusion. In April 2011, as protests raged across the region, the Moroccan government decided to send a cultural delegation to the United States. Instead of Andalusian musicians, as is often the case, officials dispatched five Gnawa masters to tour, reckoning that Americans would better identify with the bass-playing Gnawi than with the stodgy Andalusian musician in a white robe and red fez. Due to youth activism and state policy, the Gnawi is gradually becoming a symbol of Moroccan hybridity—not unlike the Brazilian samba queen—representing Morocco's ability to fuse with any civilization.

As North Africa simmers, the *sintir,* that sacred instrument which crossed the Sahara in the sixteenth century, is poised to play a greater, if changing, role. The truth is that the new generation of Gnawa musicians—the Gnawa reggae artists—are more concerned with explaining the political than with mediating the metaphysical. And when they cry, "*Dawina, dawina*—heal us, God," it is more a reference to the region's tortured politics than to spirit possession. As such, the *sintir*, whether daubed with henna or embroidered in red, yellow, and green, now represents memory and consciousness. In France and Belgium, the Gnawi is becoming a symbol of a new diaspora consciousness, an Africa-centered brand of European Muslim internationalism; in North Africa, the Gnawi stands for all that's been ignored and suppressed by the nation-state and dominant nationalism. On both sides of the Mediterranean, it's the music of postcolonial disaffection. In May 2011, Randy Weston and his longtime partner Abdellah El Gourd were honored in Manhattan by the Moroccan government. In front of hundreds of music aficionados, diplomats, women in caftans, and members of the Moorish Science Temple (in three-piece suits and tall fez hats), the Moroccan general consul in New York placed medals around the musicians' necks and congratulated them for their contribution to Moroccan culture. "I've been with the Gnawa for forty-five years," said Weston tearfully. "This music is the history of a people, songs about God and saints which enriched my life. I laid the music on the piano, but the real thing is in Morocco. And you can only absorb the Gnawa ancestors if you think of yourself not as Congolese or Senegalese or Moroccan, but as an African."

The new generation, for all its tinkering with tradition, shares the humanist vision of their Caribbean forebears—McKay, Weston—who brought Gnawa to Western attention. With a moral geography anchored in North Africa but extending east, south, and west toward the Caribbean, the new Gnawa generation see themselves as creators of what Claude McKay called an "Afro-Oriental" world.

8

"We Ain't White"

Hours after explosions struck the Boston Marathon, speculation began about the identity and appearance of the bomber(s). Muslims prayed the perpetrator of the heinous act would not be a member of their community. Liberal commentators openly hoped the bomber would not be a dark-skinned individual, as that would trigger a backlash against minorities. If the perpetrator turned out to be a "white" American, they explained, he would be seen as another gun-obsessed "lone wolf," and the crime would remain in the domain of law enforcement. If the act was committed by a darker-hued person, that would be perceived as part of a larger, ideological, existential threat, drawing in the military and national security establishment; the political fallout would include more profiling and civil rights infringements, possibly even military operations and a foreign-policy shift. On April 18, three days after the tragedy, John King of CNN declared, based on a police tip, that the bombers were "dark-skinned." The frenzy of speculation over skin tone continued for days, reaching ridiculous proportions. When the younger Tsarnaev brother was found hiding in a boat in someone's backyard, one observer tweeted, "But is it a dark-skinned boat?"

Yet when it emerged that the perpetrators were white Chechens from the Caucasus—and quite literally Caucasian—commentators insisted, despite the brothers' phenotype and geographic origin, that they were not white. That the older brother was a permanent resident and the younger brother was a U.S. citizen, and a weed-smoking hip-hop head and high-school wrestler, made no difference: "The perpetrators of the Boston Marathon bombing are not 'white Americans,'" stated *Commentary* magazine. For its special cover story on radicalization, *The Week* magazine actually darkened the skin of the two brothers. Meanwhile, liberal journalists, like Joan Walsh of *Salon* magazine, would ponder and lament "the determination to define the Tsarnaevs as non-white, no matter what the Census Bureau says."

The Boston tragedy brought to the mainstream a contradiction that Muslims in the U.S. have long been aware of: and that is just because the Census Bureau classifies Americans with roots in North Africa, the Middle East, and swaths of Central Asia as legally "white" does not mean they are considered white by society and public discourse or by other government agencies. Young Muslim activists of Iranian, Turkish, and Arab background have in the last decade been lobbying to have the American government recognize North African and Middle Eastern Americans as a minority. The push toward legal minority status is occurring beyond America's borders. Muslim communities across Europe and North America have been mobilizing around the national censuses in their respective countries, lobbying for a separate check box, and contesting the maps and geographic lines that underpin official racial and ethnic categories.

Dearborn is often described as "the Arab capital of America." Roughly one in every three Dearborn residents is Arab—generally of Yemeni, Lebanese, or Iraqi descent—part of an estimated 490,000 Arabs living in the greater Detroit area. Dearborn is home to the country's first halal McDonald's and KFC. Young, newly minted American diplomats are often sent here to achieve "cultural competency" before heading to the Middle East; delegations of European policymakers are given State Department–sponsored tours of the city to see how integrated American Muslims are. American presidential candidates visit during election season in search of the Arab-American vote. Dearborn also boasts the first largely Muslim public high school in America. Fordson High, in the city's blue-collar eastern section, is itself a fascinating mixture of Islam and Americana. The cafeteria serves halal food. Cheerleaders wear head scarves. Parents chaperone students to the end-of-year prom.

In early October 2009, the National Network for Arab American Communities (NNAAC) held its annual conference in Dearborn, bringing together leaders from around the country to discuss issues affecting the community. But between panels and in the hallways of the conference center, people were chatting not about the census but about "the amazing Rima." Two weeks earlier, Rima Fakih, a girl from Dearborn, born in southern Lebanon, qualified to represent Michigan at the Miss USA 2010 competition. Her victory was the topic of discussion at restaurants along Warren Avenue and on Detroit's Arabic radio station. At the conference, community leaders were pondering the meaning of her victory for Muslim women: Would having an Arab Muslim girl at a Miss USA pageant help mainstream American Muslim identity? Would it help counter negative images of Muslim women? Opinion was split: one camp cautioned not to place too much importance on beauty pageants ("Having women strut in evening gowns and swimsuits is *not* a sign of progress"), while others argued that beauty pageants can shape impressions, recalling how in 1927 Hannah Joseph, a Syrian-American, was selected as the first runner-up at the International Pageant of Pulchritude in Galveston, Texas—and how that helped the Syrian community's struggles for legal white status.

The subject of this year's NNAAC conference is the 2010 census and "minority status" for Arab-Americans, and that is the topic foremost on the mind of Helen Samhan as she paces down the hallway. Dressed in a white shirt, her brown hair in a ponytail, this sixty-year-old sociologist is rushing to address a group of census volunteers and community organizers (Egyptians, Palestinians, Somalis, Sudanese, Syrians) from around the country. A longtime activist, Samhan—deputy director of the Arab American Institute—is leading the 2010 census awareness campaign, and is asking the attendees to get their communities counted. "We have to get counted. Race and ethnic data is used to enforce civil rights law," she pleads to a roomful of organizers. "Data gathered from the survey helps disburse nearly 400 billion dollars in federal funding—we could use some of that funding. We *have* to get counted." Pointing to an image of the new census form projected on a wall, she circles the different categories and boxes: "Please check 'Other' and write in 'Arab.'" Helen cautions the attendants not to write down their national origin as, say, Egyptian, Mauritanian, or Syrian, as that would be coded "White" by the Census Bureau.

"We have teams of volunteers who can explain this in detail to you," says Helen. "The 2010 census form has also been translated into Arabic. Please tell your constituencies they have nothing to fear—the information is confidential. We believe the last census, which estimated the Arab-American community to be at 1.2 million, missed two-thirds of our community. We don't want that to happen again."

The activism around the national census in the U.S. is being undertaken by younger Muslim Americans who came of age during the Bush era, under the Patriot Act, who witnessed the impact of policies of deportation, rendition, profiling, and wiretapping on relatives and neighbors. These young activists, mostly lawyers and graduate students, draw on the work of Howard Winant, the eminent race sociologist at UC Santa Barbara, who two decades ago with his colleague Michael Omi made a powerful case for minority status, arguing that the ability of racially based movements—first of African-Americans, then of Latinos and Asians—to gain political recognition and minority status "permitted the entry of millions of racial minority group members into the political process." In an often-cited passage from their pioneering book *Racial Formation in the United States,* Winant explained the importance of racial classification: "How one is categorized is far from a merely academic or even personal matter. Such matters as access to employment, housing, or other publically or privately valued goods; social program design and the disbursement of local, state, and federal funds; or the organization of elections (among many other issues) are directly affected by racial classification and the recognition of 'legitimate' groups. The determination of racial categories is thus an intensely political process."

How Muslims in America are "racialized" has emerged as a hot topic debated by scholars, activists, and policymakers. The French philosopher Michel Foucault argued that state policy has been critical to the racialization of the world; for centuries, nation-states created and re-created differences (what he called "caesuras") within human populations at the national and global scale so as to be able to manage these populations. Racialization, in this perspective, is a very fluid process; race and racial categories are not fixed, but constructed through politics, and groups can experience "racial shifts." Thus, in the American experience, groups not categorized as "white" can attain legal "white" status and claim a range of benefits accorded to whites, as happened with the Irish in 1878 and then Arab immigrants in 1943; likewise, groups previously considered white can become a "nonwhite" racial minority, as happened with Hispanics, and then with Pakistani and Indian Americans in 1978. But racialization is not only a top-down process driven by state power. There is also "racialization from below," wherein social movements lobby for new categories and the expansion or elimination of old ones.

Scholars have recently argued that a transition of sorts—a "racial shift"—is taking place among North Africans and Middle Easterners in America, who although legally classified as white by the census are treated by government agencies and society as a nonwhite minority. John Tehranian, a Los Angeles–based law professor and activist, has repeatedly called on Iranians, Turks, Afghans, and Arabs in the U.S. to form a pan-ethnic Middle Eastern American identity movement and lobby for a separate check-off box on the census. In a series of articles published in law journals after 9/11, Tehranian described how while discrimination against Middle Eastern Americans had risen precipitously as a result of hate crimes and policies associated with the War on Terror, Middle Eastern Americans could do little about this, since they are not considered a minority in official government data. In his book *Whitewashed,* released in the lead-up to the 2010 census, Tehranian speaks directly to the dilemma of "compulsory whiteness."

But no pan-Islamic or Middle Eastern movement has emerged in the U.S. This is partly due to political and cultural differences among Muslim Americans and Middle Easterners. What has emerged is a host of interrelated campaigns—a Lebanese-American campaign, a Nubian and Sudanese campaign, an Iranian-American campaign—all calling for *racial* minority status at either the federal or the state level. These small but intense campaigns, led by young lawyers and students and mostly clustered around the University of California campuses, are trying to expand the country's labels of ethnic identification. To evade discriminatory immigration and naturalization laws, the early Arab immigrants to America—largely Christians who came from Syria in the early 1900s—tried to show that they were of the same (Caucasian) stock and civilization as other Americans, and struggled to demonstrate "sameness." Today's generation is loudly claiming difference and lobbying to *not* be counted as white.

The contested, shifting racial status of North African and Middle Easterners in America is a product of a number of factors: the U.S.'s complex and changing relationship with the Middle East; the particular mapping and labeling of Muslim regions by American cartographers at the State Department and Census Bureau (whereby, for instance, Chechnya is labeled "white" but Azerbaijan is "Some Other Race"); and, finally, the changing significance of minority status and criteria for membership in that category in post–civil rights America.

Jim Crow Arabia

In his six-hundred-page epic novel, *Cities of Salt,* the Saudi author Abdelrahman Munif traces the history of the Arabian peninsula from the 1930s onward, starting with the arrival of American oil prospectors. The novel begins at the oasis of Wadi al-Uyun, a lush, abundant area that has long nourished the local Bedouins. The image of a paradise on earth is suddenly disrupted by the arrival of Arabic-speaking American oil prospectors. The Americans soon return with their bulldozers ("yellow iron hulks") and begin tearing up the oasis groves, sweeping away the oasis dwellers and their families. The story then shifts from the oasis to the coastal town of Harran, where the oilmen are building a port and a pipeline linking the town to the wells they have drilled. The Americans build a small city, with an area called "American Harran," where they live, and a district called "Arab Harran," to house Arab workers and the large number of foreign laborers who are brought in.

One often-quoted passage from *Cities of Salt* involves Munif's description of the newly built city of Harran and the segregated living quarters of American Harran and Arab Harran: "The people of Harran looked at their faces and then at each other . . . Why did they have to live like this, while the Americans lived so differently? Why were they barred from going near an American house, even from looking at the swimming pool or standing for a moment in the shade of one of their trees? . . . Juma never hesitated to lash out with his whip when he found the workers in 'restricted areas.' The Americans had erected signposts warning them against loitering or going near most of the places, and they had even put barbed wire in the sea to keep them at a distance." Munif's references to barbed wires and "restricted areas" were long thought to be allegorical, symbols of separation in a metaphor-laden work of fiction. But recent research has shown that the novelist was not engaging in magical realism.

In *America's Kingdom,* political scientist Robert Vitalis set out to write a history of the Arabian American Oil Company (Aramco), set up in Saudi Arabia after World War II, and to show how this company—which at its founding was the U.S.'s largest overseas private enterprise—was critical to the American-Saudi relationship. As he researched Aramco's operations in the oil town of Dhahran in the 1940s and 1950s, Vitalis found that social arrangements in that town rested on a set of exclusionary practices and norms imported from the American West and Southwest, and his book soon turned out to be "an account of building a Jim Crow enclave on the eastern shore of Saudi Arabia at the end of World War II." Aramco's compounds were, Vitalis notes, a microcosm of the American racial order adapted to an Arabian context (not unlike American oil operations in Venezuela, Colombia, and Indonesia). Housing barracks were segregated; Americans who had contact with nearby Arab families were deported; Saudi workers were prohibited from living with their families and denied entry into the Aramco company cinema. Similarly, Chevron, which discovered oil in Bahrain in 1932, built up camps "divided into separate reservations, in this case, for Anglo-Saxons, Bahrainis, Iraqis, and Indians respectively." As described in *Cities of Salt,* the compounds were seething cauldrons of worker protest, stoppages, and confrontations at the management level between Arab, Italian, or Asian managers, and their bosses, often from Texas. Protests against Aramco's Jim Crow system started almost immediately, with a strike in 1944, and continued sporadically until June 14, 1956, when Saudi workers rose up and stormed the camp—the incident that inspired Munif's novel and led the Saudi government to ban strikes.

This history of Jim Crow practices in Arabia is today being closely studied by the Muslim-minority-status advocates, since the current policy debate over Middle Eastern racial classification in America has roots in the U.S.'s early expansion into the Middle East.

When the 1910 census was undertaken, Syrians, Palestinians, Armenians, Turks, and others from the Eastern Mediterranean were categorized as "Asiatic," or nonwhite, and were denied the right to naturalize. Chinese, Burmese, Japanese, South Asian, Hawaiian, and Filipino applicants all went to court to demonstrate their racial eligibility to naturalize, but Syrians were disproportionately represented in the racial prerequisites cases heard in U.S. federal courts between 1909 and 1923. And they were largely successful in making their case, highlighting their economic affluence and using their Christian background to make religious and civilizational arguments in favor of pseudoscientific as well as unpopular understandings of whiteness.

The early Syrian migrants were so successful in demonstrating their whiteness that Arabs (and Iranians) would be unaffected by the Immigration Act of 1917, also known as the Asiatic Barred Zone Act, whereby Congress designated a geographical area demarcating the boundaries of western Asia and specifying areas from which the U.S. would accept immigrants. Fragments of the modern-day Arab world were included in the "barred zone"—slivers of modern-day Saudi Arabia, Somalia, and Yemen—but North Africa and the Levant, the vast part of the Arab world, along with Iran, were left out. "Arabs," as sociologist Louise Cainkar has written, "were purposely excluded from immigration legislation that established the racial barrier of the Asia Barred Zone." This was because in the 1910s the U.S. was more worried about East Asian immigration (the "yellow peril") than Arab immigration, but also due to effective lobbying by the Syrian community. The Syrians successfully demonstrated that they did not come from "Turkey in Asia," so that by the early teens, Syrians in America were, in the eyes of the census, officially considered white. The Syrians underscored their Christian identity and stressed that their land of birth was closer to Europe than to either Africa or Asia. The insistence on Syria's geographic detachment from Asia and Africa had local aims as well—to prevent their being subject to any of the exclusionary laws directed at Asians and blacks in America, a strategy that would create tensions between the Arabs and these other communities.

As Muslim Arabs began to trickle into the country, the racial status of Arabs in America grew complicated. The Muslim newcomers could not use their faith to make religious arguments for whiteness. One of the first Muslims to petition for citizenship was Ahmed Hassan, who in 1942 appeared in front of a court in Detroit, a city that was slowly becoming home to a large community of Arab migrants who arrived to work in the auto industry. The presiding judge, Arthur Tittle, argued that Hassan, "an Arab," was "indisputably dark brown in color," and "a strong burden of proof devolves upon him to establish that he is a white person within the meaning of the [naturalization] act." Although Hassan's attorney argued that the plaintiff was born in the southwestern part of the Arabian peninsula—which fell outside the Asiatic Barred Zone—his petition was denied. Judge Tittle found that argument beside the point, though he did consider geography— Yemen's distance from a European border, as compared with Syria's— and religion when he denied the applicant. "Apart from the dark skin of the Arabs," wrote Tittle, "it is well known that they are a part of the Mohammedan world and that a wide gulf separates their culture from that of the predominately Christian peoples of Europe."

As more legal court battles arose around the naturalization of Arab Muslims, the Immigration and Naturalization Service undertook a review of the question of Arab Muslim classification. In 1943, less then a year after Hassan's case, the government issued a strongly worded statement affirming the eligibility of Arab Muslims to naturalize. Contravening the Hassan court ruling, the INS statement declared "a person of Arabian race *is eligible to naturalization.*" The INS declared that Arabs—of whatever religious background—were white and fully eligible for immigration and naturalization because of "shared civilization" between the Near East and the West. When Mohamed Mohriez, described as "an Arab born in Sanhy, Badan, Arabia," petitioned for citizenship in 1944, the court allowed him to naturalize. In contrast to earlier rulings that had accented the vast distance separating Arabs from European culture, Charles Wyzanski, the presiding judge, argued that the Arabs could be considered white because they had absorbed enough European culture through their role as transmitters of European civilization: "The Arab people stand as one of the chief channels by which the traditions of white Europeans, especially the ancient Greek traditions, have been carried into the present," and therefore, "the Arab passes muster as white."

The Arab Muslim's rapid "racial shift" from nonwhite to white was largely due to postwar politics and the emergence of the U.S. as a superpower with a presence in the Middle East. Before the war was over, geopolitical considerations had prompted state officials to remove racial requisites to immigration. On October 11, 1943, President Roosevelt appealed to Congress to rescind the Chinese Exclusion Act (introduced in 1882) in recognition of China's partnership in the war; Chinese immigrants were finally eligible for citizenship. In July 1946, a series of presidential proclamations and statutes granted the Philippines independence and allowed for limited Filipino and Indian immigration. In the early years of the Cold War, as it became evident that race would be used as an ideological cudgel by China and the Soviet Union, immigration policy went from being the domestic domain of Congress to a "focus of the executive branch as a tool of foreign policy." Foreign-policy elites saw treating Arabs as legally white as a way to build relations with Arab states already being wooed by the Soviet Union. As Judge Wyzanski wrote, "We as a country have learned that policies of rigid exclusion are not only false to our profession of democratic liberalism but repugnant to our vital interests as a world power"; his decision to grant Arabs in America legal status as whites was necessary "to promote friendlier relations between the United States and other nations." The U.S. government would thus shift Muslim Arabs to the "white" category on the census; but it did not, perhaps could not, prevent American oil firms from implementing segregation in Arabia.

In 1952, the Immigration and Nationality Act finally repealed all racial barriers to naturalization, and established immigration preferences for certain occupations. The overhaul of U.S. immigration policy codified in the 1965 Immigration Act led to the abolition of the national-origins quotas introduced in 1924. These new policies fundamentally changed the character of immigration to the U.S. The majority of immigrants now came not from Europe but from Latin America, Asia, Africa, and the Middle East.

Check It Right (Not Quite White)!

In the lead-up to the 2010 census, Arab-American and Iranian-American comedians launched a nationwide campaign called "Check It Right!"—explaining to their community in humorous online videos and radio segments why they're not exactly white and should check "Other." These young activists are invariably inspired by the Arab American Institute's Helen Samhan. On the eve of the 2000 census, she published an article titled "Not Quite White" that helped launch the movement for minority status and has become a manifesto for young Middle Eastern Americans. In the paper, she noted the "identity disconnect" that many young Arab-Americans feel: they are classified as white, but they have an affinity for people of color, "meaning every other non-European national origin group." The existing classification system, she wrote, "which places Arabs and other persons with origins in the Middle East and North Africa in the same white category that identifies the European majority, has been a source of confusion and a challenge." And most poignantly, in light of the growing monitoring of Arab and Muslim communities in the late

1990s, Helen argued that certain branches of the government, particularly law enforcement—the FBI and the INS—were *already* treating North African and Middle Eastern Americans as an identifiable group that was to be tracked and monitored, but the census continued to regard Arabs as the same as other white ethnics.

The community workers who Helen Samhan was addressing at the 2009 Dearborn conference are particularly supportive of the minority-status campaign. They work with and represent an immigrant community, increasingly made up of refugees resettled from Iraq, Sudan, and Somalia, that needs social services and government assistance in the areas of education and health care; but there is no data to demonstrate this need. As the minority-status advocates explain, Arab, Iranian, and Turkish Americans find themselves in a rather absurd situation: to get official minority status and a new check-off box on the census, they need to show that they suffer from systematic discrimination, and that is difficult to do, because data is not available separately for Middle Easterners. "When a police officer stops a car in Orland Park, for example, he has to mark whether that person is black, white, Hispanic or Asian," says Ray Hanania, a Chicago-based activist. "If Arabs are continually getting stopped and discriminated against, which happens, we can't access that data, because they'll be counted as white . . . It's the Achilles' heel: How can we be discriminated against when we're white?"

In the U.S., racial categories were initially used to support policies of exclusion, but after World War II, and following the enactment of the Voting Rights Act in 1965, racial and ethnic data have been used to monitor discrimination against racial minority groups and their access to equal opportunity. From the standpoint of the federal law, minority status comes not from a specific race or ethnicity but from the historic use of race and ethnicity to confer privilege or disadvantage to a particular group. Minority status has often been conferred on racial and ethnic groups—namely American Indians, Asian-Americans, blacks, and Hispanics—who have historically been victims of exclusion; but it is not contingent on ancestry or physical characteristics; even whites may be granted minority status, as is argued in reverse discrimination cases. And this is a source of great confusion: what is thought of as "race" in everyday talk—i.e., how one looks—is not how the Census Bureau defines race and minority status.

When the current census categories were created by the White House–based Office of Management and Budget (OMB) in 1977, special attention was given to disparities between Black, Latino, American Indian, and Asian-American populations in comparison with the white population based on existing data (from the 1970 census). In 2000 the OMB, in response to community activism, reformed the classification system and introduced the now famous "racial penta- gon": five categories were instituted—American Indian and Alaskan Native, Asian, Black or African-American, Native Hawaiian or Other Pacific Islander, and White. The OMB also introduced two boxes for data on ethnicity: "Hispanic or Latino" and "Not Hispanic or Latino." But the directive continued to define as white "a person having origins in the original peoples of Europe, the Middle East, or North Africa."

In late 2009, the minority-status campaigns stirred again. Arab- and Iranian-American students and activists agitated nationwide for a separate racial box. Their parents recoiled at the campaign's race- based language. The older Arab-American leadership tentatively supported a Middle East/North Africa (MENA) check-off box, but under the category White, and were opposed to a separate race box, as that would be perceived as separatist and anti-integration. The young activists felt they had to be "race activists" because their parents "sat out" the civil rights movement, when different groups lobbied and got minority status. This is not entirely accurate: there were Middle Eastern activists involved in the civil rights movement, but Arab- and Iranian-Americans did not make demands for minority status or set- asides for their community in the 1960s because they were not yet experiencing systematic defamation or discrimination. Moreover, the large influx of Middle Eastern immigrants came after the civil rights movement; it was, in fact, civil rights legislation that allowed for the ending of national-origin quotas and granted visas to immigrants.

Arab-Americans became active in civil rights after the 1967 Arab- Israeli War, which most scholars concur was a watershed moment that sparked a pan-ethnic Arab-American identity. The media coverage, public discourse, and harsh rhetoric surrounding the Palestinian-Israeli conflict prompted a group of scholars and activists to set up the Association of Arab American University Graduates (AAUG), an early precursor to the Arab Anti-Discrimination Committee, the largest Arab advocacy group in the U.S. today. This post-'67 crisis led to the "ethnicization" of the Arab-American community, galvanizing Arabic speakers—Syrians, Egyptians, Palestinians, Iraqis—and their children into a quintessentially American kind of pan-ethnic politics. But it did not prompt calls for a separate box on the census.

The discontent with white status began in the late 1980s, as Arab- and Iranian-American activists increasingly began to express their identity in racial terms. As the American presence in the Middle East deepened—the Iranian revolution, the marine bombing of 1983, and the first Gulf War—and media depiction and public perception grew more negative, Arab-Americans began to reconsider their racial status as whites. The Arab-American campaign for minority status is today particularly vocal because of the Arabic-speaking world's location across Africa and the Middle East, which means that black African populations get coded white as well. After 9/11, a new wave of activism would start; this time Lebanese-American activists would be joined by the children of Nubian and Sudanese immigrants, who are challenging the classification of North Africans as white.

Blue Nile Washington

In the last twenty years, Arab migration to the U.S. has changed dramatically due to the Diversity Visa (DV) Program (known as the Green Card Lottery), which the State Department introduced in 1995. This program provides an annual fifty thousand permanent-resident visas to individuals from countries with low rates of immigration to the U.S. Over the last century most Arab immigrants came from Syria, Lebanon, Iraq, and Palestine. To promote diversity and rectify this "historic imbalance," the DV Program has granted the lion's share of "Arab region" visas to underrepresented North African countries like Morocco, Algeria, and Sudan. The DV Lottery's geographically determined quota policy has meant that since the late 1990s tens of thousands of Sudanese, Nubians, Berbers, and Arabic-speaking Somalis have poured into the U.S., leading to a rapid growth of Arabic-speaking communities from northern Africa (according to Arab American Institute reports, the Moroccan community grew 96.5 percent between 1990 and 2000) and pushing the debate over Arab racial classification in a new direction. If the Lebanese- and Syrian-American activists are asking "Are Arabs white?" the young Nubian and Sudanese activists are asking "Are we Arab or black—or both?"

The immigrants of Nubian ancestry are of particular interest from the point of view of the census. Nubia, the region along the Nile River Valley, often described as a corridor between tropical Africa and the Mediterranean, starts at the city of Aswan in upper Egypt, at the Nile's First Cataract, and extends south to the confluence of the White and Blue Nile in the Sudanese capital of Khartoum, just above the Sixth Cataract. After centuries of Ottoman rule, Nubia was colonized by the British, and since independence in 1956, the region has been divided by a border between Egypt and Sudan. The Nubian community in the U.S., largely concentrated around the Washington, DC, area, has grown rapidly since the mid-1980s, when immigrants from upper Egypt and Sudan first began arriving, setting up hot-dog stands and driving taxis.

Nubia's location, straddling the Egyptian-Sudanese frontier, is a reason for much of the census activism; Nubians from the Egyptian part of Nubia are counted as white (if they write their country of origin), while Nubians from Sudan are "Some Other Race." The Census Bureau's exact parameters of "North Africa" versus "sub-Saharan Africa" are ambiguous; drawing on United Nations Development Program maps and country lists of the region, the census considers Egypt, Morocco, Libya, Tunisia, and Mauritania as North Africa (and hence white), but places Sudan in both the North Africa and sub-Saharan zones. Sudan was long classified white as well, until it was recently relabeled "Some Other Race." ("Pashtunistan" is another ethnic region that bestrides a state border and gets different census labels; Pashtuns in the U.S., sometimes members of the same family, will be considered Asian if born in Pakistan, but white if they write in "Afghanistan.") For the Nubian-American activists, the census categories pose a challenge. The parents who migrated from upper Egypt and Sudan will write in "Egyptian" or "Sudanese" or "Arab" in the "Other" box, not knowing or caring that they will then be considered white. The younger American-born activists, don't want to be counted as white, but are unsure what box to check.

"When I told my dad to check off 'Black' on the census, he gave me a weird look," laughs Aya Ibrahim, the daughter of Redwan, one of the founders of the Nubian Benevolence Society, a DC-based organization. Aya Ibrahim, a college junior, is one of the younger activists—she runs a group called WakeUp Somalia, which sends books to Somalia—who are contesting the classification of black North Africans as white. "The truth is I have more identities than there are boxes," says this articulate nineteen-year-old. "I'm African-American, Nubian, and Arab. When I filled out the form—I could have written 'Arab' or 'Egyptian,' but I checked off the 'Black' box."

The civil rights lawyers at ADC's national headquarters in Washington, DC, travel regularly between Dearborn—where they offer support to recent refugees from Iraq—and Minneapolis, which boasts the largest Somali population in the U.S., mostly refugees from their homeland's conflict, and Washington, DC, which today is home to tens of thousands of Arabic-speaking immigrants from upper Egypt, Sudan, Somalia, and Eritrea. A running joke among Arab-American activists is that if Dearborn is the Arab capital of America, then Washington, DC, is the "black capital of Arab-America"—the irony being that while the Arabs in Dearborn are legally white, they are rarely treated as such by law enforcement or perceived as such on the street, while many of the Arabic-speaking Africans in the nation's capital are legally classified as Arab and white but generally seen as black.

"The government is not consistent when dealing with African Arabs. The Somalis who speak Arabic may identify as African or just Somali, but they have problems with detention and law enforcement that other Arab and Muslim communities have—which is why they reach out to us," says Abed Ayoub, the legal director of ADC Washington. "And the Census Bureau may not count Somalis as Arab, but the Department of Commerce does—when we ask for minority business loans for the Arab community, they'll ask us about economic need in the Somali community. So it's confusing for everyone."

At a societal level, the "black Arab," like the "Caucasian Muslim," sounds like a contradiction in terms, and unsettles not just legal categories but cultural preconceptions. But the question of how to classify and label people from the Nile Valley and the Saharan borderlands will become more pressing in the coming years as American foreign policy turns its attention to the Sahara and Sahel region. In October 2007, the United States African Command (AFRICOM) was established, with a base at Camp Lemonnier in Djibouti, to oversee U.S. military operations all over Africa (except Egypt), and engage the "arc of instability" starting in Somalia, going through south Sudan and Darfur, cutting across the Sahelian countries of Chad, Niger, Mali, and Mauritania, and curving up toward the Maghreb. The flow of immigrants from Iraq and Somalia into the U.S. grew rapidly following American interventions in those countries in 1990 and 1993; American involvement in the Sahara—combined with the Green Card Lottery—will trigger greater migration from the Sahel-Saharan states to the U.S., making the question of Afro-Arab classification even more urgent. Not surprisingly, a campaign is currently under way, led by Egyptian-born activist Mustafa Hefny, who filed a lawsuit against the U.S. government's classification of Afro-Arabs as "Caucasian"—specifically, the OMB's Directive No. 15 geographic designations, which define whites as "having origins in the original peoples of Europe, the Middle East, and North Africa" and blacks "as having origins with the Black racial groups."

A Ramadan to Remember

Late one Sunday night in the middle of May 2010, ululations echoed from cafés and hookah lounges in Dearborn and Detroit. After tripping in her evening gown and answering a question about birth control and health insurance, Rima Fakih was crowned Miss USA. ("She dazzled judges when she took the stage in a skimpy red and orange bikini," gushed New York's *Daily News*.) Her supporters at La Pita restaurant in Dearborn—a banquet hall decorated in red, blue, and white—cheered; a woman cried. Teenage girls sported T-shirts with Rima's face, and a quote from her on the back: "It's beauty that captures your attention, personality which captures your heart." Activists hailed the local girl turned beauty queen. The mayor of Dearborn offered her a key to the city. And congratulatory messages poured in from the Middle East. The president of Lebanon, Rima's birthplace, issued a statement: "Congratulations to Rima Fakih for showing the beautiful image of Lebanon to the world." Talking heads noted how this could help integrate Muslims in America.

But before the night was over, the attacks on the beauty queen had started. Tea Party activists and right-wing commentators dubbed her "Miss Hizbullah" and "the new face of Islamic terrorism," reminding everyone that she was born to a Shia family in southern Lebanon. Others resented this "politically correct Miss USA," saying she won because of a liberal bias, part of a larger diplomatic effort to show the U.S. is accepting of its Muslim population. Things got worse. On Monday morning, pictures surfaced of Rima dancing in a stripper contest in Detroit, a competition she had won handily, taking home jewelry, gift certificates, adult toys, and "a stripper pole for home use." Soon after, it emerged that she had played the role of a police-woman in a risqué short called *Throbbing Justice* ("A film about the penal system!"). Following Donald Trump's orders, pageant officials asked to see the photos and the film, but decided not to strip the beauty queen of her crown. The snapshots of this Muslim girl in tiny red shorts and pumps, straddling a pole, dollar bills stuffed into her bra, went viral and drew criticism from within the Muslim community. Islamist journalists denounced her "un-Islamic behavior." (Hassan Fadlalah, Hizbullah's representative in the Lebanese parliament, issued a very subdued statement regarding Rima's victory: "The criteria through which we evaluate women are different from those of the West.") Meanwhile, comedians and bloggers were having unfettered fun. "Putting the ASS in 'assimilation'!" stated comedian Bill Maher, displaying a photo of Rima in a bikini. "What the Fakih?" asked one blogger. As different Arab organizations and student groups mobilized to defend the beauty queen against her attackers, Rima responded to her Muslim critics: "My family has an abundance of faith, but I'm very liberal—I'm destroying stereotypes of Islam in America." (About the photos, she said they were from an "aerobics morning event with females" and were "taken out of context.")

Rima's victory came at a low point for the minority-status activists. Seven months after their Dearborn conference, the counting had started, but the Census Bureau announced that Arabs and Iranians in America would be counted as racially white despite their write-in campaign—that is, even if they checked the "Other" box and wrote in "Arab" or "Iranian" on the questionnaire. Activists leading the campaign were finding that many within the Muslim community were not warm to the idea of minority status, saying that the political exposure that a new classification would bring far outweighed the benefits—and that there were advantages to racial ambiguity. To gain minority status, Arab-Americans would have to demonstrate that they were victims of "past racial wrongs," a process that would entail unearthing and publicizing past injustices, from Jim Crow practices in Arabia to wiretapping to negative media depictions, all of which would alienate public opinion.

These political tussles over how to self-identify and what category to adopt are also playing out in other Muslim communities. The policies derived from the Patriot Act as well as the war rhetoric from politicians about "Islamo-fascism" and "Islamic terrorism"—all of which have been shown to trigger hate crimes—have galvanized young Muslims to lobby against being categorized as white. (Maz Jobrani, an Iranian-American comedian, tries to make light of the charade of being legally white and experiencing racial harassment: "I took all the insults growing up—camel jockey, towelhead, all this other stuff—and all I had to say was, 'Dude, I'm white?!' ")

The activists pushing for minority status are American-born citizens, civil rights lawyers and doctoral students steeped in critical race theory (they speak of "racial constructs" and "sympathy gaps"), and often cannot identify with the reticence and fear of the foreign-born Muslims who live in ethnic enclaves, are either undocumented or noncitizen residents, and are reluctant to get counted or involved in any public campaign. The Census Bureau has struggled, since the early 1990s, to build trust with Muslim-American communities. In 2009, at town hall meetings, in media announcements, and in door-to-door visits, census representatives assured Muslim audiences that data gathered by the census will not be shared with the FBI, the CIA, Homeland Security, or any other state agency.

But Muslim Americans were skeptical. They knew such assurances did not stop the Census Bureau from sharing its demographic data with the Bush administration. In 2002, the Department of Homeland Security submitted a request to the Census Bureau asking for tabulated Arab ancestry data organized by zip code. (At the time such a request was not illegal, as the Census Act then only prohibited the disclosure of individually identifiable information.) In July 2004, the data sharing between Homeland Security and the Census Bureau was uncovered by a Freedom of Information Act request submitted by the Electronic Privacy Information Center (EPIC), a research center focused on civil liberties. The disclosure stunned even watchdog groups: The Census Bureau had shared statistical data with Homeland Security not long after it had issued a formal apology (in 2000) for allowing its "block-by-block" statistical data to be used to round up Japanese-Americans for internment during World War II. According to the EPIC report, the tabulations that the Census Bureau had shared showed cities—as well as zip codes—where a thousand or more, or ten thousand or more, respondents who had indicated their Arab ancestry in the census's long form resided. The Decennial Census Advisory Committee publicly denounced this sharing of demographic data, calling it "the modern-day equivalent of the pinpointing of Japanese-American communities when internment camps were opened during World War II." The Census Bureau subsequently altered its policy on sharing statistical information about "sensitive populations" with law-enforcement or intelligence agencies. A spokeswoman for Homeland Security in turn explained that the agency had requested the data to identify the airports at which to post signs and pamphlets in Arabic.

But the damage was done. When the story broke in July 2004,

Jim Zogby, president of the Arab American Institute, observed, "As this gets out, any effort to encourage people to full compliance with the census is down the tubes," adding, "How can you get people to comply when they believe that by complying they put at risk their personal and family security?" In spring 2010, as census volunteers and activists fanned out across Arab neighborhoods, encouraging people to fill out the census forms, stating that getting counted would bring more state money, services, and civil liberties protections, people on the street responded that being counted would only bring more scrutiny and informants. (In mid-2011, these fears proved true when the Associated Press revealed that the NYPD had been surveilling Muslim communities and student groups for several years and, by Attorney General Michael Mukasey's own admission, used census data to map different ethnic neighborhoods.)

Observers of the minority-status campaign were warning of a political backlash in early spring, months before the "Ground Zero" mosque controversy became a nationwide issue in August 2010. In May a pipe bomb exploded at a mosque in northern Florida. Dan Fanelli, a Republican candidate in Florida, released a political ad calling for the profiling of Middle Eastern men. Interestingly, the anti-mosque movement took off just as the census campaign began. Opposition to the construction of mosques began spreading across the South to Tennessee, Kentucky, Kansas, Texas, and Florida. After President Obama spoke in support of the construction of an Islamic center in Lower Manhattan, the anti-mosque campaign turned into a furor, reaching northern states. Soon "Leaving Islam" ads began appearing on buses and taxis in major American cities ("Fatwa on your head? Is your family threatening you? Leaving Islam? Got Questions? Get Answers"). The anti-mosque protests had familiar themes: members of a local Tea Party chapter would appear at Friday congregational prayers with picket signs that read "No Sharia in America," bringing dogs along and blaring "Born in the USA" by Bruce Springsteen. The fever-pitch rhetoric turned violent. Pipe bombs were tossed at mosques in Tennessee and upstate New York; worshippers had pork thrown at them; women had their head scarves yanked off.

The outpouring of rancor and violence against Muslims in the summer of 2010 was worse than what followed 9/11, when President Bush had stated that "Islam is a religion of peace," publicly embraced Muslim leaders, and cautioned against scapegoating "our Muslim neighbors." The Republican Party's sudden and overtly harsh stance on Islam was essentially an electoral strategy. As GOP candidates across the country geared up for midterm elections, they sought to inject the mosque issue into local races against Democrats, and largely abandoned Bush's "post–Sept. 11 rhetorical embrace of American Muslims, and his insistence—always controversial inside the party—that Islam is a religion of peace." The GOP's new policy toward American Islam was also a delayed reaction to the election of Obama, who upon gaining office had shifted the rhetorical framework of American diplomacy, speaking of "countering violent extremism" instead of the "War on Terror," "Muslim-majority states" instead of "the Islamic world," and making overtures that infuriated the Republican base.

Whatever the reasons behind it, the Republican and Tea Party movement's campaign against mosques polarized the minority-status movement. The younger activists saw the mosque and Quran-burning controversy as an opportunity to publicly make the case for minority status; the campaign was, after all, part of the GOP's "southern strategy," which exploited racial anxieties, targeting blacks, Hispanic immigrants, and now Muslims to turn out votes. Also, they argued, the Tea Party movement—the most dynamic segment of the Republican base—represented a resurgent white nationalism that was targeting Muslims, so this was the perfect time to sound off loud and clear on why Iranian- and Arab-Americans don't want to be considered white. But more seasoned activists and leaders warned that this was the worst moment for political protest: racial agitation would only lead to a sharp increase in rhetoric and hate crimes against Muslims. The months-long anti-mosque campaign had also made Muslims even more fearful and suspicious of the census.

Ironically, the anti-mosque movement also had a strong anti-census component. Aside from undocumented workers and resident aliens, the other segment of American society that was intensely distrustful of the census was the Tea Party. And while pressing for anti-sharia legislation and zoning laws to ban the construction of mosques, Tea Party activists were also—under the slogan "Stand Up, Don't Be Counted"—lobbying to withdraw funding for the American Community Survey form, which they saw as intrusive and would only give proof to the fact that whites were becoming a minority.

Late one summer afternoon in July 2010, Helen Samhan was sitting in her office in Washington, DC, overlooking K Street. The census was under way. Surrounded by boxes and stacks of paper, she counts off the headaches. "No more ancestry question, we'll be counted as white even if we write in 'Arab,' mosques being firebombed . . ." She sighs, smiling. "I'm retiring in a few weeks." Helen has been pushing for legal-minority status—a check-off box for Middle Eastern Americans—and for better census measurements for over two decades; she's become a bit of a folk hero among young Arab- and Muslim-American activists. Because of her efforts, the Census Bureau in 1995 designated a seat on the 2000 census advisory committee for Arab-Americans, the only nonminority group to get minority representation.

"I know, ideally, minority status should really be just for African-Americans and Native Americans, who have known historic discrimination. What I resist is the fact that virtually all immigrant populations outside Europe except us are considered minorities—Asians, Africans, Latin Americans are considered nonwhite, and can compete for set-asides intended for African-Americans. The South Asians, the Pakistanis—whose experience is so close to that of Arabs economically and geographically—have minority status. A Pakistani-American can compete for a small-business loan, because he's from Asia, but an Iraqi-American can't? Who decided Iraq is not western Asia?" (Minority-status campaigners in the U.S. often note how the Canadian census considers Arabs, Afghans, and Iranians as peoples of "West Asia" and classifies them as a "visible minority.")

She went on. "The complexion of Arab immigration into the U.S. has changed literally and figuratively—today we have more refugee populations, we have more Arabs who are Muslim, more

Arabs who are black. You have Nubians and Sudanese Arabs who are being counted as white—that shows the stupidity, rigidity of our system of racial classification. If they were born here, they'd be African-Americans." She pulls out a spreadsheet showing disaggregated figures from the (now extant) ancestry form. "We have a big-tent definition of Arab here at AAI—we count people from all the Arab League states—Somalis, Sudanese, people from Mauritania, Djibouti, Eritrea, and even the Comoros Islands. We count people from African states who write 'Arab' on their ancestry form, people who identify as 'Arab' whose countries of origin fall outside the Census Bureau's map of North Africa. And I'm fully aware that about one-fifth of the people here from the Arab world don't identify as Arab. Many Arab Christians don't want to be put in the Arab-American category—Chaldeans, Maronites, Assyrians." She prints out an irate letter she received from Maronite leaders in Detroit after she referred to Maronites as Arab-Americans on AAI's website. "My aunts thought like this—they spoke Arabic but didn't want to be identified with the Arab community."

Helen's family history in some ways encapsulates the changes that have occurred in the Arab-American community in the last century. Her grandfather, Salloum Mokarzel, was a prominent Maronite leader in the Little Syria enclave that emerged in Lower Manhattan in the 1900s, and founder of the *Syrian World,* the Arab-American community's first English-language journal. Mokarzel's editorials in the New York press were critical in persuading the census to see Syrians as Caucasians and not as Turkic or Asiatic. "My grandfather's generation petitioned to be considered white because it was a survival issue, but the political situation today is completely different." Helen is prepared to pass the torch to a new generation. "I'm retiring." She smiles. "I wish these kids all the best in finding allies in these campaigns. We're not the only group facing these contradictions."

Having achieved little success with the Census Bureau or their community elders, the Arab and Iranian race activists have now turned their attention to gaining minority status at the local and state levels. In early 2009, several student groups at UCLA—Iranians, Arabs, Afghans, and Armenians—launched a campaign to add a

"Southwest Asian and North African" (SWANA) box, with various subgroups, to the University of California admissions application, so as not to be identified as "White/Caucasian." They deliberately chose the category "Southwest Asian" instead of "Middle Eastern," which they saw as a Eurocentric label. This campaign also underscores the need for statistics. ("If we don't have statistics, how do we even know if we are underrepresented?" says Ghassan, a Syrian-American student at UCLA, adding, "But the point right now is to get the hell out of the 'White' box.") The effort is modeled on the Asian Pacific Coalition's "Count Me In" campaign, which in November 2007 successfully lobbied for the inclusion of twenty-three ethnic categories on the UC application, including Hmong, Pakistani, Native Hawaiian, and Samoan. The campus campaigns for minority status are also a response to police surveillance of Muslim student associations. The university administration is still deliberating, claiming that a new category for Middle Easterners could produce a sudden drop in white applicants in enrollment statistics (if those who in the past would have checked "White" were to start checking another category) and draw right-wing protest.

But this student campaign has already made national headlines. Shortly after the Boston bombing, in April 2013, amid calls by congressmen for profiling of Muslims and restrictions on student visas, the movement for a SWANA box got going again. "They may not have the direct means to successfully challenge the legal and cultural aggressions perpetrated against them, but the box schema provides a way for them to deal with their marginality and build urgent political solidarities," writes Maryam Griffin, an attorney and doctoral student at UC Santa Barbara, advising this campaign. At the national level, the minority-status advocates have now shifted their efforts from lobbying the government to building ties with other communities of color.

Jinn 'n' Juice

Arab and Pakistani Muslims have a significant presence as owners of gas stations and convenience stores in America's inner cities, particularly in the midwestern cities of Detroit, Chicago, and Minneapolis. Syrian immigrants began setting up grocery stores in Detroit in the early twentieth century; with the white flight that followed the city's riots in 1967, Syrian and Iraqi store ownership increased. At one point in the mid-1990s, 80 to 90 percent of the gas stations and grocery stores in metropolitan Detroit were owned by Chaldeans—a community of Iraqi Catholics (who as Christians were permitted to sell alcohol back in Iraq, and brought that specialization to the U.S.), but as more Muslims migrated from Iraq and Lebanon to the Motor City, the stores passed to the hands of Muslim entrepreneurs. A body of sociological literature has emerged, trying to understand the phenomenon of the "middle-man minority," wherein an immigrant minority, using its transnational ties, creates a niche in a particular business (grocery stores, gas stations, fast food), and ends up standing in between the majority population, which dominates the economy, and their customers, who are nonwhite but of a different ethnicity than their own. Yet having Muslims selling liquor in the American inner city brings a new dimension to this question.

Rola Nashef's award-winning film *Detroit Unleaded,* a love story about two youngsters who are forced to spend hours in their parents' gas station—"the cage," as they call it—subtly captures the tense relations between Middle Eastern gas station owners and their African-American customers. Lodged in impoverished, high-crime urban areas, the gas station owner will view every patron as a potential threat, selling goods and receiving money through an opening in a sunken portion of the counter, protected by a sheath of bulletproof glass. Neighborhood residents see the bulletproof glass as a symbol of the separation and distance that Muslim entrepreneurs wish to put between themselves and their customers, while the store owners see the two-inch glass as a virtual prison in which they're held for long hours every day. The film has no villains, depicting the humanity of blacks and Latinos who live in these urban wastelands, showing how the daily interactions between store owners and customers take place within the racialized and restrictive confines of the ghetto, and capturing young Arab-Americans' racial in-betweenness. The Lebanese and Iraqi kids hate working at the gas station and having to mediate between their parents and African-American and Latino clients. "I see 'the cage' as a metaphor," says Nashef. "The liquor store where these kids find themselves working under their parents' orders is a metaphor for the generational divide, the multiple restrictions facing Arab youth, and the Arab community's place between black and white."

The troubled relations between immigrant entrepreneurs and the often black and Latino majority communities around them have at times erupted into violence, as in the Los Angeles riots of 1992. This hasn't happened in Detroit, but this situation where the immigrant Muslim store owner feels threatened by his customers, and the customers see the merchant as a "bloodsucker" extracting wealth from their community, has resulted in tension and random acts of violence.

"It's not surprising that the store owners' relations with the surrounding community are tense," says Khaled Beydoun, a Dearborn native and Fordson High graduate, who is now a professor at UCLA. "You have refugees from rural parts of Iraq resettled in completely dilapidated parts of Dearborn and Detroit. The store owners often speak little English, have no sense of racial nuance. Add to that Detroit is a hyper-segregated city, and you have the current situation. Dealing with the gas station owner or liquor store owner is critical for Muslim Americans' finding a place in people-of-color coalitions."

The minority-status activists—some of whom are children of Yemeni and Lebanese grocers—see the store owner's economic "middle man" position as an obstacle to Arab- and Iranian-Americans' attaining minority status or support from communities of color. The racial status of North Africans and Middle Easterners is the result not only of the Census Bureau's legal classification, but also of society's perception of them. And minority status will require gaining the support of African-Americans and Latinos, who will sign petitions submitted to the Census Bureau and the OMB. But the Muslim grocer's highly visible presence—along with that of other immigrant merchants—engaged in aggressive profiteering, reinforces the image of Muslim immigrants as strategically aloof from and exploitative of other minorities. Like Nashef, the minority-status campaigners underline the connection between the Middle Eastern grocer's middle-man role and the Middle Eastern community's broader racial in-betweenness; the link between the "cage" and the restrictive "White" box on the census is more than metaphorical.

The presence of Muslim entrepreneurs selling liquor in inner-city areas where there are strong African-American Muslim organizations also generates intra-Muslim conflict. As May Alhassen, a doctoral student at USC and one of the activists working on this issue in the Bay Area, says, the presence of Muslim entrepreneurs selling pork, alcohol, and junk food poses a direct challenge to the authority of African-American Muslim organizations, who have historically been "the guardians of the African-American community's values and social upliftment" and find themselves in an uncomfortable situation because of their shared religious affiliation with the Muslim liquor store owners. Since the 1930s, African-American Muslim groups have stressed healthy living and a halal diet; and according to local food activists in the Bay Area and Detroit, the liquor store owner's presence has contributed to a health crisis and strained race relations.

Muslim "food justice" activists have now launched a campaign to provide Muslim store owners with financial incentives to get out of the liquor business or shift to green products. In Chicago, the Inner-City Muslim Action Network (IMAN), a social services group headquartered in the working-class enclave of Chicago Lawn, has launched a food-justice program called Muslim Run that aims to bring healthy food to black and Latino communities on the South Side. These Muslim Run green campaigns are explicitly modeled on decades-old Nation of Islam and Black Power initiatives aimed at building up neighborhoods with small businesses, many of which supplied healthy halal food. Relying on University of Chicago studies of "food deserts"—districts on the South Side that have little access to fresh produce—community organizers from IMAN will walk the streets, conducting surveys of Muslim store owners and their customers, and then help the grocers get state money earmarked for fresh food. In Flint, Michigan, Mona Sahouri, a community organizer, has launched a similar initiative and drafted a "memorandum of understanding" on how immigrant grocers should treat their customers. At the forefront of these campaigns to "quench food deserts" and bring fresh produce to low-income urban areas are coalitions of young Arab-, Iranian-, Pakistani-, and African-American Muslims. Art and music play critical roles in these initiatives. Whether it's IMAN holding a concert at the Apollo Theater in Harlem, or Beats, Rhymes & Relief—a recently formed NGO in Washington, DC—organizing live concerts in underprivileged neighborhoods while delivering free lunches and book bags, music is used to build community and raise awareness of the long history of interaction between African-American and immigrant Muslims.

These "green-*deen*" coalitions also reveal profound generational differences. The activists believe that reducing the social distance between Middle Eastern store owners and their neighbors is critical for the integration of Muslims into communities of color; the minority-status activists will argue that blurring racial borders on the ground can help shake up racial classification on the federal census. Their parents, who fled conservative societies with stifling social norms and authoritarian regimes, often dreamed of owning a small business—selling halal or non-halal products—and cannot understand the effort, led by their own children, to enforce Islamic norms in an American neighborhood. When asked why he sells alcohol, Yasser Salam told Chicago Public Radio, "It's not illegal. It's against my religion; that's in the Judgment Day." This is a common response: "Selling alcohol is not against the law in America," or "This is not a sharia state." Moreover, store owners wonder why they do not face similar halal campaigns in Latino neighborhoods. For African-American Muslim leaders, on the other hand, the enforcement of Islamic norms, including proscriptions against the consumption and sale of alcohol, is critical to bringing order and security to blighted urban areas, and to rehabilitating young men. As Imam Zayed Shaker of the Zaytuna Institute, who is spearheading a campaign in Oakland,

California, says, "Why can't we connect the high rates of [liquor] stores in the community with the high dropout rates, drug addiction rates, and high incarceration rates?"

Among the young activists there is disagreement on the best way to approach the liquor store owners: the more cautious warn that campaigns to embarrass Arab and Pakistani store owners to go green or halal rarely work. (Sometimes these young agitators organize protests where they stand outside Muslim-owned liquor stores holding placards that read, "Prophet not Profit," and chanting, "1-2-3-4, we don't want your liquor stores!") Moreover, any effort to enforce Islamic norms in a public space in an American city can inflame public opinion nationwide. This occurred in late 2006 when, citing freedom of religion, Somali cabdrivers at St. Paul International Airport in Minneapolis began refusing to drive alcohol-carrying passengers. A more effective strategy, say the activists, is to stress how "food deserts" contribute to poor health and to offer financial incentives for a change in behavior. The Muslim race activists of immigrant background—from the Iranian-American minority status activists to the Pakistani-American eco-halal workers—seem to have arrived at the conclusion that in the face of punitive state policies and organized hostility, the political incorporation of Muslim Americans is more likely to occur through the margins of American society.

Mighty in the Margins

In 2005, Sherman Jackson, a legal scholar at USC and an eminent figure in American Islam, published *Islam and the Blackamerican,* an examination of religious authority in America, and the relations between "indigenous" African-American Muslims and "immigrant" Muslims. The author argued that before 1965, Islam in America was dominated by an "indigenous black presence," but after the repeal of the National Origins Act, the influx of Muslims from Asia and the Middle East led to the marginalization of African-American Muslims, as they lacked the language commands or training in classical texts to lead American Muslim organizations. Moreover, argued Jackson, "immigrant Islam" did not understand the particular circumstances of African-Americans, the historic reasons for their "collective conversion," and the heterodox forms of Islam that had appeared in urban America. Jackson concluded by exhorting African-American Muslims to develop a mastery over the classical Sunni tradition and to build their own religious authority.

Jackson's book resonated with the so-called second generation, because in the years after 9/11, they were asking questions about race and belonging, but also because a significant political shift had taken place among American Muslims. The South Asian and Middle Eastern professionals who arrived in America after 1965 were often economic conservatives and, once naturalized, emerged as a reliable base for the Republican Party. American Muslims of immigrant background voted overwhelmingly Republican until 2004, and that's when a political convergence with African-American Muslims—who have voted for Democrats for decades—began. The GOP's pro-business policies, emphasis on family values, and Bush senior's (relatively) hard-line stance on Israel's settlement policy in 1992 made the younger Bush's candidacy in 2000 attractive to many older Arab- and Pakistani-Americans; but the Patriot Act and the invasion of Iraq, among other policies introduced by Bush, would in 2004 push American Muslims en masse toward the Democratic Party. In 2008, 90 percent of the country's Muslims voted for Obama (even though his campaign kept Muslims at arm's length), and by the time the anti-mosque and anti-sharia campaign of 2010 erupted, the exodus of Muslim Americans from the Republican Party was nearly complete.

Yet in addition to the electoral shift, a racial shift was occurring, with younger activists questioning whether the Democratic Party could deliver, claiming that the incorporation of Muslims is more likely to occur through the back channel of the civil rights movement; they argue that race is not just a legal category, but a political tool for empowerment, a site for struggle, and that activism in the ghetto can bring some kind of political belonging and protection. In one of Jackson's more intriguing passages, he states that African-American—what he terms "Blackamerican"—Muslims were not rounded up en masse like "immigrant" Muslims after 9/11 because "American blackness confers upon Blackamerican Muslims a layer of insulation beyond that of the First Amendment." He writes, "This insulation is conferred, however, as long as Blackamericans themselves are seen as embracing—and certainly not opposing—the American Constitutional order. If, on the basis of Islam or any other source, they cease to identify with that order, so, too, will American blackness cease to be a source of added insulation for Blackamerican Muslims." It's not clear where the African-American Muslims' "added insulation" comes from, their "indigeneity" or loyalty to the constitutional order; but the young Muslims' post-9/11 attraction to African-American Islam and black politics more broadly is precisely for the "added insulation" it can provide; and the belief that with state protection failing and white nationalist movements rising, joining civil rights coalitions and gaining acceptance in black movements could bring greater freedom.

Yet the questions facing young Muslim-American activists— like their counterparts everywhere—are how to balance loyalty to the "American constitutional order" with a critique of empire, and what's the tradeoff between patriotism with global Muslim solidarity. Young Muslims are drawn to African-American Islam because of its linking of the local with the global, and Noble Drew Ali's and Malcolm X's solidarity with the downtrodden worldwide, a universalism that appeals to American youth with kin in Kashmir, Somalia, and Gaza. And here was Jackson arguing that rights came by identifying strictly with the nation-state, and telling young Muslims to "embrace America" and not judge the country by its foreign policies. How, then, to—or should one—talk about race and foreign policy? The green activists and minority-status campaigners walking the streets of Oakland, Washington, Chicago, Brooklyn, and Detroit realize that they are wading into local relationships (between "indigenous" and "immigrant" Muslims) that have a complex transnational history behind them, and they are split on this question. On the one hand, there are the race activists who want to revive the solidarity and anti-imperial history of the 1960s; and on the other are those who believe that a more local, state-based patriotism is the most effective way to protect the rights of American Muslims. This wrangling—

between Muslim-American "statists" and "internationalists"—echoes and builds on the debate within the civil rights movement during the early years of the Cold War between African-American leaders who wanted to link the country's racial quagmire to the process of decolonization and those who defined the African-American situation as a domestic issue. There were figures like Paul Robeson, W. E. B. Du Bois, and Malcolm X, who thought the civil rights struggle had, as Martin Luther King would state in his Riverside speech in April 1967, to go "beyond national allegiance." In that vein, Malcolm X appealed to the UN and the newly created Organization of African Unity to protect black rights. And on the other side were leaders like diplomat Ralph Bunche, Bayard Rustin, and Adam Clayton Powell who thought the radical internationalism of the Nation of Islam, the Black Panthers, and Malcolm X simply set back the civil rights struggle. Rustin, unhappy with the way Paul Robeson criticized the U.S. while in Europe, observed, "There's sort of an unwritten rule that if you want to criticize the United States you do it at home . . . we have to prove that we're patriotic."

This debate is now taking place among Muslim race activists, with the more state-oriented arguing that given surveillance practices and laws like "material support" that punish speech critical of U.S. foreign policy, the best political strategy is one of activism on issues of racial inequality. By embracing race, the "immigrant" Muslim can become "indigenous." These Muslim-American statists will note that it was Bayard Rustin and Adam Clayton Powell's strategic patriotism and patient coalition-building that extracted important policy concessions. Radical stances on foreign policy issues only drive away allies and cast doubt on a community's patriotism. They argue that it was through careful local politicking and alliance building with Sikh and Hindu organizations that the Arab Anti-Discrimination Committee, in June 2013, was able to get the Department of Justice to recognize Arabs as a race—instead of white—on the FBI's 1-699 Hate Crimes Form. Citing the spike in hate crimes after the Boston bombing, the Department of Justice would agree to list Arabs as a race over the strenuous opposition of the OMB, which wanted the FBI to use census categories.

Their critics retort that not all speech or activism must be policy- or state-oriented; truth telling has a higher purpose, and Muslims should have the same freedom of expression that other Americans have. The question of whether to talk about foreign policy also raises complex theological issues for Muslim activists. The activists with a religious bent, in particular, argue that it is a Muslim's duty to speak out against injustice—especially when Muslims are under attack. More-over, argue the radical internationalists, another way, beyond urban renewal, to integrate Muslims into people-of-color coalitions and to bridge the distance between "immigrant" and African-American communities is by reminding people of the connections between the civil rights movement and anticolonial struggles. But these efforts to mobilize the history of the 1960s are also fraught. Many Americans don't want to be reminded of black nationalist or Third World radicalism; anti-imperial talk could alienate important domestic allies. Some organizations—like South Asian Americans Leading Together (SAALT) and the Sikh Coalition—will split the difference, talking about race, but not touching foreign policy.

The older Muslim-American leadership can understand the political shift away from the Republican Party, but not the race-based identity politics or the efforts to "stir up" the sixties. In the Arab-American community the revolts of 2011, the tumult in Egypt, Iraq, and Syria, and the subsequent out-migration of tens of thousands of Arab Christians from the Middle East have made the older generation even more suspicious of this largely Muslim-led campaign for minority status; the more established assimilated Arab Christian families (who constitute the backbone of organizations like the Arab American Institute) feel racial agitation will only alienate sympathizers that Arab Christians may have in the U.S. But other institutions, like the Arab American Museum, are quietly responding to the demographic shifts and the younger generation's demands. The Dearborn-based museum's main exhibit on the Arab-American story begins with West African Muslim slaves like Omar ibn Said of North Carolina, who wrote a narrative in Arabic script; spotlights the political work of civil rights activist Alia

Hassan, who worked closely with Malcolm X; and concludes with a section titled "Beginning Communities" that highlights the most recent Arab arrivals, Sudanese and Somalis, who have been coming in greater numbers since the mid-1990s.

Even outside the U.S., campaigns have emerged around the issue of data security, questioning the ethnic categories and maps that underpin national census forms. In Canada in 2006, activists called for a boycott of the national census, when the government decided to outsource data processing to Lockheed Martin. Protesters in Canada and to a lesser extent the UK (where the Office for National Statistics also hired Lockheed Martin) feared the American armament company would—bound by the Patriot Act—share data with Homeland Security. The revelations in June 2013 that the U.S., Britain, Canada, Australia, and New Zealand had formed a surveillance program called the Five Eyes Alliance, whereby different spy agencies exchanged vast amounts of meta-data, only fueled more suspicion.

European state officials are debating how to respond to census activism and how to count and categorize their growing Muslim communities. The National Association of British Arabs in recent years launched a campaign contesting being placed in the category "white," citing the familiar reasons that their "exclusion from official statistics" makes it difficult to track incidents of profiling and harassment, and to include undercounted communities such as Somalis and Sudanese. They called for a separate box—and unlike their American counterparts, secured a "tick-box" just in time for the 2011 census. If British Arabs were protesting "compulsory whiteness," South Asian activists and scholars have long argued that the British census is *too* race-centered; that the black-white binary was imported from the U.S. in the mid-1960s, along with various racial equality laws, by American-educated Britons, and produced a classification system that cannot conceive of discrimination that is not color-based. In the 1990s, Pakistani and Bangladeshi activists argued that they were "misplaced" into race categories when they were facing discrimination on religious grounds. In July 2000, the British Parliament passed the Census Amendment Act, permitting a "religion question" on the 2001 census; people could indicate their religious identity on the questionnaire, and official statistics were finally available on Britain's faith communities.

In France, where ethnic and religious statistics are forbidden by law, the debate over minority status is particularly acrimonious. If the American census asks about race and ethnicity, but not religion, the French census is prohibited from asking about all three; and the African, Arab, and Roma activists who are demanding that the republic relax this law, introduce "postcolonial categories" on the census, and begin collecting racial and ethnic statistics—to better monitor discrimination and profiling, and allow minorities to build support for affirmative action—are told that such counting runs against France's ideology of color-blindness and will lead to *communautarisme,* a divisive American-style identity politics. And the efforts of the American embassy in Paris to promote *statistiques ethniques,* bringing French Muslim activists to Washington for workshops with Census Bureau experts, have only inflamed French opinion. President François Hollande, in May 2013, moved to ban the term "race" altogether from the French constitution and the country's laws, saying it has no scientific basis. Minority-status campaigns across Europe are drawing opposition from societies at large. When Danish Muslims, at the height of the cartoon controversy, said that as a minority, they should be protected by law from hate speech, their critics stated that Muslims are not a minority but part of a "global majority."

The challenge over how to count and label Muslim communities in Europe and North America is creating political rifts within these communities. At root is a fundamental disagreement on how to respond to organized hostility, with younger advocates claiming that race frames political issues and determines allocation of resources, and that Muslims should mobilize accordingly; and their elders, who along with recent immigrants fear the consequences of racial agitation, prefer to blend into the majority, and have no desire to be counted, mapped, or classified.

9

American *Banlieue*

In May 2010, Bill O'Reilly invited British journalist Imogen Lloyd Webber onto his show, *The O'Reilly Factor,* to discuss France's law banning the face veil. When Lloyd Webber cited France's secular tradition as a reason for the law, O'Reilly disagreed, saying the real reason was fear of "Muslim ghettos." "The French are very worried about these ghettos, these Muslim ghettos, particularly outside of Paris, where the Muslims come to France—and they do this in England as well—and they don't integrate into society." He went on: "The same thing's going on in London. You have neighborhoods in London, they're totally Muslim, they speak Arabic. You walk in those neighborhoods, you're not in England—you're in Kuwait." Lloyd Webber looked bewildered. "I can't actually think of one in London." "Clapham Common!" bellowed O'Reilly. Lloyd Webber shot back: "Clapham Common is full of posh people with push-chairs!" O'Reilly froze. "Polish people?"

Europeans don't like it when Americans—scholars, diplomats, Fox News shouters—speak of "ghettos" on the old continent. For conservatives, ghettos are a thing of the past in Europe, and "race" is an American obsession. Left-leaning intellectuals, in turn, are irked by American chatter about Europe's failure to integrate its Muslims when it is U.S. foreign policy that inflames Muslim opinion; and they particularly resent efforts to impose American "racecraft" on Europe. In his book *Urban Outcasts,* Loïc Wacquant, a Berkeley-based French sociologist, argues forcefully against such easy transatlantic comparisons, stating that the French *banlieues*—and other urban spaces in Western Europe—have indeed been devastated by state withdrawal and the collapse of Communist parties, but in their ethnic diversity and institutional density, they are simply not analogous to the American ghetto, with its level of segregation and physical insecurity. Yet the American government, since the French riots of 2005, has been worried about how the alienation of European Muslims may weaken European allies. American diplomats and scholars are intervening in numerous ways, urging European states to adopt American-style race and security policies, funding Muslim organizations, commissioning studies on "moderate" Islam, and interceding in culture wars between Muslim artists and their governments, in ways that have embarrassed European officials and divided Muslim opinion.

This isn't the first time American diplomacy has tried to curry favor with Muslims in Europe. During the Cold War, the Munich-based Radio Liberty and Radio Free Europe broadcast behind the Iron Curtain, appealing to Muslims in the Caucasus and Central Asia, chafing under Soviet occupation. These diplomatic efforts were directed at the Soviet Union, an enemy state; the current initiatives, however, are aimed at Muslims in Western Europe—and that is new. Western states have a centuries-long record of intervening in the Muslim parts of Africa and Asia to protect and empower religious minorities. In the nineteenth century, the French sheltered the Maronites, the Russians patronized the Orthodox Christians, and American missionaries in Syria courted the Druze. The great powers assumed the protection of these religious minorities in part to expand their influence in the region. This practice continues, in different forms, to this day, but it is unprecedented for allied Western states to court each other's minorities. And yet the U.S. is spending millions of dollars to win the hearts and minds of Europe's disaffected Muslim communities, often vying with European states' own local outreach efforts.

The American embassies are not the only ones pursuing Muslim outreach strategies. Saudi Arabia, Iran, Turkey, Pakistan, and a host of Arab states are also monitoring their diasporas in Europe, assertively promoting their interpretations of Islam and trying to win the support of Europe's Muslim populations. The Great Game of the twenty-first century—the ideological and geopolitical tussles centered around postcolonial Africa and the Middle East—is increasingly playing out in Europe's immigrant neighborhoods, and it has thrust young Muslim activists and community leaders (often in their early twenties) into delicate diplomatic balancing acts.

Diversity Management

The Wikileaks cables that probably stirred the most anger in European capitals were those wherein U.S. diplomats castigated allies—France, Britain, Holland—for mistreating their Muslim minorities. The cables, released in late December 2010, showed American diplomats generally unimpressed with European efforts to combat this "new threat," and revealed that U.S. embassies were funding Muslim groups in various European cities. In August 2006, the U.S. embassy in London sent a cable to Washington stating that "little progress" had been made in combating extremism and warning of rising tensions between the Muslim community and the government. Follow-up reports stressed that while Muslims make up only 3 to 4 percent of Britain's population, outreach to this audience is vital to U.S. interests. The U.S. embassy subsequently established a project called "Reverse Radicalism," focusing on "at-risk" youth to help "raise the standard of dialogue on extremism and promote understanding between Britain's Muslim and non-Muslim communities."

The embassy also organized cultural activities, including the Ramadan Festival (first held by the U.S. embassy in Amsterdam), to highlight the diversity of British Muslims and invited various American Muslim artists. The cables stressed the importance of performances by American Muslims. "The message their performance would send—of American Muslims, proud to be both 'American' and 'Muslim'—is a powerful message that would open British Muslim eyes to American cultural and religious diversity," notes one missive, "as well as encourage reflection on the part of the British Muslim community in a positive, self-defining direction." Explaining why the U.S.-based Allah Made Me Funny comedy troupe should be invited, an officer says its "positive messages" would likely reach "thousand[s] of British Muslims, including the disproportionately high youth population." The integration of American Muslims—contrasted with the segregation of Muslims in Europe—was offered as evidence that America is not at war with Islam.

The London cables also describe the embassy's efforts to reach "moderate" Muslim communities that "lack the institutional infrastructure to actively mobilize against radicalizing influences." There is little agreement, however, on what "moderate" means. The British press was unhappy with the embassy's "secret campaign" to deradicalize British Muslims, and especially with the embassy's outreach to mosques considered "radical" in Britain, such as the Finsbury Park mosque in northern London, frequented by both "Twentieth Hijacker" Zacarias Moussaoui and "Shoe Bomber" Richard Reid. In December 2010, Ambassador Louis Susman drew criticism from conservative Britons and secular British Muslims for visiting and expressing his "great admiration" for the East London Mosque (which allegedly hosted the militant American cleric Anwar al-Awlaki some years earlier), and inviting its youth to participate in embassy-funded trips to the U.S. Dispatches from the U.S. embassy in Amsterdam describe similar displeasure by Dutch officials, and Dutch Muslim leaders worried that the embassy's outreach programs see European Muslims as a "collective problem" and associate integration with counterterrorism.

It's in France, perhaps not surprisingly, that the State Department's activities have triggered the most outrage. The dispatches from Paris are blunt in their appraisal: "The French have a well-known problem with discrimination against minorities." Some cables read like descriptions of pre–civil rights America: "The French media remains overwhelmingly white . . . Among French elite educational institutions, we are only aware that Sciences Po has taken serious steps to integrate." The thrust of the correspondence argues that the French approach to assimilation has not worked, because of an "official blindness to all racial differences." Institutions are "insufficiently flexible," unable to reflect the country's changing complexion. And the fear is not only that young French Muslims will gravitate toward extremism—"Washington takes seriously the potentially global threat of disenfranchised and disadvantaged minorities in France"—but that ethnic conflict will weaken France. Other dispatches warn that if France, over the long term, does not succeed in giving minorities true political representation, "it could become weaker, more divided and perhaps inclined toward crises . . . and a less effective ally as a result."

The U.S. embassy staff acknowledged France's reluctance to accept the American model of integration or to "partner" with the embassy, but the cables describe numerous outreach projects involving exchange programs, festivals, conferences, and media appearances to raise awareness among state and societal actors about America's civil rights movement ("sharing of our American experiences in managing diversity"). Through such efforts, and by pressing the French government and NGOs to improve the lot of French Muslims, the embassy has tried to alter French Muslim perceptions of the U.S., to show that America respects Islam and "is engaged for good in the Arab-Muslim worlds." The embassy's outreach aims to explain how America manages diversity and to help France live up to its egalitarian ideals. "While direct development assistance . . . is not likely to be available for France," notes one cable, there should be funds available "to address the consequences of discrimination and minority exclusion in France" through exchange programs, grants, and media intervention. The author underscores that given France's self-image, "such an effort will continue to require considerable discretion, sensitivity and tact on our part."

These depictions of France as a prejudiced country in need of American aid and tutelage were not well received. France has long viewed itself as immune to American-style racial politics, priding itself on providing refuge, since the late nineteenth century, to African-Americans fleeing discrimination. The cable that drew the most indignant response from French state officials was written by then ambassador Craig Stapleton at the height of the Parisian civil unrest in November 2005: "The real problem is the failure of white Christian France to view its dark-skinned and Muslim compatriots as citizens in their own rights." Speaking on a television show, former prime minister Dominique de Villepin scoffed, "This [cable] shows the limits of American diplomacy." He added that U.S. diplomats were wrongly reading the *banlieues* crisis through their own history, viewing France's urban crisis through a religious prism. The French media, in turn, was riled by revelations that the U.S. had since 2003 been deeply involved in the integration process—pushing to shift the media discourse, to get French leaders to rethink their concepts and "intellectual frameworks" regarding minorities, to generate public debate about affirmative action, multiculturalism, and hyphenated identity, as well as to reform French history curricula and to encourage French museums to exhibit the contributions of minorities. As French journalists observed, these cultural initiatives had a Cold War precedent.

A Cultural War on Terror

In the early years of the Cold War, both superpowers began using Islam as a political weapon. If the Soviets were highlighting the racial strife in the American South for propaganda purposes, the Eisenhower administration was eyeing Moscow's "Islamic underbelly" and came to see the plight of Muslims in the Central Asian territories as Russia's weak point. Just before the Bandung Conference of 1955, an Eisenhower administration official suggested using "some 'Machiavellian'" tactics to embarrass the Soviets at the conference: "I wonder if some of our friends at Bandung might not have prepared in their briefcases an exposé ["some devastating literature"] of the East's [Russia's] 'colonial' practices in its governing of the Moslem peoples of the fictitious states of Uzbek and Turkestan." The Soviets in turn would send Muslims from their Central Asian territories to hajj to show the wider Muslim world that Soviet Muslims were well-treated.

In the 1950s, there was no American Muslim community that the Truman and Eisenhower administrations could—like the Soviets— tap for public diplomacy or intelligence work. The largest Muslim community back then was the heterodox Nation of Islam, which was opposed to the U.S. government. American officials began to look toward Muslims from other regions, and soon Uzbeks, Chechens, and other Central Asian Muslims were recruited to staff the offices of Radio Liberty and Radio Free Europe and began broadcasting to Muslims behind the Iron Curtain. The broadcasts in Uzbek, Turkmen, Kazakh, Tajik, Kyrgyz, Georgian, Azerbaijani, and Chechen would—especially after Nikita Khrushchev's crackdown on Muslim institutions—highlight Moscow's repressive policies toward Islam. In 1957, the Operations Coordinating Board—a body that included officials from the U.S. Information Agency, the State Department, and the CIA—produced a report calling on the Eisenhower administration to bypass traditional Islam, and "strengthen the reformist groups" like the Muslim Brotherhood, seen as key to countering Soviet influence in the Third World. This Cold War strategy extended to Europe: in the 1960s, the U.S. would sponsor a pan-European Muslim conference, and begin courting Islamist groups like the Muslim World League and the Muslim Brotherhood (which had established a center in Geneva), all in an effort to create a sprawling, transcontinental "anti-Soviet Islamic coalition."

In her seminal *The Cultural Cold War: The CIA and the World of Arts and Letters,* Oxford historian Frances Stonor Saunders shows that the Marshall Plan and the postwar reconstruction of Europe included an elaborate cultural apparatus, one of whose main objectives was, as she put it, "to advance the claim that it did not exist." As part of its cultural offensive against communism, the CIA—through the Congress for Cultural Freedom—covertly underwrote art exhibits and tours of the Boston Symphony Orchestra in Europe, paid for the filming of George Orwell's *1984* and *Animal Farm,* bailed out struggling publications like the *Partisan Review* and the *Kenyon Review,* and in 1953 launched the liberal left-leaning literary and political journal *Encounter* under the stewardship of Irving Kristol. American intelligence even supported the Munich-based literary magazine the *Arabic Review* (*Al Majallah*), published by the anticommunist Institute for the Study of the USSR. The "War on Terror" in Western Europe today also has a cultural side. And while more discreet than covert, and often implemented through partnerships with local NGOs and private-sector actors, the current cultural offensive is underpinned by a Cold War framework—namely, the notion that the War on Terror is a battle of ideas and ideologies, and the belief that the flow of information that brought down communism can similarly defeat the jihadist ideology.

From the mid-1950s onward, the U.S. supported Cold Warriors across the political spectrum. As the late journalist Andrew Kopkind would observe, "The CIA supported socialist cold warriors, Fascist cold warriors, black and white cold warriors. The catholicity and flexibility of CIA operations were major advantages. But it was a sham pluralism and it was utterly corrupting." The U.S. today is similarly supporting a range of Muslim organizations and websites deemed "moderate." ("To win the cyber-war [in an age of global terrorism], look to the Cold War," writes Mike McConnell, former U.S. director of national intelligence, who has called for a revisiting of President Eisenhower's policies.) In France, the American embassy's efforts to empower "moderate" Muslim voices inflamed public opinion. One of the Muslim organizations supported by the embassy was the online magazine Oumma.com, described by the American ambassador as a "remarkable website." French conservatives, who see the site as extremist because of its alleged sympathies for the Muslim Brotherhood, charged that the American right and French Muslims were allying to undermine French *laïcité*. In reality, both Oumma.com supported by the State Department, and Magharebia.com, a news website launched by the United States African Command (AFRICOM), were trying to counter Salafi jihadist groups.

The Department of Defense's Minerva Research project would also stir controversy. In April 2008, Secretary of Defense Robert Gates announced the Minerva Research Initiative, inviting universities around the world to apply for an estimated $50 million for research in areas of importance to U.S. national security policy. Citing "Kremlinology," the study of the Soviet Union, as a model, Gates declared that Minerva (named after the Roman goddess of wisdom and sponsor of the arts, trade, and defense) would support social science research in areas including "Chinese military and technology research," "studies of terrorist organizations and ideologies," and "future ideological trends within Islam" with the aim of "solving terrorism challenges," and the initiative also hoped to fund a study of Iraq under Saddam Hussein (using archival material airlifted from Iraq to Washington in 2003). Gates specifically appealed to the discipline of anthropology to help with this effort.

Minerva prompted a debate between American social scientists: some argued that the academy needed to bring its knowledge to bear on policy debates, while others warned that government funding would skew research toward what the Pentagon defined as the "greatest threat"—terrorism and the rise of China—and away from issues like poverty, inequality, and global warming, which posed a bigger menace to human life. By July 2008, over a thousand anthropologists had signed a pledge to not accept Pentagon funding for counterinsurgency research on Muslims. Since the research initiative included a component identifying "moderate" Muslim networks in France, Germany, and Great Britain, Minerva would divide European opinion as well, with some universities (in France and Sweden) taking part, others refusing, fearing the "big data" project would be used for surveillance, in light of other personal data-sharing agreements between Homeland Security and the EU that passed despite opposition in the European Parliament. The Paris-based university Sciences Po, for instance, would receive a grant from DOD to partner with Arizona State University for a project titled "Finding Allies for the War of Words: Mapping the Diffusion and Influence of Counter-Radical Muslim Discourse," while scholars at the École des hautes études en sciences sociales (EHESS) would distance themselves from Minerva, "[which] promotes cultural and behavioral research in order to have a handle on possible manipulations of the sensitivities and the public opinion of occupied populations." Muslim activists in Europe and the U.S. were warning of a "global COINTELPRO," a worldwide surveillance program, throughout the post-9/11 decade. Their fears would prove true in June 2013, and the controversy over American-sponsored research in Europe would erupt again, when it emerged that the NSA was collecting the personal data of European citizens—Muslim and non-Muslim—through major Internet companies and in collaboration with the British intelligence agency GCHQ, which was intercepting data traffic between Europe and the United States.

American initiatives in Europe were also geared toward influencing cultural and artistic production. In October 2007, Farah Pandith, currently the State Department's Special Representative to Muslim Communities, and Jared Cohen, an expert on digital diplomacy and member of the Policy Planning Staff, visited the English town of Leicester, which Pandith would describe as home to the most conservative Islamic community she had seen anywhere in Europe. "Despite the many positive programmes in Leicester, the isolation of some parts of the Muslim community was striking," read one dispatch. "Girls as young as four years old were completely covered." The diplomats would propose the idea of using Bollywood films to lure young British Muslims away from militancy. They met with a British starlet named Humeira Akhter, producer Mohsin Abbas, director of Arts Versa, a film production company, and various other artists to discuss developing an "anti-extremist genre" of Bollywood films. American diplomats are no doubt aware of the popularity of Indian films among British Muslim communities and in the Middle East. Nowadays Bollywood films often have their premieres in Dubai; a Bollywood theme park is being built in that city-state. And American officials, considering how to harness Indian "soft power," conceived a film-based initiative, whereby Bollywood stars would engage young British Muslims, speak out against extremism, and also help with the reconstruction of Afghanistan.

Policymakers—in India and elsewhere—who recommend using Bollywood for counter-radicalization, argue that the genre is popular in the Muslim world for various reasons: The films reflect conservative family values and rarely have sexually explicit scenes; major Bollywood figures, like the actor Shah Ru Khan and the composer A. R. Rahman, who won an Oscar for his score of *Slumdog Millionaire,* are Muslim; the genre's sound tracks often feature Sufi music, which also has a wide appeal. Moreover, say advocates, there is already an emerging subgenre that tries to use film to promote reconciliation between India's various religious and ethnic communities. The film *Mission Kashmir* (2000), for instance, tells the story of an orphan who grows up to find out that his adoptive father is the man who killed his parents; he leaves home to live and train among Kashmiri militants. He returns a decade later to avenge his parents' death, only to fall in love again with his childhood sweetheart, a girl named Sufi, who changes his mind about retribution.

Following Cohen and Pandith's meeting with British Muslim cultural leaders, the American embassy in London sounded bullish, "Bollywood actors and executives agreed to work with the U.S. government to promote anti-extremist messages through third party actors and were excited about the idea of possibly partnering with Hollywood as well." But the plan never panned out. A couple of years after the London meeting, a number of Bollywood films—*New York* (2009), *Kurbaan* (2009), *My Name Is Khan* (2010)—were released that did address the War on Terror, but not from the "anti-extremism" standpoint the State Department was hoping for. The works generally depict the cultural angst and turmoil caused by American policies toward South Asians and American Muslims. *My Name Is Khan,* for instance, a Muslim-Hindu love story set in the U.S. before and after 2001, shows—in between courtship scenes and extravagant dance sequences—how American Muslims are involved in urban renewal projects, helping communities devastated by Hurricane Katrina, but still are not spared the post-9/11 backlash. The protagonist, an Indian Muslim named Rizwan Khan (played by heartthrob Sharuk Khan), who suffers from Asperger's syndrome, is arrested and detained by the police. He makes it his mission to meet President Bush and his successor to tell them, "My name is Khan and I'm not a terrorist." As films and plays of this type increased, American diplomacy would focus on music and the "hip-hop wars" playing out in Europe.

Jihadi Cool

One of the odder phenomena of the last decade is hearing national security elites, terrorism experts, and career diplomats discuss the finer points of "flow," "bling," and the "politics of cool." American and European terrorism experts have increasingly expressed concerns over "anti-American hip-hop," accenting the radicalizing influence of the genre. Noting that Al-Shabaab, the Somali-based Islamist group, uses "jihad rap" in its recruitment videos, Harvard scholar Jessica Stern wrote in *Foreign Affairs:* "The first- and second-generation Muslim children I interviewed for a study of the sources of radicalization in the Netherlands seemed to think that talking about jihad was cool, in the same way that listening to gangster rap is in some youth circles." Others have advocated mobilizing certain substyles of hip-hop against "jihadi cool." In Europe, hip-hop is being enlisted in a broad ideological offensive to counter domestic extremism.

As in America, some of the biggest stars on the European hip-hop scene are Muslim, the children of immigrants and/or converts, a number of whom have been embroiled in controversies about freedom of expression, national identity, and extremism. Britain became the first country to deal with the issue of "Muslim hate rap" when, in 2004, the song "Dirty Kuffar" was released online by rap group Sheikh Terra and the Soul Salah Crew. The video, splicing together images from Iraq, Palestine, and Chechnya, praises Osama bin Laden and denounces Bush, Tony Blair, Ariel Sharon, Hosni Mubarak, and Saudi Arabia's King 'Abdallah as "dirty infidels." The track drew the attention of the Home Office and Labour MPs, who saw the lyrics and imagery as advocating violence. In 2006, Aki Nawaz of the popular hip-hop techno group Fun-Da-Mental released an album, *All Is War,* with a cover depicting the Statue of Liberty hooded and wired like an Abu Ghraib prisoner, and a song ("Che Bin Pt 2") comparing bin Laden to Che Guevara. Two MPs called for his arrest.

Realizing the influence of hip-hop, when in April 2007 the Home Office introduced Prevent, an initiative to stop British Muslim youth from being lured into violent extremism, it made sure that hip-hop figured prominently. Muslim organizations in Britain would receive Prevent funding to organize "Spittin' Light" hip-hop shows, where American and British Muslim rappers with "mainstream interpretations" of Islam would parade their talents. The initiative was directed at younger Muslims, who may not have been associated with mosques or other religious institutions. Prevent's advocates claim that art can provide Muslims with "an acceptable outlet for strong emotions." Given Prevent's involvement in the arts, leaders of cultural organizations—

wooed by the American embassy and the British government—are unsure of whether to accept state funds.

"Art is inspiring, art can create conversations that we can't have in real life, and Muslim artists should be allowed to speak about anything," says Hassan Mahmadallie, a theater director and officer of the Arts Council of England. "But Prevent is in effect putting limits on the speech of Muslim artists, funding only those the government considers 'good' Muslims."

Other European governments are worrying about hip-hop and extremism. In Germany, state officials are trying to indict rapper-turned-Salafi Deso Dogg for the lyrics of a *nasheed* that allegedly inspired a twenty-one-year-old Kosovar to fire at a busload of American servicemen in Frankfurt in March 2011. In the Netherlands, the government is at a loss over what kind of rap to support. In 2007, there was a controversy surrounding the Dutch-Moroccan star Salah Eddin and his video "Het Land Van" (This Country Of), in which he describes being Muslim in an increasingly conservative Netherlands and lists what he likes and does not like about the country. Among other things, he does not like racial profiling and the red-light district—"this land that sells women behind window panes." The rapper first appears clean-shaven in a plaid shirt; as the video progresses, his facial hair grows longer until, by the end, he is wearing a scraggly beard and an orange Guantanamo jumpsuit. The uproar was not only about this content, but about the fact that Salah Eddin had received a grant from the Dutch Ministry of Culture for the video's production. Voters complained that their tax money was underwriting radicalism. Government officials felt duped: they had given Salah Eddin the grant thinking he was "moderate," but he turned out to be "radical."

European officials (along with U.S. embassy officials) are scrutinizing hip-hop practices in their cities' immigrant neighborhoods, trying to decide which Muslim hip-hop artists to legitimize and which to push aside. The debate over hip-hop, Europe's dominant youth culture, stands in for a much larger debate about race, immigration, and national identity. With many of the biggest stars being Muslim, the disputes over which Muslim hip-hop artists are "moderate" or "radical" are also disagreements over what kind of Islam to allow into the public space. This debate is playing out most poignantly in France, the country with the largest Muslim community in Europe, the second-largest hip-hop market in the world, and a place whose traditions of *laïcité* aggressively restrict expressions of religion in the public sphere.

Hamdoulah Ça Va

In the 1980s, French ministers invited American rap pioneers like Afrika Bambaataa and his Zulu Nation to come to Paris to do workshops, hoping to "channel youthful rebellion" into hip-hop's four aesthetics—rapping, DJing, dancing, and graffiti—and the Zulu Nation played a critical role spreading the culture in France. Jack Lang, Minister of Culture, in the 1980s would declare, "Even if in the beginning it [hip-hop] drew inspiration from America, I believe it has found its originality here in France." By the mid-1990s, however, politicians felt they had lost control over rap. Right-wing leaders like Jean-Marie Le Pen warned of this dangerous art form that had originated in Algeria. Hip-hop came to encapsulate France's anxieties about both American domination and Islam. Fear of Americanization, and the introduction of English words and phrases through music, led to the establishment of national quotas to protect the French language. The 1994 Carignon media law required that a minimum of 40 percent of musical programming on radio stations be by French musicians and 20 percent by contemporary French artists. This quota actually encouraged the expansion of French hip-hop, as FM mega-stations shifted their playlists from Anglophone-dominated pop and rock to rap, where they thought the French-language quotas could be met more easily. French record labels began expanding their hip-hop portfolios and sending scouts into the *banlieues,* looking for talent. And, ironically, a law designed to protect "French identity" from Americanization helped promote the French form of an American genre, one that now amplifies the voices of religious and ethnic minorities seen as a domestic threat to national identity.

As part of its cultural policy, the French government still actively promotes hip-hop, at the local and national level, bringing rappers onto the stage of the National Opera of Bordeaux, sponsoring concerts, and funding local institutions in troubled neighborhoods. The French government invests in hip-hop in an effort to recognize marginalized cultures and identities, but also to foster a hip-hop conducive to integration. Yet the question is, what kind of hip-hop best aids integration, and which rappers to invite to the Grand Palais. As sociologist Loïc Lafargue de Grangeneuve observes, "hip-hop policy" in France tries to discover artists and promote them as role models for the *banlieusards,* yet successful hip-hop artists rarely appreciate being held up by politicians as models of successful integration, often because government validation only separates them from their base. Moreover, as he notes, the "instrumentalization" of hip-hop culture risks emptying the genre of its political power and generating a different kind of contestation, between rappers validated by the state and those who are not. Precisely this process is occurring in France, as seen in the interplay between Abd Al Malik and Médine.

Probably the most celebrated French hip-hop artist of the last decade is French-Congolese rapper Abd Al Malik. A former street hustler raised in a housing project outside of Strasbourg, he embraced Islam as a teenager, joining the Islamist Tablighi Jamaat. He achieved some notoriety with his rap group New African Poets before embracing Sufism and shifting from gangsta rap to spoken-word poetry (*le slam*). Malik's poetry, accompanied by riffs of jazz and *chanson française,* speaks of the value of hard work, education, and "spirituality." In his music and his autobiography, *Qu'Allah benisse la France* (May Allah Bless France), Malik extols the republic's values—*liberté, égalité, fraternité*—saying they should be reinvigorated. He believes a Sufi universalism can accommodate the French idea of secular citizenship. Malik has won all kinds of artistic and nonartistic plaudits; he is raved about by elites as a Muslim role model and a symbol of a new multicultural France, *la France plurielle.* In January 2008 the Ministry of Culture awarded Malik the Chevalier des Arts et des Lettres, one of France's most prestigious cultural honors. As hip-hop gains public acceptance and rises to the level of high culture, French cultural and political elites are carefully monitoring the kind of Islam that is being diffused over the rap airwaves, and Malik's Sufi-inflected music embodies the kind of Islamic piety that can be permitted into the French public square. Malik's Sufism is also a useful counter to the political Islam put forth by philosopher Tariq Ramadan (the two have exchanged barbs) and the leftist rap put forth by Kery James and Médine.

If Malik's music makes no political demands, his would-be rival Médine, a popular "undergound" hip-hop artist, hits all the issues that the Sufi poet evades: the social exclusion of nonwhite French youth, conditions in the *banlieues,* and Western depredations in the Third World. Sporting a bald dome and fierce beard—which he calls "the Afro under my jaw"—Médine raps in harsh, halting tones over hard-core instrumentals, about colonialism, Malcolm X, Afghanistan, the Patriot Act, police brutality, and segregation. His videos show graphic images of war, street protests, and waterboarding. His critiques of the French model of integration are blunt and forceful. Médine, unlike Malik, is not particularly vocal about his own religiosity, speaking more about rights for Muslims. Yet the mainstream media has largely ignored him, and some radio stations boycott him, saying he promotes a Muslim *communautarisme.* The more overtly pious Malik is celebrated, in part because he declares his love for the republic, sees Islamic identity as compatible with its values, and, while he refers to the country's colonial past, is not enraged at the French state. Médine's confrontational manner, however, resonates more widely with France's disaffected youth than does Malik's approach. The more praise showered upon the clean-shaven Sufi poet, the less appeal Malik's brand of flow and Islam has with critics speaking of the rise of "lackey" hip-hop and "good Muslim" rappers versus "bad Muslim" rappers.

American embassies have slowly inserted themselves into this delicate dance between European governments and their hip-hop counter-publics. Rap is at the heart of the embassies' outreach to Muslim communities. Farah Pandith, the State Department's special representative to Muslim communities, believes hip-hop can convey a "different narrative" to counter the foreign "violent ideology" that youth are exposed to. One dispatch from the American embassy in London recommends the screening of two films, *New Muslim Cool* and *Deen Tight,* both of which describe how Hispanic and African-American converts discovered Islam through hip-hop. Muslim-American rap artists are invited regularly to perform at embassies in Europe. Local artists are invited as well. The American ambassador to France sponsors hip-hop conferences, inviting rappers to his residence, including in February 2010 the controversial K.ommando Toxik (who at the U.S. embassy performed a tribute to two boys who were killed by the French police in November 2007, an incident that triggered a wave of riots). The embassy's hip-hop diplomacy program, whereby French rappers are flown to the U.S. to spend time in Harlem and meet with artists and civil rights activists, has also raised hackles. One of the artists invited by the State Department was rapper Ekoué Labitey of La Rumeur, one of the groups that Nicolas Sarkozy, as minister of the interior, had sued for libel for their lyrics about the brutality and impunity of French police.

In France, as elsewhere in Western Europe, integration policy tries to balance Sufism and Islamism. Thus French officials backed the creation of the French Council of the Muslim Faith (some of whose leaders have Islamist leanings) as a consultative and representative body, but promote Sufism in popular culture and multicultural dialogue. The American embassy's initiative will often have a different calculus.

Pacifist Salafis

By the late 2000s, American and European policymakers began expressing doubts about the neoconservative policy of supporting Sufism in Europe. Policy advisors began redefining the Muslim Brotherhood as "moderate." In 2006, the CIA issued a report titled "Muslim Brotherhood: Pivotal Actor in European Political Islam," praising the movement's "impressive internal dynamism, organization and media savvy" and stating that "MB groups are likely to be pivotal to the future of political Islam in Europe." And while acknowledging that "more pluralistic Muslims—accuse [the MB] of hindering Muslim social integration," the report argued that "MB-related groups offer an alternative to more violent Islamic movements." This would become the view of the Obama administration, which lifted the travel ban imposed on Tariq Ramadan because of the scholar's familial links to the Brotherhood. In January 2009, U.S. officials invited German Muslim activists to visit the Virginia-based International Institute for Islamic Thought, a group founded in 1983 by Muslim Brotherhood sympathizers (and raided by the FBI in 2002).

The Obama administration's move to reengage with more conservative European Muslim groups would create rifts within the American government. As journalist Ian Johnson writes, efforts to talk to the organizations affiliated with the Muslim Brotherhood "created the strange spectacle of the legal arm of the government trying desperately to prosecute these groups while, at the same time, the diplomatic arm held them up as models of integration." American willingness to engage with Muslim Brotherhood–affiliated groups would rankle European politicians as well. In 2007, for instance, the U.S. Consulate in Munich supported the creation of an Islamic academy in the Bavarian town of Penzberg. The Conservative Party, then in power, opposed the project because the school was tied to Milli Görüş, a Turkish version of the Muslim Brotherhood. One reason German politicians resented the Americans' support of this organization is that by the mid-2000s, German (and Dutch and Belgian) leaders were beginning to see the Sufi movement Gülen as an alternative to both Salafi and Muslim Brotherhood–affiliated groups.

The Gülen movement has a strong presence in Germany's Turkish community and administers two dozen schools in Berlin alone. What strikes most observers is that this Sufi organization has a social-services and urban-renewal mission, usually characteristic of Islamist groups; yet unlike the latter, Gülen does not aim to "Islamicize" or purify society, but to integrate Muslims into the larger society. "We don't go out to convert. All we do is serve—we step in where services are needed," says Nihat Sarier, who heads the Platforme de Paris, a Gülen center in a northern Parisian suburb. "In this neighborhood, we provide Turkish and Arabic translators in public schools to help mediate between parents and teachers. French schools don't provide translators, so we assist the state. The Gülen movement is never in contradiction with the host state." Cash-strapped European states have welcomed Gülen assistance—and some officials are hoping that with the rise of Turkey, this rare Sufi movement, committed to urban development, can counter Salafi separatism. Critics, however, doubt whether this Turkish movement, which claims to be apolitical and pursues a "strategy of silence" when it comes to U.S. foreign policy, can help with counter-radicalization. Gülenists have access to capital and believe firmly in education and civic engagement, but they don't have the anti-establishment, anti-imperial message, and comprehensive self-rectification programs of the Salafis.

By 2008, unlikely coalitions began to emerge between security officials and left-leaning intellectuals calling for an engagement with Salafi groups. Scholars like Dutch anthropologist Martijn de Konning argued that Salafis, in their separatism and rejection of liberalism, are not any different from ultraconservative Christians or Jews; yet while the latter are granted a space in Western societies, the former are continuously persecuted and maligned, which often leads to further radicalization. Moreover, the ascendancy of Salafism is the result of Britain and America's continued partnerships with Saudi Arabia, and continued Saudi dissemination of their ideology. European security officials, in turn, see the (non-jihadi) Salafis' influence and street credibility as an asset in the battle against violent extremism; and it's necessary to grant Salafi activists the political space to speak out forcefully against American and British foreign policy, because that can enhance their credibility in denouncing violence. The lead proponent of this view in Europe has been Robert Lambert, director of Scotland Yard's Muslim Contact Unit, who draws attention to the Salafi community of South London and its alliance with the Metropolitan Police. The positive role played by mosques and Muslim community leaders in protecting property and restraining youth during the London riots of August 2011—which happened to take place during Ramadan—seemed to support the view that Islamist intermediaries can maintain social peace.

Similar thinking has now taken hold across the Atlantic, partly due to the ideas of Quintan Wiktorowicz, an American social scientist who wrote extensively about Salafi movements in the Middle East before becoming a resident scholar at the U.S. embassy in London, studying radicalization among British Muslims. In Britain, Wiktorowicz interviewed hundreds of Islamists, and under his counsel the U.S. embassy launched the "Reverse Radicalism" project, funding myriad NGOs and community centers in an effort to build a "counter-narrative" to jihadi Salafism. Wiktorowicz, as National Public Radio would report, brought into his anti-jihadi coalition individuals that the British found too extreme. In 2010, he returned to America and took a position at the White House as a member of the National Security Council and advisor to John Brennan, the counterterrorism czar. Wiktorowicz would echo Lambert's thinking that there should be a political space for "nonviolent extremism"—that is, Muslim leaders who reject American policies and even liberal values while denouncing jihad against the U.S. In 2011, he introduced a program to counter violent extremism called Community Partnership, which drew on the Prevent program in Britain. But unlike its British inspiration, the American program did not openly back some Muslim institutions against others; rather, the aim was to identify "credible" voices within the American Muslim community and build an "Alliance of Youth Movements" as a bulwark against extremism.

The debate continues over how to deal with Salafism. In the U.S., Salafism nowadays has a tiny presence, but security officials are still trying to groom Salafi dialogue partners, as they may be best placed to teach young Muslims that violence against the U.S. government is not permitted by Islamic law. Law enforcement is cultivating leaders like Yasir Qadhi—who as a young firebrand in the 1990s denounced Sufis and Shia as heretics, but today runs the AlMaghrib Institute in Texas and describes himself as a "pacifist Salafi" who is trying to build a community of "indigenous Salafis" in Texas akin to the orthodox Jewish community of Brooklyn. Qadhi is trying to develop a theology that balances loyalty to Islam with allegiance to America for young diaspora Muslims, who invariably ask, What does Islam command you to do when your people are dying at Western hands? He teaches his students that it is imperative to uphold the law of the land, urging his young followers to vote, pay taxes, but not to serve in the military, given the situation in Iraq and Afghanistan. He denounces "neo-imperial" American policies, but tells students that "offensive jihad"—spreading an Islamic state by force—is permissible only when ordered by a legitimate caliph, or global Muslim ruler, who does not exist today, and that joining militant groups at war with America constitutes treachery and a breach of contract with the American government, which allows Muslims to worship freely. Qadhi is emerging as an example of what American officials describe as a "moderate Salafi." This young Muslim-American cleric encourages political participation but still retains Salafism's distinct language of self-rectification and quietism: he is fond of saying that change cannot come from militancy but "begins in the heart and in the home, and it shall eventually reach the streets and shake the foundations of government."

Partly to influence the debates taking place among Muslim-American youth, in July 2013, Congress amended the 1948 Smith-Mundt Act, long known as the "anti-propaganda law." The Smith-Mundt Act was passed at a time when Congress suspected that the State Department was staffed with Communists, and prohibited websites and media outlets financed by the U.S. government—like the Arabic-language TV channel Al-Hurra—from broadcasting at home to prevent the government from aiming propaganda at its own citizens. The Smith-Mundt Modernization Act repealed this prohibition, allowing government information produced for foreign audiences to be disseminated within the United States; thus programming produced by Voice of America, Radio Free Europe/Radio Liberty, the Middle East Broadcasting Networks, and other entities controlled by the Broadcasting Board of Governors (BBG) can now be carried by local radio stations.

Scholars and journalists quickly warned of the perils of domestic propaganda. And the *Washington Post* broke a story of a "counter-propaganda" program run by the Pentagon that targeted a Somali-American journalist in Minneapolis by flooding his website, United Somalia, with comments by readers opposed to Al-Shabaab. "The Pentagon is legally prohibited from conducting psychological operations at home or targeting U.S. audiences with propaganda, except during 'domestic emergencies,'" explained the *Post,* adding that Defense Department rules also forbid the military from using psychological operations to "target U.S. citizens at any time, in any location globally, or under any circumstances." The defenders of the Smith-Mundt amendment, in turn, would argue that their law only covers information programs produced by the State Department and the BBG, not the Pentagon or the CIA, who are subject to different laws. To Muslim-American leaders, this was not reassuring.

When Obama assumed office in 2008, cultural diplomacy initiatives toward Muslim communities continued, but the Bush administration's aggressive attempts to mobilize Sufism and provoke an "Islamic Reformation" were shelved. Yet by mid-2013, perhaps in response to the sectarianism unleashed by the Arab revolts, the U.S. government again began taking a more active role in shaping Islamic discourse. Not only was the "anti-propaganda law" amended, but in July 2013 the State Department created an Office of Faith-Based Community Initiatives to engage with "religious actors," and then in September—days after Al-Shabaab launched a horrific attack on the Westgate shopping mall in Nairobi—the U.S. and Turkey announced the creation of a $200 million program to battle extremism, called the Global Fund for Community Engagement and Resilience. Critics from London to Islamabad promptly expressed concern that through "engagement" the U.S. government would be taking sides in religious debates, defining who is "moderate," and funding groups that it would not support at home.

In Europe, the upheavals in North Africa, the Syrian civil war, and the pushback from Saudi Arabia have emboldened Salafis in Belgium, France, and Germany. "The Salafis have completely overtaken the Muslim Brotherhood in Europe," says Michael Privot of the Brussels-based European Network Against Racism. "The center is weak—and that is a problem. In the 1960s, the Muslim Brotherhood was the only alternative, and the Brothers worked with Salafis for years, but then lost control of them. The Saudis had their own Marshall Plan for Europe, and they won all the cultural battles, and today, in 2013, they're still winning."

In the UK, the alliance that had formed in the mid-2000s between liberal Muslims, secular feminists, and conservatives opposed to multiculturalism, who think Salafism—quietist or activist—undermines social cohesion and impedes the integration of Muslims, mobilized again, irked that the U.S., which had cracked down on Salafism at home, was now urging engagement with Islamists in Europe. In June 2011, after a prolonged political battle within the British cabinet between Nick Clegg, the Liberal deputy prime minister who saw nonviolent extremism as a bulwark against extremism, and Prime Minister David Cameron, who argued that ideologies of nonviolent extremism—like Salafism—pave the way for violent extremism, the new Prevent program was unveiled, reflecting the prime minister's view. The new Prevent defined "extremism" broadly to include groups considered nonviolent but whose views fail to "reflect British mainstream values." The government then proceeded to cut funding to youth programs such as the Brixton-based Street UK because of their affiliation with Salafi mosques. Critics warned that this new Muslim policy would only drive extremist groups underground. Indeed, a few days after the release of the new Prevent program, yellow posters began appearing in parts of East London, plastered on lampposts and bus stops: "You are entering a sharia-controlled zone—Islamic rules enforced." "No Gambling." "No Music or Concerts." "No Porn or Prostitution." "No Drugs or Smoking." "No Alcohol."

"We Shall Overcome"

American embassies were implementing "diversity management" programs just as David Cameron, Nicolas Sarkozy, and Angela Merkel had declared multiculturalism was dead. Referring to a cultural event she organized in Denmark, Deborah Maclean, a public-diplomacy officer at the U.S. embassy in Copenhagen, explains: "We wanted to encourage these youths to realize that it is okay to be different." European officials take offense at the implicit criticism that Europeans cannot deal with difference, and that they are overwhelmed by an urban crisis that has never reached American proportions. American politicians can now take tours of "sensitive" European neighborhoods. After one such junket, in May 2008, to the northern Parisian suburb of Seine-Saint-Denis, congressional aide Kevin Casey laughed and told the French press, "You think this is the ghetto, come see the Bronx—I'm going to take photos of this to show my friends."

French journalists have expressed anger at this exercise of American "soft power," saying that the "head hunting" for future Muslim leaders constituted "direct interference" that was infringing on French sovereignty and undermining the authority of French institutions. In April 2010, when the American ambassador Charles Rivkin, a former Hollywood executive, brought actor Samuel L. Jackson to visit a community center in the *banlieue* of Bondy in northern Paris, and Jackson, addressing a group of youths, compared their struggle to the hardships of his childhood in segregated Tennessee, French media resented the comparison. Another awkward moment came at the unveiling of a painted mural for Martin Luther King at the Collège Martin Luther King in Villiers-le-Bel, another restive Parisian suburb, when a group of African and Arab children stood around Ambassador Rivkin and sang "We Shall Overcome."

The State Department's outreach to Muslims, conceived in response to Europe's "nativist surge," seems to be further inflaming the right, who see Washington's rap-infused initiatives as infringing on their sovereignty and are even more chary of their Muslim compatriots' allegiance. In April 2008, the daily *Le Parisien* ran a front-page story on alleged CIA initiatives in the *banlieues*. Today headlines are more likely to refer to the NSA's activities. If European Muslims are often accused of being loyal to their land of origin or to some transnational Islamic movement, now they are suspected of being a fifth column of the United States (just as religious minorities in the Muslim world are). French right-wingers speak of a Muslim "Trojan horse," comparing the State Department–sponsored trips taken by young French Muslims to the U.S. to the Soviet-sponsored trips of the 1920s and 1930s that took French intellectuals to Russia to experience the benefits of socialism firsthand. Overheated as such rhetoric may be, it seems true that the U.S. counterinsurgency initiatives in

Iraq, Somalia, and Afghanistan now have a kinder, gentler corollary directed at Western Europe's urban periphery.

The irony is that despite the uproar from journalists and politicians, the Muslim youth who are the targets of these initiatives are quite appreciative. If the aim of the "minority programs" was to create positive impressions of the U.S., the effort is working. European-Muslim activists appreciated the brutal candor of the Wikileaks cables. In France, in particular, perhaps because of the country's contentious alliance with the U.S., positive opinion of the U.S. has risen sharply since 2008. And young Muslims are aware of the delicate politics involved in accepting American offers. Widad Ketfi, a twenty-seven-year-old blogger who participated in an embassy-sponsored program, told the *Times* that she knows she was targeted by the U.S. embassy because of her Algerian-Muslim background, but added, "What bothers me is being the target of the French state." And while they resent the NSA surveillance and importation of American policing methods to European cities, Muslim activists and entrepreneurs think their relationship with the American embassy can help leverage better concessions from their governments. "We can ask the Belgian government for assistance, no response," says Ibrahim Akrouh, a lawyer with the Brussels-based Movement Against Racism, Anti-Semitism and Xenophobia (MRAX). "But if you get help from the U.S. embassy, then Belgian officials will respond and offer support."

Given all the governments and social movements now offering assistance in the European urban periphery, deciding whether and from whom to accept funds involves some risk. Since the financial collapse of 2008, the American embassies and the Gulf states have emerged as the funders of last resort. In 2012, Qatar decided to invest fifty million euros in the French *banlieues* to promote entrepreneurship; but after an outcry from the National Front, whose leaders said the money was intended to "Islamize" French youth, the Qataris decided to scatter the funds to include Paris proper and not just the periphery. Accepting money from the American embassy can lead to a loss of credibility as well. "If you take money from the U.S. embassy, then you can't show up at a political rally protesting American foreign policy—people will call you an American puppet," says Sami

Waqas, who runs a youth center in Berlin. "But then again, if the U.S. embassy thinks you're moderate, then the local authorities will think you're moderate and leave you alone."

Others cringe at the label "moderate." For many Muslims, the term is a top-down marker that basically means compliant, and movements that have an appeal among Muslim youth know they can lose their credibility as soon as they are embraced by local authorities or by a particular embassy. In January 2011, before the second Prevent program was released, British commentators were debating "moderate Salafism," and the *Guardian* produced a short documentary about how British Salafis monitor extremism in their midst. Abdulrahman, a soft-spoken Salafi leader from Luton, turns indignant when the interviewer praises his moderation. "Why are you calling me a moderate Muslim *now*?" he says. "Is that name not just temporary until we do your daily work for you, and remove the evil of al-Muhajirun [a militant group banned by the British government]? And then you're going to go back to calling us what? Extremists? Fundamentalist Muslims?" In a very respectful tone, he asks, "Why are you now labeling us moderate Muslims? 'Cause I still believe in the death sentence, I still believe homosexuality is incorrect morally, I still believe that the hand should be removed for the one who steals. So am I really a moderate Muslim, *really*?"

10

The X Factor

In April 2010, the State Department sent a Brooklyn-based rap group named Chen Lo and the Liberation Family to perform in Damascus. Following the show, Secretary of State Hillary Clinton was asked by CBS News about American diplomacy's recent embrace of hip-hop. "Hip-hop is America," she said, noting that rap and other musical forms could help "rebuild the image" of the United States. "You know it may be a little bit hopeful, because I can't point to a change in Syrian policy because Chen Lo and the Liberation Family showed up. But I think we have to use every tool at our disposal."

Unlike the European states that promote certain kinds of hip-hop over others, the U.S. government's approach to hip-hop at home is largely laissez-faire. But at the international level, U.S. hip-hop diplomacy is more interventionist, using hip-hop not only to rebrand America's image, but also to promote democracy and economic development and to alter the behavior of other countries. "You have to bet at the end of the day, people will choose freedom over tyranny if they're given a choice," Clinton observed, stating that cultural diplomacy is a complex game of "multidimensional chess." "Hip-hop can be a chess piece?" asked the interviewer. "Absolutely!" responded the secretary of state.

In the last decade, as hip-hop has emerged as a political force among youth, regimes have intervened to promote some substyles and sideline others in an effort to press-gang the genre to disparate political ends. In 2002, the Cuban Ministry of Culture founded the Cuban Rap Agency, along with the magazine *Movimiento,* to create a revolutionary hip-hop sound that would give voice to the "downtrodden of the world," and to make sure tracks suspected of "ideological deviation" were given no airtime. In Venezuela, Hugo Chávez funded hip-hop schools around the country and invited Bolivian *raperos* onto his Sunday television show, *Aló, Presidente.* In the U.S., Michael Steele, the first African-American to serve as chairman of the Republican National Committee, tried to give the Republican Party a "hip-hop makeover" to bring its ideas to "urban-suburban hip-hop settings." The U.S. Army, in partnership with the magazine *The Source,* has used hip-hop culture in its "Taking It to the Streets" campaign to recruit "urban teens." But it is in the War on Terror and in Western states' dealings with Muslim-majority states and Muslims in Europe that government mobilization of hip-hop is most noticeable. While European states are using the genre to integrate their Muslim populations, the U.S. has made hip-hop part of its outreach to the Muslim world. The very music blamed for a range of social ills at home—violence, misogyny, consumerism, academic underperformance—is being deployed abroad in the hopes of making America safer and better liked.

The debate about hip-hop and U.S. foreign policy came to the fore in 2011, when journalists were impressed by the role of rap in the Arab revolts. In early January of that year, as mass protests spread through Tunisia, the police burst into the home of Hamada Ben Amor, the twenty-two-year-old rapper known as El Général. President Ben Ali's regime had long harassed rappers, banning Mohamed Jendoubi—aka Psycho-M—an artist with Islamist sympathies, from the airwaves. But El Général's music had slipped past the censors. His track "Mr. President" ("Rais Lebled")—an open letter to Ben Ali excoriating Tunisia's lack of freedom and anti-veiling laws—had become the unofficial anthem of the revolt. Upon his arrest, Ben Amor was locked up for three days; the authorities banned the song, blacked out his MySpace page, and cut off his cell phone service. But Al Jazeera had already snatched up the recording: it would resound from Tahrir Square in Egypt to Pearl Circle in Bahrain.

French media would henceforth speak of "*le printemps des rappeurs.*" *Time* magazine gave the title "Rage, Rap and Revolution" to its cover story on the "Arab youthquake." The magazine would go on to name Hamada Ben Amor one of "The 100 Most Influential People of 2011," ranking him higher than President Barack Obama. And National Public Radio would claim that "Tupac encouraged the Arab Spring." It is true that, as security forces rampaged through the streets, artists in Tunis, Cairo, Benghazi, and Homs were writing lyrics and cobbling together protest footage, beats, and rhymes, which they then uploaded to proxy servers. The impromptu songs were then played at gatherings and solidarity marches in London, New York, and Washington; exile opposition groups and Muslim communities responded with musical tributes. Five Muslim-American rappers, fronted by Omar Offendum, uploaded the track "#jan25" in support of the Tahrir Square protesters on February 6; the song received forty thousand hits on YouTube overnight. "I heard 'em say the revolution won't be televised," Omar led off. "Al Jazeera proved 'em wrong; Twitter has 'em paralyzed." The rap loop between protesters and the Muslim diaspora galvanized youth on both sides of the Atlantic, but the role of music should not be exaggerated. Hip-hop did not cause the revolts any more than Twitter or Facebook did. The countries in the region with the most vibrant hip-hop scenes, Morocco and Algeria, have not seen revolts. And the cross-border spread of popular movements is not a new phenomenon in the Arab world; the uprisings of 1919, which engulfed Egypt, Libya, and Tunisia, occurred long before the advent of the Internet, social media, or rap.

The revolts in fact seemed to revive and interact with earlier eras of upheaval. The uprisings in North Africa, the Occupy movement in Europe, the standoff between the U.S. and Iran sparked an interest in the 1960s and decolonization, resurrecting figures like Che Guevara and Ali Shariati. This interest is partly because of the parallels between the "Arab Cold War" of the 1960s, which pitted Nasser's Egypt and his socialist allies against Saudi Arabia and the conservative monarchies backed by the U.S., and the current "Middle Eastern Cold War" between Saudi Arabia and her allies (American-backed monarchies) and Iran and her allies (Syria, Iraq, and Hizbullah). The rivalries of the 1960s between Egypt and Saudi Arabia, and the black freedom struggles in the U.S., would together shape Muslim communities in the West in ways that continue to resonate. Policymakers in Europe and the U.S. are noting parallels and connections between the racial militancy of 1960s America and the Islamist militancy of today. And American officials have come to believe that a cultural diplomacy centered around race, diversity, and the civil rights movement can win over Muslim youth.

The marshalling of black cultural protest—whether hip-hop or the words of Malcolm X—to counter Islamist militancy is, however, deeply ironic. Half a century ago, the U.S., wary of how racial militancy could make common cause with Third World nationalism, supported conservative Sunni movements as a counterweight to the more radical black nationalist and left-wing Islam put forth by Elijah Muhammad and Malcolm X. Today, as various interstate and intra-Muslim rivalries play out in the West, African-American Islam is again part of the ideological competition—except today, American officials are deploying black history to counter Islamism.

Sound Diplomacy

In 2005 the State Department's Advisory Committee on Cultural Diplomacy released a report that said: "Cultural diplomacy is the linchpin of public diplomacy; for it is in cultural activities that a nation's idea of itself is best represented. And cultural diplomacy can enhance our national security in subtle, wide-ranging, and sustainable ways . . . For the values embedded in our artistic and intellectual traditions form a bulwark against the forces of darkness." That same year the jazz diplomacy initiative of the Cold War was revived in a program called Rhythm Road, a partnership of the State Department, Jazz at Lincoln Center, the Brooklyn Academy of Music, and the Kennedy Center. Karen Hughes, the undersecretary of state for public diplomacy, introduced the program after being appointed by President George W. Bush in the wake of Abu Ghraib and the resurgence of the Taliban. Since its inception, Rhythm Road has included jazz and "urban/hip-hop" music, recognizing hip-hop's role as a "global musical language." The program today also invites bands of other genres to audition—bluegrass, country, gospel, Cajun, zydeco, folk—but the initiative still relies heavily on black music.

In 2005, the State Department began sending "hip-hop envoys"—rappers, dancers, DJs—to perform and speak in different parts of Africa, Asia, and the Middle East. Toni Blackman, a poet, was the first such "hip-hop ambassador." Other groups that have been sent are Chen Lo and the Liberation Family, Legacy, the Reminders, Native Deen, and Kokayi. The tours have covered the broad arc of the Muslim world, with performances taking place in Senegal and Côte d'Ivoire, across North Africa, the Levant, and Arabia, and extending to Mongolia, Pakistan, and Indonesia. The artists stage performances and hold workshops; the hip-hop ambassadors who are Muslim talk to local media about being Muslim in America and try "to correct the prevalent misperception that Muslims in the United States are oppressed."

Hip-hop, in short, is the music of choice for "perception management" and "strategic communication" with young Muslims, because of American hip-hop's long-standing relationship to Islam. Neither hard rock or heavy metal has the same appeal. In Muslim-majority states, heavy-metal artists, with their long hair and black clothes, are often viewed with suspicion, accused of "devil worship" and of eating cats. People have become even more distrustful of this genre in the last decade, as it was used on detainees in Iraq, Afghanistan, and Guantanamo. In *Sound Targets,* Jonathan Pieslak explains how metal was used in interrogations in Iraq not only because the relentless "guitar distortions" could cause "sensory deprivation," but also because American officers knew that Iraqis found the genre "culturally offensive," "satanic," and "anti-God." The sound of "industrial-style guitars" also became associated with military patrols in Iraq and Afghanistan, where young soldiers would drive around in Humvees blaring rock music. Iraqi insurgents, in turn, began circulating homemade videos of American soldiers engaged in acts of violence to the accompaniment of this loud music in order to recruit people into the insurgency. The scholarship on music and interrogation in Iraq and Afghanistan rarely mentions hip-hop. With the exception of Eminem's track "White America," the songs used to break detainees were almost exclusively hard rock and metal, with tracks like Slayer's "Angel of Death," Drowning Pool's "Let the Bodies Hit the Floor," and Deicide's "Fuck Your God" topping the interrogator's playlist. Hip-hop is used more for cultural persuasion.

The choice of jazz during the Cold War was not simply due to its international appeal. As Penny Von Eschen suggests, in the 1950s the State Department felt African-American culture could convey "a sense of *shared suffering,* as well as the conviction that equality could be gained under the American political system" to peoples who had suffered European colonialism. Similar thinking underpins the "hip-hop diplomacy" initiative. The choice of hip-hop, widely derided as libertine, to represent the U.S. in a rather conservative part of the world is not self-evident. Yet the State Department planners who are calling for "the leveraging of hip-hop" in U.S. foreign policy stress "the importance of Islam to the roots of hip-hop in America." A Brookings report authored by the program's architects notes that hip-hop resonates with marginalized Muslim youth worldwide; from the Parisian *banlieues* to Palestine to Kyrgyzstan, hip-hop expresses a "pain" that transcends language barriers. Moreover, note the authors, hip-hop's pioneers were inner-city Muslims who "carry on an African-American Muslim tradition of protest against authority, most powerfully represented by Malcolm X." The report concludes by calling for a "greater exploitation of this natural connector to the Muslim world."

The hip-hop-ambassadors program fits into a larger effort to showcase America's model integration of Muslims, to demonstrate, as the State Department publication *Muslims in America* (2009) says, that Muslim-Americans have the same freedoms and privileges as other Americans. In late 2002, the State Department began producing public-service announcements in which Muslim-American professionals spoke of the religious tolerance in America; these were televised in Muslim-majority countries. The aim was to convey that America was not at war with Islam, but with "terror," by showing how the Muslim-American population was a rich mosaic and that post–September 11 "fears and suspicions" had dipped and integration was proceeding. "Distinctions that possibly loomed larger elsewhere are instead in America 'diluted' in the deep pool of pluralism that characterizes American society," the book posited. *Muslims in America* also includes a small poster displaying African-American entertainers who are Muslim: comedian Dave Chappelle; rappers Q-Tip, RZA of Wu-Tang Clan, and Mos Def; pianist Ahmad Jamal; and Ronald Bell of Kool & the Gang.

The deployment of African-American Muslims to show how economically and politically integrated Muslims are in America is ironic on many levels. African-Americans constitute the least affluent segment of the American Muslim community, and are geographically the most segregated, with significant numbers concentrated in inner-city areas and prisons. This community—at least since Mike Wallace's 1959 documentary *The Hate That Hate Produced*—has also been portrayed as extremist, separatist, illiberal, and "not really Muslim." Yet over the last decade, diplomats have begun to celebrate the "indigenous" African-American Muslim, perhaps in a realization that as with the jazz tours, what is suspect at home can yield dividends abroad and help integration at home. When the jazz artists were dispatched, State Department officials at home scrambled to prevent images of the tours from reaching southern segregationists. In this task, ironically, they were aided by the 1948 Smith-Mundt Act, which barred the output of the U.S. Information Agency from distribution within the United States.

Perception Management

The divergent attitudes of State Department liberals and southern nativists toward Islam rose to the fore during the summer of the 2010 anti-mosque controversy. Since September 2001, Muslim activists had focused their political energy on challenging state repression—policies of deportation, rendition, profiling, wiretapping—but the anti-mosque campaign, spearheaded by the Tea Party, led them to shift gears. They launched a campaign to raise awareness about the Muslim presence in America, starting with the history of Muslim slaves brought to the New World from the 1500s onward. Community leaders told of how George Washington had two African Muslim women—a mother and a daughter, "Fatima" and "Little Fatimer"—at his Mount Vernon property. At the multiple rallies (and counter-rallies) at Ground Zero, a ubiquitous sign on the "pro-mosque" side showed a picture of an African in a white robe next to a sketch of a slave ship, under large red letters, "Islam Has Been in New York for 400 Years." Activists pointed to the African Burial Ground, discovered in 1991 on Broadway and Reade Street, a few blocks from the proposed mosque site, and recounted the story of Mahommah Baquaqua, a sailor and slave who in 1847 escaped from a Brazilian ship docked in lower Manhattan and went on to write *The Biography of Mahommah Gardo Baquaqua,* an important slave narrative that begins with a description of his Muslim upbringing in Bergoo (now northern Benin).

In the midst of the mosque furor, Imam Feisal Abdul Rauf, then the leader of the Park 51 Center, was sent on a diplomatic tour of the Persian Gulf to, in the White House's words, bring "a moderate perspective to foreign audiences on what it's like to be a practicing Muslim in the United States." Rauf had been recruited in February 2006 by Karen Hughes, public diplomacy czar, and had traveled widely in the Middle East and Asia, presenting conservative groups like Hizb ut-Tahrir with his Sufi approach to Islam and arguing that American liberalism accords with the fundamentals of sharia. Rauf, like other Muslim goodwill ambassadors, believed that patriotically representing the U.S. overseas could dampen anti-Muslim sentiment at home and create political support for his various projects for New York. (Despite his diplomatic services, when the time came, Hughes asked the imam to move the mosque as a "sign of unity" and "courtesy.") The imam's public diplomacy—and his mosque project—divided the Muslim-American community, often along North-South lines, with many disliking his overseas defense of American liberalism at a time of extreme political duress partly fomented by his project. And New York governor David Paterson's statement in support of Rauf's mosque didn't help. "This group who has put this mosque together, they are known as the Sufi Muslims. This is not like the Shiites," Paterson told CBS television. "They're almost like a hybrid, almost Westernized." Muslims in the South resented Rauf's insistence on building a center close to Ground Zero when they, below the Mason-Dixon line, were catching the brunt of the backlash. "Dear Muslims: Imam Rauf wants you to know you have it easy. While he's on State Department tours, your mosques are infiltrated. Suck it up!" tweeted Remi Kanazi, a young poet.

While Imam Rauf was touring the Gulf, hip-hop envoys were visiting other parts of the Islamic world. In July 2010, State Department–sponsored break dancers were doing shows in Morocco and Algeria; in September, rappers 50 Tyson and Kumasi were performing in Indonesia. Along with these tours, films about Islam and hip-hop in America were screened at U.S. embassies in Asia and Africa. The film *New Muslim Cool,* about a Puerto Rican rapper who embraces Islam, popped up at U.S. embassies in Jordan, Iraq, Angola, and Bahrain. Another film shown in Senegal, Gambia, and Bangladesh was *Prince Among Slaves,* which tells the extraordinary story of Ibrahima Abdul Rahman, who was born in 1762 to the king of Timbo, ruler of the Fulbe people in today's Guinea. The prince rose to take command of his father's army when, at the age of twenty-six, he was captured in war and taken across the Atlantic, ending up on an auction block in Natchez, Mississippi. His royal background and literacy would lead to his manumission in 1828, whereupon he traveled north and spoke to large audiences about his conversion to Christianity, writing in Arabic script for fascinated northerners to raise money to buy his children's freedom. In addition to films, the actual narratives of Muslims enslaved in America—pieces of parchment with Arabic script—are exhibited at diplomatic outposts. American embassies in Nigeria and Qatar have displayed the thirteen-page Arabic text written by Bilali Muhammad in 1829, a leather-bound collection of sheets in North African Arabic script, while the U.S. mission at the UN has showcased Omar ibn Said's text from 1836.

Ironically, the last time these writings drew government attention was in the mid-nineteenth century, when the young American republic sought to make inroads into the Muslim parts of Africa, specifically the Barbary Coast and the area that would become Liberia. Ibrahima, the aforementioned Fulbe prince, would gain his freedom because President John Quincy Adams, Secretary of State Henry Clay, and the American Colonization Society (which took up his cause) thought his manumission could further U.S. interests. Clay believed that Ibrahima, once freed, could be "returned" to Morocco (his Arabic script apparently betrayed North African influence) and used as a bargaining chip to release Americans held captive by Sultan 'Abd al-Rahman II.

The American Colonization Society's interest in Muslim slaves is fascinating. This organization, founded by Clay in 1817 to "repatriate" African slaves to Liberia, saw Muslim slaves with their Arabic literacy as a valuable tool for opening up West Africa to American economic and religious interests. America's African Muslims were seen as natural intermediaries in dealings with the Muslims and pagans of the West African coast; the Muslim slaves had (at least nominally) embraced Christianity, were indebted to the U.S. for their newfound freedom, and could help spread the gospel and American civilization in Africa. As the repatriation movement grew in influence, literate Muslim slaves and their narratives gained greater political significance in the U.S. Some would feign conversion to Christianity, and the American Colonization Society (or the Royal Africa Company of England) would send them to Liberia and Sierra Leone bearing Arabic-language Bibles.

Today, as the U.S. is trying to consolidate its position across the Saharan belt, the African-American Muslim is again emerging as an intermediary. It is curious that Washington would adopt this policy at a time when numerous Americans suspect that the country's first black president is secretly Muslim and join campaigns to ban sharia in American cities and to restrict the building of mosques and Islamic schools. As with the jazz tours of the 1950s, the conservatives warning of "creeping sharia" today would probably be displeased to know that the State Department is exhibiting Arabic slave narratives to show that Muslims have existed in America since the sixteenth century, that photographs of the Wu-Tang Clan grace State Department brochures, or that American embassy events are highlighting Obama's Muslim background. And the idea of the African-American as intermediary with the Muslim world is not limited to public diplomacy. "African-Americans are emerging in popular culture as leaders of the American nation and empire," writes the literary critic Moustafa Bayoumi, noting a subgenre of films—*The Siege, The Kingdom, The Traitor,* and the HBO series *Sleeper Cell*—that portray "blacks at the helm" of a liberal American imperium, people who, because of their past suffering, can achieve a level of human communication with Arabs and Muslims that whites cannot.

European states have also started sending their Muslim hip-hop artists to perform in Muslim-majority countries. The British Council twice dispatched the hip-hop duo Mecca2Medina to perform in northern Nigeria, an area of high sectarian tensions. Following a 2007 performance in Kano, one of twelve Nigerian states under sharia law, the head of the morality police who scour the streets for "un-Islamic" behavior publicly praised the rap duo for being Western yet pious. The British Council also began organizing hip-hop workshops in Tripoli and promoting Electric Steps, "Libya's only hip-hop band," as a way to encourage political reform in that country. Since 2011, the European Union has sponsored the annual Assalamalekoum Festival in Nouakchott, Mauritania, hoping that a "hip-hop music project" can help stabilize the Sahel region.

America vs. the Narrative

The American debate on extremism and jihadist violence falls roughly into two schools of thought. In one camp is a coalition of realists, leftists, and postcolonialists who think extremism is a response to an American policy or set of policies, and on the other side are those—neoconservatives and liberal internationalists—who think Islamist violence grows out of ideology and narratives, and not just opposition to American action. "After all," explains Fareed Zakaria, a proponent of this latter view, "U.S. foreign policy over the years has victimized many countries in Latin America and killed millions of Vietnamese, and yet you did not see terrorism emanating from those quarters." And if the realists advocate a less interventionist foreign policy—"offshore balancing"—as a way to prevent extremism, the neoconservatives, who think the roots of violence are cultural or theological, are more likely to advocate military intervention, and spend a great deal of effort studying Muslim scripture and cultural traditions, to find a way to disrupt the "narrative." And herein lie the roots of the new public diplomacy—Public Diplomacy 2.0—that deploys music, art, social networks, and the discourse of diversity.

When musicians—among them hip-hoppers—emerged as dissident voices during the Arab revolts, with embattled leaders like Syria's Bashar al-Assad backing "pro-stability rap" and cracking down on antigovernment artists, Western media zoomed in on hip-hop, which they saw, along with social media, as a positive, moderating force, central to the "counter-jihad" movement, and a sign that Muslim kids had embraced "our" culture. In *Rock the Casbah: Rage and Rebellion Across the Islamic World,* journalist Robin Wright would, ignoring a range of musical forms engaged in protest over the last decade, declare that "hip-hop was the first voice of political opposition, even before the street protests that erupted in 2011." Others argued that State Department hip-hop initiatives from the mid-2000s had "sowed the seeds of the Arab Spring." At a panel on hip-hop and world politics at the American Mission to the UN in February 2012, Ambassador Susan Rice spoke passionately about how she had visited hip-hop studios in Libya at the height of the civil war.

The diplomats who had advocated "21st-century statecraft" and recruited Google, Twitter, and Yahoo! to provide activists with training also felt vindicated by the Arab Spring. Jared Cohen, formerly at the State Department, currently leading antiradicalization efforts at Google Ideas, is now calling for new "content-rich alternatives" to distract young Somalis and Yemenis from extremism, a digital analogue to "dropping propaganda flyers from an airplane." The deployment of American culture and technology was seen as a success, and more studies appeared explaining how hip-hop could be further used for cultural persuasion and "countermessaging." A few months after the toppling of President Ben Ali, the American embassy in Tunis brought a group of Los Angeles–based rappers to the North African capital, and, in collaboration with local artists, produced a track in honor of Mohamed Bouazizi called "A Young Man's Spark."

European observers were less sanguine about hip-hop. "Political Islam is not going to dissolve in hip-hop!" wrote French scholar and blogger Yves Gonzalez-Quijano with exasperation. European policymakers were concerned the revolts would stir unrest in their cities—by mid-2011, self-immolations had occurred in Amsterdam, Palermo, and Marseille—and feared a flood of refugees. Leaders, it seemed, were as concerned with the flow of peoples across the Mediterranean as they were with musical flows. Twice in 2011, to much protest, BBC Radio 1Xtra would tune out the words "Free Palestine" in a song by the rapper Mic Righteous, saying it was "to ensure that impartiality was maintained." When riots erupted in London in August 2011, British commentators would place the blame squarely on rap and social media (BlackBerry Messenger in particular), but not Islam, with observers saying that it was Muslim tradition—specifically Ramadan—that had kept Muslim youth at home during the unrest.

I Am Malcolm X

In August 2011, a bookstore owner in Cairo told the newspaper *Al-Akhbar* that since Mubarak's downfall, Che Guevara's and Malcolm X's memoirs had become best sellers. The Arab revolts revived the 1960s. As thousands occupied Cairo's Tahrir Square in January of that year, Arabic-language radio stations from Brussels to Doha were playing hours of Umm Kulthum's classics, interrupted only to take phone calls from emotional listeners. "I am the people, I do not know the impossible," sang the Egyptian cultural icon, her quivering voice beckoning and reminding. "I will not be satisfied with anything less than eternity." The heady days of decolonization had returned, it seemed: youth rising up against an oppressive Western-backed state system. Muslim youth would turn to the likes of Che Guevara, Frantz

Fanon, Sayed Darwish, Ali Shariati, and Malcolm X—now immortalized on YouTube—for guidance. What would Ali Shariati think of the Sunni-Shia conflict? What would Malcolm X think of the Muslim Brotherhood coming to power? American diplomacy moved quickly to tap the revolutionary mood. In May 2011, the U.S. embassy in Tunis organized a public-speaking competition for youth who want to be like Malcolm X, "Are you the next Martin Luther King? The next Gamal Abdel Nasser? The next Malcolm X? Can you inspire and move people with your words?" Even the State Department–produced rap tributes to the Arab revolts had a distinct 1960s, pan-African pitch, "City of Compton, revolutionary moderate / They Marcus like Garvey / Bob Marley, Sékou Touré, Patrice Lumumba, Malik Shabazz, Kwame Nkrumah / Revolution free me like Mohamed Bouazizi!"

One of the more intriguing aspects of the new public diplomacy is the recurring reference to Malcolm X as a potentially radicalizing (and counter-radicalizing) influence. Government interest in the Nation of Islam leader was prompted by the case of John Walker Lindh, a young American who in October 2001 was found behind enemy lines in Afghanistan. Just how did this middle-class boy from Marin County end up joining the Taliban? His online postings, experts argued, offered a clue; in hip-hop chat rooms, Lindh often posed as black, adopting the name Doodoo or Professor J. "Our blackness does not make white people hate us, it is THEIR racism that causes hate," he once wrote. Experts would trace the young man's "journey" to radicalism to the age of twelve, when his mother took him to see Spike Lee's film *Malcolm X,* after which he read Alex Haley's *Autobiography of Malcolm X* and began listening to hip-hop. American and European officials would thereafter note the centrality of Malcolm X to Muslim youth politics, and argue that a "moderate" understanding of the "Malcolm X narrative" is critical to protecting "at-risk" Muslim youth.

Malcolm X represents different things to Muslim youth. If Islam is the unofficial religion of hip-hop culture, Malcolm X is the prophet or at the very least the patron saint; his speeches are quoted, his dress and demeanor imitated. If hip-hop celebrates the rise of the outsider, the Nation of Islam activist's awesome trajectory from street hustler to the global arena, rising above any and all states, freed from the shackles of patriotism and national allegiance, fearing only Allah, is riveting to young Muslims (and non-Muslims) chafing under state domination in the favela, the *banlieue,* or their appendage institution the prison. It is in Malcolm X's person that the forces of Islam and black history intersect, his immutability evidence of their vitality and continued spread. And as with Karl Marx and the field of Marxology—where different articles by the German philosopher have spawned myriad schools of thought—the realm of "Malcolmology" boasts a range of interpretations of Malcolm X based on a particular speech, interview, or moment in his life. There are scholars who stress the early separatist Malcolm X and his promise to gain rights "by any means necessary"; others emphasize Malcolm X the Sunni universalist, following his racial epiphany in Mecca. Young Muslims are drawn to Malcolm X's radical internationalism and embrace of a political identity that transcends the nation-state; older integrationist Muslims argue that toward the end of his life—when he delivered his speech "The Ballot or the Bullet," Malcolm had come to terms with America and the nation-state. Thus, scholar Sherman Jackson, worried by the anti-state attitudes among Muslim youth, contends, "Were Malcolm alive today, he would be able, in good conscience, as a practicing Sunni Muslim, to abandon his earlier rejectionism and proclaim without hesitation, "Yes, I am an American," adding that the African-American leader "would have come full circle from . . . from Malcolm X to 'Ibn Taym-X.' "

American and British officials took particular notice of a video that Al Qaeda released shortly after Obama's electoral victory in 2008, celebrating Malcolm X's militancy and describing the president-elect as a "house slave." American embassies began sponsoring events during Black History Month and on Malcolm X's birthday, celebrating Obama and post-hajj Malcolm X together, accenting their meteoric rise to international eminence and relationship to Islam, stressing that it was Malcolm X, a "symbol of a vital, open America," who made Obama possible. The British government also began to fund Muslim organizations that had a "moderate" understanding of Malcolm X, focusing on his post-hajj transformation. Peter Mandaville, a political scientist and member of Hillary Clinton's Policy Planning staff, argues that the resurging interest in Malcolm X, as seen in the "aggressive and confrontational" lyrics of British Muslim hip-hop acts, has implications for national security. Mandaville has praised the work of the British government in funding a "counter-radicalization" project that combined "traditional Islamic scholarship and social consciousness with hip-hop sensibilities" and sought to mobilize British Muslim youth around the "more cosmopolitanism impulses of Malcolm X after his break with the Nation of Islam and subsequent global travels."

The "I Am Malcolm X" counter-radicalization initiative sponsored by the British government and the U.S. embassy in London—whereby various Muslim rap artists from the U.S. and the UK performed pieces about the civil rights leader—has drawn mixed reactions. During one "I Am Malcolm X" performance in London in March 2009, Kumasi, an American hip-hop envoy, inserted the Muslim declaration of faith into his show, rapping one half of the *shahada* ("No god but God") and asking the audience to sing the other half ("Muhammad is His Messenger"), provoking outrage on both sides of the Atlantic. Suhaib Webb, a Boston-based American imam and former hip-hop DJ, who often comments on pop-cultural matters, would question the very idea of "Muslim hip-hop" and note that the American hip-hop envoys singing the *shahada* in London were presenting a "watered down Krush Groove Islam." "The Quran and hip-hop simply don't mix," he stated. Others took issue with the use of Malcolm X to legitimate a "Muslim hip-hop" extravaganza. "I've never in my life thought I would see the day when I would see someone on stage dancing to *la illaha ila allah* and also saying it with the backing of loads of instruments," wrote one attendee. "People were actually thinking that it was ok because it was all in the name of Malcolm X, Muslim artists and Muslim organizers." Another underlined that while Malcolm X in his youth may have enjoyed jazz and the Lindy Hop, after hajj he too would have found the mixing of hip-hop and the Quran unacceptable.

When the State Department's hip-hop envoys cross paths with Saudi-based rappers-turned-Salafis—like Loon and Napoleon—who also tour Europe trying to sway European Muslim opinion, one sees American Sufi policy and the Saudi Salafi strategy in stark juxtaposition. The State Department is deploying a cool Sufi Islam to counter Islamic—often Salafi—militancy, while Saudi Arabia is dispatching *American* Salafi converts to counter Sufism, Shiism, and hip-hop culture in general. The American envoys will present a pro-music, multicultural Malcolm X; the Saudi-based Salafi will speak of a post-hajj, post-music Malcolm X. This struggle over Malcolm X's legacy represents a larger effort by states and social movements to lay claim to black internationalism, and is reminiscent of the early 1960s, when various states and movements—at the height of the Cold War—sought to draw the African-American leader into their camp.

Propagate the Faith

One morning in February 2012, I rang the doorbell of an apartment in Gracie Terrace, a quiet, verdant cul-de-sac on Manhattan's East Side overlooking the East River. A smiling, gray-haired man in his eighties answered the door and led the way to a living-room area decorated with artifacts and paintings from Asia and the Middle East. I had come to see Richard Murphy, a retired diplomat who began his career as a vice-consul at the American embassy in Rhodesia (Zimbabwe) in the mid-1950s and went on to serve as ambassador to Syria, Saudi Arabia, Mauritania, and the Philippines. I had been doing research at the National Archives in Maryland and came across a number of embassy cables—"airgrams" as they were called—from the early sixties that spoke of Malcolm X, "Black Islam," and the Saudi Muslim World League, and they were often signed by "Richard W. Murphy," then stationed at the American consulate in Jeddah.

The cables invariably speak of America's image in the Middle East in light of the civil rights protests and urban unrest unfolding at home, and local coverage of Malcolm X's visits to the region. An airgram from the embassy in Jeddah from April 7, 1964, observes, "Displaying the same lack of information showed by their colleagues in other Arab countries, Saudi Arabian journalists in recent weeks have devoted a considerable amount of space to sympathetic stories dealing with the 'Black Muslims' in the United States. News agency reports and features on the movement have appeared almost daily, especially since Heavyweight Cassius Clay's 'conversion to (Black) Islam.'" Likewise, commenting on the coverage of Malcolm X's assassination, one cable from March 2, 1965, stated: "The local press covered his assassination thoroughly and one columnist hinted that the real assassins had not been found. However, perhaps for the first time locally the violent character of Malcolm's teachings was made clear as the press reprinted wire service commentaries on this theme."

The cables reflect the country's anxiety during the early Cold War. If American diplomats sought to harness Islam to counter the Soviet Union and Communist ideas on the European continent, officials in Washington were worried about the spread of communism within black organizations like the Nation of Islam. Elijah Muhammad claimed he rejected communism, but openly appealed to Muslim states—including Soviet clients—for support on pan-African, and pan-Islamic grounds. In 1959, the Nation of Islam leader traveled to Turkey, Lebanon, Jordan, Egypt (where he met with Nasser and Sadat), then Saudi Arabia, hoping to get ideological and financial support for his organization. American officials tried to get these Muslim-majority states to denounce the Nation of Islam for its heterodoxy and separatist language. The CIA approached Ambassador Mustafa Kamal of the United Arab Republic, hoping to get him to cancel Elijah's trip, but the ambassador would not retract Nasser's invitation to the NOI leader. Newly independent states who had long seen colonial powers woo their minorities would, upon gaining independence, begin to do the same, and appealed to minorities in the West. As early as 1956, Nasser—a key player in the Non-Aligned Movement—had declared his solidarity with African-Americans suffering in the "pure white democracy" of the U.S., offering scholarships to black students in the South. "Greetings to the Free Negroes from Free Egypt, and from all Free Men," declared one Egyptian newspaper.

As the "Arab Cold War" intensified, Nasser stepped up his rhetorical attacks on American-allied monarchies. In 1962, he sent troops to Yemen to help republican officers overthrow the country's Saudi-backed monarch. That same year the Saudis launched their own ideo-logical offensive to oppose Nasser's influence, setting up the Muslim World League. The organization aimed to consolidate various Islamist groups—Wahabis, Salafis, the Muslim Brotherhood, and the Jamaat-i-Islami—into a transnational Islamist movement to defend the Pal-estinian cause, and counter the spread of socialism and secular Arab nationalism.

The Muslim World League wanted to send emissaries around the world to spread Salafi Islam, including to Muslim communities in the West. Diplomatic cables from the early to mid-1960s show Mohammed Surur, then secretary general of the Muslim World League, ask-ing the American embassy in Jeddah for permission to set up a branch office in the U.S. to "propagate the faith" and "help raise the level of Islamic education in the US and particularly in the Black Mus-lim Movement," whose "doctrines" were "in flat contradiction to the teachings of Islam." American diplomats, in turn, were displeased by the "sympathetic stories" that Malcolm X—and "[black] Islam" in general—were receiving in the Arab press. Others were concerned about the negative coverage of racial unrest in the U.S. One dispatch from the embassy in Jeddah notes that, following the Watts riots of August 1965, the Saudi daily *Al-Bilad* described "white Americans" as "bestial butchers" who were perpetrating unspeakable atrocities on innocent Negroes." Soon American officials would come to view the Muslim World League as an antidote to Black Muslim militancy.

Richard Murphy was a young chargé d'affaires at the American embassy in Jeddah and met with Malcolm X when the latter vis-ited the embassy in September 1964. The civil rights leader seems to have made a positive impression on Murphy, who would describe the activist as "assured but surprisingly unaggressive and undogmatic" and "rather disarming." Malcolm X seemed like a transformed man. (Malcolm X in turn would note in his diary how surprisingly helpful Mr. Murphy was to him.) Malcolm X, according to Murphy, down-played his reputation as a political activist, saying he was glad to be "far away from politics" and "dwelt mainly on his interest in bringing sounder appreciation of Islam to American Negroes." Murphy recalls that Mohammed Surur of the Muslim World League had sponsored the activist's visit in 1964, as a way to "peel" Malcolm X away from Nasser's influence. "The Saudis invited Malcolm X as a reaction to Nasser—it was part of the competition with Egypt," says Murphy. "Back then, we thought Islam was a potential friend in dealing with the radical black community. We had a benevolent attitude toward what we called Wahabi Islam—the Saudis prefer to call it Salafiya. We saw the Saudis as devout, quaint, but not dangerous. Washington thought a better understanding of Islam could help deal with some of the violent tendencies in the black American community. The better Muslims they [Black Muslims] are, the less violent they'll be back home. Malcolm X was a prime example. He decided that Elijah Muhammad and his advocacy of violence was not the way to go."

Muslim-American youth today have a keen interest in the interactions between African-American and immigrant Muslims in the civil rights era, and one theory heard often in the Muslim-American community is that in the 1960s, the government used immigrant Muslims to counter or "tame" Black Muslim organizations. Community elders have said that the State Department played a key role in regulating relations between African-American Muslims and "immigrant Muslims." In his memoir, *I Buried Malcolm,* for example, the late Heshaam Jaaber, a respected imam from Newark, New Jersey, who washed Malcolm X's body and performed the *janazah* rituals, recalls the tense climate in New York in the days after the latter was gunned down at the Audubon Ballroom, and claims that the State Department "barred" foreign Muslim-born imams from performing "last rites" on Malcolm X, or even attending his funeral, as their presence would grant the slain leader an added Islamic legitimacy, or even draw reprisals.

It is difficult to ascertain the accuracy of these claims, given that thousands of FBI and CIA documents about Malcolm X remain classified. The Counterintelligence Program (COINTELPRO), set up by the FBI to monitor and infiltrate communist groups and civil rights organizations, did see the Nation of Islam as a "real racial threat," and wanted to change the movement's philosophy "to one of the strictly religious and self-improvement orientation, deleting the race hatred and separate nationhood aspects"; and law enforcement clearly preferred Warith Muhammad as a successor to Elijah (over Warith's rival, his brother Jabir Herbert Muhammad). But there is no evidence to suggest that immigrant Muslims were used to generate "factionalism" or to bolster Warith's position. According to State Department dispatches from the era and Ambassador Murphy's account, what seems to have occurred was that, as part of a broader Cold War strategy, American diplomats allowed the Muslim World League to set up a branch office in the U.S. and to dispatch teachers of orthodox Islam to Muslim communities across the United States—in part to "moderate" black militancy. And accounts in the press from that era lend support to this idea. In May 1964, the *Washington Post* published an interview—referenced to this day—with Mahmoud Shawarbi, an Egyptian national and the director of the Islamic Center of New York, who was tutoring Malcolm X in Sunni Islam and helped organize his hajj. The "Man Who 'Tamed' Malcolm," as the *Post* described Shawarbi, echoed the belief held by diplomats like Murphy in the early 1960s: that Sunni Islam could neutralize Black Muslim organizations. "Dr. Shawarbi appeared confident that Malcolm would abandon his call for Negroes to arm themselves and form rifle clubs," said the article. The Egyptian professor also predicted that if Malcolm "goes about things quietly or Islamically," many whites would join his movement. "In this way he will be serving his whole country, his own group and his new religion and setting a good example of a true Muslim for the American people."

By the early 1970s, the Muslim World League had opened up offices in Copenhagen, London, Moscow, Paris, Rome, Vienna, New York, and Washington, DC. As more Sunni Muslim immigrants arrived, and representatives of the Muslim World League and the Muslim Brotherhood began founding organizations like the Muslim Student Association (in 1963) and the Islamic Society of North America, the Nation of Islam would find itself under intense scrutiny. Elijah responded by drawing closer to Egypt and distancing himself from the Saudis: "Neither Jeddah nor Mecca have sent me! I am sent from Allah and not from the Secretary General of the Muslim League." His cozying up to Nasser—by then considered a radical—in turn drew more FBI surveillance and criticism from mainstream black leaders, who thought Black Muslim agitation set back the entire civil rights movement. In 1959, Thurgood Marshall described the Nation of Islam as "run by a bunch of thugs organized from prisons and jails and financed, I am sure, by Nasser or some Arab group." (And Malcolm X would respond by mocking the famed lawyer's light complexion and drinking habit: "Marshall + Nasser could pass for brothers, only Nasser is darker than Marshall and I hear Nasser never gets drunk [or even takes a drink.]") Elijah would also try to gain the support of orthodox Muslim leaders, appealing to Sunni clerics in Pakistan for religious validation, even reinterpreting the NOI's message to accord with Sunni orthodoxy.

When Malcolm X parted ways with the Nation of Islam, he began to navigate the Arab Cold War's shifting currents, assessing which nation-state or political movement to align his new organization, Muslim Mosque Inc., with and even presenting himself as a bridge between rival camps. He was drawn to Nasser's project of pan-Arabism and Third World socialism—just as he was to Kwame Nkrumah's revolutionary pan-Africanism—but was wary of their secularism. Malcolm X was courted by the Muslim World League and the Muslim Brotherhood, who competed to pull him into their school of Sunni Islam. In September 1964, after undergoing training in Mecca and being appointed an official representative of the organization, Malcolm would consider establishing his Muslim Mosque Inc. in Harlem as a "legal branch of the Muslim World League."

Yet reflecting his affection for Egypt and Nasser, he would also ponder setting up a branch of al-Azhar University in the U.S. In a letter to Muhammad Tawfik Oweida, secretary-general for the Supreme Council for Islamic Affairs in Egypt, Malcolm explains to the Egyptian official why he is building relations with the Muslim World League and the Muslim Brotherhood, two movements anathema to the Nasserist regime. "My heart is in Cairo," writes the civil rights leader, noting that the most progressive social forces in the Muslim world are in the Egyptian capital, but "I can be more helpful and of more value" to these progressive forces by having strong ties to the conservative forces "that are headquartered in Mecca." He adds, "When I passed through Geneva I even took time to speak with [the exiled Muslim Brotherhood leader] Said Ramadan so that I could find out what he was thinking without ever letting him know what I was really thinking."

Yet while Malcolm X admired the social conservatism of these movements and saw their Sunni orthodoxy as an antidote to NOI theology, he was wary of their insensitivity to American race issues. In his final years, Malcolm X had embraced Sunni Islam, but which ideology or state he would have aligned with is today the subject of intense debate, with observers projecting their own ideological predilections onto his future trajectory.

Two years after Malcolm's death, the Arab Cold War ended. With the 1967 War, Nasser's side was defeated and the political geography of the region redrawn, altering the direction of black and Muslim movements in the U.S. Elijah Muhammad would find himself deprived of a key ally. As states that were Soviet clients gradually entered America's orbit, they withdrew their support for leftist African-American movements. In 1973, Algeria renewed its ties with the U.S.—broken since 1967—and expelled the Black Panthers. Likewise, when Anwar Sadat left the Soviet camp, he quickly abandoned his predecessor's language of pan-Africanism and Third World solidarity. (If Nasser described himself as the "dark giant," Sadat, Egypt's Nubian head of state, would tell journalist Barbara Walters that he never liked the way the Soviets treated Egypt, like it was some "central African country.") The Saudis—flush with revenue after the OPEC oil embargo—would continue to disseminate Salafism, so that by the early 1980s, twenty-six communities in the United States were receiving the services of instructors sent by the Muslim World League.

Following Elijah Muhammad's death in 1975, his son Warith

would dismantle the Nation of Islam, abandon his father's anti-government stance, and adopt Sunni Islam, while retaining the NOI's idea of economic self-help. Muhammad's decision reflected changing domestic conditions: segregation had been outlawed, the civil rights movement had opened up opportunities for African-Americans, and his followers—thanks to the NOI's business investments—had moved up economically. But there was also a new geopolitical situation. After the Camp David Accord and the cementing of the Egyptian-Saudi alliance—which would become the linchpin of American power in the Arab world—left-leaning Black Muslim groups would find themselves bereft of economic and political support. The Saudis withdrew their support for Muslim Mosque Inc. upon Malcolm X's death. Warith Muhammad, who had studied at al-Azhar in the 1960s and knew Sadat personally, would slowly bring his movement, the largest African-American Muslim organization, now renamed the American Muslim Mission, into the Egyptian-Saudi orbit. In 1978, Saudi Arabia, Qatar, and Abu Dhabi would designate Warith Muhammad the "sole consultant and trustee" for distributing their funds to Muslim missionary organizations in the United States.

American diplomacy now had an "orthodox" Muslim leader to tap for diplomatic missions. In the 1980s, Warith Muhammad would leverage his ties in the Middle East to help release American hostages in Lebanon. In a sign of just how far he had broken with his father's anti-imperial politics, during the first Gulf War Muhammad was the only leader of a national Muslim organization to endorse the U.S.-led war against Iraq. In September 1990 he told Saudi National Radio, "I am comfortable with the decision which Saudi Arabia has taken to defend its borders and to accept the support of its friend—not only America but other friends, Muslim nations and non-Muslim friendly nations. As an American, I compliment my government for protecting its interest, the interest of the American people, the global interest, for being friendly to the Kingdom of Saudi Arabia and for respecting the religion of al-Islam." This statement would cause a rift with other American Muslim organizations, which did not support the war; and in effect, the Muslim organizations that did not support the presence of American troops in the Arabian Peninsula soon saw their funding—from Saudi Arabia—discontinued.

Warith's shift to the right left a political vacuum that was soon occupied by Louis Farrakhan. The Islamic right, mobilized as part of a Cold War strategy, had successfully pushed the heterodox Black Muslim movement toward Sunni orthodoxy, and to abandon its radical critiques of U.S. foreign policy. The political space left would be filled by Farrakhan when he revived the Nation of Islam in 1981, arguing that the orthodox Islam taught by Sunni Muslim immigrants could not address the needs of the black poor. Despite his efforts, by the late 1990s Farrakhan would find himself increasingly marginalized due to his intolerant rhetoric, and the NOI's only ally was the erratic Libyan dictator Muammar Gaddafi, the last Muslim head of state to still speak the 1960s idiom of pan-Africanism and Third World solidarity.

"Bandung Is Back, Baby!"

Gaddafi's ignominious end in October 2011 marked the end of an era, as another one had already started. Long gone were the "radical" Muslim states supporting black nationalist movements, while "moderate" American-allied states supported conservative Islamist movements; but the Arab Spring, in its rescrambling of the political map and shifting of alliances, had ignited a new interest in Bandung, the civil rights movement, and transnational solidarity. While NATO planes were strafing Libya in the summer of 2011, Sukant Chandan, a young journalist who runs the London-based group Sons of Malcolm, was reporting from Tripoli on the impact of the war on Libyan civilians. This group, which aims to fight neocolonialism "by any means necessary," is not atypical. Malcolm X is central to the political consciousness of Muslim youth in the West, and with the Arab uprisings, it wasn't just Muslim youth asking "What would Malcolm say?" and retracing his trips and statements: different regimes were trying to claim his moral mantle.

In 1984, Iran had claimed Malcolm X's legacy, releasing a stamp in his honor to promote the Universal Day of Struggle Against Race Discrimination (fifteen years before the U.S. issued its own Malcolm stamp). The Khomeini regime began to counter Saudi religious ideology with a revolutionary Shiism shortly after 1979. A study commissioned by the Iranian government in 1982 on Islam in America accused Saudi proselytizers of being in cahoots with the CIA, and said about African-American Muslims that everyone "only wants to use them for their own personal reasons as they languish." After the invasion of Iraq in 2003, as Iran seemed ascendant, a number of young Muslim activists argued that Shiism was the best way to counter Salafism. And a small Shia movement appeared in Europe arguing that Shiism, with its tradition of protest and minority consciousness, was better suited for Muslims in the West than Sunni Islam. This argument would be famously made by Malcolm Lateef Shabazz Jr., the civil rights leader's grandson, who embraced Shia Islam and moved to Syria in 2007. The twenty-seven-year-old became quite popular among Muslim youth in Europe and the U.S., lecturing and starring in political hip-hop videos, but caused an uproar at an event in Detroit in 2011 when he spoke negatively about the *sahaba* (the Prophet's companions) and declared that had his grandfather lived, he would have become Shia. One Detroit-based leader saw Malcolm Jr.'s conversion to Shiism as a result of the new "Middle East Cold War," saying that when the young man went to Syria to study, "the regime put him in a Shia 101 program at the Sayeda Zainab mosque."

The spring of 2011 also saw the publication of a new five-hundred-page biography of Malcolm X, which quickly got caught up in the cultural politics of the revolts. The new biography posits, inter alia, that Malcolm X may have been influenced by Shiism and inspired by Hussein's tragic murder in Karbala. "Like Husayn [*sic*], Malcolm made the conscious decision not to avoid or escape death," writes the historian Manning Marable. "Perhaps, like Husayn, he wanted his death to be symbolic, a passion-play representing his beliefs." In the U.S., these words revived long-standing debates about the origins of the Nation of Islam, and lent support to those who argued that Fard

Muhammad, the group's founder, was an Ismaeli Shia rather than an Ahmadi. This camp has long argued that the NOI's notions of cyclical time, numerology, divine lineage of leaders ("scientists"), and belief in *batiniyya*—that religious texts had a hidden meaning that could only be interpreted by religiously trained scholars (such as a NOI minister)—all betrayed the influence of Ismaili Shiism. Marable's book, published in April 2011, when sectarian tensions were running high and as youth in Europe were organizing reading groups around this book, seemed to support the argument made by Malcolm Jr.

The states trying to contain Iran would in turn underline Malcolm X's Sunni credentials. The Saudi-based Salafi evangelists, like Napoleon, who appear on Saudi television regularly reference Malcolm X, as do the Muslim-American hip-hop ambassadors dispatched by the State Department. Soon after Obama came to power, the Saudi government appointed a black man, Sheikh Adil Kalbani, as imam of the Grand Mosque of Mecca, so that if American diplomacy's outreach to Muslims celebrated Obama's Muslim ancestry, the Saudis would broadcast Kalbani's voice—and very conservative views—via satellite television to hundreds of millions of Muslims worldwide. ("My appointment is more significant than Obama's elections," Kalbani told the Al Arabiyya news channel, noting that American elections represented one country while the Grand Mosque is "the place of all Muslims.")

Even states not directly involved in the Sunni-Shia or U.S.-Iran standoff are laying claim to Malcolm X, and by extension to the black internationalist tradition. Sudanese nationalists contend that Malcolm X and the larger African-American Muslim movement were influenced by Sudanese Salafism, through the Sudanese scholar Ahmed Hassoun, who headed the Ansar as-Sunna movement in Khartoum before being sent by the Muslim World League to New York in 1964, where he became a close advisor to Malcolm X. The question over whether Malcolm X was more sympathetic to the Muslim Brotherhood or the Salafi movement took on a new meaning as these movements made electoral gains and secured parliamentary seats across North Africa in 2012. Supporters of the Muslim Brotherhood reject both the Salafi and the Shia view of Malcolm X; they compare the civil rights leader's death not to Hussein's martyrdom, but to that of Brotherhood founder Hassan al-Banna, who was also assassinated, claiming that in his last days, the African-American activist had grown much closer to the Muslim Brotherhood than to the Salafi movement and that the day he was killed, the letter on Malcolm X's desk was to Said Ramadan of the Islamic Center of Geneva. Liberal Muslims claim Malcolm X as well. Adil Abdel Aati, a Sudanese politician who heads Sudan's Democratic Liberal Party, argues that leftists who have long claimed Malcolm X as one of theirs ignore the extent to which he was influenced by Salafism; but, he writes, "I am convinced that had Malcolm X lived for one or two years more, he would have completely broken with Salafism, and perhaps religious thought in general," and focused on political activism to uplift all Americans.

Fifty years after his death, the Muslim conversation about the significance of Malcolm has taken a distinct theological turn and "Imam Shabazz" is gradually becoming almost a saintly figure, a *wali,* whose life offers personal and spiritual guidance. Sheikhs now debate various aspects of Malcolm X's life, his views on music, marriage, parenting, political participation, and so on. Prominent clerics like Imran Hosein of Trinidad issue opinions on whether Malcolm X's receiving an advance for his autobiography from Doubleday in 1964 constituted *riba* (interest). Young Muslims from Europe will appear at Malcolm's grave site, kneeling down with one hand on his memorial plaque, another on his wife Betty's, hoping to absorb *baraka.* When Sheikh Habib Umer, a world-renowned Yemeni scholar and Sufi master, embarked on his lecture tour of the U.S. in April 2011, his first stop in New York was Ferncliff Cemetery in Hartsdale, a few miles north of the Bronx. Standing in the drizzling rain, surrounded by adepts, the Yemeni sheikh asked God to bless the martyr.

Sound Track to the Struggle

Liberal analysts see the jazz tours of the 1950s and 1960s as a success. By showcasing racial progress, jazz diplomacy countered Soviet propaganda and created positive impressions of the United States—and, it is argued, if music worked in the 1960s, it can work in the 2010s. But hip-hop is not jazz; and the rap stars of today are not the jazz greats of the 1950s and 1960s. And for all the parallels drawn, the War on Terror is not the Cold War. The jazz tours resonated with people across Africa, the Middle East, and South Asia because the postwar U.S. was seen as an anticolonial power, a counterweight to French, British, and Italian dominance. Indeed, the U.S. did parry European colonial thrusts in Libya in 1950 and the Suez Canal Zone in 1956. Moreover, the civil rights struggle resounded globally; the black freedom movement was seen as an ally of the decolonized world. Its sounds—jazz, in particular—had a powerful moral appeal, as jazz musicians, influenced by the Afro-Asian unity discourse of Bandung and the Nation of Islam, wrote compositions like *Uhuru Afrika* and the "Freedom Now Suite" linking the civil rights movement with anticolonial struggles in Asia and Africa. But the honeymoon with America slowly came to an end as Cold War politics led to myriad interventions and proxy wars, and the U.S. gradually became, along with France and Britain, the backer of a repressive state system extending from the Barbary Coast to Pakistan. As the U.S. relationship to the region changed and the Vietnam War wore on, the jazz ambassadors would find themselves increasingly challenged by local audiences on their role in the U.S. foreign-policy establishment. Penny Von Eschen describes an incident in Algiers in April 1967, when young Algerians asked jazz ambassadors how they, as African-Americans, could represent a country that was "committing atrocities" in Vietnam.

The jazz tours would continue in the Soviet bloc through the 1970s, as did Voice of America broadcasts of jazz behind the Iron

Curtain. And black internationalism did not lose its appeal in the Muslim world. Africans and Asians languishing under authoritarian rule appreciated the statements of solidarity from the Student Nonviolent Coordinating Committee, TransAfrica, the Black Panthers, Jesse Jackson, Randall Robinson, and other black leaders. Ordinary people fasted ahead of Muhammad Ali's big fights. As hip-hop emerged, its beats and lyrics, as the public diplomacy experts correctly noted, would quickly resound with Muslim youth. But the best-loved music was the politically conscious, Afrocentric hip-hop of the 1980s and early 1990s, which paid tribute to Africa, Asia, and Islam. At some point in the mid-1990s—critics debate the precise date—"conscious" hip-hop would be sidelined by commercial rap, a form more concerned with the acquisition of wealth than solidarity with the postcolonial world.

And while references to Islam remain legion, they are not necessarily political or flattering. In December 2002, Lil' Kim appeared on the cover of *OneWorld* magazine wearing a burka and a bikini, quoted as saying "Fuck Afghanistan." 50 Cent's track "Ghetto Qu'ran" is about dealing drugs and "snitchin'." Foxy Brown charmed some and infuriated others with her song "Hot Spot," saying, "MCs wanna eat me but it's Ramadan." More disturbing was the video "Hard," released in late 2009 by the diva Rihanna, in which she appears decked out in military garb, heavily armed and straddling a tank's gun turret in a Middle Eastern war setting. An Arabic tattoo beneath her bronze bra reads "Freedom Through Christ"; on a wall is the Quranic verse "We belong to God, and to Him we shall return," recited to honor the dead, and not an uncommon wall inscription in war-torn Muslim societies. The point is that not all Islam-alluding hip-hop resonates with Muslim youth. Those American hip-hop stars—Lupe Fiasco, Mos Def, Rakim—who are beloved among Muslim youth are appreciated because they work their Muslim identity into their art and because they forthrightly criticize U.S. foreign policy. On his latest album, Lupe raps: "Gaza Strip was getting burned/Obama didn't say shit." But none of these gentlemen are likely to be invited on a State Department tour.

The Cold War jazz tours were never popular among progressive black intellectuals. Frantz Fanon and the Guyanese historian Walter Rodney both resented how Louis Armstrong and others were used as "emissaries of the Voice of America," how the music of "oppressed black people" was transformed into "propaganda." Likewise, Muslim thinkers with a Third-Worldist affiliation saw jazz as part of an expanding American imperium. Ali Shariati, the Iranian sociologist who, engaged with the ideas of Fanon and of Léopold Senghor, was wary of jazz as an instrument of cultural imperialism, and cognizant that colonial history had produced "three distinct races: one which can think, that is, the European . . . and the one which can only feel or make poetry, the Easterner, who has only mystical and gnostic feelings, and the Black, who can dance, sing and play good jazz." Likewise, when Jalal Al-e-Ahmad, the Iranian novelist and author of *Gharbzadegi* ("Westoxification"), came to participate in the Harvard International Summer Seminar in 1965—invited by Henry Kissinger—he would tell Ralph Ellison, already becoming known as a voice of American universalism, "I believe that the problem of American blacks comes from the two refuges that they have constructed for themselves: Christianity and jazz."

Similar critiques are leveled at the hip-hop diplomacy program today—again, mostly from scholars and critics outside the United States. The hip-hop ambassadors, it should be noted, have assumed some personal risk. In July 2007, as part of the Rhythm Road program, Toni Blackman was driven in an armored vehicle, flanked by a convoy of trucks carrying UN blue helmets, to perform in the largely Muslim, rebel-held north of Côte d'Ivoire. In January 2006, she was performing for an outdoor audience in Medan, Indonesia, when a throng of men on motorbikes carrying what the *New York Times* described as "anti-American banners" drove into the concert area, clambered onto the stage, shoved Blackman aside, and began shouting anti-American statements into the microphone. In August 2011, Chen Lo and the Liberation Family would perform in Bahrain at the height of the uprising as the U.S. was delivering military shipments to the Khalifah regime. In November 2011, the FEW Collective, a hip-hop dance troupe from Chicago, was detained in Pakistan, and their venue in Lahore was pressured to cancel their show. The concerts are often seen as an attempt to sugarcoat ("blackwash") unpopular policies, and African-American rap artists are asked about their newfound role as goodwill ambassadors. The Muslim hip-hop envoys are particularly aware of the way they are perceived overseas. One member of Native Deen expressed the ambivalence he felt when first approached by the State Department: " 'Should we do it?' 'Should we not do it?' Some people were saying, 'Y'all are going to be puppets, going over there saying: "Everything's O.K. We're bombing your country, but we have Muslims, too!" ' "

Realists and leftists have little illusion about the role that hip-hop can play in power politics. Samuel Huntington, in 1996, cautioned policymakers not to put too much faith in "cultural fads": "Somewhere in the Middle East a half-dozen young men could well be dressed in jeans, drinking Coke, listening to rap, and, between their bows to Mecca, putting together a bomb to blow up an American airliner." Eric Hobsbawm would also express doubt about hip-hop's geostrategic potential. "I have a blind spot or rather a blocked ear for both rap and hip-hop, and I know little about these forms of youth culture, since I am probably old enough to be the great-grandparent of those who practice them," quipped the late nonagenarian in late 2010. "My only observation is that I doubt whether the U.S. government is in a position today to launch systematic cultural offensives across the world as they did in the Cold War—or whether they would be as successful as they then undoubtedly were." As with the jazz tours, it is the liberal internationalists who believe in the geostrategic potential of music. But it's still not clear how "Muslim hip-hop" will exert a moderating influence: Will a performance by an African-American Muslim group trigger a particular calming "affect," pushing young Muslim men away from extremist ideas? What "different narrative" are groups like Legacy presenting? Nor is it clear what constitutes "Muslim hip-hop": Does the fact that Busta Rhymes is a Sunni Muslim make his music "Islamic"?

Most curious is the official claim that just as jazz embodied and disseminated democratic values, hip-hop diplomacy in the Islamic world is promoting democracy and fostering dissent because the music expresses a tradition of African-American Muslim protest, epitomized by Malcolm X. This claim is ironic, as Malcolm X, in his "personal diplomacy," explicitly repudiated the State Department's claims of racial advancement at home. This was, in fact, part of his ongoing dispute with the diplomat Ralph Bunche, who thought African Americans had a special role to play in American diplomacy, "owing to their unique ability to gain more readily the confidence of the Native." Malcolm X, in turn, dismissed the USIA's "propaganda" and "information agents," calling out Bunche himself. Moreover, the hip-hop diplomats avoid political issues in their embassy performances; local authorities, particularly in the developing world, will carefully comb through lyrics ahead of time. Yet Maura Pally, assistant secretary of state for educational and cultural affairs, contends that when Yemeni youth enter the gates of the embassy in Sanaa and witness a hip-hop show, the experience is "opening minds" and altering perceptions. The critics retort that after the show Yemeni youth are still aware of the drones falling on their country. (After an event celebrating Malcolm X's birthday in May 2013—where embassy workers in Sanaa displayed posters of the leader saying, "Happy Birthday to Malcolm X, who bravely stood up against injustice and hate"—one Yemeni wrote on the embassy's Facebook page, "I wish the American ambassador were as courageous as this man Malcolm X who stood in valor against oppression.") And this is the crux of the growing debate over hip-hop diplomacy. Proponents claim that hip-hop can have the same liberating and rebranding effect as jazz did in the 1950s, somehow overlooking Washington's close alliances with the authoritarian regimes of North Africa and the Middle East. The U.S. could use jazz to "sell" America behind the Iron Curtain and foster dissent in Soviet-backed regimes, but can American "soft power" liberate people in U.S.-backed tyrannies? The hip-hop initiatives may be more successful in generating goodwill in Europe, where Muslims are marginalized but do have political rights, or in a nonallied dictatorship like Burma, where rap artists are heavily censored, than in authoritarian regimes backed by U.S. hard power.

The hip-hop diplomacy initiatives have thus sparked a heated debate over the purpose of hip-hop: whether it is "protest music" or "party music," the "soundtrack to the struggle" (as the immensely popular London-based "underground" rapper Lowkey titled his latest album) or of American unipolarity; whether to accept embassy assistance or not; and what it means that governments—not just corporations—have entered the hip-hop game. Hip-hop activists who want to use the music to create alternative social spaces have long been concerned about how to protect their art from corporate power, but now that the music is being used in diplomacy, the conversation is shifting. "Hip-hop at its best has exposed power, challenged power, it hasn't served power," says Lowkey. "When the U.S. government loves the same rappers you love, whose interests are those rappers serving?" The State Department initiatives have stirred some debate within the American hip-hop community as well, with proponents arguing that by doing diplomatic work, the hip-hop envoys, like the jazz ambassadors, can extract policy concessions at home; the critics, on the other hand, ask how the FBI can have a "rap task force" charged with monitoring hip-hop celebrities and rap movements while the government's diplomatic arm is deploying the genre for foreign policy purposes.

Ironically, it has been law enforcement and counterterrorism specialists who have raised questions about the legality of "hip-hop diplomacy." Samuel Roscoff, a legal scholar who directed the NYPD's intelligence unit, wonders if the government's deployment of Muslim artists to engage in Islam's "battle of ideas" by putting forth a particular American Islam and liberal understanding of Islam's relationship to music does not contravene the Establishment Clause. Moreover, performances overseas are being uploaded online, where they can be viewed and commented upon by American audiences; unless explicitly authorized by Congress, such online interactions—between Americans and non-Americans—may also violate the "publicity or propaganda rider" on strategic communication. The Department of Defense–sponsored North African affairs website Magharebia.com, for instance, is designed to not allow for "two-way communications" between individuals.

"Empire of Diversity"

These clashing visions of hip-hop are playing out in Third World cities like Tunis and El Alto, Bolivia, and in immigrant neighborhoods in the West. Hip-hop NGOs that use music for pedagogy, antiwar activism, neighborhood stabilization, and "grassroots diplomacy," institutions like Gangway Beatz of Berlin, the Brooklyn-based Existence Is Resistance, and the Rebel Diaz Arts Collective in the South Bronx, all of whom invite artists and youth from similarly marginalized neighborhoods in other countries, operate in the same areas where local authorities and foreign embassies are pushing their own hip-hop initiatives. The Rebel Diaz Arts Collective, the Bronx's first "hip-hop community center," advocates for immigrants, and leads antiwar protests—for instance, staging a rap concert outside the School of the Americas in Georgia. Rebel Diaz receives some money from Citgo, the Venezuelan oil company, which provides subsidized oil to the Bronx. Not too far from the collective is the Bronx Museum, whose State Department–funded "smARTpower" initiative sends cultural ambassadors to countries, among them Venezuela, to improve America's image.

The debate about hip-hop and U.S. "soft power" has not led to a backlash against the genre, just to criticism of American hip-hop and the increasingly frequent claim that non-American rappers are rap's true standard bearers. No less a figure than Chuck D, the iconic headman of Public Enemy, has lent support to the argument that "international" hip-hoppers are more faithful to the music's mission than their American counterparts. In January 2011, while visiting South Africa, "the godfather of hip-hop" wrote a scathing open letter to American hip-hoppers, blasting its ruling elite for their materialism and lack of commitment to community, noting that the balance of power had shifted. "The world has parity now and have [sic] surpassed the USA in ALL of the basic fundamentals of HIP-HOP."

Hip-hop today is everywhere, unlike jazz in the 1960s. It is readily available over the Internet, and there are rich hip-hop scenes in cities worldwide. As a result, American hip-hop emissaries do not draw the crowds that the "jambassadors" did. The officials organizing the hip-hop tours will concede that Kokayi and the Vice Versa Alliance do not have the star power of Gillespie, Armstrong, and Ellington, but they insist that the artists are portraying an unseen side of America and that the diversity they embody can alter perceptions. "Diversity" is the buzzword of hip-hop diplomacy, encountered again and again in reports and speeches. For State Department officials, the multi-hued hip-hop acts sent overseas represent a postracial or postracist American dream.

But it is unclear how persuasive this racialized imagery is. A poll carried out by Pew in 2012 found that views of the U.S. in Muslim-majority states had not improved since the last year of George W. Bush's presidency. As with the jazz tours, the State Department's recent efforts to showcase the model integration of American Muslims, and to deploy the moral and symbolic capital of the civil rights movement, have occured against a backdrop of unfavorable (and racialized) media images of Quran burnings, anti-mosque rallies, and accusatory congressional hearings, as the Tea Party movement, one of the most alarming waves of nativism in recent American history, surged northward. And ironically, if the current cultural diplomacy is inspired by initiatives from the civil rights era, so are some of the security policies targeting American Muslims: the NYPD's surveillance program is modeled on the FBI's Ghetto Informant Program introduced in the 1960s to monitor black neighborhoods. Perhaps the greatest irony is that while State Department officials were touting the liberating effects of hip-hop and Facebook on Muslim youth, the NSA was using these very technologies for surveillance. That the top four targets of Boundless Informant, the NSA's data-gathering program, were the Muslim-majority states of Iran, Pakistan, Jordan, and Egypt did not help either. Polls dipped further in 2013. Where perceptions are poor, it is because of foreign policy as well as, increasingly, domestic policies that target Muslims.

The "diversity talk" and the use of black culture as soft power have also drawn attention to the complex relationship between diversity and empire. In *Day of Empire,* Amy Chua argues that every global hegemon, since the Achaemenid Empire of Persia, was, by the standards of its time, extraordinarily pluralistic, practicing a "strategic tolerance" during its ascent to preeminence. The United States is an exemplar, rising to world dominance in the postwar decades only after *Brown v. Board of Education* and the civil rights movement allowed the country to develop "into one of the most ethnically and racially open societies in world history." Yet ironically, Chua cautions, it is this tolerance and diversity that triggers discord and conflict and sows the seeds of imperial decline. To survive, she notes, "hyperpowers" must find ways to command the allegiance, or at least the acquiescence of the foreign populations they dominate; military force is never sufficient—hegemons need a "cultural package." American Muslims are becoming a critical component of the late American empire's cultural repertoire, part of a larger package that includes a discourse of diversity, "postracialism," and the civil rights movement. Whether black music and American Islam will help rebrand the nation's image or provoke further discord—or both—remains to be seen.

11

When the Violins Weep

Eyes closed, brow furrowed, Line Monty begins a *mawal*, her guttural, plaintive voice drawing out every vowel as if to convey the passage of time. *"Ghibt alikom ou khalit dari,"* she confides, "when I think of you all, my fire burns." She pauses, and Maurice El Medioni—her pianist and songwriter for decades—plays a few notes with his right hand, as done during the prelude (*istikhbar*) of an Andalusian *nuba*. She shakes her head, recalling her childhood home, now abandoned. "Tears have flowed, scarring my cheeks and skin." She asks forgiveness from those left behind.

When Monty finally opens her eyes, brimming with tears, a violin cries softly; the singer begs the Almighty to show mercy and take her to her loved ones. *"Ya rabi al 'ali, han aliya."* The word for "compassion" in Arabic, *hanine*, also means "love" and "nostalgia." And, her right arm outstretched toward a paradise lost, Monty's voice rises, soaring, until she hits the perfect note of love and longing. And then she stops, abruptly; and instead of a traditional *nuba*, the band breaks into a tango-waltz led by an accordion. Monty sings the opening verse of her ode to Algiers. "I love all cities, and Paris a little more"—she smiles—"but not the way I love Algiers: *Lakin mashi comme l'Algérie.*" Singing in French and Algerian Arabic, she delights the audience at the Théâtre des Champs-Élysées, referring to streets in the Algerian capital where she played as a child. As the music winds down, she intones, *"Qalbi plein de tristesse, ma nensaksh en revanche"*—despite her aching heart, she will never forget Algiers—for, as she declares at the end, "distance teaches us what's valuable."

Until her death in 2003, Line Monty was the grande dame of Judeo-Arabic music. Born Fortunée Serfati in 1926, to a Jewish family in Tunis, she grew up in the Algerian capital, studying in the city's conservatory and idolizing Edith Piaf. In her teens, she sang as Leila Fateh, but on moving to France in the early 1950s she adopted the stage name Line Monty. Record sleeves from the postwar years show a doe-eyed, dark-haired girl, fingers interlocked imploringly. She quickly became a starlet in Paris's thriving "Franco-Oriental" scene, singing at cabarets in the Quartier Latin, drawing the attention of producers and artists like Charles Aznavour. Onstage, friends recall, she could provoke any emotion she wanted. The grainy black-and-white video of Line Monty at the Champs-Élysées in 1981—possibly the only footage available of this artist—shows the diva in full effect. She saunters across the stage, shifting from medieval *nuba* to a Spanish paso doble, moving easily across centuries, continents, and language registers. Singing about the dark-eyed Andalusian boy she loved, she leans on El Medioni's piano and begins to lift-drop her hip—a signature move. Twirling the microphone cord, she promises to take him to see Hollywood—no, all of America. "I'll even take you to Cuba and teach you that rumba," she winks. Line Monty remained a central figure in France's "Oriental music" scene until the late 1990s, and when she died, she was buried at the Père Lachaise Cemetery alongside Edith Piaf and Marcel Proust.

Berthe Nachman, the owner of Librairie du Progrès, a bookstore in the Marais, Paris's historic Jewish quarter, smiles warmly when she recalls Monty. The songstress, wearing a broad white hat, would stroll into the bookshop on Sunday afternoons with her granddaughter, Johanna, an aspiring chanteuse. *"Elle était fabuleuse,"* says the eighty-five-year-old Nachman, whose family—originally from Russia—has owned the shop since 1904. The Librairie du Progrès has been selling Jewish literature and Yiddish music for over a century, catering mainly to the Polish and Russian migrants who settled in the area in the 1900s; at some point in the 1960s, the bookstore became one of the biggest distributors of Judeo-Arabic music in Europe. Nachman's late husband—who was Polish-Jewish—fell in love with the North African music he heard at Paris cabarets like Le Djazair and Le Poussin Bleu and began collecting records. When the Algerian War sent the *pieds-noirs* and Algeria's Jewish population to France, he befriended some of the Maghreb's musical luminaries. His widow recalls the greatest figures of Judeo-Arabic music frequenting her store: El Kahlaoui Tounsi, the portly, blue-eyed Tunisian percussionist, who founded Paris-based Dounia Records, which recorded these exiled artists; Reinette L'Oranaise, the blind singer and oud player, who in 1989 was named Commandeur des Arts et des Lettres by Minister of Culture Jack Lang for her knowledge of Andalusian poetry; Blond Blond, the albino comic and Reinette's tambourine player, with his white suits and diamond-crusted Cuban shoes; Luc Cherki, the white-haired guitarist, who in his eighties still favors jeans and cowboy boots; even Cheikh Raymond, the master musician of Constantine—whose assassination in 1961 would partly trigger the mass exodus of that city's Jews—was a regular visitor in the 1950s.

Berthe recalls sales falling to a trickle during World War II, rising again immediately after 1945, only to dip again during the Algerian Revolution, when police surveillance almost silenced the city's Arab cabarets. The arrival of the *pieds-noirs* in the early 1960s revitalized the music. "My husband would stand for hours turning the gramophone for our customers." By the early 1980s, Judeo-Arabic music had moved from cabarets to occasional theater productions and private settings; Dounia Records folded, and El Kahlaoui Tounsi—and other record sellers—handed over their collections to the Nachmans, who stored away crates of cassettes and records.

But a revival is now under way. "The Judeo-Arabic repertoire is popular again. Line Monty is selling rapidly, we're out of everything by Salim Halali. It's like the 1960s," says Nachman. "Young people, older people from America, the Maghreb, and Israel are buying. One gentleman gave us his entire collection fifteen years ago—now he wants to buy it all back."

Since the early fifteenth century, Andalusian music has been the music of exile and nostalgia, for both North African Muslims and

Jews, representing the loss of Spain. With decolonization and the outbreak of the Israeli-Palestinian conflict, Andalusian music would evoke a double exile. For Muslims, the sound conjures the loss of Spain and the fall of Palestine to Zionism. (The Andalusian violins, the poet Mahmoud Darwish writes, cause the very horizon to bleed.) For North Africa's Jews—Arab Jews, as some would call themselves—it is a reminder not only of Sepharad, but of the African homelands they have been exiled from. These memories and imagined geographies bleed into each other. When Line Monty sings of alleyways and abandoned homes, it's not clear if she's referring to Algiers or Granada.

For the younger generation of French Muslims revisiting the Judeo-Arabic repertoire, al-Andalus means something else. Lili Boniche and Yousef Hedjaj's lush descriptions of North Africa, their connecting southern Spain with Algiers and Tunis, doesn't only elicit nostalgia; it has implications for Muslim identity and its place in French society today. In an era of rising Muslim-Jewish tension and sharp ideological conflict, Muslim liberals believe that the words and voices of Line Monty and Salim Halali offer sonic proof of Muslim-Jewish coexistence and of a history of Andalusian *convivencia* that can help Muslims find a place in Europe today. If immigration is disturbing Europe's memory landscape, they contend, a history of musical intimacy can heal. The current musical revival—and attempts to salvage this repertoire—is also the result of a cultural and political panic, a sense that as these giants of Judeo-Arabic music pass on (in the last decade, Line Monty, Salim Halali, Lili Boniche, Raoul Journo, René Perez, and Samy El Maghribi have died), it augurs the end of Arab-Jewish civilization. The thriving Arabic-speaking Jewish communities of North Africa barely exist, their gradual extinction occurring almost exactly as the "Muslim ghetto" emerges in Europe. For young French Muslims trying to make sense of their status as Europe's new "other," the Arab Jew's songs of exile resonate.

"Les Années Folles"

The World's Fair (L'Exposition Internationale) that opened in Paris in May 1937 showcased culture from forty-six nations, including France and her far-flung colonial territories. The North African exposition featured the replica of an Arab street, a barbaresque palace, a courtyard with tents, craftsmen, artisans, and a cinema, all designed to show the progress being made by France's civilizing mission in Morocco and Algeria. But it was the entertainment at the North African section that was particularly appealing to visitors: an Arab orchestra and dancers performed for guests as they enjoyed tea and honey cakes, watched beauty pageants and films about the peoples of North Africa. The exhibit brought to Paris a group of Arabic-speaking musicians who would not only have an indelible impact on the city's music scene but would become central to the cultural life of their home countries after independence.

It was through the Paris Expo that Salim (né Simon) Halali—who would become an iconic figure of French-Arab cabaret music—encountered his compatriots Mohamed El Kamal and Mahieddine Bachtarzi. Halali was born in 1920 to a Jewish family in Annaba in eastern Algeria; in 1934, the fourteen-year-old aspiring flamenco singer found his way to Algiers and snuck aboard a French boat shipping cattle to Marseille. After trying his luck in the port city he headed to Paris, hoping to work at the Algerian pavilion of the world's fair. He soon met El Kamal and Bachtarzi. The latter was the director of El Moutribia, the first Andalusian music association of the Maghreb, and had brought thirty-one musicians to the Expo. Bachtarzi had arrived in France in 1926, when the Grand Mosque of Paris was inaugurated; already known for his powerful voice, he was invited to perform the first call to prayer. In 1931, El Moutribia had given a concert at the Colonial Exposition, held in Paris to exhibit the benefits of France's civilizing mission and to counter rival Germany's claim that France was "an exploiter of colonial societies." Bachtarzi would describe performing at the 1931 exposition, where natives (*indigènes*) from Africa and Asia were displayed in a makeshift village, as "humiliating." But in 1937, he was back at the subsequent Paris Expo, and soon Salim Halali was part of his theatrical troupe, touring in France and Italy.

In the early thirties, Mohamed El Kamel was the most ambitious and showy of the three, having founded his own theater group in Paris, called Jazz El Kamel, fusing big band and *le music hall.* Wearing a bow tie and top hat, El Kamel shuffled and tapped his feet onstage, singing vaudeville-style numbers in French and Arabic about joblessness during the Great Depression and being a carpet seller in Paris, even performing a jingle celebrating the telephone. North African artists in postwar Paris could not access the Opéra, the Folies-Bergère, or the city's other great music halls—so they would perform in cabarets and in cafés for Algerian laborers. Arab cafés had begun appearing in the French capital as migration from Algeria to France increased during World War I. French authorities, facing a labor shortage and in need of soldiers, granted Algerian Muslims freedom to travel, relaxing the Code de l'Indigénat, which had restricted them to registered communes. It was in these cafés that the French-Arab cabaret sound was born, as El Kamal, Halali, and others mixed the sounds of interwar Paris—big band, rumba, bolero, tango, flamenco—with their Andalusian training.

Halali would soon distinguish himself with his vocal range, stage presence, and interpretations of Spanish *sevillanas* in Arabic. El Kamal composed a string of Arabic flamenco-style songs—"La Sevillana," "Andalusia," "Ta'ali"—that combined oud, maracas, and castanets for Salim to sing. When another Algerian composer, Mohamed Iguerbouchene, opened the cabaret Le Djazair on Rue de la Huchette, Halali, the "boy with a giant's voice," became the star. By the late 1940s, Rue de la Huchette was known for its "Oriental" music scene; other cabarets (La Kasbah, Soleil d'Algérie, Nuits de Liban) opened up, drawing Arab students, businessmen, shopkeepers, and tourists enchanted by the belly dancers and the Arabian Nights décor. As El Kamal, Bachtarzi, and Halali traveled back and forth between France and North Africa, touring and performing, their songs were broadcast on Radio Alger and Radio Tunis, and these three artists were changing the musical landscape on both sides of the Mediterranean.

But not everyone was pleased to see or hear Algeria's Andalusian repertoire incorporated into Parisian nightlife, or medieval verse mixed with tango riffs and performed in cabarets. For the budding anticolonial movements in Algeria and Morocco, Andalusi music was the living legacy of Islamic Spain, whose verses invoked a history that the French colonial order had suppressed, and whose poetry could inspire a movement for independence.

"Genealogies of al-Andalus"

As historian Dwight Reynolds observes, until the early twentieth century it was through music—song in particular—that most Arabs experienced Andalusian culture. Across the Arab world there are diverse musical traditions described locally as "Andalusi" and thought to have developed from the musical culture of medieval Islamic Spain. These local genres differ widely; what links them together is their purported origin in medieval Iberia and their frequent use of *mawashah* and *zajal,* two strophic poetic forms that emerged in Muslim Spain.

The story of the origins of Andalusian music is one that almost every Arab child grows up hearing. Circa 822, a musician named Ziryab appeared at the court of Abdurahman II in Cordoba. This talented musician of African origin ("Ziryab" means "blackbird") was a refugee from Abbasid Baghdad, forced out by his jealous teacher, Ishaq al-Mawsili; he fled to southern Spain and rose to become one of the caliph's favorite musicians. Ziryab would go on to make Cordoba a cosmopolitan center. He developed the *nuba* musical suite—twenty-four different modes, one for each hour of the day. He introduced a new etiquette of cuisine, fashion, and refinement. The seventeenth-century historian al-Makkari would observe that before the arrival of Ziryab, the people of al-Andalus wore their hair parted in the middle and hanging loose down to the shoulders; but after seeing Ziryab's hairstyle, Cordobans "relinquished the old fashion, and adopted that which he introduced," wearing their hair with bangs down to their eyebrows, cut straight across his forehead, and pulled back with little spit curls coming out from the sides of his ears.

When Muslim Spain fell in 1492, Jews and Muslims fled and settled in North African cities, carrying their memories and *nuba* with them. According to local lore, refugees from Cordoba brought their music to Tlemcen in western Algeria, refugees from Seville brought theirs to Tunis, and those from Valencia and Granada brought theirs to Fez and Tetuan. To this day, the Andalusi genres in the Maghreb—whether the *ala* of Morocco, the *san'a* of Algeria, or the *maluf* of Tunisia—are associated with old urban centers, and underpinned by the *nuba,* the musical suite developed by Ziryab. The memory of Ziryab as a prestigious musical forebear and Islamic Spain as a fount of greatness today exists across the Arabic-speaking world; but in North Africa, the proximity to Spain, the migratory flows, the circulation of music between Spain and the coastal cities of Tangier, Tetuan, Oran, and Algiers, and the ongoing Spanish colonial presence in Morocco, have meant that the role of Spain in the Moroccan and Algerian musical imagination is particularly complex, and is as real as it is imagined.

The Algerian performers who came to thrive in Paris's 1930s music hall scene were all trained in the conservatories of interwar Algeria, at a time when Andalusi music was being claimed by both French colonial rulers and the nationalist movement. In the 1850s, French officials in Algeria were more interested in Roman artifacts and the legacy of Rome's patrimony in North Africa, which could be presented as a precursor to the French presence, than in what they termed Hispano-Mauresque patrimony. French colonial administrators would actually ban all Algerian musical traditions, including Andalusi, and Arabic would be proscribed as French became the medium of education.

In the early twentieth century, in response to French policy and centuries of Ottoman domination, a movement emerged in Algiers and Tlemcen aiming to rescue Andalusi music from oblivion. People began to write down the texts of *nuba* and to establish associations devoted to the preservation of this repertoire. In 1904, Edmond Yafil, an Algerian Jew who had studied under Mohamed Ben Ali Sfindja, the doyen of Andalusi music at the time, would publish the first compilation of *nuba* texts; the book, titled *The Collection of Songs and Melodies from the Words of al-Andalus,* continues to be a reference for musicians to this day. "We have printed this collection because we saw this art of song and words of al-Andalus vanish and diminish each day," wrote Yafil in the preface of his book. He then founded the Société El Moutribia in 1912, the first association in North Africa devoted to the preservation and performance of Andalusian music. For Yafil and other Algerian nationalists, Andalusi music bespoke a history that was suppressed by colonial rule; it embodied a tradition and identity and could inspire a nationalist consciousness: by anchoring Algerian national identity retroactively in medieval Muslim Spain, the music could point toward an independent future. This sentiment extended beyond Algeria to Morocco and Tunisia. As historian Jonathan Glasser writes, "For many North Africans seeking an identity that transcends colonialism—and perhaps transcends decolonization as well—Andalusi music is a badge of authenticity (*asala*) that points backward through the centuries."

After World War I, the French were still dismissing Andalusi music as "folklore." As the association's movement gained force, the colonial authorities began to pay closer attention, hoping to gain control of the genre. By the 1930s, Andalusi music was politically contested, claimed by the nationalist movement, colonial authorities, and various music associations, who had differing views on its purpose. After Yafil's death in 1928, for instance, Bachtarzi—who had studied under the Jewish maestro—returned from France to lead El Moutribia. But his European tours and dabbling in cabaret music displeased some of his peers; a group of El Moutribia's members broke away to establish a new association called Al Andaloussia, stating in no uncertain terms that its aim was "the propagation of the true Arab-Andalusi classical music which the tunes of the fox-trot and the refrains of the café-concert have the tendency at the present time to completely deform." Other associations soon appeared, but their work would be disrupted by World War II and Vichy.

"Arabs of the Jewish Faith"

Maurice El Medioni has a very buoyant, affable disposition onstage and off; he jokes around, feigns accents, snaps his suspenders, kisses visitors on the forehead. Exuberance pervades his music as well. A song he wrote fifty years ago, "Ahlan Wa Sahlan, Farahtu Qalbi" (Welcome, You've Warmed My Heart), a richly danceable piano tune, opens North African weddings and bar mitzvah parties around the world. So, sitting in the living room of his Marseille apartment, where he and his wife, Juliette, have lived for forty-five years, this world-renowned pianist would rather talk about the songs he wrote for Line Monty, and how for decades he worked as a tailor by day and a musician by night, than recall the war years.

"We couldn't go to school," he says with a shrug, recalling Oran, Algeria, in the early 1940s. "I would spend all day at Uncle Saoud's café, playing piano and drinking grenadine." Medioni was a twelve-year-old boy when the Vichy laws were passed in Algeria. "What happened still makes no sense," he says. The twelve-year-old and his friends were suddenly thrown out of school in Oran because legislation was passed in Paris that in effect stripped these youngsters of French citizenship.

Algeria's Jews had become French citizens in 1870, with the passing of the Crémieux Decree. This law legally separated the native Jewish population from Algeria's Muslim Arabs and Berbers, who were living under a different legal system, and granted them the same political rights that European settlers in North Africa enjoyed. The decree was the result of effective lobbying by Jewish organizations in Paris concerned about the restrictions that their co-religionists were facing, and went into effect despite the opposition of the European-settler population in Algeria. But when Vichy came to power in France in June 1940, colonial administrators swiftly embraced the collaborator government's Jewish Statute, repealed the Crémieux Decree, and divested Algerian Jews of their status as French citizens. As in France,

Jews in Algerian cities would be excluded from public service and various professions; Jewish students and teachers would be removed from the public school system. The Algerian-born novelist Albert Camus would recount how his friend André Bénichou was fired from his job as a *lycée* teacher, and on his passport the words "French citizen" were replaced with "native Jew." Likewise, the philosopher Jacques Derrida, born in Algiers, would forever recall how as a ten-year-old, he and his siblings were expelled from primary school, and only allowed back after the American troops landed in 1942.

Vichy upset the music scene as well. Theater and music hall had emerged as a voice for protest in 1930s Algeria, to such an extent that French officials were closely monitoring public performances. In 1937, they banned one of Mahieddine Bachtarzi's song booklets for inciting anti-French sentiment. Vichy placed its own restrictions on musicians. Associations, especially those such as El Moutribia and El Andaloussia, that had a significant number of Jewish members had their activities curtailed. One of the musical legends of prewar Algeria was Maurice's uncle Saoud El Medioni. Cheikh Saoud, as he was known, was a musical maestro from Oran. He trained generations of students, including Reinette L'Oranaise and Lili Boniche, and owned a popular Moorish café on Rue de la Révolution in the city's center, where young Maurice hung out.

"Uncle Saoud was very much loved," says Medioni. "In 1937, he went to perform in France. He sang a new song he had written. I still remember it was called 'Chérie, comme je t'aime.' It was very well-received—he decided to stay in Paris. He opened up a café on Rue Berger, where he would play in the evenings."

Medioni pauses. "I remember the day. It was on January 23, 1943, that my uncle was snatched off the streets of Marseille by the Nazis and never seen again. I was fourteen. He was sent to Sobibor—the camp in Poland."

The musicians who lived through the Vichy years in Algeria vividly recall those years. In the summer of 1940, the guitarist Luc Cherki, another living legend of Algerian music, had traveled with his mother and four siblings to Paris when Nazi tanks rolled into the city.

"I left school at the age of six and never went back—I don't write well, too many spelling errors!" says Cherki. "So I have been struggling to write my book." In his forthcoming memoir, Cherki—now eighty-three—has a chapter titled "Enfant caché" (Hidden Child), describing how he wore a yellow star as a seven-year-old, and how his mother sent him through city council to live with a Christian family in Paris, and then he was smuggled back to Algiers. "We were helped by our Muslim neighbors. That my mother's last name was Benhammo helped as well—a common Algerian surname."

A Night in Tunisia

When American troops landed in Oran on November 8, 1942, Maurice El Medioni was an out-of-school fourteen-year-old playing piano for tips at different cafés. Derrida was twelve and hanging out in Algiers. "At dawn, we began to hear gunfire," he would later write. "And then in the afternoon . . . we saw in front of our house soldiers with helmets that we had never seen. They were not French helmets. We said to ourselves: they are Germans. And it was the Americans." The Allied forces had landed in Casablanca, Oran, and Algiers as part of the North Africa offensive against the Axis powers, moving rapidly eastward until Tunisia was liberated in May 1943. "And that evening, the Americans arrived en masse, as always distributing cigarettes, chewing gum, chocolate, kids started going up to them."

Medioni was one of those kids. To this day he recounts—actually acts out—for his audiences his first encounters with the Puerto Rican and African-American soldiers, who taught him to play rumba and ragtime. "In Oran, I saw these tanned soldiers carrying bongos and maracas—they were Puerto Ricans, and they would say, 'Hey, ma'—hey, ma', can you play me "La Cucaracha"?'" says Medioni, slurring his speech like a tipsy sailor. "I didn't know how. But the Latino GIs taught me to sing 'La Cucaracha' and 'Quizás, Quizás.' And the black GIs taught me the boogie-woogie. In the Maghreb, pianists play with one hand—their right hand. The left hand barely moves. But the GIs played with their left hand." To demonstrate, he plays a *nuba* rhythm with his right hand; then his left comes in with Scott Joplin's ragtime classic "The Entertainer."

Meanwhile, in Algiers, Luc Cherki would have a similar experience. As a nine-year-old, he and his older brother, Rafael, would go from café to café singing in English to American and British soldiers.

"It's a looooong waaay to Teiperari, it's a long, long way to goooo!" Cherki laughs, breaking into a British World War I anthem. "We had no idea what we were saying—my brother Rafael and I just wanted coins to buy food. One day a Puerto Rican singer gave me a guitar, and I started playing—that was my first instrument."

Operation Torch, as it was called, freed Muslims and Jews from Vichy domination, and unleashed a burst of musical creativity. Luc Cherki went on to develop a pop mix of flamenco and Arabic—what he termed "DiscOriental." El Medioni in turn would learn to play rumba and jazz melodies with his left hand while simultaneously playing Andalusian *nuba* patterns with his right, wedding the two styles into an Arabic-Latin-jazz mix that he calls "Descarga Oriental." Both these subgenres are a curious result of America's encounter with the Maghreb, of Latino soldiers meeting young music aficionados in Algeria's Moorish cafés. For Americans of that generation, the tune that would forever evoke the North African campaign, conjuring up images of exotic North African settings reminiscent of the film *Casablanca*, was Dizzy Gillespie's "A Night in Tunisia." Gillespie, who had been experimenting with Latin and North African rhythms for a while, said that the bebop number—with its "very Latin, even oriental feeling"—got its title because "Tunisia was on everybody's mind at that stage of World War II." The number would become a standard, performed by the likes of Art Blakey, Ella Fitzgerald, and the State Department artists touring Africa. As one jazz critic reporting on the jazz tours in Africa wrote, "If [the Africans] failed to understand anything else, this they loved."

Gillespie's counterpart in North Africa was the Moroccan oud player Houcine Slaoui, who wrote a song in Arabic—"L'Mirikan" (The Americans)—about the American landing that beautifully captured Muslim angst about American power. Slaoui was an eighteen-year-old Gnawi musician strumming his *sintir* in Rabat's marketplace when he was "discovered" by scouts for Pathé Marconi, the French record label, and invited to perform at the Moroccan pavilion at the Paris Expo of 1937. Slaoui, the story goes, was in Paris listening to a new broadcast from Radio Cairo when he heard of the American landing in Casablanca. He boarded a ship and headed back home and soon composed the song, a simple arrangement with oud strings, a *darb'uka* drum, and women singing a chorus, describing the economic boom and the cultural anxiety that swept Moroccan society when *l'Mirikan* landed.

"The Americans brought us all kinds of good things—*Zin oul ain az-azarga jana bkul khir,*" sang Slaoui, referring to the watches, cigarettes, and chewing gum that the American GIs were passing out as they patrolled Casablanca's streets. But, he cautioned, people were feeling emboldened, especially the women; some were sporting new hairstyles, others leaving their husbands—and even grandmothers were sipping rum with the "blue-eyed ones"! "All one hears on the streets," went the chorus, is "give, give dollar," and "OK, ok, come on, bye-bye." This composition, a musical snapshot of America's arrival as a Great Power in the Arab world, and the social change it triggered, has, like "A Night in Tunisia," been remixed endlessly in the Maghreb, staged in plays and musicals, re-released following the Gulf War of 1990, then after the 2003 invasion of Iraq, and more recently as the history of World War II is being revisited by young activists.

The Ornament of the World

The film *Indigènes* (2006) starts in 1943, shortly after the American landing, showing impoverished Algerians, dressed in lend-lease American uniforms, lining up to join de Gaulle's Free French Army. One young man enlists in order to migrate to France, another for the modest salary; a third believes fighting for France will secure a better future for Muslims in Algeria. Almost a quarter of the Free French Army—around three hundred thousand in number—were troops from France's African territories; and the film follows the Seventh

Algerian Infantry Regiment as its troops battle their way through Italy, defeat the Wehrmacht in Marseille (in a historic battle where scores of Algerian fighters died in one week) and Alsace, all while facing severe discrimination within the army and being wooed by Nazi leaflets—in Arabic—urging them to join the other side. The film concludes in the present day and shows Abdelkader, one of the characters, now elderly, at a war cemetery in Alsace, visiting the graves of his fallen Muslim comrades; he then goes home to a tiny, run-down apartment.

The film—released as *Days of Glory* in the United States, and nominated for an Oscar in 2007 as Best Foreign Language Film—spurred much debate in France about the role of Muslim troops in World War II. The day after *Indigènes* premiered, Dominique de Villepin, then prime minister, announced that the government would raise the pensions for the surviving eighty thousand French veterans from the former colonies. The film is part of a larger trend: that of European activists—Muslim and non-Muslim—trying to raise awareness of the role that minorities and troops from the colonies played in liberating Europe. In Britain, activists are trying to get recognition for Nigerian veterans who fought for the British army in Burma in 1943. Across Western Europe, minority groups trying to become part of the nation-state realize how central World War II is to the identity of modern Europe. These groups believe that by narrating the stories of Africans, Muslims, and Indians who fought courageously in the French, British, and Belgian armies despite their second-class status as *indigènes,* they can show how these communities were present at the founding of modern Europe and are thus "indigenous" to the continent.

Even in America, minority activists have lobbied to have their parents or grandparents honored as members of "the Greatest Generation." In 2007, Hispanic veterans' associations and the Congressional Hispanic Caucus took filmmaker Ken Burns to task for ignoring the contribution of three hundred thousand Hispanic-American soldiers in his PBS documentary *The War.* The Arab American Museum in Dearborn has a permanent exhibit of Arab-Americans who served in the war, with photographs, diary entries, and issues of the *Knights of St. George Journal,* a publication that allowed Syrian and Lebanese soldiers to communicate with family and friends. And European governments are increasingly recognizing, if belatedly and tokenly, the contribution of the "colonial troops": In 2007, an exhibit was organized at the Imperial War Museum North in Manchester, England, honoring the African troops who fought for the British Empire. On July 14, 2010—Bastille Day—President Nicolas Sarkozy, addressing high-ranking African military officers at the presidential palace, expressed his "undying gratitude" to the African colonial troops.

Yet because of their complex relationship to World War II and the Holocaust, much of the cultural work around the memory of the war is being driven by Muslim activists. Since the outbreak of the second intifada in 2000, Muslim-Jewish tensions in Europe have occasionally run high and, especially in France, incendiary rhetoric has erupted into street brawls, random acts of vandalism, and tragedies like the shooting spree in Toulouse in April 2012, when twenty-three-year-old Mohamed Merah rode up to a Jewish school and shot dead a rabbi and three children. Muslim-Jewish conflict in Europe is largely an extension of the Palestinian-Israeli conflict peaking at moments like the Lebanon War of 2006 or the Gaza War of 2009. The rise of Salafism among European Muslim youth since the 1990s has also meant that intolerant views of non-Muslims have gotten a wider airing, as has Holocaust denial. The "denialism" present in Arab and Islamist political discourse today is, as Gilbert Achcar recently argued, part of the Arab-Israeli clash of narratives, erupting at moments of war and often deployed as a response to *nakba*-denial—that is, the dismissal of the Palestinian catastrophe of 1948. In the 1950s and 1960s, it was Arab nationalists who rejected the Holocaust, because it was seen as a justification for the takeover of Palestine; in denying the Shoah, these nationalists thought they were undermining the Zionist case—a non sequitur if there ever was one. Since the rise of Islamism in the late 1970s, it is largely Islamist groups that engage in this practice, and leaders like Iran's Mahmoud Ahmadinejad who use Holocaust denial for political purpose.

Muslim activists in Europe are pushing back against this noxious rhetoric. Integrationist Muslim leaders argue that anti-Semitic rhetoric from random Islamist preachers—which prompts journalists and American diplomats to warn that anti-Semitism is returning to the European continent—is incredibly harmful and undermines all attempts at inclusion. "The battle against anti-Semitism is critical to our integration, to our gaining full citizenship," says Samia Essabaa, a French-Moroccan high-school teacher at Noisy-le-Sec who, alarmed by the rhetoric she heard among her students after 9/11, launched a campaign to educate underprivileged French youth about the history of anti-Semitism. "In fighting anti-Semitism, we are arming our youth against intolerance in general." The younger Muslim leaders recognize that Europe's current "Muslim question" and its historic "Jewish question" are inextricably linked, and the issue of Muslim integration is often viewed in light of Europe's history of anti-Semitism. Younger leaders know that European journalists are reluctant to speak of "Muslim ghettos," because it conjures up memories of Jewish ghettos, and that a fundamental reason why even the most left-leaning French intellectuals oppose race classification and ethnic statistics is that such data were used by Vichy to locate and round up Jews. Moreover, they are aware that in terms of public perceptions, whether a European Muslim leader or organization is viewed as "moderate" or "radical" can often depend on their attitudes toward the Holocaust and Israel. As Essabaa says, "A public recognition of the Holocaust is not only morally fundamental, but necessary for the political maturation of French Muslims." In short, if Muslim-Americans post-9/11 realized that embracing black suffering is critical to their integration and are trying to highlight their role in the civil rights movement, in Europe, liberal Muslim voices argue that any effort at inclusion must pay respect to the memory of World War II and the history of Jewish suffering on European soil.

Moreover, in the last decade, a neoconservative discourse has emerged that explicitly links Islamic movements with Nazism, stressing the alleged intellectual influence of Amin Al-Husseini, the Nazi-sympathizing mufti of Jerusalem, on contemporary Islamist thought. The "Nazification" of Arabs and Muslims is not new; the actions of Al-Husseini, and others who saw Nazi Germany and Mussolini's Italy as allies in the struggle against British and French colonialism and the Zionist movement, have long been projected onto Arabs and Muslims in general. But in the last decade the trope of Arab-as-Nazi has gained greater currency, recurring in many books and articles published in the United States and Europe.

For young Muslims caught between the intolerant rhetoric emanating from within their community and the neoconservative discourse on "Eurabia," "Islamofascism," and "Arab collaborationism," it has become imperative to show not only how Muslims helped liberate Europe from Nazism, but that historically Muslims and Jews coexisted, and that there is no innate hatred of Jews in Islamic civilization. To that end, these Muslim activists are reaching for al-Andalus, talking up the "Golden Age" of Muslim Iberia, raising awareness of Andalusia's tri-religious culture. Thus, young guides in Antwerp give "Andalusian" tours through the city's Muslim and Jewish neighborhoods; Toulouse holds *convivencia* festivals; in New York, the Cordoba Initiative brings together young Muslim and Jewish leaders for dialogue. This is not new either; when besieged, Muslims have long turned to Muslim Spain. After the 1967 War, Arab nationalists began describing Muslim Spain as an "interfaith utopia" where Jews enjoyed equal status under Muslim rule, arguing that religious conflict only began with the rise of Zionism. In response to this "Andalusian myth," a countermyth emerged, a new historiography, putting forth what historian Mark Cohen calls a "neo-lachrymose" view of Jewish-Arab history, which held that Jewish life in Islamic lands was, as in the Christian West, characterized by relentless persecution and violence.

Of particular interest to Muslim activists today are the writings of the eighteenth- and nineteenth-century European Jewish intellectuals who extolled the tolerance of the Islamic world, particularly Muslim Spain. To these Jewish scholars, excluded as they were from European society during the Enlightenment, the Spanish Inquisition, and the expulsion of entire Jewish communities by other medieval Christian states did not seem to have an equivalent on the other side of the Mediterranean. "None of these excesses," writes Cohen, "seem to have a counterpart in Islam," so that by the nineteenth century the myth of the interfaith Islamic utopia was used to challenge "supposedly liberal Christian Europe to make good on its promise of political equality" for Jews. Soon the "Golden Age" of Islamic Spain—when scholar-diplomats like Hasday Ibn Shaprut, Samuel ibn Nagrela, and Judah

Halevi graced the corridors of Spanish-Muslim courts—became a recurring meme in European Jewish writing. Young Muslims today are poring over the writings of these German-Jewish scholars for various reasons. These nineteenth-century texts addressing life on the margins of society, urban exclusion, life in the *galut* (exile), while praising Islamic Spain, speak loudly to young Muslim intellectuals, who are pondering questions of minority status and diaspora and trying to respond to accusations of dual loyalty and fealty to a different legal code—canards leveled against Jews for centuries.

Moreover, what better way to counter both Muslim anti-Semitism and neoconservative talk of Islamic Judeophobia than by citing the words of these Jewish thinkers who extolled Islam's pluralism? Thus, today one finds Muslim bloggers discussing the works of Muslim-sympathizing nineteenth-century historians like the Hungarian Ignác Goldziher, who knelt in prayer at a mosque in Cairo; Heinrich Graetz, whose classic *History of the Jews* (1891) praises Jewish life in Arabia; the German Romantic poet Heinrich Heine, whose play *Almansor* was written, in 1819, following a wave of anti-Jewish violence that wracked a number of German cities. The play, set in sixteenth-century Spain, when Christians were forcing the conversion of Muslims, ends tragically when the protagonist, Almansor, and his beloved choose to leap to their deaths rather than submit to the Christians.

It is fascinating and strangely ironic that young Muslims today are studying the thought of European Jews—pre- and post-emancipation—in the hopes that the voices of these Jewish scholars who had left the shtetl can help the Muslims find their way out of their ghetto. But these "Pro-Islamic Jews," as Bernard Lewis termed them, came under heavy criticism in the late 1960s, and more recently from younger neoconservative writers. The neocons see these Jewish thinkers as biased observers who, frustrated by their exclusion in Europe, developed this "Andalusian myth" of interfaith utopia. Muslim activists today are more sophisticated when they invoke Islamic Spain than their 1960s forebears were; they don't speak of utopia, but argue that despite the restrictions placed on non-Muslims, Jews under Iberian Muslim rule experienced greater security and integration than Jews in Christian Europe. But nineteenth-century German texts can only have so much appeal among young Muslims today. The songs of Judeo-Arabic singers and their love of al-Andalus, however, have a wider and more immediate appeal; and they have yet to be discredited by polemicists.

The Archaeology of Trauma

In September 2003, Safinez Bousbia, a twenty-one-year-old Algerian studying at Oxford, was strolling through the kasbah of Algiers with a friend when they walked into a mirror store. While chatting with the seventy-eight-year-old shopkeeper, Mohammed Ferkaoui, she noticed a faded black-and-white photo on his desk of a group of musicians in dark suits and fez hats, some with violins sitting upright on their knees, others holding ouds.

"That photo is from 1956, when we played at the Algiers opera house," explained Ferkaoui. "I used to play accordion with the orchestra, and when a waltz would come on, by god, I would dance with my accordion as if it were a woman!"

The photo of Muslim and Jewish artists—pupils of the late maestro El Hadj Mohamed El Anka—who used to perform Andalusi music together at weddings, cafés, and local theaters, captivated Safinez. She set out to locate every living musician in the photo, searching through conservatory records, visiting the local municipal archive. "I just wanted to meet these artists and ask them about their memories of 1950s Algeria. They were scattered across the country," she explains, "and when I met them individually, I wanted to reunite them. When I saw how they reacted to each other, how they still had that love for each other, that gusto for the music, I decided to make a film about them."

The film, *El Gusto*, released in 2011, traces the history of *chaabi* music, a popular form of Andalusi music, from its emergence in the seaport and kasbah of Algiers through the 1940s, where local artists would barter cigarettes for banjos from American GIs, through the outbreak of the Algerian Revolution. The war of independence split the musicians as the National Liberation Front (FLN), and the secret French paramilitary force, the Organisation de l'Arméé Secrète (OAS), threatened Jews and Muslims who performed together. The film combines stunning sky shots of Algeria's coast with images of the decrepit kasbah, cafés, and houses where the musicians grew up, spliced with performances and interviews with the elder statesmen of Algerian music: El Hadj El Anka, Rachid Berkani, Ahmed Bernaoui, Redha el-Djilali, as well as the Jewish musicians now residing in France—Luc Cherki, Maurice El Medioni, Yousef Hedjaj, René Perez, and Robert Castel. It concludes with a powerful reunion concert in Marseille, where the musicians—now aged between seventy-five and ninety-five—meet after fifty years. The scenes of the French-based musicians embracing their friends on the docks of Marseille are particularly poignant.

Safinez then began organizing concerts for this 1950s Muslim-Jewish ensemble; they have performed across Europe, Asia, and in Morocco. "This is the music before the revolution," she smiles. "It's like an Algerian Buena Vista Social Club." But with the film, this accidental cinéaste also stumbled into the middle of an intractable memory war between France and Algeria. El Gusto has not received permission to perform in Algiers. "The authorities refused," says Safinez. "At a private screening for government officials, six people walked out when the Algiers synagogue appeared on the screen. Ridiculous!" Her attempt to revive Judeo-Arabic music has exposed deep fault lines in collective memory.

After World War II, Algeria's popular Andalusi music flourished. Medioni enrolled at the conservatory in Oran, becoming an apprentice of Ahmed Wahbi, the father of *rai* music. "I performed regularly at the city's opera house," Medioni recalls proudly, "part of the orchestra directed by Mahieddine Bachtarzi." In Algiers, Line Monty—then still Leila Fateh—became a pupil of Cheikh Sassi. Reinette—who was still known as Sultana Daoud—would study with Mustafa Iskandarani. Luc Cherki enrolled in the prestigious Algiers conservatory, with the maestro Abdelghani Belkaid, now his neighbor in Paris. In the postwar years, Lili Labassi would emerge as a musical giant in

Algeria and the wider Maghreb, leading an orchestra on Radio Alger with Mohamed El Anka. Starting in 1946, this master violinist and composer and his twelve-year-old son, Robert (now a member of El Gusto), would board the train from Algiers to Casablanca, stopping at towns and doing shows for Muslim and Jewish aficionados.

"The big war was over—and all seemed possible," recalls Cherki. "Ramadan was wonderful, we sang *chaabi* at cafés in the kasbah of Algiers until 3 a.m.—every night."

In postwar France, more Oriental cabarets opened in the Latin Quarter—Le Djazair, Le Soleil d'Algérie, La Kasbah, Le Tam Tam, Nuits de Liban, Le Baghdad, and so on. Algerian stars Ahmed Wahbi, Slimane Azem, and Cheikh El Hasnaoui had all settled in Paris, and all kinds of collaborations were taking place with Arab musicians visiting from Egypt and Lebanon, and even with American jazz artists.

Yousef Hedjaj, a Tunisian Jew who arrived in France in 1946 and got a job at Le Djazair, was in the thick of this musical mix. "We performed for everyone—Lebanese, Egyptians, French, American tourists," says Hedjaj, now ninety-three-years-old. "I once played in Louis Armstrong's band when he came to Paris."

One night in 1950, Hedjaj, by chance, launched the career of one of the Arab world's greatest voices. While performing at Le Tam Tam on Rue de la Huchette (the name "Tam Tam" connotes a kind of drum, but was also an acronym for Tunisia-Algeria-Morocco), he decided to give a song he had recently written about his mother to the cabaret owner's thirteen-year-old daughter to perform. The little girl, Warda, would often do a set before her bedtime at 10 p.m. Her rendition of "Ya Oumi" that night was a sensation, and the girl quickly became a child star, nicknamed "North Africa's Nightingale." She began to host a children's show on Radio Orient and grew up to become Warda Al Jazairia (the Algerian Rose), one of the Arab world's greatest vocalists, and a diva who would never forget her roots in Paris's cabaret scene.

As anticolonial ferment spread across the Maghreb, the Arab-Jewish musicians were hopeful, and traveled frequently between France and North Africa. In November 1955, when Morocco's king, Mohammed V, was returning from French-imposed exile in Madagascar back to his homeland, he stopped over in Paris. Samy El

Maghribi, a Moroccan cantor and maestro of Andalusian poetry, and Luc Cherki—who happened to be visiting France—got wind of the monarch's landing. The two ran down to a local cabaret, where El Maghribi recorded a song, "A Thousand and One Congratulations" ("Alf Haniya Wa Haniya"), celebrating the king's release. "Samy recorded the song in one afternoon, in the basement of Le Soleil d'Algérie and we hopped on the Métro and took a copy to His Majesty," recalls Cherki. "I remember—he was meeting with people at Hotel Scribe." The song would go on to become a nationalist anthem in postcolonial Morocco. In November 1956, as French, British, and Israeli jets bombarded Egypt, these Arab-Jewish artists continued performing, Yousef Hedjaj playing at Le Djazair and Le Tam Tam, and Rainette at her own recently opened Moorish café on Rue Saint-Marc.

In France, the police had been monitoring cafés and neighborhood theaters for anticolonial music since the 1930s. El Kamal's skits and vaudeville performances had attracted particular attention. In August 1938, following his troupe's tour of eastern France, a local city official, appalled by the "nationalist character" of El Kamal's show, called on authorities to take all necessary measures to protect French troops and North African laborers from the "pernicious influences" of his voice. When El Kamal died in 1953, Paris's Algerian community had grown to 120,000 or so, and the comedic theater movement he had started was going strong; laborers would gather after work in cafés and listen to songs and skits about the old country. The police would sit in as well, and if a song was deemed political, the performer would be asked to switch to another number. The musicians in turn began to sing allegorical tales. Slimane Azem, the Berber musician, who arrived in Paris in 1937, created a repertoire of protest songs qua parables that vexed the French authorities, his most famous being "Les Sauterelles" (The Locusts): "Locusts, please leave my fields," he strummed his banjo as policemen watched. His records would eventually be banned as well.

But then the Algerian War began in 1954, and the cabarets in the Quartier Latin became contested spaces. The police did spot checks every night, rounding up patrons. National Liberation Front militants appeared and warned belly dancers against drinking or dancing with Frenchmen. Shéhérazade, a retired Algerian belly dancer now in her mid-seventies, was one of the twenty-five belly dancers who performed nightly at Le Djazair. She recalls the political tension: "As [Algerian] dancers, we did not have the right to drink with the French. If a French guy bought me a drink, the next day I would be summoned by FLN people." The FLN also demanded that the dancers, like the seventeen-year-old Shéhérazade, carry the movement's banner during marches. The rallies often turned violent. It was just down the road from Rue de la Huchette that Maurice Papon, the notorious police chief, on October 17, 1961, cracked down on a march on Boulevard Saint-Michel, leaving over two hundred Algerians dead. But the nightlife never stopped, says Shéhérazade, because neither the FLN nor its rival the MNA (Algerian National Movement) wanted the cabarets shut down; they just wanted the club owners to make regular payments.

The music did stop in Algeria.

Musicians like Cherki and Medioni initially felt the pressure from the French paramilitary group the OAS, not from the FLN. "When the war started, the OAS threatened me, telling me not to sing in Arabic," says Cherki. "They said, 'We're fighting Muslims, and as a French citizen, you shouldn't sing in Arabic, or sing with Muslims.'" The OAS was invoking the Crémieux Decree, which had granted Algerian Jews citizenship in 1870 (withdrawn by Vichy and reinstated in 1943). When that law was passed, Algeria's Jews legally ceased to be "indigenous" to Algeria and were thereafter lumped in the category of *pieds-noirs* along with European colonists, having different rights than Algerian Arabs and Berbers. (This confusion continues to this day in French public discourse, where Jews of Algerian descent are described as *pieds-noirs*.) In practice, the decree positioned Algeria's Jews as intermediaries, as a "buffer community" between the French colonial state and the Muslim majority. When the war of independence began in 1954, both the settler-led OAS and a faction of the FLN would identify the Jews with French colonialism. "I was born and raised in the kasbah," says Cherki. "My closest friends were Muslim. When people started throwing bombs, I just hid out in the kasbah and sang there. I didn't dare sing in the city's cafés." In his memoir, Cherki refers to the young militants—including Ali La Pointe, who was immortalized in the film *The Battle of Algiers*—as *mes amis de kasbah*. "I knew all the so-called revolutionaries. Ali La Pointe was a good friend, *un bon copain*. He loved music—he was very nice to me," he chuckles. "We hung out with the Hamiche brothers, at their café. There was no alcohol, but there I stayed."

As the political situation deteriorated, Algeria's Jews would find themselves in a thankless situation. "As Jews, we were caught in the middle," says Cherki. "It was a tearing [*déchirure*] that we experienced."

The establishment of Israel in 1948, and the displacement of seven hundred thousand Palestinians, had stirred up Muslim-Jewish relations across North Africa. When Nasser came to power in Egypt in 1952, he proclaimed solidarity with the FLN and, to de Gaulle's frustration, began supporting the Algerian liberation movement politically and militarily. This was one reason that France joined Britain and Israel in their assault on Egypt in October 1956, following Nasser's nationalizing of the Suez Canal. The sight of French and Israeli jets strafing Egypt, just as French jets had bombarded Algeria, provoked anger. The knowledge that Israel was voting against Algeria's independence at the UN, supplying France with intelligence on FLN arms supplies from Egypt, and had even set up a special force in Algeria (the Misgeret [Framework], made up of Algerian Jews, who were also reservists in the French army), created more resentment of French and Jewish communities in North Africa, which gradually came to be seen as politically indistinguishable. When de Gaulle visited Algeria in December 1960, clashes broke out between Algerian Muslims and Europeans, cars and buildings were set on fire in Bab El Oued, and the Great Synagogue of the kasbah of Algiers was ransacked.

The FLN leadership explicitly repudiated these acts of violence. In May 1961, the FLN appealed to Algeria's Jews in an open letter, emphasizing how French colonial rule pitted Jews against Muslims by giving Jews greater rights, and how Muslims protected Jews from Vichy persecution. "Propaganda and colonial policy have they not constantly tried to make us forget the fact that Jews have been in Algeria for more than a thousand years and that they are an integral part of the Algerian People," stated the letter. Algerian Jews, who rejected both the FLN and European extremism, believed that the nation's shared Andalusian heritage, preserved in the music, could keep the country together. "The singer and musician [Cheikh] Raymond, is he not valuable to the hearts of Muslims? They love him because he has contributed to the conservation and enrichment of Algerian folklore that the colonialists wanted to extinguish," wrote one Jewish leader in May 1961 in an open letter to Algeria's Muslims. Many believed that respected musicians like Cheikh Raymond and Mahieddine Bachtarzi could use the Andalusi repertoire to bind Muslim and Jew.

But threats against musicians by FLN and OAS militants made it more and more difficult for Muslim-Jewish ensembles to gather. Music halls and cafés were blown up, artists targeted. The bitter irony surrounding the letter, hoping that Cheikh Raymond could play a conciliatory role, is that on June 22, 1961—a few weeks after its publication—the forty-eight-year-old Raymond was shot dead by an FLN militant while shopping with his daughter at Souk El Esser in Constantine. Whether he was targeted because, as his family would later say, he was a symbol of *convivencia* or because he believed in a French Algeria, the exodus of Constantine's Jewish community began almost immediately after his death. As violence increased—in November 1961, the OAS murdered William Levy, secretary-general of the Algiers Socialist Party Federation—graffiti appeared offering the *pieds-noirs* one of two choices: "the suitcase or the coffin." Most of Algeria's 130,000 Jews chose the former, despite the FLN's eleventh-hour attempts to reassure the Jews and encouraging them to join their "Muslim brothers." In January 1962, Serge Bromberger, a prominent foreign-affairs journalist, published a piece in *Le Figaro* claiming that Israel was training units of the OAS, further raising tensions. In the following months, the majority of Algeria's Jews departed for France. Luc Cherki departed for Paris shortly after Cheikh Raymond's death. "I left with two suitcases, mostly packed with documents and records—very few clothes. I have never been back since."

"C'était une *mosiba*," says Maurice El Medioni, using the Arabic word for "calamity." "We left our entrails in Algeria. We lived very well in Algeria—there was milk, there was honey. We had no desire to leave; we had no reason to leave."

His wife Juliette's eyes well up with tears as she remembers the so-called repatriation.

The Golden Age

Hundreds of thousands of *pieds-noirs* boarded ships and headed for French cities. The Algerian musicians who ended up in Paris—Labassi, Medioni, Cherki, Blond Blond, Reinette—began to congregate regularly at Le Poussin Bleu, a restaurant, on Rue du Faubourg-Montmartre, right across from the Folies-Bergère. Today it's a kosher deli. "We were all looking for each other—and we found each other at Le Poussin Bleu," says Medioni. Le Poussin provided an escape from the joblessness and hostility they faced on a daily basis. The musicians gathered around the violinist Lili Labassi, then in his late sixties and recently widowed—his wife had died from heart failure a few months after arriving on French shores. With El Medioni on piano, Blond Blond banging the tambourine, Cherki on guitar, Reinette on oud, and Samy El Maghribi shaking maracas and singing, the group had all-night sessions that they still smile about. The debate rages to this day whether the scene at Le Poussin Bleu was better than of Rue de la Huchette, where Line Monty and Salim Halali reigned. For Robert Castel, then a teenager, who would accompany his father, Labassi, there is no comparison. "The cabarets were bling, bling, for tourists *de la grenadine*—Le Poussin Bleu was heritage, tradition, for true lovers of Andalusi, *ushaq*!"

Soon a hauntingly beautiful music of exile began to emerge. On his piano, Medioni composed songs about Oran's alleyways and Paris's despondent sky, and gave them to Line Monty to perform. Three sentiments would recur in the songs—exile (*el ghorba*), separation (*el faraq*), and nostalgia (*el wahash*). The composition that would come to encapsulate this uprooted community's fall from grace was "Ana L'Werqa" (I Am the Leaf), a memorable tango by Lili Boniche. "I used to flutter on the highest branches, and now I've fallen," sang

Boniche in quavering Arabic. In this song, and others like it, Boniche moved from an Argentine tango note to an Andalusian *nuba*, keeping the same mournful tone. "I am the poor, forgotten leaf, dry and confused," he intoned, "winds push me from place to place."

It was during this epoch that the term "Judeo-Arab music" came into use, to describe these deracinated artists and their music—a contested term that Lili Boniche hated from the start. "Do we ever say a Muslim is playing Islamo-Arabic music?" he once said. "I play Arab music, that's it—period." For Boniche, whose compositions would try to make sense of the Jews' banishment from the Arab world (in one verse addressed to his Muslim compatriots, he asks, "There's only one God, *ghir rabi wahed,* you pray seated, I pray standing, *allach tu ne m'aimes pas,* why don't you love me?"), adding the prefix "Judeo" to "Arab music" simply accepted and legitimized the separation. Perhaps prior to 1962 there wasn't anything distinctive about the Jewish contributions to Andalusi music, but the genre that emerged in France explicitly tried to deal with the contradictions of being a Jew of Arab heritage in a West that perceives the Jew as the antonym of the Arab. Addressing this point soon after the 1967 war, Salim Halali, now approaching middle age, recorded an Arabic version of the vaudeville hit "My Yiddishe Mama." The original number, written in 1925 during the flowering of Yiddish theater and music in New York, voiced a nostalgia for "Old World" life, as symbolized by the Jewish mother, and anxiety over assimilation into American society. Halali's Arabic rendition did something similar, expressing longing for a different Old World, for an Arabic-speaking past; he sang of sleepless nights, recalling his childhood, tears shed for his mother, *"Ma Yiddish mama, qalbik tal alaya."* The song, articulating a New World angst in Arabic, captured the mood of the moment, as Jewish communities departed the Arab world in droves. "I still remember the night when Salim first sang 'Ma Yiddish Mama'—he put a Central European song in *istikhbar* style," recalls Luc Cherki. "The audience was mesmerized."

It was in these years that Line Monty's plaintive voice would capture French listeners. Successful on the cabaret scene in the late 1950s, when she was singing songs written by Charles Aznavour, she then went to America, hoping to make it big. In 1962, she sang at Carnegie Hall; in 1967, she accompanied Aznavour when he sang there. ("Singer Brings Paris to Mecca," declared a local newspaper.) She did cabaret nights at Oh Paris on East Fifty-third Street. She performed for months at Le Petit Paris in Washington, DC, for their "Night in Morocco" with a Latino trio, singing boleros and Edith Piaf. The *Washington Post* described her as "the petite blonde singer who had just arrived from Paris with 17 suitcases." In America, after the 1967 War, there was a sudden interest in Israeli and Mizrahi music; the Moroccan singer Jo Amar, for example, toured temples across the country performing his "Songs of Victory." But Line Monty dreamed of Hollywood and international fame. In 1982, she appeared in a film, the Miami-based organized-crime caper *Le Grand Pardon,* playing herself and singing Yousef Hedjaj's song "Ya Oumi." The film and Line's rendition are remembered to this day by France's Algerian Jewish community, as is the detail that the chanteuse twisted her ankle while filming and had to return to Paris.

The period from 1962 until Lili Labassi's death in 1969 was one of hardship and loss, but also of musical abundance—and is today remembered as *l'age d'or.* The exiled musicians were concentrated in the Paris area. El Kahlaoui Tounsi founded Dounia Records, where luckily he recorded the leading North African musicians on vinyl. The scene in Paris fed off the musical ferment in Algeria, where independence had sparked a revival led by Mohamed El Anka. The FLN—now in government—instituted a cultural policy that firmly rooted Algerian nationalism in Islamic Spain, and made Andalusi music independent Algeria's classical music.

A pop type of Andalusi music would soon cross over to the French mainstream in the 1960s, but it wasn't because of Luc Cherki, Line Monty, or any of the stars performing at Le Poussin Bleu. On October 5, 1962, French television broadcast a documentary about a twenty-four-year-old singer named Enrico Macias; curly-haired, with long, dark eyelashes, the young charmer strummed his guitar and sang a song "Adieu, mon pays" (Good-bye, My Country), drawing out his vowels in an Arabic *mawal* style. The song, about the sea, sunshine, and friends Macias had left in Algeria, sold fifty thousand copies in a few days, and the documentary made him a national sensation.

Before embracing a Spanish stage name, Macias was known as Gaston Ghrenassia. The scion of a prominent Jewish family in Constantine, he studied under Cheikh Raymond, marrying the maestro's daughter. He left Algeria shortly after his father-in-law's assassination, and apparently wrote "Good-bye, My Country" aboard the boat to Marseille. Macias and his father tried to perform traditional Andalusi music upon arriving in 1962, but the reaction from French audiences to the Arabic lyrics was so hostile, the son shifted to Mediterranean *varieté* music, tinged with "Oriental" instruments. Macias was soon embraced as the voice of the *pieds-noir* exodus, his music expressing their pain and loss, and he would become and remain to this day *the* most well-known face of Judeo-Arabic music.

Macias was also controversial from the start. During the 1967 War, he flew to Israel and performed for the Israeli Defense Forces in the Sinai and the Suez Canal; then, accompanied by General Moshe Dayan, he was one of the first Jews to pray at the Wailing Wall, his photo splashed on French newspapers. During the October War in 1973, he returned again to play for Israeli troops in the Sinai; his records were subsequently banned in several Arab states, including Algeria. Over the next twenty-five years, Macias sold some sixty million records worldwide, all the while making contradictory and polemical political statements. He wrote songs about his exile titled "Spanish Jew" and "L'Etranger," saying his exile helped him sympathize with Palestinian refugees, yet insisting that Israel had not uprooted them; he supported a Palestinian state, but wanted Jerusalem to remain the capital of Israel.

In the late 1990s, as a French Arab political movement emerged, Macias became a lightning rod for Muslim-Jewish relations. The "Beur" movement, as it was called, was modeled in various ways on the American civil rights movement, pushing for civil liberties and job programs. The political agitation sparked a North African musical fad among French youth, and the 1990s saw the rise of *rai* stars like Cheb Khaled and Mami, many of them fleeing Algeria's civil war and settling in France. The North African cultural wave revived Macias's lagging career as he, seeing the interest in Arab music, shifted from Mediterranean pop to Andalusian music, or what he called the "sacred repertoire" of his youth.

In 1999, Macias recorded an album with the Algerian violinist Taoufik Bestandji, the grandson of Cheikh Abdelkrim Bestandji; their project was meant to revive the musical communion of Jews and Muslims in Algeria. After their first concert, in Bourge, Belgium, Macias told his audience, "From this night on, two communities, Jews and Muslims, are reconciled and *retrouvés*." Then in October 2000, in the midst of the Palestinian intifada, Macias performed at a pro-Israeli rally in Paris and, in between songs, denounced the French media for their pro-Palestinian bias, saying he preferred American media for their Middle East coverage. At his next show with Bestandji, protestors lined up outside the theater in Roubaix, chanting, "Free Palestine, stop the massacre!" The very Arab youth movement that had created a new space for Macias was now calling for his boycott. As long as he was singing French pop for other *pieds-noirs,* the Beur movement could ignore his political statements as the ravings of a middle-aged has-been; but when he began singing the Maghreb's treasured Andalusi repertoire—while cheering for the IDF in between *nuba*—the youth activists could bite their tongue no longer.

Macias has, in the last decade, immersed himself deeper in the Andalusi repertoire, singing in Arabic, while swerving further to the right, which makes his shows a rather dissonant experience: onstage, he will tearfully sing classical Andalusi compositions in Arabic, then shift to Israeli nationalist anthems in Hebrew. In 2007, Macias threw his support behind Sarkozy, praising the president as a "humanist," and was even going to accompany him on a state visit to Algeria. But a public outcry erupted in Algiers, with various Islamist and conservative leaders opposing Macias's proposed visit, asking why the Algerian government would fête a man who just months earlier had been decorated by the Israeli Ministry of Defense for his "lifelong support" of the Israeli army. Algerian Jews and the *pieds-noirs* can travel freely to Algeria; but Macias, because of his position as UN goodwill ambassador and his strongly pro-Israeli discourse, is now caught in the tangle of symbolic and memory politics that hangs over the French-

Algerian relationship. Algeria wants an official apology from France for "crimes" committed in Algeria during the 130 years of colonial domination and in a war that left half a million Algerians dead. When Sarkozy visited Algeria in December 2007, he said colonialism was "unjust," but refused to express any repentance. Instead, upon returning to Paris he held a reception at the Élysée announcing reparations for the *harkis,* the Algerians who fought for France against Algeria. A guest of honor at the proceedings, Macias told France 2 that France should "categorically" not apologize for colonization, and that both sides needed to express regret for their actions during the war.

Macias has long seen himself as a carrier of the Andalusi repertoire, and a symbol of Judeo-Arab *convivencia.* "I've been a symbol of exile since 1962," he said when his 2007 trip to Algeria was canceled. "I could have become a symbol of reconciliation for all of Algeria's children." But in Algeria, musicologists see him as a lightweight, continuously milking his relationship to "Uncle Raymond." In September 2008, a concert was held in honor of the recently deceased Lili Boniche, celebrating his repertoire, and there was no mention of Macias. Macias's support for rightist policies and very conservative views of French colonialism have made him the butt of jokes in stand-up comedy and *banlieue* culture. Younger activists interested in Muslim-Jewish dialogue and memory activism see him as an obstacle. His positions have further aligned not only Algeria's Jews but their musical repertoire with French colonialism and Israel, complicating matters for activists like Safinez Bousbia, who is trying to bring El Gusto to Algiers. "Macias generates so much opposition in Algeria, he has really made our work difficult," she says. The younger generation is now looking for an alternative symbol of *convivencia,* another musician to counter Macias's fifty-year reign.

"A Muslim Schindler? An Arab Wallenberg?"

In October 2006, a few weeks after the film *Indigènes,* about Muslim troops fighting the Nazis, opened, Robert Satloff, director of the

Washington Institute for Near East Policy (WINERP), published a book titled *Among the Righteous: Lost Stories from the Holocaust's Long Reach into Arab Lands*. The aim of the book, the author explained, was to "fight the hatred of 9/11" by showing how "the Holocaust was an Arab story too." Satloff's main thesis is that when Nazi Germany controlled North Africa, from June 1940 to May 1943, the Nazis, in addition to various restrictions enforced against Jews, also placed them in a hundred or so labor camps scattered across the Maghreb. "The Arabs in these lands were not too different from Europeans: With war waging around them, most Arabs stood by and did nothing; many participated fully and willingly in the persecution of Jews; and a brave few even helped save Jews," writes Satloff. "Arab collaborators were everywhere . . . Without the help of local Arabs, the persecution of Jews would have been virtually impossible." Betrayals extended to the world of music. Satloff charged that Mohamed El Kamal, the anticolonial nationalist and vaudeville singer, had joined Radio Berlin, "the Nazis' premier propaganda organ," abandoning his partner Salim Halali, who fortunately found refuge in the Grand Mosque of Paris. The author concludes by identifying a few "righteous Arabs" who protected Jews (among them Si Kaddour Benghabrit, the rector of the Grand Mosque of Paris) and confiding that he wrote the book after 9/11 as a gesture of conciliation "to my Arab friends," hoping the study "could make the Holocaust a source of pride, worthy of remembrance—rather than avoidance or denial." Satloff subsequently launched an initiative to have the Yad Vashem Memorial in Israel recognize these "righteous Arabs."

Satloff's book was not well received in North Africa. Moroccan newspapers denounced this "monstrous" book that attacked the country's cultural memory, saying that Satloff depicts "a few brave Moroccans, but the other millions are bloodthirsty anti-Semites," all while demanding a "mea culpa," observed *Maroc Hebdomadaire*. Others pointed out the suffering inflicted on Muslims by Vichy rule and that the same Nazi camps would be used by French colonialists after the war to intern Muslims. Reviewers were particularly puzzled by the timing of the book: At a moment when American neoconservatism had caused enormous damage at home and abroad (the U.S.

invasion of Iraq had dispossessed a million and unleashed a bloody civil war; American society under Bush was polarized and reeling economically), and Israel was strafing Lebanon, why would this neoconservative American author write a book accusing Arabs—not just the mufti of Jerusalem, but general populations—of collaborating with Nazis? Satloff had extended the net of Holocaust guilt from the heads of state to the masses, and from the Levant to the Atlantic and deep down into the Sahara Desert. That the book was prefaced as a "letter to my Arab friends" was deemed particularly cynical; if he wanted to understand "the hatred that produced 9/11," wrote one Algerian reviewer, he could have examined American and Israeli policy for the last fifty years. Others dismissed the book as yet another attempt by the Israel lobby (WINERP is a spin-off of AIPAC) to intervene in the political life of the Arab world, noting that the label "righteous" was being conferred on compliant Arab figures to shore up regimes considered "moderate."

A more tempered response came at a book reception held for Satloff in Cairo in January 2007. Abdel Moneim Said, a prominent Egyptian scholar, explained that discussions of the Holocaust in the Middle East and North Africa are shaped by the collective memory of imperialism and the region's political history; the Holocaust, he explained, is seen as a "moral cover" (*ghata' akhlaqi*) for Israeli exceptionalism, from the partition of Palestine down to the Jewish state's right to nuclear weapons. This point echoes an argument made by Edward Said in the mid-1990s, when, alarmed by Arab attitudes toward the Holocaust, he wrote, "There is no reason at all, in my opinion, not to submit oneself in horror and awe to the special tragedy besetting the Jewish people," adding, "We must recognize the realities of the Holocaust not as a blank check for Israelis to abuse us, but as a sign of our humanity, our ability to understand history, our requirement that our suffering be mutually acknowledged." Yet, almost two decades hence, a reciprocal acknowledgment of suffering has not taken place; Israel has yet to acknowledge any role in the Palestinian *nakba,* and the view of the Holocaust as a "blank check" for American and Israeli policies remains widespread in Muslim-majority states and in Europe's Muslim communities.

In December 2012, the Middle East Studies Association organized a roundtable discussion called "Debating the Holocaust: Fascism and Anti-Semitism in Middle East Studies," featuring Arab, Israeli, and German historians. The dialogue focused on University of London scholar Gilbert Achcar's recently published study *The Arabs and the Holocaust.* The panelists and audience members largely agreed with Achcar's main claims that although there is a historic link between the Shoah and the Palestinian tragedy—in that Nazi policies drove European Jews to flee to Palestine when the Allies refused to grant them safe haven, and Israel would also provide refuge to Jewish survivors after the war—the two catastrophes are not comparable: the extermination of a population is morally not equivalent to mass dispossession. Likewise, the European educators in the audience had no quarrel with Achcar's suggestion that given the ongoing Palestinian-Israeli conflict, in the Muslim world, the Holocaust should be taught alongside the history of the Palestinian *nakba;* and that any attempt to teach the Holocaust without addressing the *nakba* will be viewed as propaganda. Audience members agreed, one noting that because of the widespread "Nazification" of European Muslims, teachers in German schools with large Turkish populations are including the stories of Turkish Muslims who sheltered Jews.

The fireworks began when Achcar argued that there's a "qualitative difference" between the "racism of the oppressed" and the "racism of the oppressor": that one can't equate German anti-Semitism with Arab hostility toward Jews, which after all is a response to Israeli policy and *nakba* denial. This claim drew a sharp response from Gudrun Krämer, the chair of the panel and a historian at the Free University of Berlin, saying that Achcar was being condescending. "Victims can also be racist," she argued. "If you say Arab anti-Semitism is a reaction to oppression, it's patronizing, and Israelis can say the same thing: we were oppressed." The audience split: half agreed with Achcar, citing Fanon's argument that the racism of the colonizer is not the same as the racism of the colonized, with others arguing that all racisms are morally reprehensible. At this rather tense roundtable, American attendees were exposed to a European political debate that is growing louder and more polarized. The late historian Tony Judt expressed the issue succinctly: "The recovered memory of Europe's dead Jews has become the very definition and guarantee of the continent's restored humanity"; yet how, asked Judt, to reconcile that historical memory in a postwar Europe where Jews "face no threats or prejudices comparable to those of the past," but where Muslims are increasingly the internal "other" facing xenophobic movements, War on Terror policies, and are vulnerable to the appeal of radical Islam?

Few Muslim activists or community leaders want to get involved in these sensitive debates, or to respond to books like Satloff's, fearing that publicly engaging this issue will only trigger further opprobrium against their community. Others are looking to Andalusi music for answers.

"The Children of Ziryab"

One Wednesday in September 2011, the film *Les Hommes Libres* (released in the United States as *Free Men*), opened in French theaters. Set in the Vichy era, the film tells the story of how the Grand Mosque of Paris, located on the city's Left Bank, provided refuge and certificates of Muslim identity to a small number of Jews, allowing them to evade deportation. The film centers around two real-life figures: Si Kaddour Benghabrit and Salim Halali. The former was rector of the Grand Mosque during World War II. In the film, he is seen giving German soldiers and their wives tours of the mosque while sheltering Jewish children in the basement. In one scene, Nazi soldiers strolling through the mosque's tiled courtyard pause to watch a young Algerian, with carefully coiffed black hair and an embroidered red vest, singing at the mosque's Moorish café. (A *café maure* and a *hamam* were built as part of the mosque complex in 1926 to give French visitors a taste of the Orient.) The young man is Salim Halali, the dashing Algerian cabaret singer, and one of the Jews who escaped deportation by finding refuge in the mosque. *Free Men* recounts how the mosque rector granted the crooner papers attesting to his Muslim identity and even had Halali's father's name engraved on a tombstone at the Muslim cemetery in Bobigny, to throw the Nazis off the young artist's trail. The Arab cabaret scene of 1940s Paris forms the sonic backdrop to the political intrigue. As Halali's character sings at the mosque and at a cabaret called Andaloussia, Muslims and Jews try to evade Vichy laws, and different Algerian factions—Communists, FLN and MNA activists—compete for political turf.

The initial reviews of *Free Men* were not unkind. *Le Figaro* said the film "reconstitutes an atmosphere and a period marvelously." These reviewers thought this was a side of French history that needed to be told, and found the story credible. Paris in the 1940s was, after all, home to over a hundred thousand North Africans, including thousands of Arabic-speaking Jews, who had similar names and folkways as their Muslim counterparts; and Jewish men could also pass for Muslim, as both are circumcised. The film was seen as conducive to dialogue and reconciliation ("ideal for a school setting," said *L'Express*), and hundreds of students from high schools in the *banlieues* were invited to a special screening and question-and-answer session with the filmmaker, Ismaël Ferroukhi, and the actors. Ferroukhi began lobbying the culture and education ministries to get the film shown in schools, and to place a commemorative plaque at the Grand Mosque honoring Benghabrit. "It pays homage to the people of our history who have been invisible," he said. "It shows another reality, that Muslims and Jews existed in peace." The film was also an attempt to resurrect Salim Halali, to portray him as a symbol of Andalusian *convivencia,* an Arab Jew, who in his cosmopolitanism is more inclusive and less divisive than Enrico Macias.

But then the attacks began, first from French historians who said that while Salim Halali was indeed "saved" by the mosque, there was little archival evidence to suggest that the Grand Mosque was a center of resistance. Critics argued that the story line was more a sop to contemporary politics and Israel-Palestine polemics than actual history (especially given that Halali's character was played by the Israeli-Arab actor Mahmoud Shalaby). Benjamin Stora, a historian of North African Jewry who served as a consultant to the film, responded, saying the film never claimed the mosque was a "center of resistance" and that it was just telling, in a fictionalized manner, the story of the mosque rector and the individuals he protected. "Much has been written about Muslim collaboration with the Nazis," wrote Stora. "But it has not been widely known that Muslims helped Jews. There are still stories to be told, to be written." Critics also argued that more historical evidence was needed regarding Halali's case, before the Yad Vashem Institute could make Si Kaddour Benghabrit one of the "righteous"; and if Benghabrit had protected Salim Halali, why didn't he shelter Salim's sister, Berthe Valaix (née Halali), who was deported to Auschwitz in August 1943? Ferroukhi clearly thought telling the story of Salim Halali could help bring Muslims into France's national memory; yet what drew the most ire was the educational booklet that was distributed to students at screenings, describing how the film could "illuminate" memories of World War II.

The conflict between Jews and Muslims in France—and Western Europe more broadly—is not about jobs or resources but about history and clashing narratives. As Muslims mobilize, they are putting forth alternative narratives on colonialism and Middle East politics, and that is drawing opposition. Moreover, as a Muslim underclass emerges in Europe, a historic shift is under way: Muslims are taking the place of Jews as the continent's long-standing internal "other," often moving into the same urban enclaves and housing projects where Jews were once concentrated—and that too is politically jarring. This underclass is forming against a backdrop of ongoing Middle East conflict, and the more excluded European Muslim youth feel, the more the "Gaza ghetto" comes to epitomize their own situation (of being "locked up, locked out, and locked in," in the words of a young Muslim Londoner) and global Muslim besiegement. And for some young Muslims, resentment of Jews abroad becomes entangled with resentment of Jews at home; they will speak of their Jewish compatriots as supporters of Israeli policy and representatives of international imperialism. "The experience of Muslims [in France] becomes an illustration of what Muslims are said to experience at [the] international level and is constantly associated with images of the Israeli domination of Palestinians and the violence inflicted on the Iraqi people by the Americans," explains French sociologist Michel Wieviorka. "This ghetto anti-Semitism constitutes a historical paradox: those who, in the past, lived in the ghettos . . . and have endured racist hatred have today become, in an impressive turnaround, the imagined root of the evils from which they themselves have suffered."

In the early 2000s, following the second intifada, French journalists began warning of the rising anti-Semitism among Muslims in the *banlieues* ("the lost territories of the Republic," in the words of one observer), noting the difficulty high-school teachers in the *cités* encounter when teaching the Holocaust to Muslim youth—particularly boys—who ask why Palestinian history is not being taught as well. Jewish and liberal Muslim leaders soon began organizing conferences about European Muslim perceptions of the Holocaust, underlining that paying public homage to the Holocaust was critical to Muslim integration. Liberal Muslim voices like Samia Essabaa, the high-school teacher, and Ferroukhi, the filmmaker, believe that one way to challenge these intolerant attitudes is by teaching about the Holocaust while stressing historic *convivencia* and the role that "righteous Muslims" played in sheltering Jews. These Muslim leaders will thus take lycée students to visit concentration camps and Holocaust museums as well as to cemeteries where Muslim soldiers who fought the Nazis are buried. In tours sponsored by the Aladdin Project, an initiative launched by the French Foundation for the Memory of the Shoah and UNESCO, Essabaa takes her students to visit Auschwitz and the Holocaust Museum in Washington. Ferroukhi's and Essabaa's cultural work is supported by the French government, though their talk of Muslims suffering under Nazism and Muslim-Jewish amity prior to 1948 is ruffling neoconservative feathers. Essabaa has won praise from French officials and American Jewish organizations, and in June 2013 received the Légion d'Honneur.

If *Free Men* was attacked by neoconservatives for its historical accuracy, the film also drew fire from Muslim leftists, who argued that Ferroukhi—like other liberal Muslims—had "internalized a Zionist agenda"; that just because Jews and neoconservative organizations view Muslims through the prism of the Holocaust doesn't mean Muslims have to view themselves through that lens. And the very fact that liberal Muslims are struggling to show that there were "Muslim Schindlers" means they have accepted Satloff's claim of Muslim-

Nazi collaborationism. The irony is that Ferroukhi's film was indeed inspired by Satloff's book, which suggested that Salim Halali was protected by the mosque and that his partner Mohamed El Kamal was a collaborator. In 2006, Satloff interviewed Imam Dalil Boubekeur, the current head of the Grand Mosque, who said that during Vichy the mosque issued up to a hundred certificates of Muslim identity to protect Jews, even producing a letter from the French Foreign Ministry, dated September 24, 1940, showing how German authorities warned the then rector of the mosque to cease delivering certificates to Jews. Imam Boubekeur said, "Even if it was one Jew saved, that by itself is an important fact." Muslim leftists view this issue differently: first of all, Si Kaddour Benghabrit, the mosque rector whom Satloff and liberal Muslims want honored by Yad Vashem, is hardly a hero. Until his death in 1954, he opposed Algerian independence and wanted a French Algeria. Moreover, they see the search for a "Muslim Schindler"—at a time when North Africa is erupting in revolts, and French Muslims are in dire conditions—as a pointless exercise that only serves the interests of Zionist organizations. The liberal Muslims respond that Muslims *must* include themselves in Europe's historical memory, and the stories of "righteous Muslims" like Benghabrit can help achieve that.

The memory competition raging in France—between Muslims and Jews, liberal Muslims and Islamists, government and social movements—is playing out in other parts of Europe. In the last decade, a host of left-wing movements has emerged—the Arab European League in Belgium, Pantrarna (Black Panthers) in Sweden, the Natives of the Republic in France—to challenge liberal Muslim leaders. Reminiscent of the Black Power movement, which arose in disaffection over the American civil rights movement, these new self-described "decolonial" movements are rejecting both the liberal integrationist language of mainstream European Muslim federations and the religious discourse of Islamists, and are triggering culture wars reminiscent of 1960s America.

12

The North African Syndrome

Frantz Fanon, the anticolonial philosopher, was fascinated by Andalusian music. The young Antillian first landed in North Africa in March 1944, as a volunteer fighter with the Free French Allied Forces in Morocco. Believing that "freedom is indivisible," the eighteen-year-old had joined de Gaulle's forces in the French Caribbean and boarded a navy ship bound for Africa. From Casablanca, Fanon and his comrades were transferred to Oran in Algeria, in preparation for their crossing into France. He went on to fight in the Battle of Alsace, was wounded at Colmar, and was awarded a Croix de Guerre for his military service. In 1953, Fanon returned to Algeria with a degree in psychiatric medicine and became medical chief of the Blida-Joinville Psychiatric Hospital. Intrigued by Muslim understandings of mental illness, he would observe, "In the case of illness itself, any medical ailment was interpreted as the action of an evil *djinn*." Fanon would come to see belief in jinn possession—so widespread in the Maghreb's "imaginary life"—as a way of acting out an internalized, colonial violence. Unlike Claude McKay, his fellow West Indian, interest in the jinn did not lead Fanon to the Gnawa, but rather to the nationalist effort to reclaim Andalusi music.

In the Blida ward, Fanon began experimenting with new healing methods. He took chains and straitjackets off patients, erased the murals of the Virgin Mary and French colonial history from the hospital walls. One day in 1954, two musicians—the *chaabi* singer Abderrahmane Aziz and the comedian Mohamed Touri—came to do a show at the hospital. Fanon noticed that the patients—Algerian women—responded to the music with applause and ululations (which he described as "short, high-pitched and repeated modulations"). Fanon asked Aziz, who was from Algiers, to move to Blida and help him use *chaabi* for musical therapy. Aziz, a psychiatry student, had been part of Mahieddine Bachtarzi's troupe since 1939, but as a nationalist who was writing songs about the "art" and "verse" of "Arab Spain," he didn't like his boss's use of Andalusi music for comedic theater. Aziz agreed to join Fanon on condition that patients be taught Arabic, so they could participate in the pieces that he would perform. Also, they needed a place to worship. Fanon gave him a room to be used as a mosque space, and Aziz taught patients how to perform ablution and basic prayers and brought in a local imam. Fanon began taking daily fifteen-minute Arabic lessons with Aziz. They set up a Moorish-style café with floor mats, chairs, and low *meida* tables, where men would sip tea, play dominoes, and listen to musicians perform *chaabi* music.

Even after the war erupted—and Fanon began treating Algerian torture victims and supplying FLN fighters with medical provisions—these musical *saharat* continued. At the hospital, he had developed close friendships with Muslim and Jewish colleagues and tried desperately to bridge the communities as the general situation deteriorated. Only a few Algerian Jews supported the colonial order, he insisted, arguing that the "great majority" was "a floating, highly Arabized mass with poor knowledge of French, that considered itself—by tradition and sometimes by dress—as authentic 'natives.'" Even after he was expelled from the country in January 1957, Fanon praised the FLN's appeals to the Jewish community and hoped for an independent "multiracial Algeria" for all: "Everyone is Algerian in the City that is being erected by the FLN."

Fanon died from leukemia in 1961. His book *The Wretched of the Earth,* published shortly after his death, and the film that it inspired—*The Battle of Algiers,* by the Italian director Gillo Pontecorvo—would galvanize American students and leftists through the sixties and seventies. Not so much nowadays. In a sign of the times, *Battle* is now required viewing for special-ops officers at the Pentagon; and the New

York–based fashion house Nom de Guerre released a summer collection called "Combat Continues"—replete with khaki shirts with epaulets, camouflage pants, and turbans—inspired by Pontecorvo's film. In Europe, Fanon's radical humanism and ideas about race and empire are inspiring new political movements. The European Muslim activists now resurrecting Fanon are less interested in him as a figure of Third World revolution than in how he made North Africa central to the African world, and how his writings can help young Muslims gain entry into the West through the black freedom movement.

"We came together shortly after the head scarf law of 2004," says Houria Bouteldja, the spokeswoman for the party Les Indigènes de la République. "The discourse on race in France is pathetic, the Muslim organizations are timid, the Socialist Party won't talk about race. We wanted to start a movement to defend France's postcolonial populations, so we created a political party called the Natives of the Republic."

I had come to meet Houria at a café in Stalingrad, a working-class neighborhood in central Paris, and found her sitting with two other party members, philosophy students at the Sorbonne; the three were passing around a hookah. In recent years, Houria has emerged as the most eloquent voice for the "decolonial" movements in Europe. Her appearances on television, sporting colorful head wraps, coolly debating France's "memory laws" with political figures, have become the stuff of legend among French youth. (An aficionado uploaded a video about her called "I love her to death" [*Je l'aime à mourir*], a guitar solo spliced with images of Houria's most electric TV interviews.)

Instead of *intégration,* the Natives Party manifesto calls for the "decolonization" of France, meaning that public and private institutions should reflect the country's changing demographics. The movement aims to mobilize French citizens of postcolonial origin (North Africans, West Africans, Antillians, Jews, Muslims, and Asians). Fanon's influence is evident. The term *indigène* in the party's name refers to the legal system, the Code de l'Indigénat, that was used to rule native populations in France's colonies. The Natives see France's urban crisis, and the plight of minorities in the *banlieues,* as a new chapter in a colonial story that has yet to end.

"We were helped by events. When we launched the party in early 2005, our manifesto emphasized the continuity between colonial racism and the discrimination minorities face in France today," says Houria. "A few months later the 2005 riots started, and the French state responded by enacting state-of-emergency laws not used since the Algerian War. The government's response pretty much validated our position, and we got more support."

The identity politics that the Natives put forth directly confronts the republic's ideology of color-blindness, and they are often attacked for importing an American-style race politics. "You know, it's funny that only nonwhites are accused of *communautarisme,*" says Stella Magliani-Belkacem, a party cadre, as she puffs on the hookah. "If three blacks are sitting together having coffee, it's *communautarisme;* if it's three Arabs, it's *communautarisme;* if it's three whites, well, they're just socializing—having an aperitif."

Critics who say the Natives Party is influenced by American ideas are spot-on: The French "decolonial" movement—like other race-based movements in Europe—*is* inspired by Black Power and American critical race theory. But so are their opponents. French neoconservatives, with their opposition to multiculturalism, clash-of-civilizations rhetoric, and hawkish foreign policy positions, also draw inspiration from across the Atlantic. The Natives Party—in its disdain for the concept of integration, its emphasis on race and colonial history—has emerged as a formidable opponent of French neoconservatism. The ongoing clashes between neoconservatism and "decolonizers" in Europe today are reminiscent of America in the 1960s, the difference being that in the U.S. neoconservatism arose in part as a response to Black Power, while French activists began building a race movement in reaction to neoconservatism—first Bush's, then Sarkozy's.

A curious point of contention in these European culture wars is geography—specifically, it seems, the dividing line between Africa and the Orient. The Western political imagination has long viewed the trans-Saharan region as separating "Africa" from the "Orient." This mapping is strongly contested by Europe's decolonial movements, which see the Sahara as a bridge, not a chasm, between civilizations. The transnational identity that these movements put forth of North Africa as part of an African world that is part of an even larger post-colonial world raises hackles, just as 1960s Third-Worldist rhetoric used to anger the American right. To the casual observer, the current clash of narratives and "moral geographies" between race activists and neoconservatives in Europe—with French Black Panthers clashing with Jewish Defense League members in Paris, and British government officials trying to shut down Nation of Islam–run schools in South London—seems like an eerie replay of 1960s America, until one recalls that not only have these American movements gone global, but American embassies are actively exporting the civil rights movement, training young European Muslim leaders in "diversity management," just as American organizations from the NAACP to the American Jewish Committee are trying to guide European Muslims on how to negotiate national history and memory.

A Certain Anxiety

After his expulsion from Algeria, Fanon relocated to Tunis, where he worked as a psychiatrist and editor of the FLN's newspaper *El Moudjahid*. In 1960, the Algerian Provisional Government appointed him ambassador to Ghana. Fanon died, in December 1961, a few days before *The Wretched of the Earth* was published. The French police moved quickly to confiscate copies of the book; the author was deemed a traitor who had sided with Algerian "terrorists." Fanon's work, however, went on to inspire liberation movements across the Third World and radical politics in the U.S., inspiring black leaders like Eldridge Cleaver, Amiri Baraka, Malcolm X, and even Martin Luther King, who would respond in writing to Fanon's arguments about revolutionary violence. The American landing of 1942 had already brought North Africa and its colonial predicament into the African-American imagination. The writer Harold Cruse, who became an influential scholar, wrote a fascinating short story about a chance encounter he had during his military service in Oran in 1942 with two Algerian women, who in asking about his ancestry led him to reflect on war, race, and the history of imperialism. When the Algerian War began, a number of African-American intellectuals visited Algiers and drew parallels between the Algerian uprising and the struggle back home, comparing the kasbah to the American ghetto.

Once independent, Algerian leaders returned the support. When Ahmed Ben Bella, Algeria's first head of state, traveled to New York in October 1962 to attend an induction ceremony for his country at the UN, he met with Martin Luther King for several hours. ("Ben Bella Links Two 'Injustices,'" declared a *New York Times* headline, "Tells Dr. King Segregation Is Related to Colonialism.") Ben Bella also met with Adam Clayton Powell and Malcolm X at the Abyssinian Baptist Church in Harlem. Two years later Malcolm X visited Algiers and was given a tour of the kasbah by Algerian "blood brothers." The English translation of *The Wretched of the Earth* in 1965 would make Algeria even more enthralling. Eldridge Cleaver referred to the book as "the Black Bible" and made Algiers the headquarters of the Black Panther Party. The black internationalist voices of this era did not draw a distinction between North Africa and sub-Saharan Africa, as North African cities became home to African-American artists and writers: Randy Weston and the Muslim jazzmen settled in Tangier, Shirley Graham Du Bois and Maya Angelou relocated to Cairo, and the Black Panthers set up base in Algiers. The rise of Black Power, its identification with Africa—including "Arab Africa"—soon began to unsettle black-Jewish relations in the United States.

Jewish Americans, as is well known, were deeply involved in the civil rights movement: young Jewish students joined the Freedom Riders, lawyers contested Jim Crow laws, donors supported institutions like the NAACP and the Congress for Racial Equality. The black-Jewish alliance came under strain as the civil rights struggle shifted from the South to the North and the Black Power movement began to take shape. Black discontent had risen by the mid-1960s, as civil rights legislation failed to improve conditions for the urban disenfranchised. Following the killings of Malcolm X and Martin Luther King, riots erupted across the country and a separatist mood took hold. In *The Crisis of the Negro Intellectual,* Harold Cruse's six-hundred-page tome published in 1967, the author captured the state of mind, repudiating the idea of integration ("Integrate with whom?") and calling on blacks to create their own institutions. If Jewish activists were comrades-in-arms down South, as the movement moved north, veterans of the southern struggle came to see Jews as an economic elite entrenched in the ghetto. By 1966, former civil rights activists were echoing Malcolm X's resentment of Jewish merchants in black neighborhoods, spouting rhetoric about Jews as exploitative "bloodsuckers" as a way to gain the slain leader's constituency. Stokely Carmichael, for instance, had worked closely with Jewish activists down South, but as he expanded the Student Non-Violent Coordinating Committee (SNCC) into northern urban areas, he became harshly critical of the Jewish economic presence in black communities. The Palestinian-Israeli conflict would only raise tensions.

The most prominent African-American leaders of the last century—Marcus Garvey, W.E.B. Du Bois, Paul Robeson, Ralph Bunche, and Martin Luther King—were originally committed Zionists. The biblical trope of Exodus, of the suffering Hebrews being liberated from Pharaoh and returning to the land of Israel, has long resonated with African-Americans. In the early twentieth century, many African-American leaders saw Zionism as a model for the African diaspora's eventual emancipation and return to Africa. Marcus Garvey would praise that "marvelous movement." But by the mid-1950s, black opinion began to shift, first among artists and intellectuals, then among ordinary people, as the anticolonial rhetoric of the Bandung Conference and the pan-Africanism of Gamal Abdel Nasser and Kwame Nkrumah gained sway. In some ways, the postwar conversion of thousands of African-Americans to Islam was a bellwether. "The movement among jazz musicians toward Islam created quite a stir, especially with the surge of the Zionist movement," writes Dizzy Gillespie in *To Be or Not to Bop.* "A lot of friction arose between Jews and Muslims, which took the form of a semi-boycott in New York of jazz musicians with Muslim names . . . Near the end of the forties, the newspapers really got worried about whether I'd convert to Islam."

The 1956 Suez War would further shift black opinion. In 1964 Malcolm X, who initially saw Zionism and Jewish diaspora politics as a paradigm for African-Americans to follow, made a trip to Khan Yunus refugee camp in Gaza, and thereafter stopped using Israel as an example, speaking instead of the Chinese diaspora. All this caused tensions with the Jewish community.

Tensions flared into open conflict after the 1967 War, as Black Power leaders adopted an explicitly pro-Palestinian posture. Days after the war ended, the SNCC issued a statement denouncing "the Zionists." Carmichael embarked on a tour of the Third World that also included a visit to a Palestinian refugee camp. Expressing the black "moral geography" of the era, Carmichael would declare, "We can be for no one but the Arabs because Israel belonged to them, to the Arabs, in 1917 . . . The British gave it to a group of Zionists . . . Not only that. They [the Zionists] are moving to take over Egypt. Egypt is our motherland—it's in Africa. Egypt belongs to us since four thousand years ago and we sit here supporting the Zionists." As black nationalists took an openly anti-Zionist stance, the Palestinian-Israeli conflict became part of the political competition among African-American leaders, between separatists and liberal integrationists. "The criticisms of Israel expressed by Carmichael and other SNCC members," explains historian Clayborne Carson, were "part of an effort by former civil rights workers to abandon past ties to Jewish liberals and thereby claim roles as leaders of the black urban insurgency." A familiar cycle soon developed in American politics: black militants would make anti-Zionist statements, Jewish leaders would call on more mainstream black leaders to publicly denounce their words—which, in the eyes of Black Power, only exposed the subservience of the integrationist leaders.

The rise in black militancy and the 1967 War would trigger ideological changes within the Jewish community as well. Jewish liberals, since the early 1960s, were worried by black militancy and calls for affirmative action; and the black consciousness movement of the 1960s would spur the Jewish political awakening of the 1970s. Following a dispute over the Ocean Hill–Brownsville school district in Brooklyn in 1968, Rabbi Meir Kahane created the Jewish Defense

League, explicitly modeled on the Black Panthers; this group posed a challenge to the liberal Jewish leadership comparable to that which black separatists posed to black integrationists. The rise in black-Jewish tension reflected black disappointment with integrated political movements, and fed off the rise of consciousness and communal identity within both communities. "Black power and Jewish power were on different sides of the Israel-Palestine debate, but they agreed that their own group must exercise a measure of exclusive political control on matters involving vital group interests," observes Carson.

This new Jewish political consciousness would find expression in neoconservatism. For all that has been written about neoconservatism in the last decade, little has been said about how this ideology emerged partly in response to black radicalism and the discourse of Afro-Arab solidarity put forth by African-American leftists. For the neoconservatives—most of whom were leftists in their youth—the militancy of Black Power, the calls for racial quotas, the Soviet Union's oppression of Soviet Jews, and the radical left's embrace of the Palestinian cause only bolstered their anticommunism and defense of a hyper-liberalism. Scholars like Nathan Glazer, long wary of the Black Muslims, and others (Norman Podhoretz, Irving Kristol, Midge Decter) would outline neoconservatism's response to Black Power in the pages of *Commentary* magazine. As Podhoretz put it, the 1967 victory triggered a sense of euphoria and "passion of solidarity" for Israel at a moment when Jewish vulnerability in Israel was entwined with Jewish anxiety at home, and pushed many American Jews to fight black militancy and the radical left, seen together as the "enemy of liberal values" and a threat to Jewish security. Ironically, it was also during this euphoric post-'67 period that many Americans would gain an interest in the music of Mizrahi Jews. In February 1968, Enrico Macias was invited to perform at Carnegie Hall for the first time.

That the black nationalists and African-American Muslims were claiming solidarity with the Arab world, describing Islam as color-blind and not talking about the trans-Saharan slave trade, was particularly galling to the neoconservatives. "We can understand why many blacks would give up the name and language of the white men who bought them as slaves, but why on earth would they want to adopt the name and language of the Arabs who sold them into slavery?" asked Bernard Lewis. Lewis, a British scholar of Islam, had been warily watching the rise of Islam among African-Americans from his perch at the University of London. In 1970, he published *Race and Color in Islam,* which directly challenged Malcolm X's view of Islam as color-blind and questioned the epiphany he experienced at hajj. Lewis wrote that although "Malcolm X was an acute and sensitive observer . . . the [Islamic] beliefs which he had acquired . . . prevented him from realizing the full implication of 'the color pattern' he saw" in the Arab world. Rather than an "interracial utopia," Lewis argued, a quick reading of *The Arabian Nights* showed the "Alabama-like quality" and "Southern impression" of Arab life. Lewis would go on to publish subsequent books critiquing Edward Blyden, the father of pan-Africanism, for creating the "myth of racial Islamic innocence," which "mythologized and idealized Islam provid[ing] a stick with which to chastise Western failings," just as the European Jewish Orientalists had done, in the 1800s, when they "appealed to a legendary golden age in Muslim Spain."

Meanwhile, the U.S. government was trying to separate the Black Power movement from its international supporters. Algeria wanted to renew relations with the United States, broken off since the 1967 War. Normalizing ties would hinge on Algeria's renouncing support for black radicalism. A dispatch of a 1972 meeting between the Algerian minister of foreign affairs, Abdelaziz Bouteflika, and Nixon's secretary of state, William Rogers, reports that "Bouteflika said GOA [Government of Algeria] is interest[ed] in developing relations with U.S. and added that Black Panthers do not make any effective contribution to Algeria from a revolutionary, ideological and moral standpoint." Hoping for a one-billion-dollar plan to export natural gas to the U.S., the Algerian government withdrew its support for the Black Panthers. The Panthers would depart Algiers for France, where they would battle extradition to the U.S. Similarly in Egypt, Anwar Sadat, hoping to leave the Soviet camp, would upon assuming office in 1970 abandon Nasser's pan-Africanism. In the U.S., black militancy would also be neutralized, as orthodox Islam and the Salafi movement gained influence in inner-city areas and law enforcement targeted radical black organizations. Today, aside from Farrakhan's occasional outbursts, tensions between black and Jewish nationalism, which have interacted and shaped each other since the late nineteenth century, have largely abated. The rise of Bush and the neoconservatives in the 2000s would resurrect black radicalism—but across the Atlantic.

Decolonizing Europe

In February 2000, a dozen or so Belgians of Lebanese and Moroccan descent founded an organization called Al Rabita ("the link" in Arabic). Based in Brussels, the group was meant to promote Arab-European relations and the interests of Belgium's Muslim community. Some months later the organization relocated to Antwerp, joined forces with the Federatie van Marokkaange Verenigingen (FMV), an immigrant umbrella federation, and changed its name to the Arab European League. By the end of 2003, the Arab European League was one of the most organized and militant youth organizations in Western Europe. With followers in several countries, the AEL hoped to mobilize Muslim youth across borders, lobby governments to make Arabic one of the official languages of the European Union, and gain state funding for Islamic schools. Aside from its confrontational, anarchist language, what struck observers was how American this Antwerpian movement was, and how heavily it drew on the Black Power movement. The AEL organized Black Panther–style patrols to "police the police," with groups of unarmed youth dressed in black following the police around Antwerp and Brussels, carrying video cameras and flyers that read, "Bad cops: AEL is watching you." The AEL flag, with its red, black, and green colors, resembles the Garveyite movement's pan-African flag, displaying two interlocked crescents.

"We're a civil rights movement, not a club of fundamentalist fanatics who want to blow things up," Dyab Abou Jahjah, the movement's charismatic leader, told the *New York Times*. "In Europe, the immigrant organizations are Uncle Toms. We want to polarize people, to sharpen the discussion, to unmask the myth that the system is democratic for us." The media soon began referring to these youths as the "Arabian Panthers" and the movement's Lebanese-born leader as the "Arab Malcolm X." Abou Jahjah embraced the role. He appeared at media events surrounded by bodyguards, speaking in short sound bites, declaring that integration was "degrading," demanding "100 percent rights" from the Belgian authorities and a mea culpa for thirty years of discrimination; he warned that European Muslims would get their rights "By Any Means Necessary!"

The Arab European League openly acknowledged its debt to Fanon—and to Malcolm X. The group's leaders mined black internationalism's history of solidarity with the Muslim world. In fact, Abou Jahjah refers to Fanon as his "guide." The AEL website still displays photos of Malcolm X with President Nasser of Egypt. But the truth is, the organization never set out to be a militant Black Power–style movement. It started off as a local immigrant-advocacy organization and grew more radical and racially minded in response to Vlaams Blok, a far-right party that had gained power in Flanders. The AEL's radicalization was also fueled by international developments—the Palestinian intifada and the invasion of Iraq—as well as the Belgian government's reaction to the movement.

The AEL's confrontational language and police patrols angered law enforcement from the start. In early 2003, Belgian authorities invoked a 1930s law that proscribed private militias to ban the AEL's police patrols. In response, the AEL changed its tactics, calling on its members to vote and participate politically, rejecting Salafi-style disengagement. The movement gained supporters across the border in Holland, and the AEL leadership began envisioning a transnational movement that would organize in various states. But despite its popularity among Dutch Muslim youth, in March 2003 Dutch authorities prevented the AEL from setting up a local branch. "The Dutch government simply did not want a far left Muslim movement in the country—and that ended up further radicalizing Muslim youth, pushing them to Salafism," says Dutch anthropologist Martijn de Koning of Radboud University. "The government's preventing the AEL from setting up in Holland actually drove some youth to jihadi groups—that was the only radical alternative left."

The Arab European League in response moderated its separatist language, and by 2005 was trying to become a political party (the "Muslim-Democratic Party"). But the Belgian and Dutch governments continued their efforts to crush the movement. The AEL soon found itself politically hemmed in, the target of several lawsuits. The AEL leadership's anti-Zionist rhetoric and militancy toward the Jewish community of Antwerp didn't help. One member had declared that "Antwerp is the stronghold of Zionism in Europe, and that's why it should become the Mecca of pro-Palestinian action." In February 2006, reacting to the Danish cartoon controversy and public debates about blasphemy and freedom of expression, the AEL published cartoons about the Holocaust on its website. This drew even more legal action. The AEL issued a statement: "All we are trying to do is to confront Europe with its own hypocrisy [and 'double morals'] using sarcasm and cartoons." This episode proved to be the nail in the movement's coffin.

On May 8, 2012, the day after François Hollande was elected president, thousands of youths marched through the neighborhood of Barbès in northern Paris. Students wore shirts with statements by Frantz Fanon and Aimé Cesaire (and carried placards with the faces of slain African leaders Thomas Sankara, Steve Biko, and others). Activists from the Brigade Anti Négrophobie, dressed in black uniforms and combat boots, and members of the Natives Party held up black-and-yellow posters that read, "Colonial crimes: Sétif, Guelma, Madagascar, Tiaroy Cameroon, Deir Yassin," and "WE are here because YOU were there." This rally, organized by the Natives Party, drew an array of black, feminist, and antiwar groups, and was held on a historic day for France and Algeria: May 8, 1945, is Victory Day, when de Gaulle announced the end of World War II, but also the day the French colonial army killed hundreds of demonstrators in the Algerian town of Sétif. And this march, brought together a coalition of groups that had boycotted the presidential election, aimed to remind France of its colonial history and to signal to the president-elect that there was a youth movement to the left of his Socialist Party.

The Natives of the Republic Party emerged in France just as the Arab European League was falling apart, and seems to have learned from the latter's errors. The Natives Party has a wider appeal, defending the rights of all postcolonial populations, not just Muslims or Arabs. The Natives are also more media savvy than the AEL. A stable of European-based professors and social scientists from Berkeley to York University in Canada serve on the party's advisory committee, helping develop an "indigenous strategy," lending their credibility to the party's manifestos. The party's publications are replete with references to Stokely Carmichael, Huey Newton, and modern-day American race sociologists like Tommie Shelby, Cornel West, and Kimberlé Crenshaw. But the party's intellectual guru is Sadri Khiari, a Tunisian political scientist, who was active in the Communist Party in Tunis for decades before being exiled to France by the Ben Ali government. Per his advice, the Natives Party boycotts elections and focuses strictly on "discursive activism"—on shifting France's political discourse. In maintaining a critical distance from the "white political arena," the Natives have also avoided the clashes with the police that sank the AEL. The party also builds on Malcolm X and Fanon's linking of the African world with the Orient; in particular, Fanon's insights into colonial hierarchy are seen as a way to transcend ethnic differences in Europe's urban periphery.

When the nineteen-year-old Fanon was stationed outside of Casablanca, his Free French division was organized hierarchically: with European volunteers and fighters from the West Indian colonies like himself at the top, Senegalese and sub-Saharan infantry at the bottom, and Moroccan and Algerian troops in between. The European fighters, Fanon noticed, got better-quality headgear and tents. At times the French commanders would "whiten" the army, leaving out Senegalese troops but taking Moroccan and Algerian fighters or, better yet, the French Maquis. It was these racial practices that he witnessed within the army—Africans being called *Nègres* or *bougnoles,* Algerians being called *indigènes*—that would lead Fanon to advocate a pan-African anti-imperialism. Today the North African's awkward racial in-betweenness, positioned between European whiteness and sub-Saharan blackness, is something that the "decolonials" are explicitly trying to address (in ways reminiscent of the minority-status campaigns in the United States).

"The French sociologists who study race in France will defend Caribbean communities," says Houria. "They pushed for the Taubira Law of 2005"—which recognized slavery as a crime against humanity—"but they don't want to deal with our movement. And that's because we speak of Algeria—which is still taboo in France. And Palestine—super-taboo. And because we bring together North Africans with sub-Saharan Africans. We are the only organization in France—aside from the Salafis—who do bring Berbers, Arabs, and blacks together. And that is also controversial. I think France prefers Salafis, who separate themselves from society than a group like us that mobilizes all minorities across categories." The "decolonial" activists argue, following Fanon, that the fact that the term *bougnole,* which means "black" in Wolof, was used in the nineteenth century as a term for West Africans but is today applied to North Africans, is an indication of how rapidly Arabs and Berbers in France have been racially downgraded—and pushed away from whiteness.

In July 2010, another Black Power–inspired movement emerged in France. The New Black Panther Party was founded in Paris by Kemi Seba, a young activist who studied in Los Angeles under the late Khalid Muhammad of the Nation of Islam. The French Black Panthers began appearing on street corners in Paris dressed in black fatigues and berets, teaching "knowledge of self" (*connaissance de même*) and calling for unity among "imperialism's wretched." The group has positioned itself against the Salafi movement—whom they call "Arab supremacists"—and against the mainstream CRAN, the Representative Council of Black Associations of France founded shortly after the 2005 riots. Seba refers to France's mainstream black leaders as *oncles Toms,* telling interviewers, "I want to live and die like Stokely Carmichael." In response to a notorious speech that Sarkozy gave in Senegal, declaring that "the African has never really entered history," the Panthers began demanding the right to run community centers for black children in France where they could teach Négritude: "We want to shape our own destiny." The group has dozens of followers, but as with the Arab European League, the movement's anti-Zionist rhetoric and penchant for altercations are drawing government suppression. (The Panthers will get into run-ins with French Jewish Defense League members; both sides will face off, fists raised, hurling invective at each other about whether Islam is racist or not.) The French left, which in the 1970s rallied around the American Black Panthers in Paris battling extradition to the United States, has not lent its support to this local offshoot.

Saharan Blues

The French have since the 1940s been concerned about the influence of African-American culture on their minorities. In *No Name in the Street,* James Baldwin described the "uneasy" reaction he would get when, while in Paris in 1948, he would "claim kinship" with the Algerians living there. ("The fact that I had never seen the Algerian casbah was of no more relevance . . . than the fact that the Algerians had never seen Harlem," he mused. "The Algerian and I were both, alike, victims of this history [of Europe in Africa].") When Malcolm X was invited to address the Federation of African Students in Paris in February 1965, he was denied entry. The de Gaulle government thought his "undesirable" presence might "provoke demonstrations." Today the more French youth speak of race and Malcolm X, the more French conservatives denounce this as American-style "victim politics." In 2010, Pascal Bruckner, a French neoconservative, published *The Tyranny of Guilt,* railing against multiculturalism and French youth "of distant immigrant origin" who hate France "but have nowhere else to go." What is striking is that Bruckner's critique of French multiculturalism and the West's guilt complex is inspired by *American* conservatism and is symptomatic of a broader trend: that of European neoconservatives reading American authors to understand their Muslim compatriots, thinking that American observers—

because of their country's racial history—have a special insight into Europe's Muslim problem. Since 9/11, American conservatives have published a number of books—*While Europe Slept, The Last Days of Europe, Menace in Europe, Reflections of the Revolution in Europe, The West's Last Chance*—that warn of an Islamic invasion of a weak and appeasing Europe and have found readers across the Atlantic.

The "Eurabia" genre is informed not only by a Cold War outlook but also by the memory of Black Muslim agitation and the racial tumult of the 1960s. "It's the Farrakhan problem," wrote one American observer of the French scene. "Mosques do rescue youths from delinquency, idleness, and all sorts of other ills. But in so doing, they become power brokers in areas where almost all disputes are resolved by violence and the most tribal kind of *woospeh* ["respect" in a French accent, presumably]. And it is that mastery of a violent environment—not the social-service record—that these groups call on when they make demands on the larger society." Angst over the popularity of African-American culture ("an adversary culture") among European Muslims runs through much of this literature. Pondering the alternative identities available to young Muslim men in Europe, *New York Times* columnist David Brooks writes, "After 9/11, everyone knew there was going to be a debate about the future of Islam. We just didn't know the debate would be between Osama bin Laden and Tupac Shakur." This literature also singles out Tariq Ramadan, the Egyptian-Swiss theologian, for reproach. One reason is that Ramadan's grandfather was the founder of the Muslim Brotherhood; another is that the dapper, globe-trotting scholar, popular among Muslim youth worldwide, evokes the specter of Malcolm X. "Ramadan is said to have been influenced by the example of Malcolm X in the United States, or at least by Spike Lee's Malcolm X," writes Paul Berman, another American leftist-turned-Eurabia-alarmist, in a twenty-eight-thousand-word profile of the Oxford professor published in the *New Republic,* though granting that "Ramadan, who has something of Malcolm's air of touchy dignity, has nothing of Malcolm's demeanor of unstated threats."

The 1960s anxieties about Islam and pan-Africanism resurfaced in post-9/11 America in surprising ways. The first anti-mosque campaign—which would snowball into the broader anti-sharia and anti-mosque movement of 2010—began in early 2003 in opposition to a mosque on Malcolm X Boulevard in the Roxbury section of Boston. (The mosque would eventually open its doors in 2009.) The campaign was led by Charles Jacobs, a wealthy conservative who, in 1994, founded the Anti-Slavery Project to monitor slavery in the Saharan borderlands. In 2002, in response to an increase in Arab and Muslim campus activism, he launched the David Project to monitor Middle East studies departments across the United States for anti-Israel bias. And when the Sudanese regime began to brutally suppress the insurgency in Darfur, Jacobs—along with the American Jewish World Service—launched the Save Darfur campaign. In April 2004, the U.S. Holocaust Memorial Museum issued a "genocide alert" about Darfur—the first in the institution's history—and Save Darfur turned into one of the largest, most impressive humanitarian campaigns ever organized around an African conflict. The coalition brought together a range of groups and organizations. Rallies were held in many cities, kids updated their Facebook status to "Save Darfur," MTV ran documentaries on Darfur and sponsored a "Darfur Is Dying" video game, and vigils took place on college campuses across the country, while students in green T-shirts hoped to start a Sudan divestment campaign similar to that waged against apartheid-era South Africa. The Holocaust Museum partnered with Google Earth to provide a crowd-sourced online service mapping the atrocities in Darfur.

One recurring theme at these rallies was that the Darfur campaign provided a historic opportunity to revive the black-Jewish alliance of the civil rights movement, since Sudan, at the intersection of Africa and the Middle East, was where African-American and Jewish-American internationalisms overlapped. (When asked why he was moved by the Sudan conflict, Charles Jacobs said that the "same people doing this to the Darfuris are planting bombs in pizza parlors in Israel.") Organizations leading the campaign soon began arranging trips for African-American leaders to visit both Darfur and Yad Vashem. But the main African-American organizations, like the NAACP, and the larger Africa advocacy groups, like Action Africa, were noticeably absent from the coalition—as were Muslim and Arab organizations. These groups were wary of the calls for regime change heard at rallies, and skeptical of the curious obsession with Sudan, when various conflicts were raging across Africa. "I want to remind everyone that 3 million people died in the Congo recently," declared hip-hop mogul Russell Simmons at a rally for Darfur in Washington in April 2006. "I don't want us to forget the suffering all over the continent of Africa." Worried that the Darfur issue was being used to counter Palestine activism on college campuses, and put off by the framing of an intra-African conflict as one between "Arab settlers" and "indigenous blacks," Muslim organizations largely kept a distance from the Save Darfur coalition. Consequently, a conflict where Arab and African identities were clashing, which should have given rise to a coalition of African-American and Muslim-American communities, ended up being a largely white, Judeo-Christian affair.

Across the Atlantic, European observers were puzzled by how this corner of northeast Africa had so captured the American imagination. "And why Darfur?" one reporter asked George Clooney at the Cannes Film Festival in 2007, where the actor was holding a fundraiser for the conflict's victims. "Why not Congo? Chechnya? Lebanon?" The Hollywood star mentioned the accessibility of the Darfur region to humanitarian workers. European and African observers were intrigued by how domestic politics had made Darfur resonate so powerfully in the United States, how Sudan's location—and the Saharan borderlands—had come to be seen as a "civilizational faultline." Yet there was an antecedent to this thinking. If American neoconservatives in the 1960s and 1970s were dismayed by black radicalism's affinity for Islam, by 2001 American (and European) neoconservatives were worried by a politicized younger Muslim generation's penchant for black radicalism and the new solidarities forming between Islam and pan-Africanism. And so the issue of "Arab slavery" was revived, often by the same political agitators of the 1960s. Historian Bernard Lewis, who forty years earlier had repudiated Malcolm X's idealization of the Muslim world, was by the early 2000s an advisor to Dick Cheney, and writing about Sudan and the "new anti-Semitism." Jazz critic Nat Hentoff, who had written critically about Black Power and the appeal of Algeria, also became an advocate for Darfur.

The Save Darfur campaign soon spread to France, with public figures like Bernard Kouchner, Bernard-Henri Lévy, and André Glucksman establishing the Collectif Urgence Darfour to push for intervention in Sudan. French journalists warned that the Darfur activism could roil the *banlieues* as Jewish activists countered Muslim activism around Palestine with the Darfur campaign. The Urgence Darfour movement, as in the United States, would split African and Muslim opinion, with liberal Muslim groups arguing that it was in the Muslim community's interest to be part of this "moral coalition," while the left-wing activists spurned this "trans-Atlantic Zionist" movement with its neoconservative agenda. Soon a counter-coalition began to form against the French Darfur coalition, led by left-wing African and Muslim activists trying to wrest the issue of Darfur and intra-Muslim conflict away from neoconservatives.

In democracies, the political scientist E. E. Schattschneider once observed, conflict is essential to agenda-setting. And Muslim-Jewish conflict in Europe today is largely about what issues will be talked about publicly. What's surprising is how the Sahara has become a proxy site for these agenda wars. As Muslim activists reach out, figuratively speaking, across the Sahara to form coalitions that bring together citizens of sub-Saharan and North African origin, and embrace a pro-Islamic pan-Africanism, their political adversaries respond by introducing "trans-Saharan slavery" into public discourse, or by highlighting a conflict in the Saharan borderlands, where Arab Africans dominate non-Arab Africans. In the United States, historically, when black-Jewish relations are good, the Sahara is depicted as an oceanlike divide; when that relationship is tense, the Sahara is a "civilizational bridge." In Europe, representations of the trans-Saharan region are being similarly shaped by domestic and geo-politics. The more AFRICOM tries to "pacify" the trans-Sahara—Mali, Mauritania, Niger, southern Algeria—the more these military incursions inflame Islamic identity in Europe's urban periphery, particularly among Salafi groups. The more North African migration increases into Europe and the louder the Salafis get, the deeper Holocaust guilt is extended toward the Sahara; the more North African Arabs and Berbers in France and elsewhere gravitate toward pan-Africanism, the more the trans-

Saharan slave trade is deployed to separate "white" North Africans from Caribbean and sub-Saharan populations. "Arab slavery"—and to a lesser extent "African slavery"—is becoming a recurring meme in European politics, just as it emerged as a domestic issue in the United States, from the late 1960s onward.

"Every time we try to build coalitions between Caribbean youth and North African youth, the right will bring up trans-Saharan slavery," says Sandew Hira, a Surinamese sociologist who heads the International Institute for Scientific Research, a "decolonial" organization in Amsterdam. "These people will literally go to a Surinamese kid standing on a street corner, and tell him, 'Your Moroccan friend's ancestors enslaved your ancestors.' So we're trying to build a counternarrative, to explain to our youth how slavery in Africa was not the same as the trans-Atlantic one."

In this climate of recrimination, it is not clear what music can achieve. But, again, liberal Muslims and liberal Jews are deploying Andalusi music in all kinds of ways.

I Know They Love Me

> I am of a strange country
> And of a strange breed . . .
>
> —SALIM HALALI

When the film *Free Men* was released in October 2011, Salim Halali had been dead for six years, and it had been thirty years since his final media interview—and yet the singer would become more popular than he had been since the 1960s. "We are completely sold out of Salim records, only cassettes left," says Berthe Nachman of the Librairie du Progrès. Hearing "Ashaqtu fil andalussia" (I loved an Andalusian girl), one of Salim's 1950s flamenco songs popularized by the film *Free Men,* floating from store speakers in the Marais in the spring of 2012 is a bit spooky and perhaps not surprising. In the 1940s, the singer lived in the neighborhood—on Rue François Miron, not far from Nachman's shop. Down the road from him on Rue des Écouffes, Samy El Maghribi, the Moroccan cantor and maestro of Andalusi and *melhoun,* owned a record shop specializing in North African music. The Marais—nicknamed Le Petzl ("little place" in Yiddish)—with its cobbled streets and historic buildings, has for centuries been a center of Jewish life in Paris. Since the 1980s, the district has also become known for its gay culture, so it's not uncommon today to see bars with rainbow flags next to Renaissance buildings and houses of worship. That Salim's silken tenor would be filling the Marais's ancient walls in the early twenty-first century, as armed police patrol the neighborhood, seems strangely appropriate. Salim mixed identities and cultures with great ease, a fact not lost on today's youth, who are trying to resurrect him as an Arab-Jewish artist, gay icon, and a symbol of *convivencia.*

When World War II ended, Salim opened his own cabaret, called Ismailia Folies, on Avenue Montaigne. But in 1949, he and his companion, Pierre, moved to Casablanca and opened the fabled Coq d'Or, a cabaret that has become almost mythical in North African musical lore. Situated in the city's medina, just across from the grave of Lala Kadiria, a female saint venerated by the Jilali Sufi order, and near the home of Rabbi Haim Pinto, then Casablanca's head rabbi, the club had a Muslim-Jewish orchestra and clientele from its inception. The interior, recall patrons, resembled a Victorian parlor, adorned with ruby-red Persian carpets, crystal chandeliers, and Orientalist paintings. "Pierre would handle the cash register, while Salim managed the kitchen, making sure every lamb tagine had its prunes," chuckles Luc Cherki, who in 1951 took the train from Algiers to Casablanca and spent weeks performing at the club.

Every night at ten o'clock (except on Fridays), the house orchestra would begin playing Moroccan popular music and Egyptian songs. Salim would let young aspiring artists take the stage for a couple of hours. Around midnight, the clientele would hear a familiar voice goading them, "You are all the scum of the world, *la dernière race,* the worst of humanity." And Salim, as he was known, would walk down a spiraling metal staircase from his "private quarters," microphone in hand. Whether dressed in a black tuxedo, as an Oriental prince in a satin robe, or as a Spanish matador in gold-threaded pants, midcalf stockings, and a cape, Salim would walk through the ululating crowd, teasing and kissing friends, while singing his nostalgia-bathed opening *mawal,* "Ya hasra ala dik Liyam" (O for the days) until he reached the stage, and then he'd begin his signature song "Sidi Hbibi Fein Howa" (Where Is My Sweetheart?).

Salim would sing for hours on end—mixing Moroccan and Egyptian Arabic, French, and Spanish. "Salim was a volcano onstage!" recalls Maurice El Medioni. "He would come down while singing, walk around, look into a woman's eyes, then her husband's eyes. He would curse the hell out of anyone who dared talk while he sang." Luc Cherki, Line Monty, and Blond Blond would fly down from Rue de la Huchette to perform at Salim's cabaret; Umm Kulthum and Mohamed Abdel Wahab, giants of modern Arab music, would visit from Egypt and witness Casablanca's belle époque. Today when asked about Le Coq d'Or, the patrons of the 1950s smile, *"Ya hasra."* They recount the night when, as Salim was sauntering across the stage, a young American GI in the audience caught his eye; the crooner began to sing to the *Mirikani,* composing impromptu "El Ain Zarga" (The Blue Eye), which would become one of his most memorable songs. Michel Kakon, a seventy-four-year-old businessman who grew up in Casablanca, recalls those nights in the mid-1950s. "We would arrive at 9 p.m. and we would leave in the morning. And almost every night Salim would finish off a *darbuka.*" This story is told often: Salim was a vocalist but also an accomplished percussionist, and at some point just before dawn he would tuck his gold-encrusted, ceramic *darbuka* under his armpit, kneel down, and beat the drum with such passion that the skin would burst. The crowd would cheer wildly—and the skin would be replaced in time for the show the following night.

In the early 1960s, Le Coq d'Or shut down abruptly. No one knows why: some claim an arson destroyed the place; others say Salim had achieved what he'd wanted, a reputation across the Maghreb. The cabaret's sudden and unexplained demise only added to its legend. Salim returned to France and began recording again—songs about love, separation, and lost homelands, mostly in Arabic, recounting the magical nights he spent in Casablanca, Tangier, and Tunis. Album covers from that period—recorded with Polydor—drip with Orientalia. The album cover of *Dourt Essahra* (I Wandered the Sahara) shows him seated on the floor in a rose-colored gown, holding up his oud; next to him is a treasure chest covered with a black silk robe, a pair of black-and-golden slippers peeking out from underneath. The cover of *Salim Halali en Public* shows the crooner in full Orientalist splendor: sprawled on a bed of pillows, against a tapestry of birds and peacocks, Salim is barefoot, decked in a red satin gown with gold lapels, part of his leg showing.

Salim was more open about his sexuality and love of men than about his religious identity, enjoying, even encouraging, curiosity about his background and alleged conversion to Islam. When with Muslims, he fasted Ramadan; when among Jews, he fasted Yom Kippur. In one heartrending song "Arjaa Lebladek" (Return to Your Homeland), written in the 1960s as migration out of North Africa was growing, Salim implores those leaving their country to return. Listeners to this day debate what he meant when he sang, "Say I'm an Arab Muslim—*qul ana arbi muslim.*" Was he addressing the Jews leaving the Maghreb for Israel? Muslim migration, after all, had yet to begin in earnest. Salim is enjoying renewed attention today because he was also the most flamboyant of an already colorful crop of Arab-Jewish musicians; his art was ostentatious, but also angst-ridden. He sang "My Yiddishe Mama" in Arabic, shortly after Tom Jones sang an English version on his 1967 album *Live at the Talk of the Town.* Salim would, however, one-up the Welsh crooner by making a music video, one of the first in French history. In the clip, he is dressed in a black tuxedo, walking between boulders and bridges inside a studio; a somber violin moans as he, in operatic style, longs for the past.

In his memoir, Mahieddine Bachtarzi, who died in 1992, describes Salim as "the most beautiful Arab male voice of the postwar era." The latter had "discovered" Salim in the mid-1930s and watched him entrance audiences over the decades. Singing almost exclusively in Arabic, he also won the praise of Umm Kulthum and Mohamed Abdel Wahab. His subtlety worked its way into the hearts of many Arab listeners, his refrains incorporated into everyday talk. As wars broke out between Arab and Jew, he would repeat a medieval Andalusi verse, hoping poetry could reconcile peoples. "The children of al-Andalús understand allusions, it's the Christians who only know war." In the early 1970s, Salim recorded an astonishing cover of flamenco singer Imperio Argentina's 1930s classic "Los Piconeros"; his fans loved the lightly accented Spanish but wondered why he chose a song by Argentina, who had traveled to Germany in 1938, performed for Hitler, and described the führer "as a very attractive man." "My heart knows no horizons or frontiers," Salim would say. "The song of a guitar and my soul changes . . . My homeland is love."

And then Salim faded from public view. In the early 1980s, he and Pierre moved into a mansion in Cannes, which had an Arabian Nights décor similar to his cabaret in Casablanca, and a garden where two pet tigers roamed. As late as 1992, he was flying down to Morocco and Tunisia to perform at private galas and weddings, but he did no interviews and asked not to be filmed. He wanted to be remembered for his glory years. For about twenty years, from 1980 to 2000, as a generation raised on his music grew older, Salim's star faded. And then almost overnight his music began to attract the attention of a younger generation. "Sidi Hbibi," an old folk song he popularized, was recorded in various languages, including a version by the rock singer Manu Chao. In 2005, some months after Halali's death, a music festival in Morocco was organized to celebrate his legacy. The youth now discovering Salim see him as a man for the moment: a modern-day Ziryab, Nazi resister, bon vivant, openly gay man, an avatar of Andalusian cosmopolitanism. The film *Free Men* shows Salim's character performing at the cabaret Andaloussia, defying the decree of June 1942 banning Jews from performing, and seducing a man dancing in front of him—under the watchful eyes of Vichy officials. The youth discovering Salim today think his music can help blur the boundaries set up by hard-liners. And it doesn't hurt that the singer remained above the fray of Muslim-Jewish conflict, never went to Israel, and loved the youth of the *banlieues*.

The attempts to revive Salim have drawn mixed reaction. In Morocco—where he has been part of the music scene since the American landing—liberal reformers concur with their counterparts in France: that reviving his musical repertoire can raise awareness of

Arab-Jewish history, counter the collaborationist charge, improve the country's image, promote tourism, and build better ties with Europe. Yet the country's cultural elite, who see themselves as guardians of the Andalusi repertoire, think that while Salim is more sympathetic than Enrico Macias, he's still a pop singer, not to be compared to giants like Abdelkrim Rais, who memorized and transmitted dozens of medieval *nuba*. "I don't understand this focus on Salim Halali," said the late Simon Levy, professor of Hispanism at Université Mohammed V in Rabat. "Why celebrate a cabaret pop singer who never wrote a single song—when we have Lili Labassi and Samy El Maghribi?" And of course religious conservatives across the Maghreb are reluctant to see a gay Jewish cabaret singer become the symbol of Andalusian civilization.

Much of the opposition also comes from the fact that the current revival of Judeo-Arabic music is seen as an effort to placate American and French neoconservatives. While it was Robert Satloff's 2006 book, *Among the Righteous,* that brought Salim Halali's story to French and American readers and suggested that his friend Mohamed El Kamal was a collaborator, Muslim youth interest in Arab-Jewish music actually began almost a decade earlier, prompted by rising Muslim-Jewish tensions in Europe, and the slow disappearance of North Africa's Jewish communities. In July 1997, the Moroccan weekly *Maroc Hebdo* ran an issue titled, "Why Are Our Jews Leaving Us?" asking why the country's Jewish community had declined from three hundred thousand at independence in 1956 to almost 5 percent of that. Yet with the ongoing campaign to find a "Muslim Schindler" and gain reparations for North African Jews, it's not surprising that the current American and French interest in Arab-Jewish music is seen as another attempt by the Israel lobby to intervene in the Arab world's musical life. (People remember how in July 2001 McDonald's terminated Egyptian singer Shaaban's ad for its McFalafel sandwich, after the American Jewish Committee protested his anti-Israeli stance.) In Algeria, the ongoing dispute with France over an apology for colonialism, and the musician Enrico Macias's role at the center of the matter, has also caused many to view this musical revival with suspicion. In 2010, the Algerian historian Fawzi Sadallah published a cantankerous book asking why so much attention was being paid to Jewish-Algerian musicians, who had all but forgotten Arabic and been separated from their cultural roots for decades, when there were dozens of outstanding Muslim musicians across the Maghreb who command the Andalusi repertoire.

In France, this music is now a point of contention between Muslim liberals and Muslim leftists, partly because of how films like *El Gusto* and *Free Men* are being used to promote "interconfessional sociability" and "deradicalization." "My film is not about reconciliation," says Safinez Bousbia about *El Gusto*. "I made the film because I fell in love with these artists and their passion for music. Yet journalists and reviewers keep describing it as a 'project of reconciliation.' If it leads to reconciliation, good—if not, so be it."

The Natives Party leadership sees art as a critical part of the decolonization project. And the party's music critic writes often about music—especially Andalusi music—as essential to the empowerment of European Muslims, but sees no reason to highlight the Arab-Jewish dimension. "French Muslims are obsessed with Jews, it's a bit much," says Houria. "So what if Muslims protected Jews during the Holocaust? Do we have to make films about it? Now these films—*Free Men, El Gusto*—are shown in the *banlieues*, promoting the idea that Muslims used to be tolerant, but somehow became intolerant." The liberal French Muslims reply that the story of Salim Halali must be told to counter public perceptions, and—echoing liberal American Muslims—argue that alliances with liberal Jewish organizations are necessary for Muslim integration.

The American civil rights movement looms large in this discussion, as activists debate which route to take, Bayard Rustin's or Harold Cruse's. To the integrationists, the admirers of Rustin, a central feature of the American struggle was the alliance between black and Jewish civil rights agencies that kept anti-Zionist activists at bay and successfully pushed through legislation. The race activists are not convinced. Both sides are keeping a close eye on events across the Atlantic. And the leftists will point out that even in the United States, Muslim-Jewish coalitions rarely succeed; that Imam Feisal Abdul Rauf of New York distanced himself from conservative Muslims and allied with liberal Jewish groups, but conservative Zionist organizations still blocked his "Ground Zero mosque"; that a Brooklyn-based schoolteacher's attempt to establish an Arab-American high school, the Khalil Gibran Academy, was defeated by the Stop the Madrassah campaign, despite support from liberal Jewish leaders. When Debbie Almontaser, the school's founder, was removed from office in August 2007, Rabbi Michael Paley, a progressive local leader who supported the school, told the press that such xenophobic campaigns would simply produce an Arab-American community that was more isolated, "like the Arabs in France." In France, meanwhile, activists were watching the drama in Brooklyn and seeing the futility of interfaith organizing.

The "decolonial" critiques of Zionist politics—that Zionist organizations promote policies harmful to Palestinians, intervene in North African politics supporting "moderate" heads of state, call for the removal of "radical" leaders, back non-Arabs against Arabs in the Sahara, and so on—resonate profoundly among Muslim youth. But the integrationists warn that criticizing—even speaking of Zionism publicly—will further isolate the Muslim community. "Ninety-nine percent of Americans believe in Zionism. If we criticize Zionism, we immediately drive away sympathizers. We put international issues over local concerns—and remain politically irrelevant," says Mazen Asbahi, a Chicago-based lawyer and Democratic Party politico, who served as Obama's liaison to the American Muslim community in 2008.

The "decolonials" brush off this political pussyfooting and reject the idea that Jewish support and alliances with (liberal) Zionist organizations will help integrate Muslims into the mainstream. Echoing Harold Cruse, who dismissed the idea of "the American Jew [as] a political mediator between Negro and Anglo-Saxon," the French race activists take a similarly dim view of the Arab Jew as a "bridge," and think such coalitions will only divide the Muslim community and divert the Muslim agenda toward externally determined goals. Part of this wariness is a reaction to the "deradicalization" work that American Jewish organizations are doing in the *banlieues* around the issue of Darfur, taking Muslim youth on trips to Auschwitz and Yad

Vashem—initiatives that, according to AJC France, aim to "move beyond post-colonial compassion." But more broadly, a key difference between liberal Muslims and leftist Muslims in Europe is that the liberals, for all their (private) reservations about Zionist politics, see much to emulate in the Jewish path to integration. Liberal Muslim leaders—and policymakers—are closely studying the emancipation of Jews, scrutinizing institutions established during the nineteenth century linking Jewish religious authorities to the state. (Former French prime minister Michel Rocard, who established the first state Islam consultation, often draws a parallel between the situation of Muslims and that of Jews in nineteenth-century France, highlighting the importance of Napoleon's getting Jewish religious authorities to accept the civil code ahead of religious law.)

The "decolonials," on the other hand, prefer the black freedom movement, and will cite British scholar Stuart Hall's definition of diaspora as having more to do with the hybridity of a postcolonial identity than of "scattered tribes whose identity can only be secured in relation to some sacred homeland to which they must at all cost return, even if it means pushing other people into the sea." The decolonials will invoke the voices of African-American scholars and leaders—like James Baldwin, who lived in France half a century ago—and were openly sympathetic to France's Muslims. The moral authority of these black voices is summoned to bolster the "decolonial" critiques of integration, *laïcité*, and empire. Not surprisingly, the race activists see little point in invoking the voices of medieval Andalusian poets, German Orientalists, or Arab-Jewish singers as attestors of Muslim tolerance. All the *convivencia* talk and the nostalgia for Andalusia are in fact scoffed at. "All this yearning for Andalusia comes from an inferiority complex," says Houria Bouteldja. "As Muslims, we want to claim Andalusian civilization to match the supposed grandeur of Western civilization. We prefer to anchor our history in Andalusia or the Pharaonic era, a civilization recognized by Westerners, rather than admit that we come from a small village in Mali."

Transnational history is disturbing; it unsettles national narratives and hard-fought bargains between governments and social groups. Across Europe a fractious politics is bubbling around the memory of

World War II and the colonial past. In December 2011, the Netherlands apologized to Indonesia for massacres committed in 1947 during their war of independence. A few months later the Reichstag threw out a motion introduced by the Left Party calling on the German government to recognize massacres committed by German troops in Namibia a century ago as a genocide. Between 2001 and 2007, the British Muslim Council refused to commemorate Holocaust Memorial Day, calling instead for a Genocide Memorial Day that would honor the dead in Bosnia, Palestine, and Rwanda. A government official from the Home Office's Race Equality Commission rebuffed these demands, saying it risked diluting the day's message with "too much history." Liberal British Muslims, in turn, sharply criticized the British Muslim Council, calling the boycott "morally abhorrent (and strategically stupid)." As in France, Britain's liberal integrationists say Muslims should pay unequivocal tribute to the Holocaust but ask that the government honor Muslims who fought the Nazis, such as Noor Inayat Khan, an Indian Muslim woman who was part of Churchill's Special Operations Executive before being captured and sent to Dachau.

As these culture wars intensify, it's not clear if the memory of World War II will expand to include events outside Europe or if other memory fulcrums will appear alongside that of the war. State officials are pondering how to respond; in some ways it's easier to dismiss Salafi denialism than the new race movements that, following Fanon and Hannah Arendt, see the Holocaust as the culmination of a colonial policy that the Third Reich brought home to Europe. The Oxford historian Timothy Garton Ash, a coauthor of a Council of Europe report on diversity and integration, has recommended that all memory laws (criminalizing denial of the Holocaust and the Armenian genocide) be repealed, but dismissed as "rubbish" calls by the European Commission to "rewrite European history" in a way that would cast the medieval era as one of *convivencia* and intellectual exchange, when classical philosophy came to Western Europe through al-Andalus.

"Too Much History"

"You're looking at the last of the Mohicans—*les derniers des Mohicans,*" says Maurice El Medioni, referring to himself, Luc Cherki, and Robert Castel. The three are the lone survivors of the belle époque of Judeo-Arabic music that emerged in the kasbahs of postwar Algeria and then migrated to France's cabarets. The three octogenarians have been touring nonstop with El Gusto since 2008, playing to sold-out audiences in Europe, Asia, and the United States along with a forty-member orchestra populated by some of the biggest names in contemporary Algerian music. Each concert opens with a prayer by a rabbi and an imam, the rabbi reciting an old Algerian prayer asking that God protect Jews and Muslims from their Christian enemy. Then Castel, with his father's violin on his knee, sings tunes that Lili Labassi wrote almost seventy years ago; Cherki on guitar performs numbers he composed in 1951, when he toured Morocco with Halali. But Medioni steals the show. Introduced as "our Cheikh Medioni," the pianist—now recognized as an elder statesman of Andalusi music—begins with a long *nuba* solo on piano, then launches into "Ahlan Wasahlan," his signature composition. For two hours, Medioni, the de facto conductor of El Gusto, takes the audience on a journey through the Maghreb, playing songs of love and deprivation from southern Morocco to eastern Tunisia. He concludes with "L'Mirikan," Houcine Slaoui's ironic take on American power, which unfailingly gets audiences onto their feet. El Medioni's jazzed up ragtime rendition, his endearing tics, and exaggerated delivery get the crowd—all too aware of the perks, quirks, and hypocrisies of American power—in a raucous mood. "OK, OK, come on, bye-bye," they sing back.

Every Sunday morning for decades now, Medioni leaves his apartment on Boulevard Périer in Marseille and strolls down, hands clasped behind his back, to the café La Samaritaine in the city's old port, right across from the fish market. It's here that he meets the young musicians and researchers who fly up from Algeria to talk to him about their country's past. ("In 1492, the Spaniards gave us—Muslims and Jews—a kick in the pants, and all we took from Spain was a suitcase of songs," he begins.) Since he left Oran in 1962, El Medioni has never returned to Algeria, and vowed not to, but he has been very active in the Algerian music scene, working with artists in the current renewal movement, from *Les Orientales,* a trio of women who in 2004 released *Music Hall d'Algerie,* an album of covers honoring Line Monty, Lili Boniche, and Medioni himself, to Cheb Khaled's most recent 2012 *C'est la Vie,* a tribute to Salim Halali and René Perez. Medioni and his colleagues have been getting more attention since the release of *El Gusto.*

In September 2012, after much political wrangling, *El Gusto* was screened in Algiers. Safinez Bousbia, the filmmaker, got a standing ovation at the end, but during the Q&A, Abdelkader Bendamache, an official from the Ministry of Culture and a historian of the FLN's music policy, stood up and tore into the film for alleged historical inaccuracies. "He said the film was based on lies, that it gave the impression that *chaabi* music was invented by Jews—and why did the film have to mention that Ali La Pointe was a pimp?" says Safinez. Despite its ambivalence about *El Gusto,* the Algerian government is capitalizing on the interest in Andalusi music that the film has generated at home and abroad, establishing a new conservatory for *chaabi* music in Algiers, a *chaabi* festival, and even a national orchestra for *chaabi.*

The efforts now under way in North Africa to reclaim Andalusi music—particularly, the Judeo-Arabic repertoire—are strikingly reminiscent of the movements that sought to safeguard the genre a century ago amid enormous political tumult. If, in 1904, nationalists like Edmond Yafil were writing down and circulating printed copies of *nuba* to inspire a nationalist movement and historiography anchored in Islamic Spain, today's activists are uploading old LPs onto YouTube, blogging, and making documentaries about Arab-Jewish music at a time of political turbulence in the hopes that the music—proof of past Muslim-Jewish musical amity—can arouse a pluralist nationalism.

Music has emerged as a weapon in the ongoing debates about

national identity and memory in North Africa. In Egypt, as Judy Barsalou notes, activists are pushing for the reform of textbooks and the creation of new museums, using historical narratives and "memorialization" to promote their agendas, just as the state is limiting access to historical materials (books, photos, videos, and audio recordings) that may cause more controversy in interpreting the country's contemporary history. If state officials are refusing to make critical recordings available to the public, and state-owned stations, for political reasons, are not playing the nationalist songs of Jewish artists from decades past, civil society groups and individual activists are bypassing the state, disseminating footage online from half a century ago to challenge official historiography. For a younger generation that has only encountered Arab Jews through their music, the crackling 1950s vinyl recordings now uploaded on YouTube provide a window into a fascinating, unresolved past. The young Algerian and Moroccan activists see every song recorded by Lili Labassi or Samy El Maghribi as a repository of memory, that can provide clues into what happened at the founding of the postcolonial state.

The interest in Judeo-Arabic music across North Africa today bespeaks a larger question that is provoking much self-reflection: Why have North Africa's two-thousand-year-old Jewish communities all but disappeared? Along with the new music compilations and commercial films probing Paris's cabaret history, a spate of books and documentaries about the departure of these communities is being released. The narrative that the Jews of Morocco, Algeria, and Tunisia were committed Zionists who eagerly migrated to Israel is being contested by the democratic movements (as is the analogue narrative that after the 1967 War, Arab Jews were scapegoated and forced to flee). These young activists don't deny that the Jews suffered a backlash, but they want the historical record set straight: What role did local regimes play in this departure? Why did the postcolonial regimes of Morocco and Tunisia not protect Jewish communities from persecution? What role did Israel play in stirring up violence against local Arab Jewish communities, as with the infamous Operation Shosana of 1954, when Israeli agents planted bombs in Cairo to delay British and French withdrawal from the Suez Canal, and to speed up the emigration of Jews? What role did American and French Zionist organizations play during this period of tumult? Did heads of state receive payment from American Jewish organizations in exchange for permitting local Jewish communities to leave for Israel?

These debates about minorities and national identity are taking place just as Saudi Arabia and Qatar are pushing back against leftist youth movements with an Islamism that is neither pro-music nor particularly fond of non-Muslims. And questions about how Zionist organizations intervened in postindependence North Africa are being publicly raised just as these organizations, unnerved by the current political change, are embarking on a new round of interventions. The Washington Institute for Near East Policy, still trying to make the Holocaust part of national memory in North Africa, is now embroiled in a dispute with Tunisian politicians over an article in the Tunisian constitution about normalization of ties with Israel. In fall 2012, the World Jewish Congress was lobbying the UN for reparations for Jews from Arab nations, while the Iraqi government broke off archaeological cooperation with the United States after the State Department refused to return archives of historical records of Iraq's Jewish community, which had been found at police headquarters in Baghdad by American troops in 2003 and airlifted to Washington. The debate over who owns Arab-Jewish history also touches on music, of course. In Morocco, student activists objected when researchers with the American Jewish Joint Distribution Committee bought up troves of old records and cassettes by Moroccan Jewish artists, driving up prices locally and depriving students of primary material.

The past, long silent, is now clamoring for attention on both sides of the Mediterranean. The slogan "the suitcase or the coffin," once directed at European colonists in Algeria, now appears as graffiti in Muslim neighborhoods. François Hollande is trying to calm these "history wars." In July 2012, he stated that France bore responsibility for the killings of thousands of Jews who were detained in France by local police and deported to Nazi camps; on October 17, 2012, exactly fifty-one years after the police shot at a pro-independence rally in Paris, killing two hundred Algerians, Hollande paid homage to the victims, "who were killed in a bloody repression." Members of the conservative UMP Party promptly criticized him for undermining "national cohesion" and saddling the republic with more guilt and political responsibility. The antagonism continues. After the shooting in Toulouse, the French government cracked down on Salafi imams, but outbreaks of anti-Semitic vandalism persist. One afternoon in October 2012, Houria Bouteldja was leaving her office at the Institut Monde Arabe, when she was assaulted by Jewish Defense League militants. French JDL militants regularly clash with Muslim youth and the New Black Panther Party; on one occasion, the latter marched into the Marais, onto Rue des Rosiers, a few yards from Berthe Nachman's bookshop, looking to scuffle with JDL members.

In this climate, it's not surprising that El Gusto has not received permission to perform in Algeria. A public performance of a high-profile Muslim-Jewish ensemble would symbolize reconciliation. But as long as the subjugation of Palestinians continues, and the French state has yet to express remorse for a century and a half of colonial domination—for using Jews to lord over Muslims, and for waging a savage war against the FLN—such a gesture of reconciliation would be viewed as premature by broad segments of Algerian opinion. The Algerian government does see benefits to sponsoring El Gusto concerts overseas, however—at the Kennedy Center in Washington, for instance—just not in Algiers. "I spoke to a dozen officials in the ministry of culture and ministry of foreign affairs. And in July 2012 I finally got an appointment with the prime minister, who was very nice, praised our work, and said he would think about it," says Safinez. "As soon as I left his office, his assistant called, and said El Gusto can perform in Algiers, but only the Muslim members." At their next event in Paris, Safinez summoned the orchestra members—all fifty-two musicians—after rehearsal and told them of the prime minister's offer. "We decided to vote," she recalls. "And every single musician said no. They would not perform in Algiers without their Jewish colleagues. I sat down and cried."

This vote of confidence, affirmation of belonging, was emotionally overwhelming for the three Jewish musicians, especially Medioni. Castel has gone back to Algeria frequently, Cherki hasn't but wants to, but El Medioni has long vowed—since 1962—to never return. "I know my generation loves me, *ils jurent par moi,*" he says, "but I don't know about the younger generation." His reconnecting with friends from the 1950s, and the bonds forged with the Muslim musicians while touring with El Gusto, seem to have softened his stance. He's now talking about visiting Algeria "for the sake of my new friends."

As the politics swirls around them—the Arab revolts, right-wing movements in France, Islamists, Black Panthers—the octogenarians seem unperturbed. They're unfazed that songs about Jewish exile—that recorded their life experiences—are now being bequeathed to a younger Muslim generation. Onstage, Castel will stand up, tuck his jacket hip into his teeth, and swivel his waist; Mohammed Ferkaoui, the accordion player, will stand across him and do the same. El Medioni will leave his piano and begin to shake his soft belly. "This music will live on. I'm not concerned," says Castel with a smile. Their main concern seems to be how they're viewed in their land of birth. Castel appears confident that Algerians love him, and has a letter of appreciation from President Bouteflika declaring his father a giant of Andalusian music. As he writes in his memoir, "I think (in fact I believe) that the Algerians love me a bit. I think I know why. Okay, I will let you in on a secret: President Bouteflika has told me in person and in writing. But I didn't announce it to Agence France-Presse or Reuters or CNN." It's not clear why he won't make this letter public. Likewise, Cherki has a letter of appreciation from the king of Morocco for his contributions to Andalusi music but is unsure whether he will publish it in his forthcoming memoir.

At the end of every El Gusto concert, before the curtain comes down, the elders line up for a collective bow. Since the ensemble began touring, four musicians have died, and as audience members wave back, many in tears, one senses that they—like the musicians—realize that this is no ordinary farewell tour; the audience has gotten a glimpse of the past as well as of an alternate future—of what could have been—but they know they're actually witnessing the end of a civilization.

"Every night for the last fifty years, I listen to Radio Alger," says Luc Cherki. "In 1951, when I was seventeen, I had my own show on the station. Since then, every night, I go to sleep listening to Radio Alger, hoping to hear one of us again."

Acknowledgments

I'm not sure where the origins of this book lie. Perhaps it was during my days as a graduate student, when I moonlighted as a journalist, covering Harlem and the Bronx for Africana.com and the London-based *New African*, or maybe it was later, during my postdoctoral year at the David C. Driskell Center for the Study of the African Diaspora at the University of Maryland, when I first began thinking seriously about race, Islam, and internationalism. What is clear is that in producing this book, I have accumulated debt on both sides of the Mediterranean and the Atlantic. This project has taken me to many cities. I've talked to and learned from dozens of colleagues from Paris to São Paulo to Berkeley, and interviewed musicians, journalists, belly dancers, diplomats, imams, DJs and congressional staffers. I regret that I cannot thank everyone.

In writing *Rebel Music*, I have been privileged to be part of a remarkable intellectual community at Columbia—straddling the School of International and Public Affairs, the Institute for Research in African-American Studies, and the Institute of African Studies. I have been enriched by conversations with Zaheer Ali, Richard Betts, Souleymane Bachir Diagne, Mamadou Diouf, Najam Haider, Ousmane Kane, Brinkley Messick, José Moya, Al Stepan, and Steve Sestanovich. In my time at Columbia, as a student and lecturer, I have relied on a number of people, but I'm particularly indebted to Lisa Anderson, Mahmood Mamdani, and the late Manning Marable, for their guidance and steadfast support over the years. Chapters in this book were originally written as research papers for seminars I took with Paul Gilroy (then at Yale) and Robin Kelley (then at Columbia). I'm deeply grateful to Paul and Robin for their instruction and example. I want to thank the friends who read chapters, or the manuscript in its entirety, and offered comments: a special *shukran* to Joel Gordon, Paul Silverstein, Chris Toensing, Daniel Schroetter, Kambiz Ghaneabassiri, David Levering Lewis, Philip Schuyler, Charles Hirschkind, Zareena Grewal, and Rami Nashashibi.

Other scholars who bear some responsibility for what intelligence this book may contain: Ted Swedenburg at the University of Arkansas; Sherman Jackson at the University of Southern California; Amina McCloud and John Karam at DePaul; Paulo Pinto and Jorge de la Barre at the Fluminense Federal University in Rio de Janeiro; Fernando Conceição and João José Reis at the Federal University of Bahia; Bernabé López García of the Universidad Autonoma de Madrid; Riva Kastoryano and Luis Martinez at Science Pos; Vanessa Paloma at the Sorbonne; the late Simon Levy at Université Mohammed V in Rabat; Iman Lechkar and Nadia Fadel at the University of Leuven; Martijn de Koning at Radboud University; and Farid Hafez at the University of Vienna. In addition, I thank: Thomas Whitcomb, Abdullahi Boru, Gustavo Chacra, Alice Cherki, Tim Fuson, Arun Kundnani, Ayesha Hasan, Zain Abdallah, Rasul Miller, Erik Love, Louis Cristillo, Arash Davari, Maryam Griffin, Oliver Wang, Keith Feldman, Shahid Hasan, Mayanthi Fernando, Farid El Asri, Sara Crafts, Brian Karl, Harold Morales, Qasim Rashid, Junaid Rana, Laith Ulaby, and Hamada Zahawi.

A number of scholars in America and Europe invited me to present bits of my research. I must thank colleagues at the David C. Driskell Center at the University of Maryland in College Park—Robert Steele, Daryle Williams, and the late Clyde Woods—who invited me to speak on black internationalism and North Africa in April 2005. I'm also grateful to Hatem Bazian and Munir Jiwa for inviting me to Berkeley; Salah Hassan for inviting me to Michigan State University; Juliane Hammer for inviting me to George Mason University; and Rosemary Hicks for inviting me to Tufts. On the European side, I thank Peter Morey and Amina Yaqin for inviting me to their "Framing Muslims" conference at the School of Oriental and African Studies in November 2009; Jeanette Jouili and Annelies Moors for inviting me to their "Secular Sounds, Islamic Sounds" conference at the Amsterdam Institute for Social Science Research in October 2010; and Trica Keaton for including me in her wonderful "Black France" conference in Paris, in memory of Aimé Césaire and Michel Fabre.

Among the activists and community leaders I interviewed, I want to thank Dawud Walid of the Council on American Islamic Relations in Detroit; Zaid Shakir of Zaytuna College; Ma'alem Abdullah and Asad Jafri of the Inner City Muslim Action Network in Chicago; Mobeen Butt of the Asian Youth Alliance in Croydon, London; Ahmed Versi of *Muslim News,* Nadeem Kazmi of Al-Khoei Foundation, and Shaista Gohir of Muslim Women's Network, all in London; Majid El Jarroudi and Fati Tanriverdi of Adive in Paris; Olad Aden of Gangway Beatz in Berlin; Betul Yilmaz of Muslim Voices, also in Berlin; Ico Maly of Kif Kif, and Mourad Bekour of 'Nuff Said, both in Antwerp; Michael Privot of the European Network Against Racism (ENAR) in Brussels, and Ibrahim Akrouh of MRAX, also in the Belgian capital; Neila Tazi of REZO Productions in Casablanca; Antônio Carlos Vovô of Ilê Aiyê in Salvador, Bahia; Sheikh Abdul Hameed Ahmad of the Centro Cultural Islâmico da Bahia; Janaina Fari at the Centro de Memória do Carnaval in Rio; and Fernando Casado Cañeque of the CAD (Centro de Alianzas para el Desarrollo) in Barcelona.

This research project would not have been possible without the support of the Carnegie Corporation of New York and the Open Society Foundation. At Carnegie I thank Patricia Rosenfield and Hillary Wiesner. As an Open Society Global Fellow, I was able to access an extraordinary transcontinental network of scholars and specialists, and the Open Society staff was helpful in everything from arranging interviews with community leaders to providing visa letters. I'm especially grateful to the New York team: Lenny Bernardo, Stephen Hubbell, Aryeh Nair, Bipasha Ray, Hernan Bonomo, Lisena DeSantis, and Christine Seisun. In London, a very special thanks to Nazia Hussein, director of OSF's "At Home in Europe" program, for connecting me with a number of artists and community leaders. I also thank Helene Irving for organizing the Rich Mix event on art and Muslim cultures in Europe. At the Brussels office, I extend my gratitude to Tarana Ahmadova, Heather Grabbe, Ellen Riotte, and Jacqueline Hale. At the Baltimore office, I thank Diana Morris. And at the Washington office, I thank Rachel Neild and Akwe Amosu. Over the last few years, I have also benefited from my affiliation with the Institute for Social Policy and Understanding, and their work on Muslim Americans. I thank Farid Senzai, Siwar Bizri, Muzammil Ahmad, and Mazen Asbahi.

I spent several months in Washington, D.C., researching public diplomacy and I am grateful to the retired career diplomats—Chas Freeman, Richard Murphy, and Frank Wisner—for sharing their knowledge of American diplomatic maneuvering in the Middle East during the 1960s. I'm particularly thankful to the Muslim- and Arab-American public servants and government officials who shared their thoughts on everything from census classification to political participation: Shahed Amanullah, Rima Dodin, Rita Estefan, Yousra Fazili, Saba Ghori, Suhail Khan, Mouaz Moustafa, Ahmed Al-Rumaihi, Maryum Saifee, and Jihad Saleh Williams. In Harlem, I'm grateful to Aisha Al-Adawiya and Steven Fullwood at the Schomburg Library; Sharon Harris at IRAAS at Columbia has also been a great support. Some of my research appeared in *Souls* journal and *Middle East Report;* I'm grateful to Barbara Ransby and the *Souls* Editorial Working Group, and to Chris Toensing, editor extraordinaire of *MERIP*. In Brooklyn, Zaheer Ali's "Artists & Intellectuals" dinners were an ongoing seminar on Muslim youth culture: I thank Su'ad Abdulkhabeer, Arshad Ali, Nisaa Ali, Nsenga and Nzinga Knight, and Kauthar Umar. A special shout out to all the young artists who were so forthcoming: Omar Offendum, Outlandish, Malika Zarra, Brahim Fribgane, Christie Z, Jorge Pabón, Toni Blackman, Hamza Perez, Mohammed Yahya & Poetic Pilgrimage, Mecca2Medina, Ben Herson and Magee McIlvaine of Nomadic Wax, Hoba Hoba Spirit, The Narcicyst, The Kominas, The Reminders, Tommie Evans, Ali Jamal Shabazz (Khaffu), Honerê al-Amin Oadq, and Posse Hausa.

A heartfelt thanks is due to my literary agent, Jane Gelfman, who first encouraged me to write a book about Muslim youth. I also thank my editor, Shelley Wanger, and her assistant, Juhea Kim, at Pantheon.

In writing this book, I have been sustained by the love and support of friends and relatives. I'm particularly grateful to Atefa Shah—

only she knows how much I've relied on her. I'm also grateful to my comrades Rambo Osanya, Newman Horton, Moumie Maoulidi, and Carlos Suarez. In Paris, I would have been bereft without the help of Safinez Bousbia, and the company of my cousin Hayate, my aunt and uncle Farida and Omar. Back home in Tangier, I thank Abdallah El Gourd of Dar Gnawa, for some magical evenings in the medina. I also thank his neighbors, Bernabé López García and Cecilia Fernández Suzor of the Instituto Cervantes for their hospitality. I'm grateful to my mother, Rachida, for so many things, but in this case, simply for being a reciter, and trying to impart her vast knowledge of Maghrebian music to me and my sisters.

Finally, a special thanks to the musical elders who were so generous with their memories and recordings: Randy Weston, Maurice El Medioni, Yusef Lateef, Abdallah El Gourd, Kenny Gamble, Robert "Kool" Bell, Ahmad Jamal, Luc Cherki, Ira Cohen, Marcel Abitbol, Robert Castell, Jacques Muyal, Maurice Ahouasse, and Mohammed El Ferkioui. Two individuals closely inhabited my thoughts as I wrote, and these were Randy Weston and Maurice El Medioni. It's always a delight when the phone rings and I hear "It's Randy Weston" or *"C'est Maurice!"* Now in their late eighties, their humanism and creative fire undimmed, Randy's and Maurice's conversations and compositions have energized me; their life stories shaped the course of this book.

November 2013
Harlem USA

Selected Discography and Videography

Discography

Abbey Lincoln and Max Roach, *We Insist!—Max Roach's Freedom Now Suite* (Candid Productions, 1989).

Abd Al Malik, *Gibraltar* (Atmosphériques, 2006).

Amazigh Kateb, *Marchez Noir* (Iris Music, 2010).

Arabian Knightz, featuring Shadia Mansour, "Prisoner" (song of the Egyptian Revolution), *Uknighted State of Arabia* (Magnum Opus Music, 2012).

Archie Shepp Quartet and Dar Gnawa, *Kindred Spirits, Vol. 1* (Archie Ball, 2011).

Art Blakey and the Jazz Messengers, *A Night in Tunisia* (Blue Note, 1960).

Burhan G, "Who Is He," *Breakout* (Copenhagen Records, 2007).

Darga, "Africa," *Stop Baraka* (Box Music, 2008).

Deicide, "Fuck Your God," *Scars of the Crucifix* (Earache Records, 2004).

DJ Cut Killer and 3ème Oeil, "Si Triste," *1 Son 2 Rue (L'Album)* (Double H Production, 2002).

Drowning Pool, "Bodies," *Sinner* (Wind-Up Entertainment, 2001).

El General, "Rais Lebled (Head of the Country)," *Our Dreams Are Our Weapons: Soundtracks of the Revolutions in Tunisia and Egypt* (Network, 2013).

Enrico Macias, "Adieu Mon Pays," *Ses Plus Belles Chansons* (EMI Music France, 1994).

Enrico Macias with Taoufik Bastandji and L'Ensemble Foundok, *Hommage à Cheikh Raymond* (Trema, 1999).

Frank Zappa, *Trance-Fusion* (Zappa Records, 2006).

Fun-Da-Mental, *All Is War* (5 Uncivilised Tribes, 2006).

Gnawa Diffusion, *Bab El Oued Kingston* (7 Colors Music, 1999).

Hamid El Kasri, "Lalaamira" and "Lalaaïcha," *Soirées Gnawa Neurasys Remaster, Vol. 2* (Sacavneurasys, 2010).

Hanine y Son Cubano, *Arabo-Cuban* (Warner, 2005).

Hanine y Son Cubano, "Rahou," *Radio Beirut* (Galileo Music Communication, 2012).

Harold Melvin and the Blue Notes, "Wake Up Everybody," *Wake Up Everybody* (Philadelphia International Records, 1975).

Haroldo Lobo, Carlos Galhardo, and Antônio Nássara, "Alah-lá-ô," *Marchinhas de Carnaval, Vol. 8* (MNR Media, 2011).

Hoba Hoba Spirit, "Basta Lahia," *Hoba Hoba Spirit* (Moroccan Music Division, 2002).

Houcine Slaoui, "El Marikan Ain Zerka," *Best of Houcine of Slaoui (20 Années de Success)* (Edition Cléopâtre, 2011).

John Coltrane, "A Love Supreme, Pt. 1: Acknowledgement (Live)," *A Love Supreme* (Deluxe Edition) (Verve Music Group, UMG Recordings, 2002).

Junoon, "Sayonee," *Azadi* (EMI Pakistan/Universal Music, 1997).

Kery James featuring Youssoupha & Médine, "Contre Nous," *Dernier MC* (AZ, 2013).

Kool & the Gang, *Celebration* (De-Lite, 1980).

Kool & the Gang, *Open Sesame* (De-Lite, 1976).

Koringa, "Dança Sensual," *A Caminhada* (Som Livre, 2012).

La Rumeur, "L'Ombre sur la Mesure," *L'Ombre sur la Mesure* (EMI Music France, 2003).

Les Orientales, *Music-Hall d'Algérie* (Mk2, 2005).

Lili Boniche, "Ana El Owerka (Algerian Tango)," *Grand Cafe Oriental (1953–1963 Recordings)* (VintageMusic, 2013).

Lili Boniche, "Il n'y à qu'un seul Dieu," *Anthologie* (Harmonia Mundi S.S./World Village, 2012).

Line Monty, "Ana Ene Hobbek," *Trésors de la Chanson Judéo-Arabe* (MLP, 2001).

Lowkey, "Terrorist?" *Soundtrack to the Struggle* (Mesopotamia Music, 2011).

Luc Cherki, "Andalousia," *Mazal* (Time Zone Records, 2000).

Luc Cherki, "Ya Ghadi l'Sahra," *Trésors de la Chanson Judéo-Arabe* (MLP, 2006).

Lupe Fiasco featuring Skylar Grey, "Words I Never Said," *Lasers* (Atlantic Recording Corporation for the United States and WEA International, 2011).

Maâlem Abderrahmane Paco, "La Ilaha Illa Llah," *Gnawa Music Collection* (Alchemy, 2012).

Maleem Mahmoud Ghania with Pharoah Sanders, *The Trance of Seven Colors* (Axiom, 1994).

Maurice El Medioni, "Ahla[n] Ouassahla[n]" and "Ana n'Habek," *Pianoriental* (Buda Musique, 2005).

MC Créu, "Dança do Creu," *Funk do Brasil* (Shark Entertainment, 2010).

Médine, "Du Panjshir à Harlem," *Jihad—Le Plus Grand Combat est Contre Soi-Même* (Din Records, 2005).

Médine, *Protest Song* (Because Music, 2013).

Mohamed El Kamal, *Algérie: Fantaisistes des Années 30* (Buda Musique, 1998).

Nass El Ghiwane, *Hommage à Boudjemma* (Editions Cléopâtre/Brahim Ounassar, 2011).

Orchestre El Gusto, *El Gusto* (Quidam & Remark, 2012).

Orchestre National de Barbès, *En Concert* (EMI Music France, 1997).

Outlandish, "Callin' U," *Closer Than Veins* (Deluxe Edition) (Sony BMG Music Entertainment Music Denmark, 2005).

Philadelphia International All Stars, "Let's Clean Up the Ghetto," *Let's Clean Up the Ghetto* (Philadelphia International Records, 1977).

Randy Weston, *Blue Moses* (King Japan, 1972).

Randy Weston, "Little Niles," *African Rhythms* (Planet Woo, 1969).

Randy Weston, *Uhuru Afrika* [Freedom Africa] (Roulette, 1960).

Randy Weston and the Gnawa Master Musicians of Morocco, "El Wali Sidi Mimoun," *Spirit! The Power of Music* (Sunnyside, 2003).

Rubén Blades, "La Mora," *Bohemio y Poeta* (Fania, 1979).

Salah Edin, "Het Land Van," *Nederlands Grootste Nachtmerrie* (Top Notch, 2007).

Salim Halali, "Arjaa Lebladek," *En Algérie* (Oriental, 1990).

Salim Halali, "El Andalous," *Les Hommes Libres* (Original Motion Picture Soundtrack) (Atoll Music, 2011).

Salim Halali, "Live" [Los Piconeros], *L'Album D'Or, Vol. 2* (Atoll Music, 2010).

Salim Halali, "Ma Yiddishe Mama," *Best of Salim Halali* (Ascot Music, 2001).

Salim Halali, "Moi Je Suis D'un Pays" and "Sidi H'Bibi," *L'Essentiel* (Atoli Music/Fifty-Five, 2005).

Sami Yusuf, *My Ummah* (Awakening Worldwide, 2005).

Shakira, "Ojos Así," *Dónde Están los Ladrones?* (Sony Latin, 1999).

Slayer, "Angel of Death," *Reign of Blood* (American Recordings, 1986).

The Kominas, "I Want a Hand Job," *The Taqwacores* (Original Motion Picture Soundtrack) (Insolent Cad Records, 2010).

Various Artists, "A Young Man's Spark (Bouazizi)" (Remarkable Current, 2011).

Various Artists, "Danca Das Serpentes," *Danças do Ventre de* O Clone (Sonhos & Sons, 2005).

Various Artists, *Maktub II: La Danza de los Siete Velos (de la Telenovela* El Clon*)* (Original Soundtrack) (Universal Music Latino, 2002).

Yusef Lateef, *Blues for the Orient* (Fantasy Studios, 1974).

Videography

Algérie Djmawi Africa, "Hchich et Pois Chiche," accessible at www.youtube.com/watch?v=et3KzrhRnS4.

Khaled M. featuring Lowkey, "Can't Take Our Freedom?" (Bliz Beats, 2011). Accessible at: www.youtube.com/watch?v=hapPFY8tvzY.

Line Monty (Leila Fateh), "Alger, Alger," written by Lili Boniche (Pathé Marconi, 1952). Accessible at: www.youtube.com/watch?v=-sT9Z6auBbg.

Malê Debalê, "Fantástico," *Que Bloco É Esse?* (Berimbau Filmes, 2012). Accessible at: www.vimeo.com/40274972.

MC Jair Da Rocha, "Funk Do Trenzinho," (*Camisa Verde e Branco,* 2008). Accessible at: www.youtube.com/watch?v=PDIJSiZsMSQ.

Omar Offendum, "#Syria" (2012). Accessible at: www.youtube.com/watch?v=TXjEWrhkb6g.

Omar Offendum, the Narcicyst, Freeway, Ayah, and Amir Sulaiman, "#Jan25 Egypt" (2011). Accessible at: www.youtube.com/watch?v=sCbpiOpLwFg.

Warda, "Ya Oumi," written by Yousef Haggag (1951). Accessible at: www.youtube.com/watch?v=rWhvEGOCuOY.

Notes

Prologue

xii **As the *New York Times* reported:** "Feeling Slighted by France, and Respected by U.S.," *New York Times,* September 22, 2010; "With Obama's Victory, Europe's Minorities Sense New Possibilities," *Christian Science Monitor,* November 7, 2008.

xiii **"I'm boycotting France":** "Je boycotte la France," *Bondy Blog,* September 10, 2011; "Où le musulman vit-il le mieux: aux Etats-Unis ou en France?" *Bondy Blog,* November 1, 2010.

xiv **An easy consensus seems to have emerged:** Francis Fukuyama, "Identity, Immigration and Liberal Democracy," *Journal of Democracy,* April 2006; see also Paul Barrett, *American Islam: The Struggle for the Soul of a Religion* (New York: Farrar, Straus and Giroux, 2006).

xv **In *Among Empires:*** Charles S. Maier, *Among Empires: American Ascendancy and Its Predecessors* (Cambridge: Harvard University Press, 2006), p. 10.

xviii **The U.S.'s National Intelligence Council's:** *Global Trends 2025: A Transformed World—The National Intelligence Council's 2025 Project* (National Intelligence Council, November 2008).

xix **The challenge for all governments:** Jonathan Laurence, *The Emancipation of Europe's Muslims: The State's Role in Minority Integration* (Princeton, NJ: Princeton University Press, 2012).

xx **But while having European Muslim:** Anita Elash, "U.S. Reaches Out to Poor Immigrants in France," *Morning Edition,* NPR (July 2, 2008).

xxii **Explaining how the accused:** Olivier Roy, *Globalized Islam: The Search for a New Ummah* (New York: Columbia University Press, 2003). For another study of globalized Islam that neglects the role of race and African-American Islam, see Peter Mansfield, *Global Political Islam* (New York: Routledge, 2003).

xxii **Similarly, the scholars:** Susan Buck-Morss, *Thinking Past Terror: Islamism and Critical Theory on the Left* (London: Verso, 2003).

xxii **Youth activists often ponder:** Ali Etera, "The Making of the Muslim Left," *The Guardian,* October 16, 2007.

xxv   **In Europe today, Muslim youth:** Arjun Appadurai, *Modernity at Large: Cultural Dimensions of Globalization* (Minneapolis: University of Minnesota Press, 1996), p. 15.

xxv   **In 1929:** Rami Nashashibi, "Ghetto Cosmopolitanism: Making Theory at the Margins," in Saskia Sassen, ed., *Deciphering the Global: Its Scales, Spaces, and Subjects* (New York: Routledge, 2007).

xxvi   **In *What the Music Said*:** Mark Anthony Neal, *What the Music Said: Black Popular Music and Black Public Culture* (New York: Routledge, 1999).

xxvi   **As the Canadian-based neuroscientist:** Steven Brown and Ulrik Volgsten, eds., *Music and Manipulation: On the Social Uses and Social Control of Music* (New York: Berghahn Books, 2006).

xxvii   **French and American observers:** Nicolas Simon, "Young, Male and Angry," *The Jerusalem Report*, May 6, 2002; Marion Festraëts, "Enfants d'Allah et de l'Amérique," *L'Express*, April 3, 2003.

xxvii   **Before the riots were over:** "Rap 'Not Cause of French Riots,'" *BBC News*, November 25, 2005.

xxviii   **"drug dealers, imams":** Farid Laroussi, "Why I Became an American," *Yale Alumni Magazine*, May/June 2004.

xxviii   **what French journalists call:** "Opération Séduction des USA dans les Banlieues Français," *Le Figaro*, July 1, 2008.

xxix   **The ideological ferment:** Michael A. Gomez, *Black Crescent: The Experience and Legacy of African Muslims in the Americas* (New York: Cambridge University Press, 2005), p. 209.

1 · The Enchanted Mooress

5   **Soap operas in Brazil:** Lila Abu-Lughod, *Dramas of Nationhood: The Politics of Television in Egypt* (Chicago: University of Chicago Press, 2005).

7   **In underlining Brazil's mixedness:** Jeffrey Lesser, *Immigration, Ethnicity, and National Identity in Brazil: 1808 to the Present* (New York: Cambridge University Press, 2013), p. 2.

7   **It was the "interpenetration":** See Gilberto Freyre, *The Masters and the Slaves: A Study in the Development of Brazilian Civilization* (New York: Knopf, 1964), pp. 12–13.

8   **The Moorish era was critical:** Gilberto Freyre, *New World in the Tropics: The Culture of Modern Brazil* (New York: Knopf, 1966).

8   **Yet Freyre's account:** Alexandra Isfahani-Hammond, "Aristocratas da Senzala: Gilberto Freyre na Interseção do Orientalismo e dos Estudos de Escravidão," *Afro-Ásia* 37, no. 1 (2008).

9   **In 1942, the House of Representatives:** Congressional records, Proceedings

and Debates of the 77th Congress, Second Session, October 2, 1941; March 30, 1942, cited in Maria Lucia G. Pallares-Burke, "Gilberto Freyre and Brazilian Self-perception," in Francisco Bethencourt and Adrian J. Pearce, eds., *Racism and Ethnic Relations in the Portuguese-Speaking World,* Proceedings of the British Academy (New York: Oxford University Press, 2012), pp. 113–32.

9 **The regime would also:** Daryle Williams, *Culture Wars in Brazil: The First Vargas Regime, 1930–1945* (Durham, NC: Duke University Press, 2001), p. 86.

10 **But the scholar's defense:** João Felipe Marques, "Les Racistes c'est les Autres: Les Origines du Mythe du «non racisme» des Portugais," *Lusotopie* 14, no. 1 (June 2007), pp. 71–88.

11 **There are roughly one million:** Paulo G. Pinto, "Arab Ethnicity and Diasporic Islam: A Comparative Approach to Processes of Identity Formation and Religious Codification in the Muslim Communities in Brazil," *Comparative Studies of South Asia, Africa and the Middle East* 31, no. 2 (2011).

11 **Arab Brazilians own:** John Tofik Karam, *Another Arabesque: Syrian-Lebanese Ethnicity in Neoliberal Brazil* (Philadelphia: Temple University Press, 2007).

13 **"We need to say no":** "Muçulmanos Ganham Destaque em *O Clone,*" *Folha de São Paulo,* September 23, 2001.

13 **The allegations snowballed:** "Bin Laden Reportedly Spent Time in Brazil in '95," *Washington Post,* March 28, 2003; Jeffrey Goldberg, "In the Party of God," *The New Yorker,* October 14, 2002.

13 **In Portugal, the soap:** Julie McBrien, "Brazilian TV & Muslimness in Kyrgyzstan," *ISIM Review* 19, no. 1 (Spring 2007), pp. 16–17.

14 **A journalist visiting Quito:** Kimi Eisele, "The Multicultural Power of Soap Operas," *Pacific News Service,* November 25, 2002.

15 **"Made in Brazil":** Gina Montaner, "El Clon, un Año Después," *Nuevo Herald,* June 9, 2004.

15 **In New York, the Spanish:** Interview with Rosa Margarita of *El Diario–La Prensa,* August 8, 2003. "El Clon"–inspired fashion can be viewed online at http://www .laoriginal.com/especiales.htm.

15 **When CNN aired:** "Terrorists Find Haven in South America," CNN, November 8, 2001.

15 **It printed posters:** "Laughing in the Face of Terrorist Reports: Brazilian City Lures Tourists with Humor," *Washington Post,* April 11, 2004.

15 **In February 2002:** Ella Shohat and Robert Stam, *Flagging Patriotism: Crises of Narcissism and Anti-Americanism* (New York: Routledge, 2006), p. 103.

16 **A 2009 dispatch:** "U.S. Embassy Cables: Brazil Covered Up Existence of Terrorist Suspects," *The Guardian,* December 5, 2010.

17 **"U.S. cultural imperialism":** Michael Kimmelman, "Turks Put Twist in Racy Soaps," *New York Times,* June 17, 2010.

18   **Samba singers—in satin:** Marcia Christina da Silva, "Gaviões Destaca Grandiosi-
       dade de Dubai," Estadao.com.br, February 23, 2011.

18   **"The naked, seductive women":** Roberto DaMatta, *Carnivals, Rogues, and Heroes:
       An Interpretation of the Brazilian Dilemma* (South Bend: IN: University of Notre
       Dame Press, 1991), p. 106.

19   **In June 2010, a group:** Rafael Valladao et al., "La Contribución Árabe-Musulmana a
       la Formación de la Cultura Corporal Carioca," Efdeportes.com, June 2010.

19   **At the launch for the Arabic:** "Rabat: Hommage au Sociologue Brésilien Gilberto
       Freyre," *Libération,* December 18, 2002.

19   **"Freyre saw the Oriental":** "Festa Literária Internacional de Pernambuco," *Jornal
       do Brasil,* November 9, 2011; Ana Raquel, "O Legado Árabe no Brasil," *Ibérica:
       Revista Interdisciplinar de Estudos Ibéricos e Ibérico-Americanos,* no. 16 (May–August
       2011).

19   **And the enchanted Mooress:** "A Moura Encantada: Os Mouros e a Presença da Cul-
       tura Árabe na Música Tradicional do Brasil," *Guia da Folha,* September 2008.

20   **She would appeal:** Julio Caro Baroja, *Vidas Mágicas e Inquisición,* vol. 1 (Madrid:
       Ediciones Akal, 1967, rpt. 1992), p. 182.

20   **The Spanish and Portuguese:** Michael A. Gomez, *Black Crescent: The Experience and
       Legacy of African Muslims in the Americas* (New York: Cambridge University Press,
       2005), p. 28.

21   **In 1526, Charles I:** José Manuel García Leduc, *Apuntes para una Historia Breve de
       Puerto Rico: Desde la Prehistoria hasta 1898* (San Juan, Puerto Rico: Isla Negra, 2003),
       p. 123; James Lockhart, *Spanish Peru, 1532–1560: A Social History* (Madison: Univer-
       sity of Wisconsin Press, 1994).

21   **In New Mexico:** Ramon A. Gutiérrez, *When Jesus Came, the Corn Mothers Went Away:
       Marriage, Sexuality, and Power in New Mexico, 1500–1846* (Palo Alto, CA: Stanford
       University Press, 1991), p. 44.

21   **Yet the Moorish seductress:** Sérgio Buarque de Holanda, "Da Alva Dinamene à
       Moura Encantada," in *Tentativas de Mitologia* (São Paulo: Perspectiva, 1979), pp. 85–
       97; Narda Henríquez, *El Hechizo de las Imágenes: Estatus Social, Género y Etnicidad en
       la Historia Peruana* (Lima: Póntificia Universidad Católica del Perú, Fondo Editorial,
       2000), p. 77.

22   **"You can hear Moorish":** Oswaldo Truzzi, "Sentindo-se em Casa: Os Árabes se
       Adaptaram Muito bem ao Brasil," *Revista de História* 46 (July 2009).

23   **Brazilian officials and cultural elites:** Elisa Larkin Nascimento, *Cultura em Movi-
       mento: Matrizes Africanas e Ativismo Negro no Brasil* 2 (São Paulo: Selo Negro,
       2008/2009), p. 284.

23   **Why exactly, feminist critics:** Vera Lucia Maia Marque, "Sobre Práticas Religiosas e
       Culturais Islâmicas no Brasil e em Portugal: Notas e Observações de Viagem," Disser-
       tation, Sociology Department, Universidade Federal de Minas Gerais, Brazil, October

2009, p. 103; interview with Fernando Conceição, Universidade Federal da Bahia, Salvador, Brazil, July 17, 2013.

23 **But today he is openly:** Alberto Mussa, "A Poesia Perdida dos Sambas de Enredo," *O Globo,* February 9, 2013.

2 · Sugar's Secrets

24 **"'As-salamu 'alaykum'":** 'Abd al-Rahmān al-Baġdādī, *The Amusement of the Foreigner* (*Musalliyat al-gharib*), translated by Yacine Daddi Addoun and Renée Soulodre–La France (Toronto: York University, 2001), p. 11. See also Rosemarie Quiring-Zoche, "Bei den Malé in Brasilien: 'Das Reisebuch des 'Abdarrahmān al-Baġdādī,'" *Die Welt des Islams* 40, no. 2 (July 2000), pp. 196–273.

27 **Bilali's literacy was always:** Joel Chandler Harris, *The Story of Aaron (So Named), the Son of Ben Ali* (1896) and *Aaron in the Wildwoods* (1897).

27 **"The Spaniard was accustomed":** Jaime Borja, "Barbarizacion y Redes de Indoctrinamiento en los Negros Cartageno XVII y XVIII," in Astrid Ulloa, ed., *Contribution Africana a la Cultura de las Americas* (Bogota: Instituto Colombiano de Antropología y Colcultura, 1993), p. 249.

27 **Discontent had simmered:** João José Reis, *Slave Rebellion in Brazil: The 1835 Muslim Uprising in Bahia* (Baltimore, MD: Johns Hopkins University Press, 1995), pp. 109–115.

28 **The Malê Revolt:** See the *Times* (London), March 3, 1835, cited in João José Reis, *Rebelião Escrava no Brasil: A História do Levante dos Malês em 1835* (São Paulo: Companhia das Letras, 2003), pp. 520–22.

29 **Today, as the Orient beckons:** Paulo Daniel Farah, "Um Imã nos Trópicos," *Revista de História,* June 2008.

30 **Members note casually:** "Brésil: l'Essor de l'Islam dans les Favelas," *France 24,* April 2, 2010.

31 **In his classic *Sweetness and Power*:** Sidney W. Mintz, *Sweetness and Power: The Place of Sugar in Modern History* (New York: Penguin Books, 1985), p. 25; Omar Ramadan-Santiago, "Rhyming *Insha'Allah* with *Ojala:* Puerto Rican Muslim Hip Hoppers (Re) Defining Boricua Identity," Master's thesis, CUNY, January 2011.

32 **"Since I became Muslim":** Eliane Brum, "Islã Cresce na Periferia das Cidades do Brasil," *Época,* January 30, 2009.

32 **"In 2000, there were":** Fatiha Benelbah and Sylvia Montenegro, eds., *Al Muslimun fil Brasil: Qadaya al-hawiyat wal Intima' lil jama'at wa tawaif wal muasasat* (Rabat, Morocco: ONR Editora, 2013).

32 **Rap took root in São Paulo:** George Yúdice, *The Expediency of Culture: Uses of Culture in the Global Era* (Durham, NC: Duke University Press, 2004).

33 **"Funk with a Police Record":** João Freire Filho and Micael Herschmann, "Funk Music Made in Brazil: Media and Moral Panic," in Idelber Avelar and Christopher Dunn, eds., *Brazilian Popular Music and Citizenship* (Durham, NC: Duke University Press, 2011), pp. 23-39.

34 **Brazil watchers will observe:** Vitória Peres de Oliveira and Cecília L. Mariz, "Conversion to Islam in Contemporary Brazil," *Exchange* 35, no. 1 (March 2006).

34 **It is rather ironic:** David Kenner, "Helium Diplomacy and the Jamaican Menace," *Foreign Policy,* September 2, 2011.

36 **"the black struggle":** Jerry Dávila, *Hotel Tropico: Brazil and the Challenge of African Decolonization, 1950–1980* (Durham, NC: Duke University Press, 2010).

36 **Is the Afro-Brazilian distrust:** Claudia Maria de Assis Rocha Lima, "Heranças Muçulmanas no Nagô de Pernambuco: Construíndo Mitos Fundadores da Religião de Matriz Africana no Brasil," *Revista Brasileira de História das Religiões* 1, no. 3 (January 2009).

37 **As in the U.S.:** Akbar Ahmed, *Journey into America: The Challenge of Islam* (Washington, DC: Brookings Institution Press, 2010), pp. 165–67.

37 **The church brochure says:** Manuel Raumundo Querino, *Artistas Bahianos* (Rio de Janeiro: Imprensa Nacional, 1909), p. 206, cited in Gomez, *Black Crescent.*

38 **The Moorish Atlantic:** Hisham Aidi, "The Moorish Atlantic: Moors, Aztecs, and the Invention of the Americas," paper prepared for seminar, Sociology Department, Yale University, New Haven, CT, May 2003.

38 **The Mexican novelist:** Carlos Fuentes, *The Buried Mirror: Reflections on Spain and the New World* (Baltimore, MD: First Mariner Books, 1999), p. 15.

38 **But his compatriot:** Octavio Paz, *El ogro filantrópico: historia y política 1971–1978* (Barcelona: Editorial Seix Barral, 1979), p.128.

38 **In Brazil, the conservative economist:** Antônio Paim, *História do Liberalismo Brasileiro* (São Paulo: Editora Mandarim; Instituto Tancredo Neves, 1998), p. 280.

38 **To woo foreign customers:** Vera M. Kutzinski, *Sugar's Secrets: Race and the Erotics of Cuban Nationalism* (Charlottesville: University of Virginia Press, 1993), pp. 48, 196.

38 **In 1893, as the Berbers:** José Martí, "Espana en Melilla," *Cuba: Letras* 2 (Havana: Edición Tropico, 1938), p. 201.

39 **In 1926, the novelist:** Waldo Frank, "Habana of the Cubans," *New Republic,* June 23, 1926.

39 **But the music of 1950s Havana:** Vernon W. Boggs, *Salsiology: Afro-Cuban Music and the Evolution of Salsa in New York City* (London: Greenwood Press, 1992), p. 82.

39 **"We all have":** Cited in René Dépestre, "Carta de Cuba Sobre el Imperialismo de la Mala Fé," *Por la Revolucion, por la Poesia* (Havana: Instituto del Libro, 1969), p. 9.

41 **Even Colombia, the sole:** Max Fisher, "A Staggering Map of the 54 Countries That Reportedly Participated in the CIA's Rendition Program," *Washington Post,* February 5, 2013; Greg Grandin, "The Latin American Exception: How a Washington Global

Torture Gulag Was Turned Into the Only Gulag-Free Zone on Earth," *Tom's Dispatch*, February 18, 2013.

41 **Latin American leaders would:** Greg Grandin, *Empire's Workshop: Latin America, the United States, and the Rise of the New Imperialism* (New York: Metropolitan, 2006); see also "From El Salvador to Iraq: Washington's Man Behind Brutal Police Squads," *The Guardian*, March 6, 2013.

41 **speaking at the Security Council:** Renata Giraldi, "Na ONU, Dilma Repudia Preconceito contra Islamismo e Ataques aos Norte-Americanos," *Agência Brasil*, September 25, 2012.

3 · Ghettos in the Sky

46 **"The first time":** *Deen* (religion); *shahada* (the Muslim profession of faith: "There is no god but Allah, and Muhammad is the messenger of Allah"); Zamzam (holy water obtained from the well of Zamzam located in the Grand Mosque in Mecca); *iman* (faith); *shabab* (youth).

47 ***Thobe*-wearin', *Miswak*-chewin':** *Miswak* (a small tooth-cleaning twig, usually drawn from the arak tree).

48 **In *Global Salafism:*** Roel Meijer, ed., *Global Salafism: Islam's New Religious Movement* (New York: Columbia University Press, 2009), p. 22.

48 **While there is a jihadi-Salafi fringe:** Quinton Wictorowicz, "Anatomy of the Salafi Movement," *Studies in Conflict and Terrorism* 29, no. 3 (April–May 2006), pp. 207–39.

51 **Conservative Muslims mock:** Jenice Armstrong, "Philadelphia Locals Adopt Muslim-Inspired Menswear," Philly.com, August 23, 2011.

51 **When the officer appealed:** Sophia Pearson, "Philadelphia Tells Muslim Police to Trim Beards or Lose Jobs," Bloomberg News, October 19, 2005.

52 **He is the founder of:** John A. Jackson, *A House on Fire: The Rise and Fall of Philadelphia Soul* (New York: Oxford University Press, 2004).

52 **in the early 1990s:** Joy T. Bennett, "For the Love of Philly: Gamble & Huff Revitalize Community and Inspire the Music Industry," *Ebony*, June 2008, pp. 104–108. See also Gamble's interview with Saudi channel TV2, "Music Mogul Kenneth Gamble Embraced Islam," http://www.youtube.com/watch?v=0KQQ0Vw167o.

53 **He purchased a plot:** Matthew Teague, "King Kenny," *Philadelphia Magazine*, December 2007.

55 **These debates continue:** "Islam & Music," *Beyond Belief*, BBC Radio 4, July 26, 2010.

55 **Sufi thinkers, who see music:** Charles Hirschkind, *The Ethical Soundscape: Cassette Sermons and Islamic Counterpublics* (New York: Columbia University Press, 2009), p. 35; Kristina Nelson, *The Art of Reciting the Quran* (Cairo: American University of Cairo Press, 2001), pp. 32–48.

57 **One morning, after reading:** Interview with Robert Bell, August 25, 2008.

57 **"The initial idea":** Adam White and Fred Bronson, *The Billboard Book of Number One Rhythm & Blues Hits* (New York: Billboard Books, 1993), p. 278.

58 **"The poets mentioned in the Quran":** Umar Quinn, "Let Jahiliyya Go! The Evils of Hip Hop Culture," Rtbot.net, January 23, 2010.

59 **Conservative clerics have:** Suhaib Webb, "A Response to a Well-Intentioned Hiphop Brother," SuhaibWebb.com, July 20, 2009.

59 **Imam Talib, in his Chicago:** *Hadith* (a collection of the sayings or actions of the prophet Muhammad and his companions); *dua* (supplication); *minbar* (the pulpit structure within a mosque from which the imam speaks).

59 **Imam Talib thus defends:** Suad Abdul Khabeer, "Rep That Islam: The Rhyme and Reason of American Islamic Hip Hop," *Muslim World* 97, no. 1 (2007), pp. 125–41.

60 **But the political excitement:** Umar Lee, "The Rise and Fall of the Salafi Dawah in the US," *Liberator Magazine,* January 2008.

61 **A very small minority:** Ihsan Bagby et al., "The Mosque and the American Public Square," in Zahid Hussain Bukhari et al., *Muslims' Place in the American Public Square* (Lanham, MD: AltaMira Press, 2004). Bagby estimates that 1 percent of the mosques in the United States are Salafi-affiliated.

62 **In response to American pressure:** "For Conservative Muslims, Goal of Isolation a Challenge," *Washington Post,* September 5, 2006.

63 **The Salafi movement has:** Patrick Haenni, *L'Islam de Marché: L'Autre Révolution Conservatrice* (Paris: Seuil, 2005).

63 **Moreover, from the late 1970s:** Tariq Modood, "Moderate Secularism, Religion as Identity and Respect for Religion," *Political Quarterly* 81, no. 1 (March 2010).

63 **In suburban Detroit:** Sally Howell, "Competing for Muslims: New Strategies for Urban Renewal in Detroit," in Andrew Shryock, ed., *Islamophobia/Islamophilia: Beyond the Politics of Enemy and Friend* (Bloomington: Indiana University Press, 2010), p. 227. See also "Muslims Start Patrol to Fight Crack in Brooklyn," *New York Times,* January 23, 1988.

64 **In their pioneering study:** Nathan Glazer and Daniel Patrick Moynihan, *Beyond the Melting Pot: The Negros, Puerto Ricans, Jews, Italians and Irish of New York City* (Cambridge, MA: MIT Press, 1968), pp. 82–83.

64 **In the 1990s, the Salafi:** Samir Amghar, "Les Salafistes Francais: Une Nouvelle Aristocratie Religieuse?," *Maghreb-Machrek,* no. 183 (Spring 2005), pp. 13–31.

65 **In France, authorities estimate:** Piotr Smolar, "Mouvance Éclatée, le Salafisme s'est Étendu aux Villes Moyennes," *Le Monde,* February 22, 2005.

65 **Sociologists continue to debate:** Glenn C. Loury et al., *Ethnicity, Social Mobility, and Public Policy: Comparing the USA and UK* (New York: Cambridge University Press, 2005), p. 12.

67 **This group was centered around the Jamaican convert:** Elaine Sciolino and Dan Van Natta, Jr., "For a Decade, London Thrived as a Busy Crossroads of Terror,"

The New York Times, July 10, 2005; "Profile: Sheikh Abdullah al-Faisal," BBC.com, May 25, 2007.

68   **"Before the emergence of Rastafari":** Robert Beckford, *Dread and Pentecostal: A Political Theology for the Black Church in Britain* (London: SPCK, 2000).

4 · 9,000 Miles . . . of Sufi Rock

70   **In the keynote, Lewis:** Zeno Baran, ed., "Understanding Sufism and Its Potential Role in U.S. Policy," Nixon Center, Washington, DC, March 2004.

71   **Colonial treatises:** Bernd Radtke, "Between Projection and Suppression: Some Considerations Concerning the Study of Sufism," in F. de Jong, ed., *Shi'aIslam, Sects and Sufism: Historical Dimensions, Religious Practice and Methodological Considerations* (Utrecht: M.Th. Houtsma Stichting, 1992), pp. 70–82.

71   **In 1900, the French ethnologist:** Edmond Doutté, *Les Marabouts* (Paris: Ernest Leroux, 1900), p. 118, in Donal Cruise O'Brien, "Towards an 'Islamic Policy' in French West Africa, 1854–1914," *Journal of African History* 8, no. 2 (1967), pp. 303–16.

71   **More than fifty years:** Nathan J. Cintino, *From Arab Nationalism to OPEC: Eisenhower, King Saud and the Making of US–Saudi Relations* (Bloomington: Indiana University Press, 2002), p. 96.

72   **"It was 2003":** Suzy Hansen, "Fethullah Gülen and International Islam," *New Republic,* November 10, 2010.

72   **A monograph published by the US:** Stephen P. Lambert, *Y: The Sources of Islamic Revolutionary Conduct* (Washington, DC: Center for Strategic Intelligence Research, Joint Military Intelligence College, 2005).

72   **This ideological project:** Saba Mahmood, "Secularism, Hermeneutics, and Empire: The Politics of Islamic Reformation," *Public Culture* 18, no. 2 (2006), pp. 323–47.

73   **In August 2006:** "To combat terror the government has focused extensively on domestic legislation. While some of this will have an impact, the government must not ignore the role of its foreign policy," said the letter.

74   **He echoed Margaret Thatcher's:** Jack O'Sullivan, "If You Hate the West, Emigrate to a Muslim Country," *The Guardian,* October 7, 2001.

74   **Hamza Yusuf in particular:** Sadek Hamid, "The Development of British Salafism," *ISIM Review,* no. 21 (spring 2008).

75   **In the 2000s, he relaxed:** Hamza Yusuf, "What Happened to Poetry," lecture at Spiritual Rumi Conference, Fremont, CA, March 2002.

76   **Local activists, like Salma Yaqoob:** "Britain and Its Muslims: How the Government Lost the Plot," *The Economist,* February 26, 2009.

76   **Others worried that mobilizing Sufis:** Michael Mumisa, "The Civil War Among Muslims in Britain," *The Independent,* December 1, 2010.

78 **In honor of Rumi's:** "Secretary-General Says Commemoration of Poet Maulana Rumi Can Motivate Work of United Nations Alliance of Civilizations," press release, Department of Public Information, June 27, 2007; "Alliance of Civilizations Project Inspired by Mevlana," *Today's Zaman,* March 14, 2001.

78 **"You counter radicalization":** Richard Kerbaj, "Muslim Rocker Wields Guitar in Rock 'n' Roll Jihad," *Sunday Times,* May 16, 2010.

78 **"The latest folly":** "Government Use [*sic*] Rock n Roll to Defeat Muslim Extremism," *London Muslim,* May 19, 2010.

80 **Hasan filed a lawsuit:** "Local Author Says Muslim Writer, Band Defamed Her," *Denver Post,* October 24, 2007.

80 **Basim would pen:** Basim Usmani, "This Musical Event Cheapens Sufism," *Guardian,* August 4, 2010.

80 **Historians generally agreed:** Anatol Lieven, *Pakistan: A Hard Country* (New York: PublicAffairs, 2011).

80 **When two young men:** Sameer Arshad, "Pak Sufis Become Victims of West's Great Expectations," *Times of India,* April 10, 2011.

80 **After 9/11, the State:** *Changing Minds, Winning Peace: A New Strategic Direction for U.S. Public Diplomacy in the Arab & Muslim World,* Report of the Advisory Group on Public Diplomacy for the Arab and Muslim World (October 2003) http://www.state.gov/documents/organization/24882.pdf.

81 **As one American official:** David Kaplan, "Hearts, Minds and Dollars," *US News & World Report,* April 17, 2005.

81 **Commenting on how USAID:** Jesse R. Merriam, "Establishment Clause-Trophobia: Building a Framework for Escaping the Confines of Domestic Church-State Jurisprudence," *Columbia Human Rights Law Review* 41 (2010), pp. 699–764.

81 **Even in Britain:** Peter Edge, "Hard Law and Soft Power: Counter-terrorism, the Power of Sacred Places, and the Establishment of an Anglican Islam," *Rutgers Journal of Law & Religion* 12, no. 2 (2010).

81 **British security officials:** Brian Whitaker, "Keep Anti-terrorism and Theology Apart," *Guardian,* August 5, 2010.

81 **Robert Lambert:** Robert Lambert, "Salafi and Islamist Londoners: Stigmatised Minority Faith Communities Countering al-Qaida," *Crime, Law and Social Change* 50 (May 2008), pp. 73–89.

83 **In European cities:** Richard Reddie, *Black Muslims in Britain: Why Are a Growing Number of Young Black People Converting to Islam?* (Oxford, England: Lion Hudson, 2009), p. 194.

84 **With the rise of anticolonial:** Nile Green, *Sufism: A Global History* (Malden, MA: Wiley-Blackwell, 2012), p. 189.

5 · The Jazz Caliphate

87 **What the jazz musicians:** Francis Newton, *The Jazz Scene* (London: Macgibbon & Kee, 1959), pp. 214–16.

91 **One of his columns:** Mufti Muhammad Sadiq, "The Only Solution of Color Prejudice," *Moslem Sunrise,* October 2, 1921, p. 41.

92 **"devoted to the interests":** Colin Grant, *Negro with a Hat: The Rise and Fall of Marcus Garvey* (New York: Oxford University Press, 2010), p. 40.

92 **"child of Allah":** Richard Brent Turner, *Islam in the African-American Experience,* 2nd ed. (Bloomington: Indiana University Press, 2003), p. 88.

93 **"The spread of":** *Moslem Sunrise* 2, nos. 2–3 (April 1923), p. 263, cited in Kambiz GhaneaBassiri, *A History of Islam in America: From the New World to the New World Order* (New York: Cambridge University Press, 2010), p. 213.

93 **When he arrived:** Michael A. Gomez, *Black Crescent: The Experience and Legacy of African Muslims in the Americas* (New York: Cambridge University Press, 2005), p. 278.

96 **"even if it's":** *Sunnah* ("habitual practice" in Arabic; referring to the way of life prescribed for Muslims based on the example of the prophet Muhammad).

98 **Listening to these "pioneers":** Ralph Ellison, *Shadow and Act* (New York: NAL, 1966), pp. 283–84.

99 **This "Asiatic Barred Zone Act":** Vivek Bald, *Bengali Harlem and the Lost Histories of South Asian America* (Cambridge, MA: Harvard University Press, 2012).

100 **Later, as the band's personnel:** Robin D. G. Kelley, *Thelonious Monk: The Life and Times of an American Original* (New York: Free Press, 2009), p. 127.

100 **The mass conversion:** "Moslem Musicians Take Firm Stand Against Racism," *Ebony,* April 1953, p. 111.

100 **"'Man, if you join'":** Dizzy Gillespie, *To Be or Not to Bop* (New York: Doubleday, 1979), p. 291.

101 **He saw how Ahmadi jazz:** Amina Beverly Mccloud, *African American Islam* (New York: Routledge, 1995), pp. 20–21.

102 **The preferential treatment:** While Ibrahima's case was in the headlines, just before his return to Africa, others began claiming Muslim descent and Oriental ancestry, including "Abdullah Mohammed," who claimed to have been abducted from his native Syria by pirates, and "Almourad Ali," who "collected $1500 for 'my passage back home to Turkey' before it was discovered that the only home he had was in Albany, New York." Terry Alford, *Prince Among Slaves* (New York: Oxford University Press, 1977), p. 137.

102 **Booker T. Washington:** Booker T. Washington, *Up from Slavery* (New York: Carol Publishing Group, 1993), p. 103.

102 **In 1913, Noble Drew Ali:** As the historian Richard Turner writes, Ibrahima, the prince, "had used a pretended connection to Morocco to gain his freedom. If this

strategy for liberation worked in the nineteenth century, Noble Drew Ali probably reasoned that it might also work for black people in the twentieth century." Turner, *Islam in the African-American Experience,* p. 96.

103 **A firm believer in civic:** Michael A. Gomez, *Black Crescent: The Experience and Legacy of African Muslims in the Americas* (New York: Cambridge University Press, 2005), p. 274.

103 **Across the country:** Historian Robert Dannin thinks the Moorish Americans' dress was "reminiscent of early 19th century attempts to commemorate the African Islamic heritage of some slaves." Robert Dannin, *Black Pilgrimage to Islam* (New York: Oxford University Press, 2002), p. 27.

103 **"What a terrible gang":** Arthur Huff Fauset, *Black Gods of the Metropolis: Negro Religious Cults of the Urban North* (Philadelphia: University of Philadelphia Press; London: H. Milford, Oxford University Press, 1944), p. 43.

104 **The Brooklyn-born bassist:** Robin D. G. Kelley, *Africa Speaks, America Answers: Modern Jazz in Revolutionary Times* (Cambridge, MA: Harvard University Press, 2012), p. 92.

104 **Likewise, the Juilliard-educated:** Robert Dannin, *Black Pilgrimage to Islam* (New York: Oxford University Press, 2002), p. 63.

105 **"Before long, jazz will become":** "Remote Lands to Hear Old Democracy Boogie," *New York Times,* November 18, 1955.

106 **The jazz tours targeted:** Penny Von Eschen, *Satchmo Blows Up the World: Jazz Ambassadors Play the Cold War* (Cambridge, MA: Harvard University Press, 2005), p. 5.

106 **"They sent us to every post":** Quincy Jones, *The Autobiography of Quincy Jones* (New York: Doubleday, 2001), p. 14.

106 **during his performance:** "Duke Ellington Pledges Himself to Role in Negro's Rights Push," *Detroit Courier,* November 23, 1963.

107 **Harvard scholar Ingrid Minson:** Ingrid Minson, *Freedom Sounds: Civil Rights Call Out to Jazz and Africa* (New York: Oxford University Press, 2007).

107 **"When I announce":** Fred Kaplan, "When Ambassadors Had Rhythm," *New York Times,* June 29, 2008.

108 **"We stood at a flat plaque":** Michael Muhammad Knight, *Blue-Eyed Devil: A Road Odyssey Through Islamic America* (Brooklyn, NY: Soft Skull Press, 2009), p. 141. *Fatiha* (the opening chapter of the Quran).

109 **"black man with":** Askia Muhammad, "Farrakhan Addresses World at Saviours' Day 2008," *Final Call,* March 5, 2008.

111 **Satti Majid would never:** Abu Shouk, J. O. Hunwick, and R. S. O'Fahey, "A Sudanese Missionary to the United States: Satti Majid, 'Shaykh al-Istim in North America,' and His Encounter with Noble Drew Ali, Prophet of the Moorish Science Temple Movement," *Sudanese Africa* 8 (1997), pp. 137–91.

112 **Sufi *dhikr:*** *Dhikr* (a form of prayer, associated with Sufism, often involving the repetition of God's name).

112 **They cite his biography:** C. O. Simpkins, *Coltrane: A Biography* (Baltimore, MD: Black Classic Press, 1989), pp. 39–40. Simpkins writes, "John's exposure to Islam may have played a role in his struggle with drugs."

112 **"NO MATTER WHAT":** For more on the debate around *A Love Supreme,* see Moustafa Bayoumi, "East of the Sun (West of the Moon): Islam, the Ahmadis, and African America," *Journal of Asian American Studies* 4, no. 3 (October 2001), pp. 251–63.

113 **Rashied Ali, who was:** Steve Rowland, "Tell Me How Long Trane's Been Gone," *CultureWorks* (documentary), episode 3 (2001).

113 **For today's kids:** For recent Sufi-inflected renditions of *A Love Supreme,* see Daoud Kringle's *Allah Supreme* in homage to Coltrane. "Mystic Jaz Is Sitarist Dawoud Kringle and the New Cultural Ensemble: Paying Homage to Coltrane," *New York Beacon,* February 13, 2002.

115 **"The Arabic transliteration is":** Interview with Yusef Lateef, September 22, 2009; Yusef Lateef with Herb Boyd, *The Gentle Giant* (Irvington, NJ: Morton Books, 2006), p. 54.

6 · The Blue Spirit Chose Me

120 **North African state officials:** "The French had encouraged the orders in Morocco, recognizing their leaders and festivals, as part of their attempt to maintain a balance between the different forces in the country, especially opposing them to the orthodox, reformist, and progressive. Muhammad V (reg. 1927–1961) supported the Salafis and prohibited the processions and *mawasim* of the Isawiyya and Hamdushiyya, as well as sacrifices (*naha'ir*) offered to saints and other prohibited practices. He was successful in promulgating a decree (1946) prohibiting the establishment of new orders and the building of new *zawiyas* without authorization from the king." John Spencer Trimingham, *The Sufi Orders in Islam,* 2nd ed. (New York: Oxford University Press, 1998), p. 255.

120 **Eugène Delacroix's famous painting:** Joanne Sharpe, *Geographies of Postcolonialism* (London: Sage Publications, 2008), p. 22.

121 **But in Morocco:** Pierre-Alain Claisse, *Les Gnawa Marocains de Tradition Loyaliste* (Paris: Éditions L'Harmattan, 2003), p. 172.

121 **"This lady was older":** Zineb Majdouli, *Trajectoires des Musiciens Gnawa* (Paris: L'Harmattan, 2007), p. 213.

122 **Likewise, prominent feminists:** Fatima Mernissi, *Beyond the Veil: Male-Female Dynamics in Modern Muslim Society* (Bloomington: Indiana University Press, 1987), p. 43.

124 **After World War I:** David Levering Lewis, *When Harlem Was in Vogue* (New York: Penguin Books, 1997).

124 **In New York:** William A. Shack, *Harlem in Montmartre: A Paris Jazz Story Between the Great Wars* (Berkeley: University of California Press, 2001).

125 **France's appeal to African-Americans:** Michael Fabre, *From Harlem to Paris: Black American Writers in France, 1840–1980* (Urbana: University of Illinois Press, 1991).

127 **Later that evening:** Jessie Fauset, "Episodes in Tangier," *Metropolitan: A Monthly Review* 1, no. 1 (January 1935), pp. 8–12, Yale Collection of American Literature, Beinecke Rare Book and Manuscript Library, Yale University.

128 **Paul Bowles describes McKay:** Paul Bowles, *Without Stopping* (New York: Ecco Press, 1985), p. 148.

128 **"The Gueanoua were exorcising":** Claude McKay, *A Long Way from Home* (New York: Lee Furman, 1937), p. 297.

130 **Whether it was his rising profile:** Randy Weston and Willard Jenkins, *African Rhythms: The Autobiography of Randy Weston* (Durham, NC, and London: Duke University Press, 2010).

133 **Yet the French public's relationship:** Elizabeth Vihlen, "Jammin' on the Champs-Elysées: Jazz, France, and the 1950s," in Reinhold Wagnleitner and Elaine Tyler May, eds., *Here, There and Everywhere: The Foreign Politics of American Popular Culture* (Hanover, NH: University Press of New England, 2000).

133 **In 1947 Sartre:** Jean-Paul Sartre, "Présence Noir," *Présence Africaine I* 29 (1947).

137 **In May 2000, the pan-African festival:** "Randy Weston: Le Maâlem de la Blue Note," *L'Humanité Hebdo,* July 22, 2000.

7 · In Trance We Trust

139 **It's not clear:** "Aicha Kandicha," documentary, *Yuhka Ana,* Channel 2M, April 2012.

139 **"The fact is, any time":** "Kandisha: Une Vision Actuelle de la Femme Marocaine," Radio France Internationale, December 31, 2011.

140 **The truth is that when:** Deborah Kapchan, *Traveling Spirit Masters: Moroccan Gnawa Trance and Music in the Global Marketplace* (Middletown, CT: Wesleyan University Press, 2007), p. 206.

141 **In Europe, where Sufism:** Frédéric Calmès, "Les Gnawas de Belgique," Luxe Radio, November 5, 2012.

141 **"The main message here":** "Le Procès de l'Exorcisme aux Assises," Télé Bruxelles, May 15, 2012.

142 **In June 2010:** "Des Gnawas PS Payés par la Commune à Molenbeek?," RTBF.be, June 5, 2010.

142 ***Le Monde's* music critic:** Véronique Mortaigne of *Le Monde,* cited in "Gnawa Diffusion/Amazigh Kateb," *Spectacles et Musiques du Monde* http://www.musiquesdumonde.fr/GNAWA-DIFFUSION,51.

143 **Yacine purposely named:** The Berberphone movements of Algeria, Morocco, and

Niger prefer the name Amazigh to Berber, as the latter term derives from the Latin "barbarian"; today Imazighen is the term used to describe the various Berber-speaking communities of North Africa.

143 **"My father gave me":** "Kateb, de Père en Fils," interview, Radio Alger, May 2008.

144 **Amazigh's worldview is typical:** "Kateb, Père et Fils," *El Watan,* April 12, 2007.

149 **Upon gaining independence:** Amina Touzani, *La Culture et la Politique Culturelle au Maroc* (Casablanca: Éditions La Croisée des Chemins, 2003).

149 **As the Italian ethnomusicologist:** Alessandra Ciucci, "Poems of Honor, Voices of Shame: The 'Aita and the Moroccan Shikhat," dissertation, Department of Ethnomusicology, City University of New York, 2008.

150 **Their songs resonated strongly:** Philip Schuyler, "A Folk Revival in Morocco," in Donna Lee Bowen and Evelyn A. Early, eds., *Everyday Life in the Muslim Middle East* (Bloomington: Indiana University Press, 1994), pp. 287–93.

150 **Paco, already known:** Jimi Hendrix played with Malem Si Mohamed Chaouqi while in Essaouira; Chaouqi remembers Hendrix warmly: "He loved to smoke kif. He was always high *(mekiyif)*." For Paco's relationship with Hendrix, see *Nostalgia: Abdelrahman Paco,* documentary, 2M, July 2003, http://www.youtube.com/watch?v =Vbsu8AvEIoE. Denizens also swear that guitarist Carlos Santana recorded his cover of "Black Magic Woman," after an encounter with Aisha Kandisha in Essaouira in 1970.

151 **In their lyrics:** Timothy D. Fuson, "Musical Imagining in Morocco: The Voice of the Gnawa in the Music of Nas al-Ghiwan," manuscript, 1997.

151 **Most troubling to the state:** Youssef Aït Akdim, "Paco, le Mâalem Ghiwani," *Tel Quel,* November 3, 2005.

152 **Now an estimated seventy festivals:** Amina Boubia, "Les Festivals de Musique au Maroc: Fusions Artistiques, Cultures Globales et Pratiques Locales," in Nicolas Bénard Dastarac, ed., *Festivals, Rave Parties, Free Parties: Histoire des Rencontres Musicales Actuelles, en France et à l'Étranger* (Rosières-en-Haye, France: Camion Blanc, 2012), p. 371.

152 **And the more aficionados:** Cynthia Becker, *Amazigh Arts in Morocco: Women Shaping Berber Identity* (Austin: University of Texas Press, 2006).

152 **It's seen as a genre:** Paulla A. Ebron, *Performing Africa* (Princeton, NJ: Princeton University Press, 2002), p. 58.

153 **By the mid-1990s:** "Morocco Taps African Roots with Gnawa Music Revival," Reuters, September 13, 2008.

153 **The cultural liberalization:** Ted Swedenburg, "Arab 'World Music' in the US," *Middle East Report* 219 (Fall 2002), pp. 34–41.

153 **"In most Middle East countries":** Fayçal Chehat, "Entretien avec Amazigh Kateb: Les Sources du Maghreb Sont au Sud," *Africultures: La Revue des Cultures Africaines,* no. 13 (December 1998).

154 **Songs make reference:** Hoba Hoba Spirit thus sing of "Exodus—Movement of Haraga!" referring to the boat people.

154 **Islamists regularly denounce:** Songs like Bob Marley's "Zion's Train" and "Iron Lion Zion." References come from Psalm 137:1, "By the rivers of Babylon, there we sat down, yea, we wept, when we remembered Zion," and Psalm 87:4, "I will make mention of Rahab and Babylon to them that know me: behold Philistia, and Tyre, with Ethiopia; this man was born there."

155 **The Gnawa reggae groups':** Reda Allali, "Les Nouveaux Fascists," *Tel Quel,* July 5, 2006.

155 **"This whole 'we are Arabs'":** Interview with Reda Allali, July 10, 2013.

155 **Yet for all their agitating:** "Al Malik Yad'am Musiqah Yarfuduha al-Islamiyyun" ["The King Supports Music Rejected by the Islamist"], *Al-Quds Al Arabi,* May 30, 2008.

155 **After the civil war:** Isabelle Werenfeis, "Promoting the 'Good Islam': The Regime and Sufi Brotherhoods in Algeria," *IPRIS Maghreb Bulletin,* Summer 2011, pp. 2–3; Abdellatif El Azizi, "La Guerre des Zaouïas," *Actuel,* no. 66, October 23, 2010.

155 **Nationalists opposed French Sufi:** Said Hajji, "How the Arab East Sees Us," *Majallat al-Maghrib,* October 1934, cited in Emilio Spadola, *Calls of Islam: Sufis, Islamists, and Mass Mediation in Urban Morocco* (Bloomington: Indiana University Press, forthcoming 2014).

156 **Pro-regime Sufi orders:** "Maroc: Les Soufis de Sa Majesté," *Jeune Afrique,* June 11, 2011.

156 **At the regional level:** Samia Errazzouki and Mona Kareem, "*Arab Idol* and Policing Identities," *Bil3afya,* May 20, 2013.

156 **The Saudi government's:** M. D. Humaidan, "Haia Officers Get Training to Combat Black Magic," *Arab News,* April 4, 2011.

157 **"What we are doing":** Alain Brunet, "Djmawi Africa: l'Algérie est d'abord . . . Africaine," *La Presse,* October 27, 2010. See also Djmawi Africa's interview with Nessma TV, June 4, 2011.

8 · "We Ain't White"

160 **Meanwhile, liberal journalists:** Joan Walsh, "Are the Tsarnaev Brothers White?" *Salon,* April 22, 2013; Peter Beinart, "Are the Tsarnaevs White?" *Daily Beast,* April 24, 2013.

162 **In an often-cited passage:** Michael Omi and Howard Winant, *Racial Formation in the United States: From the 1960s to the 1990s* (New York: Routledge, 1994), p. 3.

163 **The French philosopher:** Michel Foucault, *Society Must Be Defended* (New York: Picador, 2003), p. 253.

165 **"The people of Harran":** Abdelrahman Munif, *Cities of Salt* (New York: Vintage, 1987), p. 595.

165   **In *America's Kingdom*:** Robert Vitalis, *America's Kingdom: Mythmaking on the Saudi Oil Frontier* (Palo Alto, CA: Stanford University Press, 2007).

166   **Chinese, Burmese, Japanese:** Sarah M. A. Gualtieri, *Between Arab and White: Race and Ethnicity in the Early Syrian American Diaspora* (Berkeley: University of California Press, 2009), p. 2.

166   **The early Syrian migrants:** Asia Barred Zone 1917—U.S. Congress, Immigration Act of 1917, Feb. 5, 1917, 39 Stat. 874.

166   **"Arabs," as sociologist Louise Cainkar:** Louise A. Cainkar, *Homeland Insecurity: The Arab American and Muslim American Experience After 9/11* (New York: Russell Sage Foundation, 2009), p. 73.

168   **Contravening the Hassan court:** US INS, "The Eligibility of Arabs to Naturalization," *Monthly Review* 1 (October 1943), p. 12.

168   **In the early years:** Philip Dolec, "The McCarran-Walter Act and the Conflict over Immigration Policy During the Truman Administration," in Frank J. Coppa and Thomas Curran, eds., *The Immigrant Experience in America* (Boston: Twayne Publishers, 1976), pp. 215–31.

170   **"When a police officer":** Suzanne Manneh, "Census to Count Arabs as White, Despite Write-in Campaign," *New American Media,* March 25, 2010.

170   **In the U.S., racial categories:** 1973, pp. 3–4; Juanita Tamayo Lott, *Asian Americans: From Racial Category to Multiple Identities* (Lanham, MD: AltaMira Press, 1997), p. 34.

170   **Minority status has often:** Lott, *Asian Americans,* p. 37.

171   **The older Arab-American:** Randa Kayyali, "US Census Classifications and Arab Americans: Contestations and Definitions of Identity Markers," *Journal of Ethnic and Migration Studies* 39, no. 8 (March 2013), 1299–1318.

171   **The young activists felt:** Abed Ayoub and Khaled Beydoun, "Building African-Arab Connections During Black History Month," *Al Jazeera,* February 8, 2012.

175   **At a societal level:** Bedour Alagraa, "The Elephant in the Racialised Room: The Conundrum of Black-Arabness," *Body Narratives,* July 14, 2013.

175   **Not surprisingly, a campaign:** Aylin Zafar, "Egyptian Immigrant Wants to Be Reclassified as Black," *Time,* September 7, 2012.

177   **Activists leading the campaign:** For a defense of the racial ambiguity of white status, Andrew Shryock, "The Moral Analogies of Race: Arab American Identity, Color Politics, and the Limits of Racialized Citizenship," in Amaney Jamal and Nadine Naber, eds., *Race and Arab Americans Before and After 9/11* (Syracuse, NY: Syracuse University Press, 2008).

178   **According to the EPIC report:** Lynette Clemetson, "Homeland Security Given Data on Arab-Americans," *New York Times,* July 30, 2004. See also "Freedom of Information Documents on the Census: Department of Homeland Security Obtained Data on Arab Americans from Census Bureau," Electronic Privacy Information Center, available at http://epic.org/privacy/census/foia/.

179 **In mid-2011, these fears:** Michael Mukasey, "NYPD True," *Daily News,* December 22, 2011.

180 **The Republican Party's sudden:** Ben Smith and Maggie Haberman, "GOP Takes Harsher Stance Toward Islam," *Politico,* August 15, 2010.

180 **And while pressing:** Daniel Nasaw, "Barack Obama Opponents Urge Census Boycott," *Guardian,* January 29, 2010.

182 **Her grandfather, Salloum Mokarzel:** In an op-ed in the *New York Times* on September 30, 1909, titled "Is the Turk a White Man?," Salloum Mokarzel argues that Syrians are not Asiatic or Turkic, despite being Ottoman subjects: "Is it not a fact that the peoples conquered by the Turks of old retain an indisputable claim to their racial descent? In other words, how could the Caucasian blood of the Greek, the Slav, the Armenian, the Arab and the Syrian be contested, since they were the aborigines of the lands where they now live?"

183 **The effort is modeled:** "Students Push UC to Expand Terms of Ethnic Identification," *Los Angeles Times,* March 31, 2009.

183 **Shortly after the Boston bombing:** "SWANA Campaign News on UC Campuses," IranianAlliances.org, April 30, 2013.

183 **"They may not have":** Maryam Susan Griffin, "We Ain't White: Forged and Forging Terrains of Racial Identity for SWANA Students at the University of California," master's thesis, Sociology Department, University of California, Santa Barbara, September 2010.

184 **Neighborhood residents see:** Gary C. David, "Behind the Bulletproof Glass: Iraqi Chaldean Store Ownership in Metropolitan Detroit," in Andrew Shryock and Nabeel Abraham, eds., *Arab Detroit: From Margin to Mainstream* (Detroit, MI: Wayne State University Press, 2000), pp. 151–79.

186 **As May Alhassen, a doctoral student:** Maytha Alhassen, "The Liquor Store Wars," *CounterPunch,* July 23, 2010.

186 **Relying on University of Chicago:** Natalie Y. Moore, "Chicago Food Deserts: The Search to Find Fresh Food in America's Inner Cities," TheRoot.com, April 15, 2010.

187 **At the forefront:** Ibrahim Abdul-Matin, *Green Deen: What Islam Teaches About Protecting the Planet* (San Francisco, CA: Berrett-Koehler, 2010).

187 **When asked why he sells:** "Muslim Coalition Targets Arab-Run Stores in Food Deserts," *Eight Forty Eight,* WBEZ 91.5, February 18, 2010.

188 **Sometimes these young agitators:** Reginald James, "Will the Real Muslims Please Stand Up?" *San Francisco Bayview,* February 6, 2006.

189 **In 2008, 90 percent:** Suhail A. Khan, "America's First Muslim President," ForeignPolicy.com, August 23, 2010; Farid Senzai, "The Political Incorporation of American Muslims," manuscript, Santa Clara University, September 2012.

190 **"American blackness confers":** Sherman Jackson, *Islam and the Blackamerican: Look-*

ing Toward the Third Resurrection (Oxford, New York: Oxford University Press, 2005), p. 133.

190 **And here was Jackson:** "Don't judge my country by its foreign policy," Sherman Jackson told thousands at a memorial conference in Washington, DC, on September 11, 2011. "Don't ask me to disavow my country just because my country doesn't live up to your expectations!"

190 **This wrangling—between:** Nikhil Pal Singh, *Black Is a Country: Race and the Unfinished Struggle for Democracy* (Cambridge, MA: Harvard University Press, 2004), p. 109.

191 **And on the other side:** Brenda Gayle Plummer, *Rising Wind: Black Americans and U.S. Foreign Affairs, 1935–1960* (Chapel Hill: University of North Carolina Press, 1996), pp. 23–24.

191 **They argue that it was:** Sara Suleiman, "CAIR-Chicago Efforts Lead to EEOC Officially Recognizing 'Arab' as Race," CAIR-Chicago, October 13, 2011.

192 **Moreover, argue the radical internationalists:** Sohail Daulatzai, *Black Star, Crescent Moon: The Muslim International and Black Freedom Beyond America* (Minneapolis: University of Minnesota, 2012).

193 **In Canada in 2006:** Chris Browne, "This Lockheed Martin Contract Tarnishes the Census," *Guardian,* March 18, 2011.

193 **The National Association of British Arabs:** Tariq Modood, *Multicultural Politics: Racism, Ethnicity, and Muslims in Britain* (Edinburgh: Edinburgh University Press, 2007). The Office of Population Census recently announced that a new section for Arabs would be added to the 2011 census. See Ismail al-Jalili and Maureen Jalili, "Arab Population in the UK: Study for Consideration of Inclusion of Arab as an Ethnic Group on Future Census Returns," National Association of British Arabs with the British Arabs Forum, November 2004.

9 · American *Banlieue*

195 **In his book *Urban Outcasts*:** Loïc Wacquant, *Urban Outcasts: A Comparative Sociology of Advanced Marginality* (Cambridge, MA: Polity Press, 2008).

198 **There is little agreement:** Tim Ross and Steven Swinford, "WikiLeaks Cables: US Launched Anti-extremist Campaign to Reverse UK Radicalisation," *Telegraph,* February 4, 2011.

198 **In December 2010:** Shiraz Maher, "Empowering Islamists: Repeating U.K. Mistakes, Obama's Ambassador to Britain Reaches Out to Muslim Radicals," *Wall Street Journal,* December 1, 2010.

200 **Just before the Bandung Conference:** Memorandum from Mr. Dumont to Mr. Jones, February 16, 1955, cited in Ian Johnson, *A Mosque in Munich: Nazis, the CIA,*

and the Rise of the Muslim Brotherhood in the West (Boston: Houghton Mifflin Harcourt, 2010), p. 72.

201 **The broadcasts in Uzbek:** Robert Dreyfuss, *Devil's Game: How the United States Helped Unleash Fundamentalist Islam* (New York: Metropolitan Books, 2005), p. 250.

201 **In 1957, the Operations:** "Strengthen the reformist groups," NSC 5428, "U.S. Objectives and Policies with Respect to the Near East," cited in Johnson, *A Mosque in Munich,* p. 128.

201 **In the 1960s, the U.S. would sponsor:** Zbigniew Brzezinski, *Power and Principle: Memoirs of the National Security Adviser 1977–1981* (New York: Farrar, Straus, Giroux, 1983).

201 **American intelligence even supported:** Johnson, *A Mosque in Munich,* p. 134.

202 **"The CIA supported":** Cited in Frances Stonor Saunders, *The Cultural Cold War: The CIA and the World of Arts and Letters* (New York: New Press, 2000), p. 409.

202 **"To win the cyber-war":** Mike McConnell, "Mike McConnell on How to Win the Cyber-War We're Losing," *Washington Post,* February 28, 2010.

202 **French conservatives, who see:** Caroline Fourest, "Oumma.com et l'ambassade Américaine," *France Culture,* December 12, 2010.

203 **By July 2008:** Hugh Gusterson, "When Professors Go to War," *Foreign Policy,* July 21, 2008.

203 **Since the research initiative:** Jennifer Baker, "European Parliament Agrees to Send Airline Passenger Data to US," ComputerWorldUK.com, April 19, 2012; Patryk Pawlak, "Homeland Security in the Making: American and European Patterns of Transformation," in Christian Kaunert et al., eds., *European Homeland Security: A European Strategy in the Making?* (London: Routledge, 2012).

203 **The Paris-based university:** Alain Joxe, "Should the Social Sciences Contribute to the Art of War in the Era of Securitization? Or to the Crafting of Peace?," *Social Science Research Council,* October 27, 2008; Maximilian Forte, "What Are the Pentagon's Minerva Researchers Doing?," *Zero Anthropology,* July 12, 2009.

203 **Muslim activists in Europe:** Hatem Bazian, "Muslims—Enemies of the State: The New Counter-Intelligence Program (COINTELPRO)," *Islamophobia Studies Journal* 1, no. 1 (Spring 2012), pp. 165–206.

204 **They met with a British starlet:** Dean Nelson, "US Tried to Recruit Bollywood to Stop British Muslims Being Radicalized," *Telegraph,* December 15, 2010; Jason Burke, "U.S. Wanted Bollywood Stars to Tour and Help in the 'Reconstruction' of Afghanistan: WikiLeaks," *Hindu,* December 17, 2010.

204 **Moreover, say advocates:** Shikha Dalmia, "Bollywood's Soft Power," *Reason,* January–February 2011.

206 **Noting that Al-Shabaab:** Jessica Stern, "Mind Over Martyr: How to Deradicalize Islamist Extremists," *Foreign Affairs,* January–February 2010.

206 **In 2006, Aki Nawaz:** Ted Swedenburg, "Fun^Da^Mental's 'Jihad Rap,'" in Asef

Bayat and Linda Herrera, eds., *Being Young and Muslim* (Oxford: Oxford University Press, 2010).

207 **In Germany, state officials are trying:** Souad Mekhennet, "German Officials Alarmed by Ex-Rapper's New Message: Jihad," *The New York Times,* August 31, 2011.

208 **In the 1980s, French ministers:** Halifu Osumare, *The Africanist Aesthetic in Global Hip-Hop: Power Moves* (New York: Palgrave Macmillan, 2008), p. 85.

208 **Jack Lang, Minister of Culture:** Samir Meghelli, "Hip-Hop à la Française," *The New Yok Times,* October 15, 2013.

208 **French record labels began:** Paul Silverstein, "Guerrilla Capitalism and Ghettocentric Cosmopolitanism on the French Urban Periphery," in Melissa S. Fischer and Greg Downey, eds., *Frontiers of Capital: Ethnographic Reflections on the New Economy* (Durham, NC: Duke University Press, 2006).

209 **Moreover, as he notes:** Loïc Lafargue de Grangeneuve, *Politique du Hip-hop: Action Publique et Cultures Urbaines* (Paris: Presses Universitaires Mirail, 2008), p. 226.

209 **Malik has won all kinds:** Jeanette Jouili, "Rapping the Republic: Who Should Muslim Youth Listen to in Secular France?," unpublished paper presented at the Amsterdam School of Social Research, University of Amsterdam, October 2010.

210 **Malik's Sufism is also:** Patrice van Eersel, "Soufisme: Une Porte Musulmane Vers la Modernité," and "Soufisme vs Intégrisme—Racisme vs Integration," *CLÉS,* 2009.

210 **The more praise showered:** Faycal Riad, "Un Truc de Malade: Abd Al Malik, ou la Pétainisation du Slam," *Les Mots Sont Importants,* January 2009.

210 **Farah Pandith, the State:** Farah Pandith, "Muslim Engagement in the Twenty-First Century," speech at the Atlantic Council's South Asia Center, April 21, 2010.

211 **The embassy's hip-hop:** "Des Jeunes Rappeurs Français 'ambassadeurs' des USA," *Le Figaro,* March 4, 2010.

212 **And while acknowledging:** Robert S. Leiken and Steven Brook, "The Moderate Muslim Brotherhood," *Foreign Affairs,* March/April 2007.

212 **One reason German politicians:** Interview with Johan Leman, University of Leuven, Belgium, January 11, 2011.

213 **Cash-strapped European states:** Mehdi Nabti, "Des Soufis en Banlieue Parisienne: Mise en Scène d'une Spiritualité Musulmane," *Archives de Sciences Sociales des Religions* 140 (October–December 2007), p. 68.

213 **The positive role played:** "London Riots: Residents Fight Back," *Telegraph,* August 9, 2011.

214 **Law enforcement is cultivating:** Zareena Grewal, *Islam Is a Foreign Country: American Muslims and the Global Crisis of Authority* (New York: NYU Press, forthcoming 2013), p. 197.

215 **This young Muslim-American:** Andrea Elliott, "Why Yasir Qadhi Wants to Talk About Jihad," *New York Times,* May 17, 2011.

215 **Partly to influence:** John Hudson, "U.S. Repeals Propaganda Ban, Spreads

Government-Made News to Americans," *Foreign Policy,* July 14, 2013; Craig Whitlock, "Somali American Caught Up in a Shadowy Pentagon Counterpropaganda Campaign," *Washington Post,* July 7, 2013; Rosa Brooks, "The Case for American Propaganda," *Foreign Policy,* July 17, 2013.

216 **Not only was the "anti-propoganda law" amended:** Melani McAlister, "State Department Finds Religion, But Whose?" *Religion Dispatches* (online), August 12, 2013; Huma Yusuf, "A Flawed Approach," Dawn.com, September 30, 2013.

217 **The government then proceeded:** Duncan Gardham, "Counter-terrorism projects worth £1.2m face axe as part of end to multiculturalism," *The Telegraph,* February 11, 2011.

217 **Referring to a cultural event:** Sherry C. Keneson-Hall, "Bridging Cultures," *State Magazine* 542 (February 2010), p. 13.

218 **After one such junket:** Bruno Pinel, "Le Blanc-Mesnil, c'est Loin d'être le Bronx," 20Minutes.fr, May 28, 2008.

218 **In April 2008:** "Les Enquêtes de la CIA," *Le Parisien,* April 21, 2008.

218 **French right-wingers speak:** Erwan Ruty, "Etats-Unis: À Quand le Retour du (Vrai) Plan Marshall Pour les Banlieues," *Presse & Cité,* July 8, 2010.

220 **In a very respectful tone:** "Muslim Resistance: The Struggle Within," *Guardian,* January 17, 2011.

10 · The X Factor

222 **In 2002, the Cuban:** Sujatha Fernandes, *Cuba Represent! Cuban Arts, State Power, and the Making of New Revolutionary Cultures* (Durham, NC: Duke University Press, 2006).

222 **The U.S. Army, in partnership:** Whitney Joiner, "The Army Be Thuggin' It," *Salon,* October 17, 2003.

223 **And the cross-border spread:** Lisa Anderson, "Demystifying the Arab Spring," *Foreign Affairs,* May/June 2011.

224 **In 2005 the State Department's:** "Cultural Diplomacy: The Linchpin of Public Diplomacy," *Report of the Advisory Committee on Cultural Diplomacy,* U.S. Department of State, September 2005.

225 **The artists stage performances:** American embassy press release, Kuala Lumpur, Malaysia, September 2011.

225 **In *Sound Targets,* Jonathan Pieslak:** Jonathan Pieslak, *Sound Targets: American Soldiers and Music in the Iraq War* (Bloomington: Indiana University Press, 2009), p. 168.

225 **Iraqi insurgents, in turn:** J. Martin Daughtry, "From Voice to Violence and Back Again," manuscript, New York University, April 2012.

226 **As Penny Von Eschen suggests:** Von Eschen, *Satchmo Blows Up the World,* p. 77.

226 **Yet the State Department:** Cynthia Schneider and Kristina Nelson, *Mightier Than*

the Sword: Arts and Culture in the US-Muslim World Relationship (Washington, DC: Brookings Institution, June 2008), pp. 48, 57.

228 **Community leaders told:** George Washington, *The Papers of George Washington,* Colonial Series, eds. W. W. Abbot et al., vol. 10 (Charlottesville: University of Virginia Press, 1995), pp. 137–38.

228 **And New York governor David Paterson:** "Paterson: Mosque Developers 'Hybrid, Almost Westernized' Muslims," CBS New York, August 26, 2010.

230 **Clay believed that Ibrahima:** Terry Alford, *Prince Among Slaves* (New York: Oxford University Press, 1986).

230 **Some would feign conversion:** See Kambiz GhaneaBassiri, *A History of Islam in America: From the New World to the New World Order* (New York: Cambridge University Press, 2010).

231 **"African-Americans are emerging":** Moustafa Bayoumi, "The Race Is On: Muslims and Arabs in the American Imagination," *Middle East Report Online* (March 2010).

231 **"After all," explains Fareed Zakaria:** Fareed Zakaria, "When Terror Loses Its Grip," *Newsweek,* May 20, 2011; Thomas Friedman, "America vs. the Narrative," *New York Times,* November 28, 2009. See Stephen Walt's response, "Why They Hate Us (II)," *Foreign Policy,* November 30, 2009.

232 **In *Rock the Casbah*:** Robin Wright, *Rock the Casbah: Rage and Rebellion Across the Islamic World* (New York: Simon & Schuster, 2012).

232 **At a panel on hip-hop:** "In Defense of Hip-Hop Diplomacy," *The Root,* January 27, 2012. Comments by Susan Rice, "Hip Hop and International Diplomacy: Is There a Bridge?," U.S. Mission to the United Nations, February 27, 2012.

232 **Jared Cohen, formerly at:** Eric Schmidt and Jared Cohen, *The New Digital Age: Reshaping the Future of People, Nations and Business* (New York: Knopf, 2013), p. 180.

232 **The deployment of American culture:** Anthony Lemieux and Robert Nill, "The Role and Impact of Music in Promoting (and Countering) Violent Extremism," in *Countering Violent Extremism: Scientific Methods & Strategies,* Air Force Research Laboratory and U.S. Department of State, September 2011.

233 **"Political Islam is not going":** Yves Gonzalez-Quijano, "L'Islam Politique n'est Pas Soluble Dans le Rap!," *Culture et Politiques Arabes,* January 23, 2012.

233 **In August 2011, a bookstore:** Mohammed Shair, "Malcolm X wa Guifara wa . . . al-dustur al-masri" ("Malcolm X and Guevara and . . . the Egyptian Constitution"), *Al-Akhbar,* August 2011.

234 **American and European officials:** Mark S. Hamm, "Terrorist Recruitment in American Correctional Institutions: An Exploratory Study of Non-Traditional Faith Groups," *National Institute of Justice,* December 2007; Clarence Page, "The 'White Negro' Taliban?," *Chicago Tribune,* December 14, 2001.

235 **"Were Malcolm alive":** Jackson, *Islam and the Blackamerican,* p. 168.

235 **American embassies began:** Gregory Garland, "The US-Africa Relationship and the

Presidential Transition," Bureau of African Affairs, U.S. Department of State, January 29, 2009. See also "This Day in African American History," February 21, 2013, United States Diplomatic Mission to Nigeria, http://nigeria.usembassy.gov/bhm2013 .html. This event stresses that Malcolm X abandoned "the hard-line anti-white prejudice of his early years." The American consulate in São Paulo does "a series of outreach presentations on President Obama" to Brazilian Muslim audiences (http://wikileaks .org/cable/2009/11/09SAOPAULO653.html).

236 **Mandaville has praised:** Peter Mandaville, "The Rise of Islamic Rap," *Yale Global Online,* August 2010.

236 **"watered down Krush":** Suhaib Webb, "A Response to a Well-Intended Hiphop Brother," SuhaibWebb.com, July 20, 2009; Suhaib Webb, "Muslim Hip Hop an Important Conversation," SuhaibWebb.com, July 19, 2009; Yusuf Rios, "Hip Hop in the 21st Century," SuhaibWebb.com, July 9, 2009.

237 **"Displaying the same lack":** "Black Muslims," Department of State, Aerogram filed by E. Marthinsen, Jeddah, Saudi Arabia, April 7, 1964.

238 **"The local press":** "Assassination of Malcolm X," Department of State, Aerogram filed by Richard W. Murphy, Jeddah, Saudi Arabia, March 2, 1965.

238 **"Greetings to the Free Negroes":** Richard H. Nolte, "Pure White Democracy: Egyptian Reactions to the Affair of Autherine Lucy," *American Universities Field Staff Reports,* Northeast Africa Series 4, no. 1 (1956), pp. 1–8.

239 **Diplomatic cables from the early:** Richard W. Murphy, "Memorandum of Conversation," aerogram, Department of State, Jeddah, Saudi Arabia, October 30, 1965, Nicholas G. Thacher, "Muslim World League Representatives to Visit U.S. to Investigate Black Muslims," aerogram, Department of State, Jeddah, Saudi Arabia, May 26, 1964, A-397.

239 **One dispatch from the embassy:** "Monthly Review for Saudi Arabia," Department of State, Aerogram filed by Richard W. Murphy, Jeddah, Saudi Arabia, September 14, 1965. Notes the cable: "Efforts by the Public Affairs Officer to ascertain the identity of the author of these articles were unsuccessful but his representations with the Acting Editor of *al-Bilad* may have had some beneficial effect since no further such articles have appeared."

239 **Richard Murphy was a young:** "Malcolm X Visits Jidda," Department of State, Aerogram filed by Richard W. Murphy, Jeddah, Saudi Arabia, September 29, 1964.

239 **The civil rights leader:** "Activities of Malcolm X," Department of State, Aerogram filed by Richard W. Murphy, Jeddah, Saudi Arabia, September 29, 1964.

240 **"The Saudis invited":** Interview with Richard W. Murphy, New York, February 15, 2012.

240 **He decided that Elijah Muhammad:** Another diplomat who expressed this view was John Badeau, who was the American ambassador to Egypt in 1964, when the heavyweight champion Muhammad Ali (Cassius Clay) announced that he was going to visit

the Egyptian capital. Badeau wrote to one of Nasser's closest advisors, "If Cassius Clay came to Cairo, he should be received as a boxer and not as a 'Moslem.' Indeed, were I a member of the Islamic community, I would try to covert [sic] him to true Islam and wean him away from the false and vicious notions which characterize the Black Muslims." John S. Badeau. "Black Muslims and Cassius Clay," airgram, Department of State, April 25, 1964, Cairo A-782.

240 **In his memoir:** Heshaam Jaaber, *I Buried Malcolm: The Final Chapter* (Los Angeles: New Mind Productions, 1993), pp. 76–77.

240 **It is difficult to ascertain:** Letter from Director's Office to Chicago Agent Marlin Johnson Counterintelligence Program, FBI File Date, January 7, 1969, cited in Karl Evanzz, *The Messenger: The Rise and Fall of Elijah Muhammad* (Durham, NC: Duke University Press, 1999), pp. 476–77. See also Matthias Gardell, *In the Name of Elijah Muhammad: Louis Farrakhan and the Nation of Islam* (Durham, NC: Duke University Press, 1996), pp. 101, 369.

241 **In May 1964:** Jesse W. Lewis Jr., "Man Who 'Tamed' Malcolm Is Hopeful," *Washington Post,* May 18, 1964.

241 **By the early 1970s:** "Muslim Networks and Movements in Western Europe," *Pew Forum,* September 15, 2010.

241 **As more Sunni Muslim immigrants:** Mohamed Nimer, "The Americanization of Islamism," *American Interest,* July/August 2011.

242 **And Malcolm X would respond:** Speech Notes, Reel #5, Box #5, p. 8, Malcolm X Collection, Schomburg Center for Research in Black Culture, New York Public Library.

242 **Elijah would also try:** Sylvester Leaks, "The Messenger of Allah as Seen by an Islamic Leader in Pakistan," *Muhammad Speaks,* May 8, 1964.

242 **In September 1964:** M. S. Handler, "Malcolm X Reports He Now Represents World Muslim Unit," *New York Times,* October 11, 1964; "Azhar" Travel Diaries, Box #5, Folder #14, p. 70, Malcolm X Collection, Schomburg Center; Letter to H. S. Muhammad Tawfik Oweida, the Supreme Council for Islamic Affairs, Cairo, UAR, November 30, 1964, Reel #3, Box #3 (Correspondence), Folder #4, Malcolm X Collection, Schomburg Center.

243 **If Nasser described himself:** Steven Gregory and Roger Sanjek, eds., *Race* (New Brunswick, NJ: Rutgers University Press, 1994), p. 188.

243 **The Saudis—flush with:** Edward Curtis, "Islamism and Its African American Muslim Critics: Black Muslims in the Era of the Cold War," in Manning Marable and Hishaam Aidi, eds., *Black Routes to Islam* (New York: Palgrave Macmillan, 2009), p. 62.

244 **The Saudis withdrew their support:** Richard W. Murphy, "Muslim World League No Longer Assisting Muslim Mosques, Inc," airgram, Department of State, Jeddah, Saudi Arabia, June 26, 1965, A-378.

244 **In 1978, Saudi Arabia:** C. Eric Lincoln, "The American Muslim Mission in the

Context of American Social History," in Earle Waugh et al., eds., *The Muslim Community in North America* (Edmonton, Canada: University of Alberta Press, 1983), pp. 230–31.

244 **This statement would cause:** The director of the California-based United Muslims of America has described the first Gulf War as "a watershed event for Muslim leaders taking Saudi money." He told the *San Francisco Chronicle:* "Most of those who did not openly come out and condemn Saddam received no more money . . . They (the Saudis) are trying to have influence here, but many American Muslims are professionals now and have their own money. Many say they do not want Saudi money. They want independence." Don Lattin, "Some U.S. Muslims Question Saudi Largess," *San Francisco Chronicle,* January 19, 1994, quoted in GhaneaBassiri, *A History of Islam,* p. 335.

246 **A study commissioned:** Muhammad Said, *Questions and Answers About Indigenous US Muslims,* unpublished manuscript, Tehran, 1982.

246 **And a small Shia:** Jelle Puelings, "Fearing a 'Shiite Octopus': Sunni-Shi'a Relations and the Implications for Belgium and Europe," Egmont Paper, Royal Institute for International Relations, Brussels, January 2010.

246 **One Detroit-based leader:** Interview with Dawud Walid, CAIR Detroit, November 13, 2012.

246 **"Like Husayn [*sic*], Malcolm":** Manning Marable, *Malcolm X: A Life of Reinvention* (New York: Viking Press, 2011), p. 431.

246 **In the U.S., these words:** Gardell, *In the Name of Elijah Muhammad,* p. 182. Others would point to Malcolm X's relationship with Mohammad Taki Mehdi, the Iraqi-American author and activist, who was of Shia background. See John Andrew Morrow, "Malcolm X and Mohammad Mehdi: The Shi'a Connection?," *Journal of Shi'a Islamic Studies* 5, no. 1 (Winter 2012); see also "Malcolm X's Shi'ite influences," Discussion Forum, ShiaChat.com, November 2012.

247 **Sudanese nationalists contend:** Mohammed Waqi Allah Ahmad, "Arba'a muathirat sudaniya fi fikr Malcolm iks wa masiratihi dawiya" [Four Sudanese Influences on Malcolm X and His Advocacy], *Hay'at Al-A'mal al-Fikiriya, Kursat Fikiriya* 15 (2006).

247 **Supporters of the Muslim:** Ahmad Khaled Tawfiq, "Malcolm X: Al Muslim Al-Amriki al-tha'ir [Malcolm X: The Muslim American Revolutionary], Ikhwanwiki. com. Accessed November 2011. Debate about Malcolm X on the Muslim Brotherhood's website.

248 **Adil Abdel Aaati:** "Malcolm X: Between Salafism and the Revolutionism" ("*Malcolm Iks: Bayna Salafiya wa Thawriya*"), Sudaneseonline.com, April 17, 2007.

251 **Frantz Fanon and the Guyanese:** See Frantz Fanon, "This Africa to Come," *Toward the African Revolution* (New York: Grove Press, 1967), p. 178; Walter Rodney, *How Europe Underdeveloped Africa* (Washington, DC: Howard University Press, 2009), p. 26.

251 **Ali Shariati, the Iranian sociologist:** Ali Shariati, *Reflections of Humanity: Two Views of Civilization and the Plight of Man* (Houston, TX: Free Islamic Literatures, 1980).

251   **Likewise, when Jalal Al-e Ahmad:** Roy Mottahedeh, *The Mantle of the Prophet: Religion and Politics in Iran* (New York: Pantheon, 1985), p. 321.

251   **Similar critiques are leveled:** Paul Gilroy, *Darker than Blue: On the Moral Economies of Black Atlantic Culture* (Cambridge, MA: Harvard University Press, 2010).

251   **In November 2011:** "US Hip-Hop Diplomacy Fails to Heal Rift with Pakistan," *Telegraph,* November 23, 2011.

252   **One member of Native:** Mark Oppenheimer, "A Diplomatic Mission Bearing Islamic Hip-Hop," *New York Times,* July 22, 2011.

252   **"I have a blind spot":** Communication with Eric Hobsbawm, December 6, 2010.

253   **This claim is ironic:** "U.S. Race Problem," *The Spark* [Accra, Ghana], October 25, 1963.

253   **This was, in fact, part of his ongoing dispute:** Bunche argued: "Carefully chosen American Negroes could prove more effective than whites, owing to their unique ability to gain more readily the confidence of the Native on the basis of their right to claim blood relationship." Malcolm X would call Bunche an "international Uncle Tom." Charles P. Henry, *Ralph Bunche: Model Negro or American Other?* (New York: New York University Press, 1999), p. 126.

254   **The State Department initiatives:** Julianne Escobedo Shepherd, "How the State Department Uses Rap to Spread Propaganda Abroad," *Alternet,* January 4, 2012; "Why Hip Hop Belongs at the State Department," *The Root,* January 27, 2012.

254   **Moreover, performances overseas:** Daniel Silverberg and Joseph Heimann, "An Ever-Expanding War: Legal Aspects of Online Strategic Communication," *Parameters* 39, no. 2 (Summer 2009), p. 82.

255   **"The world has":** Chuck D, "Chuck D's Open Letter on Media, Messages & Pimps," AllHipHop.com, January 3, 2011.

256   **But it is unclear:** "Global Opinion of Obama Slips, International Policies Faulted," Pew Research Global Attitudes Project, June 13, 2012.

256   **And ironically, if the current cultural diplomacy:** Matt Apuzzo and Adam Goldman, *Enemies Within: Inside the NYPD's Secret Spying Unit and bin Laden's Final Plot Against America* (New York: Touchstone, 2013), p. 130.

11 · When the Violins Weep

This chapter is based on interviews with Safinez Bousbia, Karine Boniche, Luc Cherki, Maurice El Medioni, René Perez, Jose de Souza, Paul Sultan, and Maurice Ahouasse of Radio Shalom.

259   **Until her death in 2003:** The term "Judeo-Arabic" is contested. In some cases it refers to the language of Arabic-speaking Jews that has its own distinct morphology; in France, the term "Judeo-Arabe" is used to describe the culture—including the music—of North Africa's Jews. I use the term in the latter sense. See Emily Benichou

Gottreich, "Historicizing the Concept of Arab Jews in the Maghrib," *Jewish Quarterly Review* 98, no. 4 (Fall 2008), pp. 433–51.

264 **Across the Arab world:** Dwight F. Reynolds, "Musical 'Membrances of Medieval Muslim Spain," in Stacy Beckwith, ed., *Charting Memory: Recalling Medieval Spain* (New York: Garland, 2000), pp. 155–68.

264 **The seventeenth-century historian:** Chris Lowney, *A Vanished World: Medieval Spain's Golden Age of Enlightenment* (New York: Free Press, 2005), p. 66.

265 **According to local lore:** Alexis Chottin, *Tableau de la Musique Marocaine* (Casablanca: Imprimeries Réunies, 1938), pp. 90–95.

266 **"We have printed":** Jonathan Glasser, "Edmond Yafil and Andalusi Musical Revival in Early 20th-Century Algeria," *International Journal of Middle East Studies* 44 (2012), pp. 671–92.

266 **But his European tours:** Cited in Jonathan Glasser, "Genealogies of al-Andalus: Music and Patrimony in the Modern Maghreb," dissertation, University of Michigan, 2008, p. 269.

267 **"Arabs of the Jewish Faith":** Joshua Schreier, *Arabs of the Jewish Faith: The Civilizing Mission in Colonial Algeria* (New Brunswick, NJ: Rutgers University Press, 2010).

268 **The Algerian-born novelist:** Olivier Todd, *Albert Camus: A Life* (Boston: Da Capo Press, 2000), p. 151.

269 **"We were helped":** Luc Cherki, *Itinéraire d'un Chanteur Juif Pied-noir Déraciné,* manuscript, 2012.

269 **"And that evening":** Cited in Martin Evans, *Algeria: France's Undeclared War* (New York: Oxford University Press, 2012), p. 77.

270 **As one jazz critic:** Norman C. Weinstein, *A Night in Tunisia: Imaginings of Africa in Jazz* (New York: Limelight Editions, 1993), p. 57.

271 **The Ornament of the World:** María Rosa Menocal, *The Ornament of the World: How Muslims, Jews, and Christians Created a Culture of Tolerance in Medieval Spain* (New York: Back Bay Books, 2002).

274 **"The battle against":** Samia Essabaa with Cyril Azouvi, *Le Voyage des Lycéens: Des Jeunes de Cité Découvrent la Shoah* (Paris: Stock, 2009).

275 **Of particular interest:** Nadia Marzouki, "Les Lumières Juives ou la Réforme de l'Islamologie," *Revue Mouvements,* no. 36 (November–December 2004), pp. 15–21.

275 **"None of these excesses":** Mark Cohen, *Under Crescent and Cross: The Jews in the Middle Ages* (Princeton, NJ: Princeton University Press, 1995), p. 4.

276 **The play, set in sixteenth-century:** Leïla Salam, "Juifs et Arabes: Histoire d'une Symbiose," Oumma.com, February 7, 2005.

280 **In August 1938:** Rabah Aïssaoui, "La Culture Mobilisée par le Nationalisme," in Driss El Yazami et al., eds., *Générations: Un Siècle d'histoire Culturelle des Maghrébins en France* (Paris: Gallimard, 2009), p. 93.

281 **It was just down:** Catherine Guilyardi and Charlotte Roux, "Les Cabarets Orientaux

à Paris, des Années Folles aux Années Raï," documentary aired on *France Culture, La Fabrique de l'histoire,* November 25, 2009.

282 **The sight of French:** Ian Black and Benny Morris, *Israel's Secret Wars: A History of Israel's Intelligence Services* (New York: Grove Press, 1987), p. 173.

282 **"Propaganda and colonial policy":** Mohammed Harbi and Gilbert Meynier, eds., *Le FLN: Documents et Histoire 1954–1962* (Paris: Fayard, 2004), pp. 594–96.

283 **"The singer and musician [Cheikh] Raymond":** Signed Appeal by "Un Groupe de Patriots Algériens Juifs," *Droit et Liberté,* May 1961, cited in Benjamin Stora, *Les Trois Exiles: Juifs d'Algérie* (Paris: Stock, 2006), p. 159.

283 **As violence increased:** Benjamin Stora, "L'impossible Neutralité des Juifs d'Algérie," in Mohammed Harbi and Benjamin Stora, eds., *La Guerre d'Algérie: 1954–2004, la Fin de l'Amnésie* (Paris: R. Laffont, 2004), p. 441.

283 **In January 1962:** Michael M. Laskier, "Israel and Algeria amid French Colonialism and the Arab-Israeli Conflict, 1954–1978," *Israel Studies* 6, no. 2 (Summer 2001), p. 12; Benjamin Beit-Hallahmi, *The Israeli Connection: Who Israel Arms and Why* (London: Taurus, 1988), p. 45. Historians largely concur that Israel trained Misgeret units in Algeria, though there is less agreement on whether Israel was training or backing the OAS. Laskier sees no evidence of such involvement, whereas Beit-Hallahmi mentions reports from 1961 and 1962 of "Israeli support" for the right-wing paramilitary force.

285 **"Do we ever say":** Rémi Yacine, "Disparition de Lili Boniche," *El Watan* (Algiers), March 24, 2008.

286 **The *Washington Post* described:** Nancy Ross, "Her Voice Has a Familiar Tone," *Washington Post,* March 29, 1966.

289 **A guest of honor:** "Nicolas Sarkozy Impose Enrico Macias aux Algériens," *Le Matin Algerie,* November 14, 2007.

289 **"I've been a symbol":** "France-Algerie: Les Cicatrices de l'histoire," *Ripostes* France 5, December 2007.

289 **But in Algeria, musicologists:** Abdelmajid Merdaci, *Dictionnaire des Musiques Citadines de Constantine* (Constantine, Algeria: Les Editions du Champ Libre, 2008), p. 151.

290 **"The Arabs in these lands":** Robert Satloff, "The Holocaust's Arab Heroes," *Washington Post,* October 6, 2006; "Arab Schindler Provides Valuable Lesson to Arabs Today," *Jerusalem Post,* May 7, 2007.

290 **Moroccan newspapers denounced:** Abdellah Rajy, "Notre Histoire Revisitée," *Maroc Hebdomadaire,* November 3, 2006.

291 **That the book was prefaced:** Amira Soltane, "Quand le Maghreb Protégeait l'Étoile de David," *L'Expression* (Algiers), June 5, 2010.

291 **Others dismissed the book:** Karim Boukhari and Hassan Hamdani, "Histoire d'un Tabou: Les Camps de Concentration au Maroc," *Tel Quel,* May 27, 2007.

291 **Abdel Moneim Said:** "Meeting Dr. Robert Satloff," Ahram Center, Cairo, Egypt, January 16, 2007, (Arabic), http://acpss.ahram.org.eg/ahram/2001/1/1/CONF57.HTM; see also Laura King and Batsheva Sobelman, "Egyptian Hero's Kin Reject Honor by Israel's Holocaust Museum," *Los Angeles Times,* October 20, 2013.

292 **The late historian Tony Judt:** Tony Judt, "The 'Problem of Evil' in Postwar Europe," *New York Review of Books,* February 14, 2008.

294 **The initial reviews:** Elaine Sciolino, "How a Paris Mosque Sheltered Jews in the Holocaust," *New York Times,* October 3, 2011.

294 **Critics argued that:** Michel Renard, "Résistance à la Mosquée de Paris: Histoire ou Fiction?" Rue89.com, October 1, 2011. Writes Renard: "Il est exact que le chanteur Selim (Simon) Halali fut sauvé par la délivrance de papiers attestant faussement de sa musulmanité."

295 **Critics also argued that:** Jean Laloum, "Cinéma et Histoire. La Mosquée de Paris et les Juifs sous l'Occupation," *Archives Juives: Revue d'Histoire des Juifs de France* 45, no. 1 (2012), pp. 116–28.

295 **Moreover, as a Muslim underclass:** Peter J. Bloom, "The State of French Cultural Exceptionalism: The 2005 Uprisings and the Politics of Visibility," in Charles Tshimanga et al., eds., *Frenchness and the African Diaspora* (Bloomington: Indiana University Press, 2009), pp. 229–30.

295 **And for some young Muslims:** Paul A. Silverstein, "The Fantasy and Violence of Religious Imagination: Islamophobia and Anti-Semitism in France and North Africa," in Andrew Shryock, ed., *Islamophobia/Islamophilia: Beyond the Politics of Enemy and Friend* (Bloomington: Indiana University Press, 2010).

295 **"The experience of Muslims":** Michel Wieviorka, *The Lure of Anti-Semitism: Hatred of Jews in Present-Day France,* trans. Kristin Couper Lobel and Anna Declerck (Leiden: Brill, 2007), p. 140.

296 **Essabaa has won praise:** Samia Essabaa, *Le Voyage des Lycéens: Des Jeunes de Cité Découvrent la Shoah* (Paris: Stock, 2009); Ethan Katz, "Did the Paris Mosque Save Jews? A Mystery and Its Memory," *Jewish Quarterly Review* 102, no. 2 (Spring 2012), pp. 256–87.

12 · The North African Syndrome

298 **Intrigued by Muslim understandings:** David Macey, *Frantz Fanon: A Biography* (London: Granta Books, 2001), p. 548.

299 **Aziz agreed to join:** "Abdelrahman Aziz: Portrait," *Hanine,* aired on Radio Television Algérie, February 2, 2000.

299 **They set up a Moorish-style:** Ghania Hammadou, "Fanon-Blida, Blida-Fanon," *Revolution Africaine* 11 (December 1987).

299 **Even after he was expelled:** Alice Cherki, *Frantz Fanon: A Portrait* (New York: Cornell University Press, 2006), p. 136.

299 **In a sign of the times:** "Mode: Quand la Guerre d'Algérie Inspire les Branchés New-Yorkais," *Rue 89,* March 21, 2010.

302 **Fanon's work, however:** John C. Hawley, ed., *Encyclopedia of Postcolonial Studies* (Westport, CT: Greenwood, 2010), p. 167.

302 **The writer Harold Cruse:** Harold Cruse, *Rebellion or Revolution* (Minneapolis: University of Minnesota Press, 2009), p. 191.

305 **In 1964 Malcolm X:** Travel Diary, Entry for Friday, September 4, 1964, Reel #5, Folder #14, p. 66, Malcolm X Collection, Schomburg Center.

305 **"The criticisms of Israel":** Clayborne Carson, "Black-Jewish Universalism in the Era of Identity Politics," in Jack Salzman and Cornel West, eds., *Struggles in the Promised Land: Toward a History of Black-Jewish Relations in the United States* (New York: Oxford University Press, 1997), p. 188.

305 **Jewish liberals, since the early 1960s:** Jonathan Kaufman, *Broken Alliance: The Turbulent Times Between Blacks and Jews in America* (New York: Charles Scribner's Sons, 1988), p. 213.

306 **As Podhoretz put it:** Norman Podhoretz, "A Certain Anxiety," *Commentary,* August 1971, pp. 4–10.

306 **"We can understand":** Dinesh D'Souza, *The End of Racism: Principles for a Multiracial Society* (New York: Touchstone Books, 1996), p. 377.

307 **Rather than an "interracial utopia":** Bernard Lewis, *Race and Color in Islam* (New York: Harper and Row, 1971), p. 3.

307 **Lewis would go on:** Bernard Lewis, *Race and Slavery in the Middle East* (New York: Oxford University Press, 1992), p. 101.

307 **A dispatch of a 1972:** Samir Meghelli, "From Harlem to Algiers: Transnational Solidarities Between the African American Freedom Movement and Algeria, 1962–1978," in Manning Marable and Hishaam Aidi, eds., *Black Routes to Islam* (New York: Palgrave Macmillan, 2009), p. 114.

308 **"We're a civil rights":** Marlise Simons, "An Outspoken Arab in Europe: Demon or Hero?" *New York Times,* March 1, 2003.

310 **The AEL issued a statement:** Dirk Jacobs, "Arab European League (AEL): The Rapid Rise of a Radical Immigrant Movement," *Journal of Muslim Minority Affairs* 25, no. 1 (2005), pp. 97–115.

311 **It was these racial practices:** Frantz Fanon, "The North African Syndrome," *L'Esprit,* February 1952.

312 **Seba refers to France's mainstream:** "Qui est le Farrakhan Français?" *Jeune Afrique,* July 31, 2006.

314 **Since 9/11, American conservatives:** Justin Vaïsse, "What the 'Eurabia' Authors Get Wrong About Islam in Europe," *Foreign Policy,* January/February 2010.

314   **"It's the Farrakhan problem":** Christopher Caldwell, "Allah Mode: France's Islam problem," *Weekly Standard,* July 6, 2002.

315   **The Holocaust Museum:** "Google Earth, Holocaust Museum Focus in on Sudan's Darfur," Associated Press, April 11, 2007.

315   **But the main African-American:** "US Jews Lead Darfur Rally Planning," *Jerusalem Post,* April 27, 2006.

316   **Worried that the Darfur:** Hisham Aidi, "Slavery, Genocide and the Politics of Outrage: Understanding the New Racial Olympics," *Middle East Report,* no. 234 (Winter 2005).

316   **"Arab slavery":** Olivier Pétré-Grenouilleau, *Les Traites Négrières, Essai d'histoire Globale* (Paris: Gallimard, 2004).

316   **Historian Bernard Lewis:** Bernard Lewis, "The New Anti-Semitism," *American Scholar,* Winter 2006.

317   **French journalists warned:** Fabrice Weissman, "Urgence Darfour: Les Artifices d'une Rhétorique Néoconservatrice," in Olfa Lamloum, ed., *Médias et Islamisme* (Cahiers de l'Ifpo, 2010), pp. 113–32.

317   **The Urgence Darfour movement:** Muslim organizations such as FRAMCA (Fraternité musulmane contre l'antisémitisme) would sign the "europetition" Urgence Darfour, while others refrained. See Daniel Bensoussan-Bursztein, "Etude 2011: Le Dialogue Judéo-Musulman en France d'hier à Aujourd'hui," *Revue Regards* (Bruxelles), December 1, 2011.

317   **Soon a counter-coalition:** Charles Onana, *Al-Bashir et Darfour: La Contre-Enquête. Menaces sur le Soudan et Révélations sur le Procureur Ocampo* (Paris: Duboiris, 2010).

318   **"These people will":** Sandew Hira, "Decolonizing the Mind: The Case of the Netherlands," *Journal of the Sociology of Self-Knowledge* 1 (Winter 2012), pp. 53–68.

321   **In his memoir, Mahieddine Bachtarzi:** Mahieddine Bachetarzi, *Memoires 1919–1939,* vol. I (Alger: Editions Nationales Algériens, 1968), p. 167.

322   **And it doesn't hurt:** "Mon pays c'est l'amour et j'aime avec outrance les enfants des faubourgs." From Salim Halali, "Moi je suis d'un pays," *L'Essentiel: Salim Halali* (Atoll Music 2005).

323   **In July 1997:** "Pourquoi nos Juifs nous Quittent?," *Maroc Hebdo,* (July 19 and 25, 1997).

323   **People remember how:** Joel Gordon, "Singing the Pulse of the Egyptian-Arab Street: Shaaban Abd al-Rahim and the Geo-Pop-Politics of Fast Food," *Popular Music* 22, no. 1 (2003), pp. 73–88.

323   **In 2010, the Algerian historian:** Fawzi Sadallah, *Yahud al Jazair: Majlis al-Ghina wal Tarab* (Algeria: Dar Al Qortoba, 2010), pp. 396–97.

324   **To the integrationists:** "La Lutte Pour la Défense des Droits Civiques aux USA: Hommage à Deux Grands Penseurs Martin Luther King et Abraham Heschel," papers presented at symposium, "Lutte Droits Civiques USA," Mairie de Paris, February 4, 2009.

325 **When Debbie Almontaser:** Larry Cohen-Esses, "Jewish Shoot-Out over Arab School," *Jewish Week,* August 17, 2007.

325 **Part of this wariness:** Emmanuel Brenner, *The Lost Territories of the Republic,* trans. Bob Chodos and Susan Joanis (New York: American Jewish Committee, 2006), p. 7. See also *What Do We Do with a Difference? France and the Debate over Headscarves in Schools* (Brookline, MA: Facing History and Ourselves, 2008).

326 **Former French prime minister:** Laurence, *The Emancipation of Europe's Muslims;* Esther Benbassa, *La République Face à ses Minorités: Les Juifs Hier, les Musulmans Aujourd'hui* (Paris: Fayard, 2004), p. 130.

326 **The "decolonials":** Stuart Hall, "Cultural Identity and Diaspora," in Jonathan Rutherford, ed., *Identity: Community, Culture, and Difference* (London: Lawrence & Wishart, 1990), pp. 222–37.

326 **"All this yearning":** Houria Bouteldja, "Une Autre Civilisation S'Impose," conference/debate, Parti de Indigènes de la République and Groupe de Associations de Bagnolet, Bagnolet, France, May 7, 2012.

327 **A government official:** Cited in Robert Fisk, *The Great War for Civilisation: The Conquest of the Middle East* (New York: First Vintage Books, 2007), p. 345.

327 **Liberal British Muslims:** Mehdi Hasan, "Muslim Attitudes and the Holocaust," *New Statesman,* January 27, 2012.

327 **The Oxford historian:** Timothy Garton Ash, "Muslims in Europe! The Challenges to Liberalism," Tony Judt Memorial Lecture, New York University, September 27, 2011.

330 **In Egypt, as Judy Barsalou notes:** Judy Barsalou, "Recalling the Past: The Battle over History, Collective Memory and Memorialization in Egypt," *Jadaliyya,* June 22, 2012.

331 **Did heads of state:** This argument, initially made by Agnès Bensimon (*Hassan II et les Juifs* [Paris: Le Seuil, 1991]), was examined more recently by Al Jazeera, in an episode of its show *Milaf: Yahud Al Arab* (September 2010).

331 **In fall 2012:** Glenn Kessler, "Iraq Demands Return of Its Jewish Archive," *Washington Post,* April 30, 2010; Lisa Leff, "Were Iraqi Jewish Treasures Displayed in D.C. Stolen?" *Tablet,* October 7, 2013.

331 **In Morocco, student activists:** Interview with Vanessa Paloma, Casablanca-based scholar and musician, December 11, 2012.

331 **"history wars":** Eric Foner, *Who Owns History? Rethinking the Past in a Changing World* (New York: Hill and Wang, 2002).

333 **As he writes in his memoir:** Robert Castel, *Je Pose Soixante-Quinze mais Je Retiens Tout* (Paris: Editions Ramsay, 2008), p. 27.

Index